Praise for *The Way Out*

"Peter T. Coleman's latest is a tour de force: eminently readable, with compelling stories from the streets of Watertown, MA, and the negotiating tables of Northern Ireland yet replete with frameworks and insights that help Americans understand—and chart a way out of—our polarized national condition. *The Way Out* is a road map to a more perfect union."

—SHAMIL IDRISS, CEO OF SEARCH FOR COMMON GROUND

"*The Way Out* offers the most comprehensive and succinct understanding of how polarization leads to harm and dysfunction in our current American landscape. With the clarity of empirical evidence and open imagination, these pages explore the opportunities available to engage and transform these dynamics toward far healthier and responsive interactions that reinvigorate our social contract and democracy. A treasure trove of insight and instruction, this is the best scientific and practical guide I have read about toxic polarization. Coleman's gift of a book could not be better timed or more laser focused."

—JOHN PAUL LEDERACH, AUTHOR OF *THE MORAL IMAGINATION: THE ART AND SOUL OF BUILDING PEACE*

"In *The Way Out*, Coleman tackles a critically important issue, a topic on everyone's mind: the emergence of a unique brand of polarization, centered less on policy disputes than on tribal instincts. Not only do we disagree with the other side, but we are convinced that their views are dangerous and that they are the true threat to the nation. Coleman lays out a new perspective regarding the roots of this hyperpolarization in a lively, accessible way and, most importantly, offers a detailed map out of the quagmire."

—DANIEL M. SHEA, AUTHOR OF *WHY VOTE? ESSENTIAL QUESTIONS ABOUT THE FUTURE OF ELECTIONS IN AMERICA*

"The great value of Coleman's book consists in setting out positive approaches that can be pursued where disputes on political issues relate to people's differing values and priorities and where our emotional impulses prevent effective engagement with other people: for this reason, the book should be widely read and used by conflict-resolution practitioners."

—*PROCESS NORTH*

THE
WAY
OUT

HOW TO OVERCOME TOXIC POLARIZATION

PETER T. COLEMAN

Columbia University Press
New York

Columbia University Press gratefully acknowledges the generous support for this book provided by a Publisher's Circle member.

Columbia University Press
Publishers Since 1893
New York Chichester, West Sussex
cup.columbia.edu

Paperback edition, 2023

Library of Congress Cataloging-in-Publication Data
Names: Coleman, Peter T., 1959- author.
Title: The way out: how to overcome toxic polarization / Peter T. Coleman, PhD, Columbia University.
Description: New York : Columbia University Press, [2021] | Includes index. | Identifiers: LCCN 2020051516 (print) | LCCN 2020051517 (ebook) | ISBN 9780231197403 (hardback) | ISBN 9780231197410 (pbk.) | ISBN 9780231552158 (ebook)
Subjects: LCSH: Conflict management–United States. | Polarization (Social sciences)–United States. | Political participation–United States. | Interpersonal relations–United States.
Classification: LCC HM1126 .C573 2021 (print) | LCC HM1126 (ebook) | DDC 303.6/9–dc23
LC record available at https://lccn.loc.gov/2020051516
LC ebook record available at https://lccn.loc.gov/2020051517

Cover Design: Julia Kushnirsky

This book is dedicated to the 86 percent of Americans who are currently exhausted, miserable, and desperately seeking a way out of our culture of contempt.

CONTENTS

Preface: While Rome Burns ix

Acknowledgments xiii

1. Introduction: Our Crisis and Opportunity 1
2. Why We Are Stuck 16
3. Attracted to Conflict 41
4. Think Different—Change Your Theory of Change 63
5. Reset—Capture the Power of New Beginnings 81
6. Bolster and Break—Locate Latent Bubbles 109
7. Complicate—Embrace Contradictory Complexity 135
8. Move—Activate Novel Pathways and Rhythms 161
9. Adapt—Seek Evolution for Revolution 182
10. Conclusion: New Rules for *The Way Out* 204

Afterword 219

Appendix A: Takeaways 221

Appendix B: Assessments and Exercises 229

Notes 231

Index 271

PREFACE

While Rome Burns

It feels both urgent and frivolous to sit with my laptop and opine about the science on reducing toxic forms of polarization while my various devices send me constant updates on the reality of the increasingly tense, poisonous, fractured, state of our union. Initially, the context was birtherism, Benghazi, and Brexit, but then it jumped to Russian hacking of our elections, the Mueller inquiry, and Trump's impeachment. Then, amid this crisis of Western democracy, my family and I suffered the profound, unexpected loss of a dear, twenty-seven-year old friend, the only son of our closest friends. Immediately afterward came COVID-19 (which we contracted in February), a nearly complete worldwide social and economic shutdown, and unprecedented levels of civil unrest in our streets triggered by the perpetual stream of brutal killings of unarmed Black Americans at the hands of our own police.

I am deeply shaken. We are destabilized.

In the context of this maelstrom, I wrote this book. It will not rid us of predatory despots, racists, misogynists, anarchists, or other types of extremists and opportunists who take advantage of our divisive human tribal tendencies to gain power. These pathologies are afflicting societies around the world and are nearing epidemic levels in the United States. Many in politics and the media have learned to play these forces like maestros. It is clear to me that they must be actively challenged, fought, blocked, controlled, and legally constrained if our original vision of American democracy—of optimism and egalitarianism and fairness and *E pluribus unum* (out of many, one)—is ever to be realized. However, this book is *not* about how to win this fight.

It *is* about finding another way out of it.

I grew up in middle America in a lower working-class family who struggled to make ends meet. Born in Chicago, my mother, siblings, and I fled a dangerous situation there (my father drank, gambled, and owed money to violent men) and moved to Iowa when I was ten, where I was thereafter raised in a single-parent home. Although my mom worked to exhaustion, we found ourselves needing to go on welfare, so to help out I began working at the age of ten. Since then, I have held more than fifty different jobs, many of them menial labor, to make my way out of hard times. Despite being pigeonholed as an indigent "Industrial Ed" kid in high school, I attended college at a state school, moved to New York City, eventually got a PhD, and today live on the Upper West Side where I am proud to be a professor of peace and conflict studies at Columbia University.

All this to say that I feel a genuine connection with, and concern for, both Americas: rural and urban, poor and well-off, progressive and conservative. No, I am not a fan of Donald Trump, and I feel his mean-spirited divisiveness; trivialization of facts, truth, and science; and profound selfishness and recklessness are dangerous in a president. But I understand why some see him as a folk hero, so I am an advocate for many Trump voters as well as adamant anti-Trumpers—I understand how they got there. Because I, too, am angry.

There is an old tale about a Cherokee elder who was teaching his grandchild about life and said, "A fight is going on inside you. It is a terrible fight between two wolves. One wolf represents fear, anger, envy, greed, arrogance, and ego. The other stands for joy, peace, love, hope, kindness, generosity, and faith. The same fight going on inside you is inside every other person too." The child thought about it for a moment and then asked, "Which wolf will win?" The old man replied, "The one you feed."

These days, my enraged, fearful, arrogant wolf is well-fed. I feel perversely energized by my distain for leaders on the other side of our political chasm and bewildered by their followers. I feel constantly pulled into fits of self-righteous certainty and disgust. There is an obsessive, addictive, contagious quality to all this. Our violent wolves are battling their vicious wolves to the death—damn the consequences! All the while our kinder, more generous, hopeful wolves are left battered, withered, and quivering on the ropes. Writing this book is my attempt to resuscitate our compassionate wolves.

A hundred years ago, Mary Parker Follett, one of the great unsung heroes of the twentieth century, did exactly this by offering a vision for quelling violent labor strife and oppressive management practices in the United States. Follett was an American social worker by trade who wrote prophetic essays about business, industrial relations, and management. In the early 1900s, she offered a view on reducing worker-management enmity (class warfare) that was a radical departure from the prevailing orthodoxy, which believed in the raw use of threat, coercion, and control to overwhelm one's opponent. At a time when management philosophy was deeply rooted in what came to be known as "Theory X" (the belief that workers are basically lazy, irresponsible, and greedy and need to be controlled by a strong hand)[1], and when coercive, "power-over" approaches to employee management and union strategy prevailed, she offered an alternative:

> It seems to me that whereas power usually means power-over, the power of some person or group over some other person or group, it is possible to develop the conception of power-with, a jointly developed power, a co-active, not a coercive power. . . . Coercive power is the curse of the universe; co-active power, the enrichment and advancement of every human soul.[2]

In Follett's view, one of the most effective ways to reduce the use of abusive forms of control and stem the battle in industry was to make them less relevant—by developing the idea, the capacities, and the conditions that foster coactive power and integrative solutions for all involved. As such, she was able to rise above the poisonous, polarizing struggles between labor and management that had threatened the survival of many communities of her time by appealing to those in the middle and encouraging both sides to see the value of working together to improve their mutual conditions. Although it took decades, Follett's vision was ultimately transformational, spawning widespread movements in participatory leadership and inclusive management practices, constructive conflict resolution, and employee empowerment and teamwork in organizations that continue to enrich our lives today.

My aim is similar. I fully recognize that the battles against our more destructive political forces and tendencies must continue unabated, but I hope to offer an alternative way out of our current dystopian struggles that will be sufficiently hopeful, attractive, and feasible to make the more combative approaches to them become much less germane. In the end, although we may need both wolves to survive, our humanity, our decency, and our sense of community and solidarity depends on the capacities of our kinder ones to thrive.

Recent events have reminded me, once again, of the incredible promise of the human spirit and of the devastating fragility of life and brevity of our time on this planet. They have made me refocus my energies on doing everything I can to make our world a more just and generous place. So, in good faith, I offer this book to my America, to *our* America, with the genuine hope that it can help us all to find a better way out together.

ACKNOWLEDGMENTS

I wish to acknowledge a few people for making this book and these days possible.

First and foremost are Leah, Hannah, and Adlai, the foundational pillars of my life. Every moment of every day is warmed and brightened by our love.

Next are Debi, David, Sam, and Tiny, my dear sweet friends. Our lives together are forever entangled through our shared joy and pain. Much of this book was inspired by your courage and resilience.

I also want to thank Becca Bass, whose partnership and constant support on this project were vital. Becca's keen intelligence, creativity, sensitivity, conscientiousness and heart have made me and this book so much better.

An enthusiastic thank you to my close and most outstanding colleagues and friends, Katharina Kugler, Andrea Bartoli, Larry Liebovitch, and Naira Musallam, whose intellectual, practical, and emotional contributions to this book are priceless. And a special thanks to my excellent colleagues Bodi Regan, Allegra Chen-Carrel, Robert Anderson, Danielle Coon, Jaspar Leahy, and Andy Chan, whose insights into how to communicate and teach the concepts from this book have been vital.

I want to also express my deep appreciation to my literary agent, Jessica Papin, for believing in me all these years and encouraging me to write this book, and to my editors at CUP, Eric Schwartz and Lowell Frye, for supporting and tolerating me.

Finally, I want to thank all those colleagues whose work knowingly and unknowingly contributed to this book, including Morton Deutsch, Mary Parker Follett, William Zartman, Robin Vallacher, Andrzej Nowak, Lan Bui-Wrzosinska, John Gottman, Julie Gottman, Paul Diehl, Gary Goertz, Connie Gersick, Dietrich Dörner, Jonathan Haidt, Carol Dweck, Laura Chasin, Susan Podziba, Douglas Fry, John Paul Lederach, Rob Ricigliano, Danny Burns, Cedric De Coning, Josh Fisher, Nick Redding, Kyong Mazzaro, William Ury, Michelle LeBaron, Tory Higgins, Christine Webb, Carol Dweck, Danny Bar-Tal, Eran Halperin, Boaz Hameiri, Philip E. Tetlock, Orit Gal, Meghan Phelps-Roper, Amanda Ripley, Norman Cousins, the team at the *Morton Deutsch Center for Cooperation and Conflict Resolution*, the team at *More in Common*, and so many more. You are the visionaries who see light amidst darkness.

1
INTRODUCTION
Our Crisis and Opportunity

In this book I address an urgent question: What can we do to escape the grip of partisan contempt in our divided society and get back to solving our most pressing problems?

TROUBLED TERRITORY

The city of Boston, Massachusetts, is no stranger to toxic conflict. Here's a little history. Founded in 1630, by the 1670s it figured centrally in King Philip's War (also known as the First Indian War), a rebellion by the Algonquian nation against the rapidly encroaching New England colonialists, which is considered to be the bloodiest war per capita in U.S. history.[1] In the 1770s, it was the site of the Boston Tea Party and the Siege of Boston, which kicked off the Revolutionary War against the British. Then, in the 1840s, it became a hotbed for the anti-Catholic, anti-immigrant Know Nothing movement, which began

1.1 This is the Chinese character for *crisis* (*wēijī*), which translates to *danger at a point of juncture*, but it is often misconstrued to mean a combination of *danger + opportunity*. Either way, it is appropriate to our situation today. We are both navigating a time of considerable crisis that is fracturing us and may sink us *and* being presented with an opportunity to choose a path less-traveled and head in a more promising direction. The trick is knowing how to do it.

as a secret society but blossomed into a far-right nativist political party. In the 1970s, Boston was forced into more than a decade of federal court-mandated busing to promote racial desegregation in their schools, which triggered years of protests and riots. And, of course, more recently we saw the Patriots' coach Bill Belichick's notorious Spygate (2007), Spygate 2.0 (2019), and Deflategate (2015) controversies.[2] In other words, Beantown is an "attractor" for deeply polarizing conflict.*

Consider, for instance, the more recent tensions surrounding Boston's cherished Red Sox baseball team. The 2018 Boston Red Sox was arguably the greatest team in their franchise's storied 117-year history, with a record 108-game-winning season, a definitive 3–1 game trouncing of the New York Yankees for the Division Championship,† and a 4–1 game rout of the Los Angeles Dodgers to win the World Series. They were formidable.

Then, something went awry. Although they had managed to retain their most talented players, the team inexplicably imploded in the next season and failed to even make the play-offs–. Fans and pundits were baffled. How could their best team by far—and one with a $236 million annual price tag—become such an embarrassment so soon? Speculation and after-action analyses of the 2019 season spawned many theories, but one source of the collapse stands out.

In May 2018, after their World Series victory, President Donald Trump invited the Red Sox team to the White House to celebrate. Soon after, the Red Sox coach Alex Cora, who is Puerto Rican, and several other players of color declined the invitation.[3] In all, fifteen players and coaches refused to attend the White House celebration, while twenty-two other predominantly white team members attended. In response, *Boston Herald* sports columnist Steve Buckley tweeted, "Alex Cora has confirmed newspaper reports he will not make the trip to meet the president. So basically it's the white Sox who'll be going." The Red Sox's pitching ace, David Price, also declined the president's invitation and retweeted Buckley's tweet to his 1.8 million followers, which got everyone's attention.

Similar tensions had been erupting within sports teams since candidate Trump's early disparaging remarks regarding Colin Kaepernick's protests of the

---

* Attractors are stable patterns that draw us in repeatedly and resist change—like a strong attitude, habit, or addiction.

† Full disclosure: I am a long-suffering Chicago Cubs fan who has also succumbed to the lure of the New York Yankees, so I claim no neutrality here.

National Anthem in 2016, when Trump suggested that the quarterback should "find another country."[4] In fact, between 2017 and 2019, only eleven of twenty-five championship teams in major U.S. professional and college sports agreed to celebrate with President Trump at the White House, even though more than 50 percent of Americans felt they should.[5] Although Coach Cora and the Red Sox front office said that the players' decisions not to attend the celebration were personal and would not affect their play on the field, several members made comments alluding to their grievances over Trump's positions on Black Lives Matter protests and immigration. These were the strains that accompanied the team into their lackluster 2019 season.

In June 2020, as protests over racial injustice once again roiled our country in response to police killings of unarmed Blacks, more revelations came. Torii Hunter, a former professional outfielder who had played for other teams, released a statement about his experiences playing at the Red Sox's Fenway Park. He describes frequently being harassed with racial slurs by Boston fans, such as being called the N-word "100 times." The Red Sox front office soon released a statement in response: "Torii Hunter's experience is real. If you doubt him because you've never heard it yourself, take it from us, it happens."[6]

This rather remarkable statement from a professional sports franchise—one of the flagships of our national pastime—seemed to acknowledge the fact that the sources of the racial, cultural, and political divisions tearing at the Sox clubhouse went far beyond Trump and the players. They were situated much more deeply in a society, culture, and nation that feeds them.

I don't mean to pick on Boston. In fact, I could have described hundreds of other communities across the United States that have been hotbeds for divisive conflicts. I will point out, though, that Suffolk County, in which Boston resides, was recently ranked in the top 100th percentile of politically prejudiced places out of all three thousand counties across the United States—indicating that, in addition to its challenges with racial injustice, it is currently at the top of political intolerance.[7]

THE BAD NEWS

By many accounts, the United States is more polarized today than ever before in our history. To be sure, we have had bad patches in the past—the battle over states-versus-federal rights during the founding of our nation, the U.S. Civil War, the civil rights movement, the Vietnam War, and Watergate—but nothing quite like this. This period has been longer, deeper, and more complicated, and is likely to be more threatening to the future of our country (and the world order) than the others. We are in the grip of a more than fifty year escalating trend of political, cultural, and geographical polarization, and it is damaging our families, friendships, neighborhoods, workplaces, and communities to a degree not previously seen in our lifetime.[8]

On a personal level, many of us are *feeling* much colder toward, and more fearful and contemptuous of, those on the other side of our political divide.[9] Today these feelings are increasingly affecting who we hire, date, marry, and choose to hang out with in our free time.[10]

Our *perceptions* are also way off. Today Democrats and Republicans imagine that almost twice as many people on the other side of the political fence hold more extreme views than really do.[11] And the more media we consume, including newspapers, social media, talk radio, and local news, the more our views become divorced from reality. We are also paying less careful *attention* to the specifics of the issues that divide us—such as health care, immigration, and gun control—opting instead to blindly follow what we are told by our party leaders.[12]

In Washington, D.C., our leaders in Congress have reached an unprecedented stage of almost complete opposition in legislative voting. It is increasingly rare for members of one party to cross the aisle and support legislation proposed by the other, and it is ever more common for them to publicly disparage, ridicule, and condemn members of the other party.[13] The result is deadlock, dysfunction, and national decay. The *New York Times* characterized the 2019 State of the Union speech in this way: "The entire spectacle—reflected in the vibrating hostility between the two sides trapped together in the House chamber—evidenced the true state of the union: Fractured, fractious, painfully dysfunctional."[14]

No, this is not about President Trump, or at least it is not only about him. Our current heated divisions over the Trump presidency are largely a symptom of a decades-long trend in our society that goes back to at least the late 1960s. In other words, our current political crisis grew from the soil of our widening geographical and cultural divisions, which are much more deeply rooted and enduring than any single politician. This trend created the conditions that led to such a divisive presidency in the first place, and it is the underlying trend, much more than the current administration, that we should be concerned about. Yes, Trump seems

Team America A Views Trump as...	Team America B Views Trump as...
• Anti-intellectual – Anti-science	• Born smart with great instincts – Who needs science?
• Hyper-consumerist capitalist	• Successful, rich, and happy
• Obese glutton	• Healthy appetite
• High maintenance appearance	• Really pulls it together
• Violent and punitive	• A strong leader
• Media-addicted	• An informed and curious communicator
• Economically rational – ends justify means	• Practical and pragmatic
• Ethnocentric	• Puts America first
• Status-obsessed	• Ambitious and powerful
• Disconnected from nature	• Sophisticated urbanite
• Dishonest – Amoral – Criminal	• A flexible politician
• Nepotistic	• A family man
• Disloyal	• Doesn't suffer fools
• Selfish and self-serving friendless loner	• Fiercely independent
• Hyper-competitive – Winning is the *only* thing	• A winner
• Impulsive reactionary	• Goes with his gut
• Machiavellian – Autocratic	• A clever leader
• Privileged, greedy, and entitled	• A self-made man
• Hostile, blaming, contentious bully	• A scrappy fighter
• Divisive	• Has moral clarity re good and evil
• Cowardly	• Prudent and cautious
• Fragile narcissist – Emotionally needy	• Sensitive and caring
• Misogynous, Racist, Xenophobic, Nationalist	• Who isn't?

1.2 American psychosis.

to relish fueling and fanning the flames of division and contempt, but presidents come and go. This deeper pattern has become increasingly more complicated, consequential, and intractable, and today the schism seems to be approaching a form of *mass national psychosis*—with the two sides experiencing fundamentally different realities. Do the two realities described in figure 1.2 look familiar? One is reasonable and one is completely insane, right? But which is which?

If you spend an evening flipping back and forth between MSNBC and FOX News, this is exactly the language you will hear. Sean Hannity and Rush Limbaugh speak one language, and Rachel Maddow and Stephen Colbert are fluent in the other. Or if you spend any time at all with a friend, neighbor, or relative from the other team, same thing—two completely divergent accounts of the actions of the same individual.

Now, as a psychologist, I am aware that *psychosis* is a strong word. This is how the National Institute of Health describes it:

> The word psychosis is used to describe conditions that affect the mind, where there has been some loss of contact with reality. During a period of psychosis, a person's thoughts and perceptions are disturbed and the individual may have difficulty understanding what is real and what is not. Symptoms of psychosis include delusions (false beliefs) and hallucinations (seeing or hearing things that others do not see or hear). A person in a psychotic episode may also experience depression, anxiety, sleep problems, social withdrawal, lack of motivation, and difficulty functioning overall.[15]

Let's see . . . anxious, depressed, not sleeping, withdrawing socially, not functioning, and having difficulty understanding what is *real* or *true* anymore. That sounds like most Americans I know today!

As entertaining as living in a psychotic nation may be, serious problems arise when we exist in two parallel but conflicting realities while living in the same home or community, not the least of which is that it becomes increasingly impossible to communicate, work together, and solve *real* problems. Our divisions are a first-order problem; they impair our capacities to problem solve as a society. As a result, we cannot even begin to agree on what our national priorities should be. Even when Americans do agree on some issues—raising taxes on the ultrawealthy (75 percent bipartisan support), guaranteed paid maternity leave (67 percent), net neutrality rules for broadband (83 percent), background checks for gun purchases (90 percent), and the need for Medicare to be able to negotiate lower drug prices (92 percent)—we can't come together long enough to deliver on what the supermajority want!

This is toxic. Today 83 percent of Americans find the future of the country to be a "significant source of stress"[16]—the highest ever reported—which leads to an increased likelihood of chronic health problems.[17] According to the American Psychiatric Association's 2019 public opinion poll, 32 percent of adults reported feeling more anxious than in the previous year,[18] and approximately 40 million adults in the United States struggled with anxiety disorders.[19] In 2017, 17.3 million

U.S. adults had at least one episode of major depression,[20] and among adolescents, the rate of moderate to severe depression increased from 23.2 percent in 2007 to 41.1 percent in 2018.[21] This has contributed to a suicide rate that increased 35 percent between 1999 and 2018.[22] In 2020, 72 percent of Americans reported "that this is the lowest point in the nation's history that they can remember,"[23] and when voters were asked to imagine a loss of the presidency in 2020, 22 percent of Democrats and 21 percent of Republicans said that partisan violence could be justified. This is the noxious state of our union.[24]

The widening divisions and anxieties we are seeing in the United States today also appear to be part of a global trend that is erupting across democracies, including in France, Germany, the UK, Italy, Hungary, Austria, Sweden, Poland, Brazil, Turkey, India, and the Philippines. This broader pattern of left-versus-right tribalism and democratic-versus-autocratic dysfunction has led some to characterize this time as a "historic crisis point." Speaking at the World Economic Forum in 2019, Tim Dixon, cofounder of an initiative called More in Common, summed it up like this:

> As we approach the 2020s, there's growing evidence that we're at a historic crisis point for modern democracies and pluralist societies. Political systems across the world are simultaneously experiencing deep disruption, with a startling escalation of polarization and tribalism. . . . This makes pluralist societies less resilient, more vulnerable to social stresses, and less able to navigate the typical 21st-century crises such as political deadlock, rapid demographic change, economic slumps, climate events, technological change and threats to national security.[25]

It is in contexts like these that teams like the Boston Red Sox, and perhaps communities and families like yours, come apart.

REASONS TO BE HOPEFUL

Fortunately, scientists have been studying long-standing, polarizing, change-resistant conflicts like ours for decades. The research on *how to begin to end* such divisive conflicts has taught us that three things matter most for getting warring groups to pause their battle and begin to consider other ways of resolving their differences.[26]

The first condition is *instability*. When it becomes completely normal, expected, and encouraged to feel and act with contempt toward another large group of people—most of whom you have never met but you are certain are dead set on harming our country—it often takes an earthquake of sorts to really change things up. Such jolts to a community can come from internal sources such as severe economic hardship, dysfunctional or scandalous leaders, unsettling incidents of violence, or from outside sources such as natural disasters or the entrance of radically new leaders. A change in strong normative patterns is thought to require a disassembly and resetting of their deep structures—essentially the assumptions, values, and incentives that determine our most basic decision-making processes.[27] Research on this type of change has found that significant shocks are often a necessary, albeit insufficient, condition for bringing about an end to deep intergroup divisions[28] and sustained, transformational change.[29]

Fortunately, for these purposes, we are currently a mess. Today we are living through a profoundly destabilizing series of shocks—including the radically unorthodox nature of the Trump presidency, a deadly global pandemic, the ensuing derailment of our basic social and economic foundations, and a resurgence of national and international protests around racial injustice. Let's call it Instability^4, which is somewhat akin to the experience of a major earthquake, tsunami, extreme wildfires, and a plague hitting the same community in succession. The effects of these events are unknowable beyond the fact that they will destabilize us profoundly.

The second and third conditions associated with ending prolonged divisions are related to timing. There are, of course, better and worse times to stop fighting a war and consider an alternative course of action. The best time is when two other conditions are present: a *mutually hurting stalemate* arises between the groups and is coupled with a sense of a *mutually enticing opportunity*.[30] A mutually hurting stalemate happens when disputants in a conflict (the reds, blues, and the independent "leaners" in our case) see the situation they are in as chronically stuck and unlikely to be unilaterally "won" by either side (in other words, a stalemate), and when the disputants are experiencing enough pain, regret, or dread right now to motivate them to find an alternative way out. However, it is important that they also believe that enough of the disputants on the other side of the aisle are feeling the same level of trepidation and longing for resolution, which makes it *mutually* painful. So, enough people on both sides must feel really awful.

The good news is that today most Americans are miserable. A study after the 2016 election found that 67 percent of more moderate Americans on both sides of the divide—a group the authors of the study call the "exhausted majority"—were fed up with our state of dysfunction, despised our contemptuous condition of polarization, and were eager to find ways to talk, compromise, and work together again.[31] In fact, after the 2018 midterm elections, the same group found that 86 percent of Americans felt exhausted by our political divisions and worried that they would lead to more violence, and 89 percent said they want both parties to find places to compromise. This group represents the "hidden tribes" in the political middle, not the more extreme groups on either side. Nevertheless, this growing *miserable middle majority* provides a solid foundation to build on—suggesting that a significant segment of the population may be open to a dramatic reset.

However, a third condition is also necessary to break out of a hostile quagmire. All sides to these disputes also need to begin to sense that there might be a *mutually enticing opportunity* to exit. In other words, they need to begin to sense that there may be a way out in which they can get unstuck, change course, and move on with their lives without having to lose face or give up too much.

This book offers a way out.

Let's return to our conflictual city of Boston to see what this might look like.

DISTURBING SACRED GROUND IN BOSTON

One of America's most Catholic cities (roughly 36 percent of its population), Boston has a long history of tense acrimony between its highly active pro-choice and pro-life communities that is legendary, going back as far as the late nineteenth century. The highly sensitive and personal nature of the issues around abortion, combined with gender, class, and religious politics, and the seesawing of federal and state abortion laws over decades, often resulted in each camp despising and publicly vilifying the other.

In Boston in the 1980s and 1990s, tensions over abortion peaked. The pro-life community organized large, daily protests at abortion clinics in the area. They would wield grotesque, poster-size images of aborted fetuses, kneel outside the entrances, and pray loudly or shout and condemn women attempting to enter the clinics. The pro-choice community held firm in its conviction of a woman's right to choose, bolstered by the *Roe v. Wade* ruling a decade earlier, and organized counterprotests at the clinics on weekends. Around this time, volunteers began to provide "escorts" for the women trying to enter the clinics, walking on either side of the patients to shield them from the onslaught of the protesters.

Such was the landscape in the otherwise quiet Boston suburb of Brookline on the morning of December 30, 1994, when John C. Salvi III, dressed all in black, walked past the pro-life protestors outside and entered the Planned Parenthood Clinic where he methodically shot and killed Shannon Lowney, a 25-year-old receptionist, and wounded three others. Salvi then drove down Beacon Street to the Preterm Health Services clinic and opened fire again, shooting 38-year-old Leanne Nichols, a volunteer, ten times with a rifle at point-blank range, saying, "That's what you get. You should pray the rosary."[32] By the end of the day, two women were dead and five others were seriously wounded.

After the shootings and the arrest and conviction of the killer, security was increased at the clinics, and the Catholic Church called for a moratorium on protests. But nothing much of great significance seemed to happen in response to the underlying tensions around abortion. Although Brookline was traumatized, the pro-choice community devastated and fearful, and pro-life proponents ashamed and appalled, the only public response to the tensions came twelve days later when the governor of Massachusetts, William F. Weld, and Cardinal Bernard Law of the Catholic archdiocese of Boston called for "common ground" talks between the two camps.

A call for talks. That was it. But after all, what *really* could be done to stem the tide of hate and violence over this issue after decades of belittlement, battle, and blame? It seemed so vast and immoveable.

Then, six years later, something quite remarkable came to light. On January 28, 2001, an article appeared in the *Boston Globe* coauthored by six local leaders and called "Talking with the Enemy." The authors described an extraordinary process in which they had been involved—under secret cover—over several years. They were six women, all activists who had been fighting for decades on the frontlines of the war over abortion. They were a lawyer, a rector, a chemist, a president and CEO, and two executive directors of not-for-profits. Three were pro-life leaders, and three were pro-choice leaders.

Their article in the *Globe* cataloged a harrowing journey. Driven to come together to prevent more gruesome violence in the aftermath of the Brookline shootings, they nevertheless feared and abhorred those on the other side. They had never met with leaders across this divide and only knew of each other through the media, but they had devoted much of their lives to blocking and countering their opponents' every move. When Laura Chasin, Susan Podziba, and the Public Conversations Project in Cambridge reached out quietly to these six women and asked them to consider meeting for a clandestine dialogue, the response of the women was largely one of fear and disgust. Nevertheless, they agreed. They agreed to meet with their enemy.

The process was excruciating at first. Before the initial meeting, the pro-life group met in a booth at a nearby Friendly's restaurant and prayed together for protection and forgiveness for their sins (for sitting down with evil women). The six women then all met together, face-to-face, in a small windowless office in Watertown, Massachusetts.

Laura and Susan, both expert facilitators, laid the groundwork for their talks: safety, confidentiality, discretion, and clear, respectful ground rules for how they would speak together. Despite their agreement at the onset to behave in a respectful manner toward one another, tempers often flared. The participants had to constantly fight their instincts to shame and condemn the other side, feeling driven by a searing combination of rage and righteousness. Yet each time they somehow managed to push through.

The women initially agreed to meet together four times for four hours each over a month. After the fourth meeting, despite continued concerns over violence, they agreed to extend their sessions to the one-year anniversary of the shootings. Subsequently, they chose to prolong them further, although they found it necessary for security reasons to vary the location of their meetings, and they spoke with few others about the process. In all, they met together in hiding for five and a half years. Ultimately, they learned to work together in spite of their initial sense of the futility of such talks and their very real concerns for their own personal safety and professional standing.[33]

The talks had several extraordinary effects. First, after years of painful but increasingly constructive dialogue—learning about the others' personal lives, courage, and integrity and working collaboratively to avoid further violence in the community—*the women nevertheless found themselves even more polarized* over the issue of abortion. That's right. Ironically, by agreeing to drop their inflammatory rhetoric and to speak personally and precisely about their feelings on the issues, the participants all learned more about their own principles and eventually found themselves even more deeply committed to their original position. They wrote, "Since that first fear-filled meeting, we have experienced a paradox. While learning to treat each other with dignity and respect, we have all become firmer in our views about abortion. . . . We saw that our differences on abortion reflect two world views that are irreconcilable."[34]

Second, despite their profound moral and ideological differences, *the relationships between the women became much closer*. As one of the participants shared years later during a 2011 public forum,

> As you hear us and see us today, I think the thing that might not be seen here are the very painful moments that were also part of the dialogue. I mean we were discussing for five years, with great passion and intensity, our trying to get to deeper understanding of our differences over the abortion issue. . . . It was painful and there was hurt and difficult moments. I think the thing that we were surprised at at times was that we pushed through those moments, that even though I can remember feeling that, "Well, I think we've taken this as far as it's gonna go," there was something else that was going on about a connection to one another that was sort of, had kind of crept up on us unawares, in that we were falling in love with one another.[35]

To this day, twenty-five years later, the group continues to get together occasionally to provide support to one another during times of loss and to celebrate joyous occasions. When Susan Podziba was asked recently how this is possible, she remarked simply, "We share much more than we differ."

Third, *the women also reported learning a great deal about the complexity, trade-offs, and contradictions* inherent in their own positions on abortion. One participant realized that

> We never talk on our own sides about the shades of gray. When you are involved in a political movement like we are, we are focused on mobilizing the troops and the way you do that is we paint things in the starkest possible terms so that people are moved to act, so they know what to do. We don't

> have conversations about things we have doubts about or are more murky. I really valued the conversations we had with the women who shared my perspective on the reproductive choice issue.

The challenges the conversations presented and the quality of how the women engaged seemed to open their minds to previously neglected aspects of their own views, which ultimately broadened their thinking and feeling and changed their approach to their advocacy.

Finally, *the transformation of these six community leaders seemed to affect the broader climate* of the debate over abortion.[36] The day after publication of their article in the *Boston Globe*, the leaders held a public press conference and were shocked to find the room filled with journalists and camera crews from all the major networks. Media requests, invitations to speak at universities, and emails of (mostly) thanks and support poured in from around the globe. Some were quite personal, sharing sentiments such as, "If you all can find the courage to do this, I can certainly speak with my mother about our differences." In other words, the group's decision to go public, particularly given the risks they took, their perseverance, and their status within their communities resonated widely.

Years after the article was published, another journalist observed, "The reduction in angry rhetoric that resulted from the dialogue may have helped assign to history that ugly chapter in the abortion controversy."[37] Despite the fact that the controversy continues to grind on in the United States, the violence and vitriol of the debate in the Boston community has largely subsided. In other words, they seemed to have fashioned a way out of some of the most perilous terrain of this protracted conflict.

THE WAY OUT

The tensions and events surrounding the Boston abortion conflict share many parallels with our current climate of political polarization in the United States and offer some hints of *the way out*. Here, too, was a deeply rooted, increasingly tense, and seemingly intractable conflict between two camps of mostly true believers that had persisted for many decades. There was no obvious way of de-escalation. This was largely due to the fact that there were so many pieces to this particular puzzle that kept it heated—religious beliefs and personal ethical decisions, legal and medical issues and scientific advances, politics and angry rhetoric, friendships and enemies, and secrets and shame. These elements can combine to create treacherous landscapes that feel impossible to escape. Even the catastrophic violence of the clinic shootings seemed to have little significant impact on the underlying tensions until years later when the effects of the leaders' dialogue process were revealed. And this required a significant reset: a careful, intentional, well-facilitated process that involved courageous, influential leaders from the community who were able to persevere over a long period of time. But even more than that, it required the fruits of these transformational encounters to permeate out through networks of influence into the broader community to affect societal-level change. Despite the fact that the leaders made little progress in reconciling their ideological differences over the issue of abortion, they nevertheless transformed their relationships, enhanced their own understanding of the dilemmas inherent to their own positions, helped to stem violence in their community, and quieted the rhetoric and contempt affecting the larger ethos around both movements.

Much of what can be gleaned from the Boston case has been borne out in the systematic study of other cases of deeply entrenched, divisive conflict.[38] These conflicts tend to be highly complex and mercurial, with many interrelated causes. They are often unresponsive to well-intentioned efforts to address them and respond strangely to significant shocks to their system (such as violence) often only years later. So nothing much changes for years, and then everything seems to change. Genuine, sustained change usually requires a concerted effort by leaders and citizens at various levels (particularly local, grassroots leaders) both to reduce the likelihood of additional violent, polarizing or otherwise destructive incidents and to increase the chances of more positive, prosocial types of language, encounters, and activities between members of the previously warring groups.

Of course, the nationwide trend of toxic polarization we are currently experiencing is a much larger quagmire than that faced in Boston in the 1990s. Today the many layers of causes of our divisions are constantly discussed and analyzed by academics and the media, but they are often poorly understood. One premise of this book is that none of the usual suspects cited for this pattern of divisiveness—our neural tribal tendencies, red-versus-blue moral differences, a loneliness epidemic, a blistering pace of technological and cultural change, sensationalist media, the business model of the major internet platforms, divisive political leadership, foreign interference, and so on—is really the cause of our current crisis. All of them are. It is more accurate to say that the intractable trends seen in our current divisions are not caused by any one thing but rather by how the many different sources of these tensions combine and feed off one another in ways that create landscapes for our lives that are difficult to change. In other words, we need to look beyond the motives that present as the surface features of these problems and gain a better understanding of their underlying structural dynamics.

Today we understand quite a bit about these kinds of strong, complicated, change-resistant patterns. Physicists and other scientists have long studied these types of dynamics in many areas of the physical and social world, including the change-resistant nature of some cancer cells, the contagious spread of hate speech on social media, the intractability of certain patterns of violence in cities, and protracted wars between nations. Scientists call these *attractors.*

Attractors are simply patterns that are revealed when you measure something (e.g., attitudes, marital relations, voting behavior, or intergroup tensions) that seems to resist change for a long period of time. These patterns are fed by many different elements interacting and reinforcing one another in complicated ways. Like a strong whirlpool or maelstrom, they display dynamics that, in fact, draw us into their patterns—they attract us. Think of them as a chronic habit, addiction, or abusive relationship in which we get stuck. They draw us in repeatedly to toxic patterns of thinking, feeling, and behaving that can begin to feel impossible to escape. Today we are all stuck in an us-versus-them attractor that is much larger and more powerful than any one of us.

The phenomenon of attractors has powerful implications for understanding and addressing pathological forms of polarization, and they are the focus of this book. Attractors are created by many different elements working in concert, but they also present us with almost as many ways out of them. These, of course, can be hard to see unless you know where to look.

As you read these pages, I will show you where to look. New insights from current research illustrate how seemingly unchangeable problems can and do, in fact, change. I will suggest what *you* can do—the actions, skills, and competencies that will help you navigate these times most effectively—as well as what to look for in *groups and organizations in your community* that are already at work making America more functional again.

Clearly, we all need a break from our mass national psychotic break.

2
WHY WE ARE STUCK

THE BOOMING BUSINESS OF BESTING

A while back, I was invited (via Twitter) to a "pop-up" meeting in New York City about the alarming rise in hate speech and polarization on social media, hosted by one of the founders of a popular community advocacy group. The gathering was small but included an accomplished group of leaders from the big social media platforms (yes, those), some tech journalists, and a few of us scrawny academics. We met at lunchtime during a snow storm in a temporary meeting space in the Fashion district. It happened to be on the day that the *New York Times* published a scathing front-page exposé about the "delay, deny and deflect" leadership of Mark Zuckerberg and Sheryl Sandberg at Facebook in response to Russian agents weaponizing their platform to leverage hate and sow division to sway the 2016 U.S. presidential election.[1] A current executive and one of the founders of Facebook (no, not him) was in the room for our meeting. I was riveted.

The meeting began with the convener writing on a white board, "What type of dialogue should we be having on social media to promote a healthy virtual society?" Given that I was the least qualified person to speak about social media in the room, I spoke first, suggesting, "Well, it depends on what you mean by *dialogue*." When this was met with stony silence, I clarified, explaining that there is widespread misunderstanding about what the process of dialogue actually entails. Most people using the term are referring to debate or criticism or other forms of oppositional confrontation, which are more closed communication processes of persuasion and influence aimed at winning a disagreement. Dialogue, in fact, is completely the opposite. It is a process of open and reflective speaking, hearing, learning, and discovery that is unfamiliar to most of us. It is more like what you would hear at a Quaker meeting or an AA meeting.

After another long silence the cofounder of Facebook spoke up and said, "Oh, well, if *that* is dialogue, then there is nowhere online where people can go to dialogue—other than Zoom. It just doesn't exist." The group seemed to agree.

Now let's get this straight. Online social media—increasingly our primary channel for communication and source for entertainment, news, and information, and one of the more accessible avenues of contact we have these days with people who disagree with us—is built primarily for debate, criticism, competition, social comparison. and contention. It does not offer much space for promoting reflective listening and mutual understanding. In other words, the underlying algorithms on which the major social media platforms are currently based are actively pitting us against each other.

Of course, this makes sense. Consider, for instance, the legendary (but disputed) origin story of Facebook. In 2003, nineteen-year-old, 5 ft. 7 in., Harvard sophomore Mark Zuckerberg gets jilted by a girl and then goes to his room, drinks beer with his friends, and builds a website called "Facemash," which invites viewers to compare photos of fellow Harvard classmates and choose which one is "hotter." The site "blows-up"—attracting 450 visitors and twenty-two thousand photo views in its first four hours—temporarily shutting down Harvard's IT system. This intentionally addictive, probably vindictive, exclusive, social competition site is the framework for what in 2004 becomes Facebook, one of the big tech platforms today, serving approximately 2.4 billion users worldwide (and there are only 7.5 billion of us on the planet).

Facebook's espoused mission today is "to give people the power to build community and bring the world closer together." But what kind of community is it building? Even ignoring the instances when it has been intentionally weaponized for political gain[2] or to promote genocidal violence (such as in Myanmar[3] and South Sudan[4]), is a community based fundamentally on competition and social comparison what is needed to promote a "healthy virtual society"? And given the platform's addictive quality and unprecedented levels of success, can we be surprised that its leadership is loath to change its basic business model? Or that other platforms have happily followed in its footsteps?

Take a moment and consider what this means for our increasingly divisive, device-oriented society. This led a colleague of mine to quip recently during a presentation on technology and terror, "Social media is to polarization and violence what carbon is to climate change."[5] Namely, a basic accelerant.

And this is just one piece of what we are up against. A growing constellation of forces beyond social media is working in concert today to pit us against each other and to pull this country apart. Some of them simply create a strong climate of self-focus, interpersonal competition and one-upmanship. Others build on this ethos and start to draw moral lines in the sand between groups—good versus bad, right versus wrong, us versus them. Others are more blatant in depicting certain out-groups as genuine threats. Still others go further and vilify and dehumanize members of some out-groups, calling for their complete exclusion or elimination. The result is a more tense, toxic, fractured society.

In this chapter, I explore some of the many forces fueling our culture of divisiveness today. I begin with a brief discussion of our main topic—polarization—explaining what it is and why humans are often so susceptible to its lure. I then briefly summarize what decades of research on polarization suggest is driving the current pattern and explain why these researchers have gotten it partly right, but mostly wrong. This sets up chapter 2, in which I introduce the idea of *attractors*, the main focus of our story, and explain how attractors provide a more accurate and fruitful way of understanding our current situation—and of envisioning a way out.

THE ATTRACTION OF POLARIZATION

In 1940, the German Nazi army occupied Paris. Four years later, French philosopher Jean-Paul Sartre wrote a short piece in *The Atlantic* that provides a glimpse into one of the deeper and most effective drivers of polarization, moral certainty.

> Never were we freer than under the German occupation. We had lost all our rights, and first of all our right to speak. They insulted us to our faces every day—and we had to hold our tongues. They deported us *en masse*—as workers,

as Jews, and political prisoners. Everywhere,–upon the walls, in the press, on the screen–we found that filthy and insipid image of ourselves which the oppressor wished to present to us. And because of all this we were free.[6]

Sartre's main thesis in this haunting essay illustrates the emancipating power of free will and solidarity under the worst possible circumstances. Yet his words also suggest that there is something liberating, almost comforting, about living in a world of clear good and evil. No messy gray areas, no confusion, and no need to compromise–just a sturdy sense of certainty, of a place to take a stand. We are good and they are evil, and that is that. Our purpose is therefore simple–stand and fight in solidarity and resist them at every turn. The Boston leaders described a similar pull toward clarity of purpose in their advocacy work on abortion. Many "red and blue" Americans are feeling it today. Such cleaving of the world into good and evil feels particularly necessary and reassuring under conditions of high threat, anxiety, and uncertainty–when life feels scary and chaotic and unpredictable (like today).

Psychologists have situated this need for moral certainty in what is known as the *consistency principle.* This is a very robust finding across much of psychology and behavioral economics: People seek consistency in their lives–in how they think, feel, and act, in what they value, and in their relationships.[7] This means that it usually feels bad to contradict ourselves publicly (flip-flop) or to behave in ways that go against our more important values (like enjoying the company of our enemy) or to have close friendships with people who are friendly with others we despise (how could they?) or to challenge the basic beliefs of our more cherished identity groups (yes, my friends, the *New York Times* has been shown to be highly biased too[8]). Inconsistencies and contradictions like these just don't feel right. When life gets particularly tense, unpredictable, or dangerous, we seek consistency and certainty even more desperately. So it follows that in more threatening times (like today) we find comfort and solace in moral certainty.

In Nazi-occupied France during WWII, the threat to the French people was an objective reality. But in America today, threat is often a political device; we weaponize the threat of the other: "They are coming for your guns!" "They are coming for your SUVs!" "They are coming for complete control of women's bodies!" These stories are told to us and our children daily by much of the media, by our political leaders, and by friends and acquaintances in our local and social media tribes who continue to become more and more distant from and contemptuous of the other side. Of course, there are real threats to our life, liberty, and happiness out there, but manufacturing threat is a booming industry today. And the effects of real and manufactured threats are often quite similar; they pull us into feeling a sense of fear and repulsion from "them," safety and comfort among "us," and the need to put as much distance between them and us as possible.

WHAT IS POLARIZATION, ANYWAY?

Polarization is a bit hard to define because it has meant different things to different people.[9] Essentially, it is an observable phenomenon first described by scientists in the early 1600s that involved light, radiation, or magnetism moving in specific directions—usually toward one pole and away from another. Initially, scientists understood polarization as the result of two forces acting between one body and another in an empty space, similar to a ping-pong match. But in the 1800s, Hans Christian Oersted and Michael Faraday conducted a series of brilliant experiments on electromagnetism that challenged this basic view. They demonstrated that between two opposing magnetic poles, instead of empty space, lies a *complex field of forces acting to attract and repel* the poles (figure 2.1).

Fantastic, right? Hold this image in your mind for a moment.

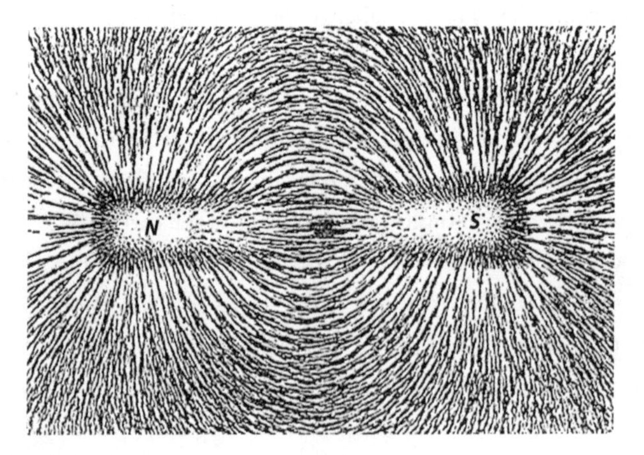

2.1 Magnetic polarization.

In politics, polarization has long referred to the divergence of political attitudes toward more ideological extremes, such as I described between the Boston pro-life and pro-choice camps. However, more recently, scholars have begun to distinguish between different aspects of attitude divergence, such as between *affective polarization*, the tendency of members of oppositional groups to feel negatively about the opposing group members and positively about members of their own group, and *ideological polarization*, the divergence of attitudes on substantive issues.[10] Recall that the Boston leadership dialogue group was able to slowly disentangle these two forms, and their feelings and ideological beliefs eventually diverged.

Political polarization is somewhat different from both affective and ideological polarity, referring instead to cases in which an individual's stance on a given issue, policy, or person is more likely to be influenced by identification with a particular political party or ideology (e.g., progressive or conservative) than with understanding the issue or the person. Political polarization has been found to be associated with higher levels of out-group hostility, aggressiveness, and more intensive conflicts—but also with more active political engagement.[11]

More recently, scholars have also begun to study something called *perceptual polarization*, the degree to which a gap exists between what Americans believe to be the attitudes of the opposing party on an issue and what their attitudes actually are. A recent study showed that most Americans believe that members of the other party dehumanize, dislike, and disagree with their own party about twice as much as they actually do.[12] Today many Americans are demonstrating some combination of all the above.

Of course, political polarization is not necessarily a bad thing. In fact, some degree of ideological divergence has long been seen as a functional aspect of healthy, two-party system democracies.[13] In fact, research has shown that under certain conditions more polarized ideological differences can lead to higher-quality decision making in teams.[14] However, when political differences become extreme, chronic, and increasingly intolerant, they are often toxic and pathological.

A FEW CONCERNING TRENDS IN AMERICA TODAY

Many books and articles on polarization are being published today, so I will not elaborate on the many ways our society is and is not currently divided.[15]

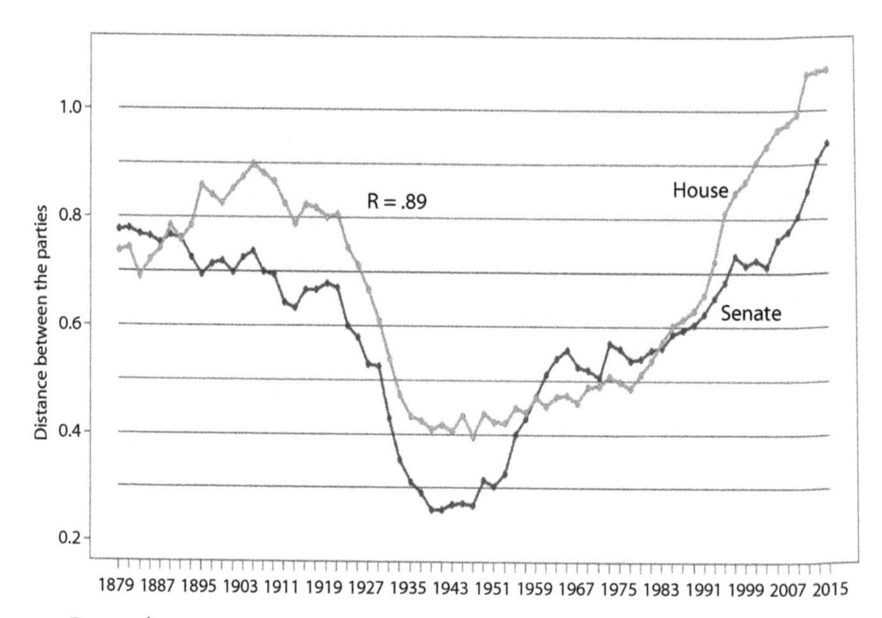

2.2 Party polarization 1879–2015: Degree of division and bipartisanship over time.

However, I do want to stress a few important points. First, it is critical to understand that we are in the midst of a decades-long trend of escalating polarization. Figure 2.2 displays voting patterns in the U.S. Congress (both Senate and House) from 1879 until 2015.[16] The lower the lines, the more cooperation and compromise we saw between the parties on legislative voting; the higher the lines, the more polarization.

According to these data, the last time the U.S. Congress was nearly as politically polarized as it is today was in the late 1800s, after the end of the U.S. Civil War. Beginning in the 1920s, we saw a marked decrease in partisan division, which ushered in decades of more functional bipartisanship in Congress. But since around 1979, we have seen a steady increase in polarization in legislative voting, which continues today and contributes to the bitter, fractious, and dysfunctional climate currently on display.

These trends are not only evident among political elites. A study on data from the American National Election Studies (ANES) database found that ideological polarization has also increased dramatically among the public in the United States since the 1970s.[17] The authors found significant differences in outlook between Democrats and Republicans, between red and blue state voters, and between religious and secular voters. These divisions were not confined to a small minority of activists but involved large segments of the general public—with the deepest divisions found among the most interested, informed, and engaged citizens. So Main Street and K Street (home of D.C. lobbyists) have apparently been in sync on this for quite some time.

Nevertheless, it may be interesting to note that despite the stand-offs we are seeing in Washington, D.C. today, the American public is *not* more polarized in terms of political party (Democrat-Republican) or ideological (Progressive-Conservative) affiliation than in recent decades. Polling from Pew and ANES suggests that these trends have been mostly flat or in decline for about seventy years.[18]

Strange, right? This suggests that the current divisions we are experiencing are not necessarily about stronger identification with *these* groups, or at least if they are, they are more nuanced and complicated than the red-versus-blue America stories we are told.[19] It most likely suggests that some of the subdivisions within these groups (such as pro- and anti-Trump conservatives) are increasingly meaningful today.

Second, the data on the American public does point to two other particularly concerning ways that we are more divided today; our *feeling* and our *thinking* about our national political landscape have become more simplistic, dichotomized, and tribal. Emotionally, Americans are feeling much colder toward and contemptuous of those on the other side of our political divide than in past decades, and they are feeling a much greater sense of warmth and loyalty for members of their own in-group.[20] For instance, the proportion of people who hold "very unfavorable views" of the opposite party has more than doubled since 1994. A recent study from our lab found that strong majorities (around 80 percent) of both Democrats and Republicans view members of the other party as "more immoral, dishonest, and close-minded" than members of their own. So many of us are experiencing much higher levels of affective polarization.[21]

This high level of contempt for members of the other party has resulted in a preponderance of *negative partisanship*, in which Americans largely mobilize *against* the other party rather than align with their own.[22] This, of course, is a common tactic of political campaigns, but it is usually accompanied by a candidate and a platform that also attracts voters. Today's partisans care less and less about their own party leaders' policies or actions because their real concerns are the many perceived threats posed by those on the other side. Threats from out-groups can be profoundly motivating[23] (especially with the hyperbole of an aggressive political campaign), and in this context even a highly flawed candidate and party are seen by their own as the lesser of two evils.

Finally, data also show that our understanding of the major challenges our nation is facing is becoming much more superficial and simplistic. The Pew Research Center's "ideological consistency scale" measures the degree of overlap people hold—both within and between parties—on attitudes about ten distinct but often polarizing issues in the United States, including views on governmental waste and efficiency, homosexuality, welfare policies, and environmental regulations. Since 1994, Pew has tracked the correlations of all ten of these issues within and between our main political groups. The data show that the split between Democrats and Republicans (and the convergence of attitudes across the ten issues within each party) has grown markedly over the past twenty years. This suggests that we, as individuals, are paying much less attention to the specifics of the issues that divide us, opting instead to believe and follow the party line on these matters.[24] Yes, there was a time in the not-so-distant past when many of us held more nuanced views of our world—when, for example, we had more fiscal conservatives with liberal views on some social issues, and vice versa. Today they are a vanishing breed.

This suggests that of us today are putting much less time and energy into seeking accurate information about the people on the other side of the divide or on the many different challenges facing our world, choosing instead to think and feel in ways that are consistent and conforming with our tribes. We are devoting much more energy to obtaining a sense of *belonging* and comfort from our groups than to seeking accurate information about our increasingly complicated world. Psychologically, the need to acquire accurate information and the need to belong to groups are often competing motives that humans need to navigate between and manage optimally (sometimes we choose to ignore the problems within our groups for the sake of harmony, other times we just can't).[25] Today the need for belonging is clearly trumping the need for accuracy (pun intended).

Stanford political scientist Matthew Gentzkow recently summed up the state of the American political landscape.

> Putting the evidence together, it seems clear that polarization is a real, and serious phenomenon. Americans may or may not be further apart on the issues than they used to be. But clearly what divides them politically is increasingly personal, and this in many ways may be worse. We don't just disagree politely

> about what is the best way to reform the health care system. We believe that those on the other side are trying to destroy America, and that we should spare nothing in trying to stop them.[26]

This statement, in fact, echoes Sartre's sentiments regarding moral certainty in 1944 Nazi-occupied Paris.

OUR ENDURING PATTERN OF POLARIZATION

Why are we so stuck? What are the main drivers of our decades-long pattern of escalating division? Existing research on polarization suggests a wide variety of competing theories on this. These vary from basic, person-level factors and tendencies to broader, macro-level policies and structures. Figure 2.3 provides a snapshot of a few.

These are all reasonable theories with decent scientific evidence supporting most of them. Some argue for the importance of basic biological differences in brain sensitivities to threat between red and blue Americans, with conservatives being more inclined to be motivated by perceptions of danger.[27] Others argue that differences in moral priorities (e.g., some research suggests that conservatives prioritize the values of loyalty, authority, and purity and liberals prioritize values of care and fairness[28]) and related personality disparities such as authoritarianism and social dominance orientation drive partisan preferences.[29] Others emphasize community-level drivers, including competition over scarce jobs, unequal educational opportunities, or changing demographics. Further out, others focus on the nature of our competitive and dysfunctional political processes, legacies of racism and sexism, rising economic inequality, and the hypercompetitive pressures emanating from unregulated capitalism. A few even look beyond our borders at how foreign powers intentionally target and exacerbate our internal divisions.

And, of course, they are right. They are all right sometimes and to different degrees. In statistics-speak, this means that each of these factors might explain some small percentage of the variance of polarization in some studies but not in others.

Nevertheless, I disagree with the premise that any of these drivers can account for a more than fifty-year pattern of increasingly intractable division. We scholars

Micro-Level Drivers

- Partisan differences in evolutionary brain wiring for threat sensitivity
- Amygdala (fear) stimulation from mere outgroup images
- Role of "hot" emotions in political decision making
- Human ethnocentric tendencies and tribal psychology
- Reduction in mixed-partisan marriages and families
- Socialization of negative outgroup antipathy
- Basic processes of selective perception and confirmation bias
- Partisan differences in authoritarianism and obedience to authority
- Partisan differences in motivated reasoning and need for closure
- Differences in moral value priorities between Libs and Cons
- Preferences for economic vs. social rationality
- Cognitive rigidity of more extreme/engaged partisans
- The rise in loneliness and alienation in the United States
- Power of group identity to affect perceptions
- Inclination to conform to group norms
- Salience and rumination over partisan differences
- Frustration displacement onto outgroups
- Reliance on stereotypes under high cognitive demand
- A crisis of meaning as families and communities fracture
- Decreasing contact with members of the other side
- Competition for scarce resources (jobs) and power
- Dissatisfaction from governmental dysfunction/gridlock
- Technological advances that threaten our livelihoods
- Increasing information overload
- Increasing pace of change = uncertainty and anxiety!

Macro-Level Drivers

- Our two-party, winner-takes-all political system
- Effectiveness of negative political campaigning and governing
- Ingroup sanctioning against outgroup contact/communication
- Voter suppression efforts
- Failure of our divided educational systems (wealthy and poor)
- Rapidly rising inequality
- Historic injustice and ethnic group fissures in our communities
- Destabilization from political shocks (since late 1960s)
- Citizens United decision and $ in politics
- Gingrich's restructuring of Congress's social structure (contact)
- Political gerrymandering
- "Primarying" of moderate candidates
- Manipulation of fear by political leaders
- The competitive, normless, anonymous internet
- Our hypercompetitive capitalist business model
- Interference from foreign actors/internet trolls
- Profit motives that drive news media sensationalism
- 24-hour news cycles increase threat perception
- Internet algorithms that sort us into preference groups
- Loss of trust in the fairness of our institutions
- Increases in cybersecurity threats and data sharing
- Increasing isolation of wealthy elites
- Rapid demographic changes and shifting population majorites
- Stark increases in natural and social threats (terrorism)
- Honor cultures of toxic masculinity

2.3 Micro- and macro-level drivers of political division.

and pundits too often fall prey to the *single sovereign theory fallacy.*[30] After spending years studying a major cause of a problem or writing a book on it, we start to overvalue its singular importance. Here are a few examples.

"Our problem is really about moral value differences between rural conservative and urban progressive groups."

"No, it's about political maneuvering, gerrymandering, and the intentional suppression and manipulation of voters."

"No, no, no, it's about how differences in the threat sensitivity of the brains of reds versus blues lead to completely different worldviews! It's in our neurons!"

"Can't you see, this is really about our profound loneliness epidemic and our desperate need to belong to our tribal groups!"

"No! It's all about the money in media. Just look at FOX, MSNBC, and social media. They're all chasing dollars and clicks at the expense of the common good."

"How can you not see that this is essentially about racism and white backlash in response to the success of President Obama—it is so obvious!"

"It is clearly about men. Our political system was born from toxic masculinity, and its hypercompetitive, dominance-oriented, phallic devotion (see the Washington Monument) still fuels it today."

"Nope. It's our parents' fault. They either raised authoritarian children who are threatened by everything or snowflake progressives who are offended by everything!"

"The problem is clear. Robots. Robots and artificial intelligence are taking over our jobs and our decision making, and no one is paying attention. It is making us all crazy anxious because we know they're coming and we can't stop it—so we look for someone to blame."

All good points.

Don't get me wrong, however; I am not equating all of these drivers. Clearly some of these factors go deeper and play a much more central role in dividing us than others do. In fact, we conducted a recent search of the published review papers and meta-analyses (statistical summaries) on the science on drivers of polarization to see which ones stood out.[31] Although the results of this search did not prove conclusive in identifying *the* most powerful drivers, three stories emerged—the people, the group, and society.

1. **The People Story: Humans are highly emotional, esteem-thirsty, cognitive misers.** As sophisticated as human cognition is relative to that of other species, it is also sorely limited. First, we process information in fundamentally emotional ways. Even when we think we're being highly rational, the emotion centers in our brain light up bright when we talk and think about political issues. Second, we are also highly threat sensitive and attend much more carefully to its perceived sources. We prefer to take in information that affirms our existing beliefs and values, both for consistency and so we can boost our feelings of self and group-based esteem. We just love to belong to highly esteemed groups. Third, we take many cognitive shortcuts, categorizing one another in overly simplified ways to help us reduce the cognitive load on our brains. Differences in personality factors such as authoritarianism and social dominance orientation also play a part in preferring in-group superiority. Finally, differences in how we prioritize our core moral values lead to self-righteous divisions. All this adds up to a basic susceptibility to being split and divided into us versus them.
2. **The Group Story: Humans form group preferences quickly, and groups tend toward conformity and extremity.** We all tend to favor our in-groups (to increase our self-esteem), and a close cousin of this is the tendency to disfavor and discriminate against out-groups. Even when groups are based on nothing more than coin tosses or estimates of the number of jelly beans in a jar, we quickly show in-group favoritism. Over time, in-groups tend toward conformity and uniformity in thought and deed—we care a lot about our in-group's approval of us!—and new member selection, socialization, and sanctioning perpetuates this. We are also more likely to share information consistent with in-group opinions, and these processes result in shifts toward more extreme group attitudes. Feelings of relative group deprivation—not getting what your group deserves when compared to another group—are also highly motivating in pitting us against other groups. Using these levers, it is relatively easy for leaders and outsiders to manipulate group divisions and gain power by dividing and conquering.

3. **The Societal Story: Differences in societal norms and structures matter, with hostilities accumulating over time.** Humans tend to move toward people who are similar to them (and away from those who differ)—something called homophily—and therefore establish physical, social, security, and economic structures in their communities that reflect this homogeneity. There also appears to be a universal tendency toward hierarchical group structures in large societies, with certain groups (particularly men) often ascending to the top and then dominating and holding on for dear life. These tendencies become intensified under difficult conditions of perceived threat. Where we are located in these structures (top or bottom) affects what we care about, our sense of identity, and what resources and information we can access. More insolated and competitive structures and norms between groups inherently drive polarization, and when you add power struggles and scarcity over important resources, it is even more likely. The negative emotional consequences around these divisions often accumulate over time and create volatile conditions for intergroup strife.

In other words, we found that the intransigence of our current divisive trend is simply not due to any one cause. Rather, it is the result of how many different individual, community, and macro-level tendencies and influences start to line up and fuel each other in complex and ever-increasing ways, establishing *vicious cycles*. This *is not* how most of us, including most scientists and policy makers, tend to think about and study problems, but *it is* the nature of many of our more wicked problems.

VICIOUS CYCLES, CYCLONES, AND SUPERSTORMS

Here is a simple illustration of a vicious cycle. Say, in 2016 you had a slight preference for Donald Trump or Hillary Clinton for president. When you caught the news or scrolled through Twitter, you would have tended to process the information you came across in a manner that reinforced your feelings about your preferred candidate (figure 2.4) and ignored or disregarded information that contradicted your feelings (remember, we don't like inconsistency). Psychologists

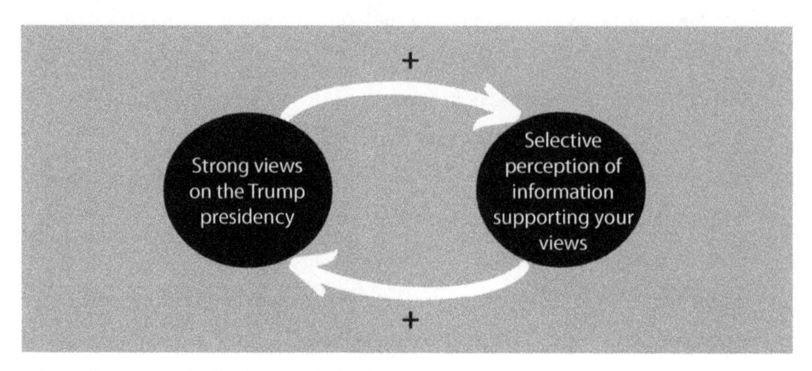

2.4 A reinforcing cycle that strengthens division.

refer to this process as *confirmation bias*, which is a form of motivated reasoning. We don't process new information neutrally, instead we are motivated to make sense of it in ways that are consistent with our existing worldview. We all do it. Consuming more attitude-consistent information would have strengthened your original views, and the stronger they became, the more likely you would be to continue to do this, in turn bolstering your preference even more. This illustrates a very simple *reinforcing feedback loop* in which your initial attitude affects your information processing, which reinforces and strengthens that attitude, and away you go! This scenario suggests that increasingly polarized attitudes are due less to existing opinions or biased information processing than to how they can escalate each other over time.

Of course, vicious cycles also can be more complicated (figure 2.5). For instance, if you strongly supported President Trump, it is likely that you shared his philosophy of "American Carnage" that the United States is a country under perpetual attack by countless sources of internal and external threat and decay. If you spurned Trump, you would have tended to view *him* and his policies as a major existential threat to the survival of the United States. Either way, you would be likely to feel higher levels of anxiety about our future. Given this increase in anxiety, you would have been much more likely to seek out and tune into news and information about events in our country, but largely select and prefer sources that are consistent with your views (and therefore more comforting). And given our twenty-four-hour news cycle, you would also have been likely to be more frequently exposed to these one-sided presentations of the news by

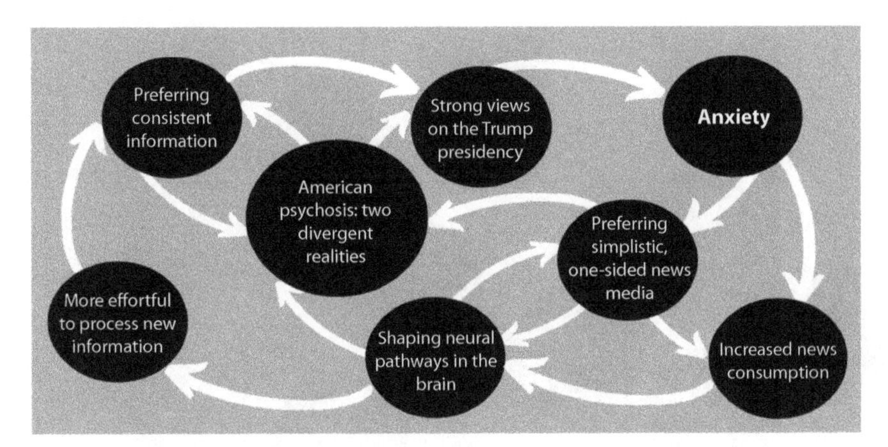

2.5 Vicious cycles that increase divergent realities.

your preferred media outlets. This higher level of exposure to consistent information can eventually reconfigure the neural pathways in your brain, making it harder and more effortful to process and comprehend contradictory perspectives on the issues. This makes it less likely that you would even think about changing the channel or following someone from the other team on Twitter. This, in turn, leads to more exposure to the original sources, higher anxiety, and so on. The result is spiraling levels of divergent realities: our American psychosis.

But that's not all. This set of vicious cycles is mostly happening within our own heads. It, in turn, can be fed by other feedback cycles related to other aspects of information flow, including in-group socialization processes, homogenous social networks, internet sorting algorithms, an exponential rise in the pervasiveness of social media, political weaponizing of distrust in media, and other related forces, forming what I call *vicious cyclones*, like the one shown in figure 2.6. Simply mapping the constellation of these cycles begins to reveal how different polarizing forces can work in concert with one another to make our patterns of division stronger, more complex, and ever-more difficult to change.

This set of cycles is only looking at bias in our flow and processing of information. These vicious cyclones can also be affected by other economic, political, cultural, and psychological factors at the individual, community, national, and international levels, which can create *superstorms of polarization* that begin to seem impossible to address (figure 2.7).

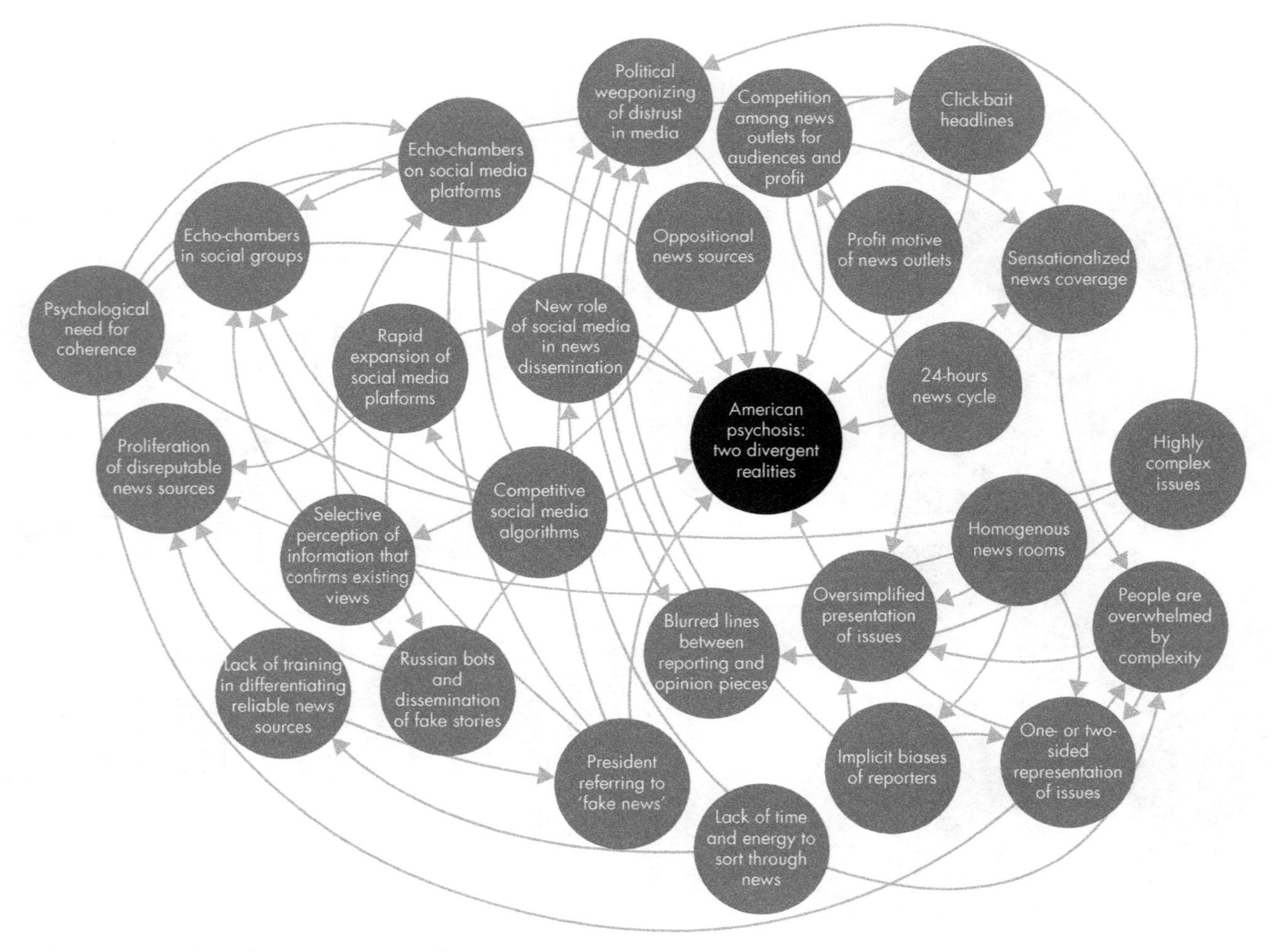

2.6 A vicious cyclone of news consumption factors.

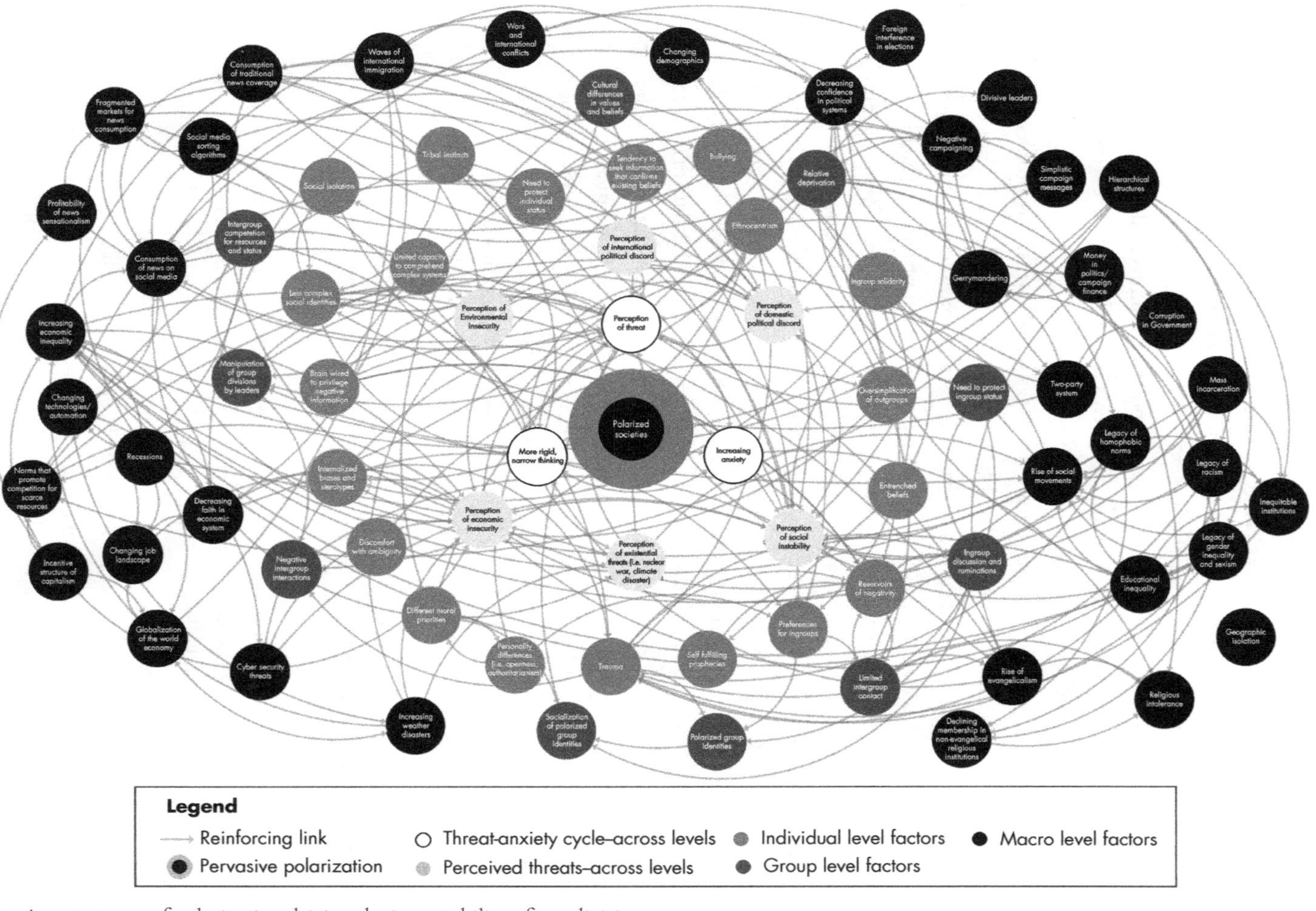

2.7 A superstorm of polarization driving the intractability of our divisions.

Help!! Together these forces create a dangerous landscape for our lives that readily attracts us into toxic, pathological patterns of repulsion and contempt for their side and love and loyalty of our own.

Now recall the image of electromagnetic polarization revealed by the experiments of Oersted and Faraday in the 1800s. This is exactly what they were trying to tell us. The problem, you see, is complex.

My emphasis on the complex nature of the system of interacting problems we are facing today does *not* mean that I believe all of these problems are of equal consequence. Some of the current drivers of our division, such as the actions of race-baiting politicians in the context of our deep legacy of racism; the blanket vilification and delegitimization of our mainstream media (our Fourth Estate), which could otherwise act as a check on our divisions; the incitement of violence against one's political opponents; and the disdain and disparagement of rigorous scientific findings when they are politically inconvenient not only do great harm in the present but also deeply offend large swaths of our population and trigger deep-seated reservoirs of indignation and outrage. These (and other) drivers can have a considerable *direct* impact on our level of intergroup enmity and polarization. Nevertheless, despite their direct effects, they too operate in a system of forces that has become largely self-perpetuating and consequently increasingly intractable and therefore must be understood and addressed as a system. In other words, attempting to address a system of problems by attending to any one problem at a time—is part of the problem. This is why we are stuck.

CLOUD PROBLEMS

In a brilliant lecture in 1965,[32] Karl Popper, one of the most influential philosophers of science of the last century, argued that how scientists—and all humans for that matter—think about problems metaphorically matters, and he proposed a crucial distinction between two different types of problems: clock problems and cloud problems (figure 2.8). *Clock problems* are those, like "a very reliable pendulum clock," that are of a more mechanical, knowable, controllable, and predictable nature. They can be disassembled and analyzed—broken down into their component parts and precisely measured and studied in order to reveal the source of the problem—and then can be repaired and reassembled to resume their

Clock Problems —————————————— **Cloud Problems**

Based on **The Newtonian Revolution** (1687), which led to "Physical Determinism," the view that all physical events can be described by physical laws.	**Karl Popper**	Based on **Quantum theory** (1920s), which led to "Physical indeterminism," the view that not all physical events are "predetermined with absolute precision."
Clock problems are those, like "a very reliable pendulum clock," that are of a more mechanical, knowable, controllable, and predictable nature.	**Of Clouds and Clocks**	***Cloud problems*** are those, like clusters of gnats or gaseous clouds, that are of a highly irregular, disorderly, uncontrollable, and unpredictable nature.
All cloud problems are actually clocks, it's just that our ignorance of their underlying laws leads us to see them as clouds.		**All clock problems are in fact clouds,** as randomness and chance affect everything, known as the *uncertainty principle*.
Clocks can be disassembled and analyzed–broken down to component parts, precisely measured and studied to reveal the source of the problem–and then can be repaired and reassembled to resume their original functionality.	**1965**	Clouds are considered *complex* because many aspects of these problems interact over time in unpredictable ways and therefore they evidence erratic behavior and outcomes.
Clock problems can be fixed through problem-solving methods.		**Cloud problems prove unresponsive to standard problem-solving techniques and require alternative methods.**

Automobiles · **Solar system** · **Cannonballs** · **Tides** · **Changing seasons** · **Plants** · **Animals** · **Man** · **Gnat cluster** · **Gaseous clouds** · **Drops of storm water**

2.8 Clock problems and cloud problems.

original functionality. Typically, problems with automobiles, jet engines, computers, and even traffic and city planning can be categorized as clock problems.

At the other extreme are *cloud problems*. These are challenges of a highly irregular, disorderly, and unpredictable nature. Popper classified scientific phenomena such as water droplets in storm clouds, individual molecules in a gas, and clusters of gnats as cloud problems. Cloud problems also include human problems such as change-resistant forms of corruption, poverty, discrimination, homelessness, violence, and political polarization. These are not simply more complicated problems. They are considered *complex* because many aspects of these problems interact over time in unpredictable ways, evidence erratic behavior, and typically prove unresponsive to standard, proven solutions or attempts at problem solving. As a result, our good-faith attempts to address them often have no identifiable effects whatsoever, result in problems going away in the short term but resurfacing in the longer term, or serving to make matters worse.

Popper argued that clocks became *the* organizing metaphor in science around 1686 due to the unprecedented success of Newtonian mechanics, the first really successful scientific theory in human history, which triggered one of the greatest scientific revolutions of all time. Newton's theory showed that some simple laws of nature could explain very complex problems, such as the movement of the planets, tides, and cannon balls. The theory has remained unchanged since its discovery by Newton, and its extraordinary predictive power raised the hopes and aspirations of most scientists of the time (and many today) that all problems in science are ultimately measurable, predictable, and controllable.

Given that scientists are our most celebrated (and systematic) problem solvers, the clock metaphor became the standard for how we think about problems and problem solving more generally. The Newtonian revolution ushered in an era of *physical determinism* (the belief that all physical events can ultimately be described by physical laws), which is still alive and well today. It holds that the only thing standing between us and full control over our physical and social worlds is our current state of ignorance, which can be overcome through rigorous scientific inquiry. This belief was articulated by Popper as "all clouds are clocks—even the most cloudy of clouds."

However, physical determinism and clock thinking was seriously challenged and downgraded in science in the 1920s when quantum theory was first proposed in physics. Today the theoretical basis of modern physics, quantum theory explains the nature and behavior of matter and energy at the atomic and subatomic levels. At these levels, most everything is cloudy—variable and virtually impossible to measure precisely. Popper writes, "This made the world an interlocking system of clouds and clocks, so that even the best clock would, in its molecular structure, show some degree of cloudiness." This advance ushered in a period of what was called *physical indeterminism*, the understanding that not all events in the physical world are "predetermined with absolute precision, in all their infinitesimal details." This, in effect, debunked the idea that all cloud problems are clock problems. In fact, it argued that all clocks are in fact clouds because randomness and chance affect everything; this became known as the *uncertainty principle*.

Nevertheless, the assumption that all clouds are clocks—that all complex problems can be broken down into component parts to be fixed—is still prevalent in many societies today and continues to shape our views of problem solving, with direct consequences. Popper stated that "in spite of the victory of the new quantum theory, and the conversion of so many physicists to indeterminism, de Lamettrie's doctrine that man is a machine has today perhaps more defenders than ever before among physicists, biologists, and philosophers; especially in the form of the thesis that man is a computer." The popular tendency to worship technology and engineering today, particularly in the era of smartphones, the internet, genetic engineering, big data, and artificial intelligence, is a testament to this. Despite the warnings of everyone from Isaac Asimov to Stephen Hawking to Elon Musk on the potentially dire consequences of such technological idolatry, many of us still cling tightly to our clock assumptions, which affects how we think about problems, change, and our future. Our mainstream understanding of science still provides a narrative that reinforces the errors our linear brains make in our increasingly complex, nonlinear world.

Ultimately, Popper believed that most of our problems lie on a continuum somewhere between clouds and clocks, with our more complex and volatile problems closer to clouds: "Only clouds exist, though clouds of very different degrees of cloudiness." However, he emphasized two prescient points. First, he cautioned that we must be careful to approach predominantly clocklike and primarily cloudlike challenges with different strategies that fit with their distinct natures. In other words, we must employ clock tools for clock work and cloud methods for cloud work. Second, Popper argued that given the prevalence of imprecision and cloudiness in our world, we must be vigilant to view our solutions to cloudy problems critically and vigorously, to seek out and correct for our inevitable errors. He quoted the physicist John Archibald Wheeler, who said, "Our whole problem is to make the mistakes as fast as possible." This problem is solved by consciously adopting a perpetually critical attitude. Popper concluded, "This, I believe, is the highest form so far of the rational attitude, or of rationality."

If the polarizing conflicts we are facing increasingly in our lives today are cloud problems, then thinking we can "fix" them directly by administering one or more technical solutions—like just bringing reds and blues together to talk or blocking gerrymandering through legislation—is like thinking we can use a screwdriver to fix a cloudy day. The fix is totally inappropriate and inadequate for bringing about the change we desire. Still, most of us are much more familiar and comfortable with clock tools: reductionist thinking and linear change processes that give us a feeling of being in control of seemingly uncontrollable problems. We simply lack the same level of familiarity and comfort with cloud methods.

But here is a key: simply recognizing the fact that the problems we are facing around polarization are categorically different from most conflicts we face in our lives is step one. Acknowledging this fact encourages us to approach these types of problems in fundamentally different ways. It's similar to the difference between treating a flu and treating leukemia—they may initially present as similar ailments, but they require fundamentally different approaches to treatment.

THE BIG COLLAPSE

There is a second reason why complex, cloudy problems resolve into strong, simplistic patterns—we can't tolerate complexity. Given our deep need for consistency, people tend to hate extreme complexity.[33] Most of us find problem sets and images like the superstorm of polarization overwhelming, anxiety-provoking, and threatening. It feels impossible to make any sense of them, let alone do anything about them. As a basic defense against this, we tend to automatically, prematurely, oversimplify them.

Decades of research supports this. Hundreds of studies on cognitive and emotional processing have shown that they both tend to collapse under highly complex and demanding circumstances. Our cognitive processing evidences much lower levels of *cognitive complexity* (the capacity to see different sides to a problem), higher degrees of *cognitive rigidity* (dichotomous, black-and-white thinking), and we experience more *need for closure* (an aversion to ambiguity and desire for clear, expedient answers) and start to think in shorter time spans (less *consideration of future consequences* of our actions).[34] So, overall, we think smaller.

Our *emotional complexity* becomes degraded as well. We lose the capacity to tolerate feeling contradictory emotions such as frustration and appreciation for others and become more anxious, which leads us to hold more dogmatic worldviews and become more intolerant of outsiders.[35] So, overall, we feel tighter as well.

We also collapse socially. In demanding situations, we tend to *fractionalize* more, trusting smaller circles of people, splitting into tinier subgroups, and shrinking our *moral scope* of people we see as deserving of fair treatment. Today our distinct partisan and racial identities are merging as well, feeding the negative partisan effect.[36] We also develop a preference for more dominant, autocratic, and militant leaders to represent our groups, and increasingly stereotype, scapegoat, and vilify out-groups.[37] In fact, research at the national level has found that societies around the globe that have developed in the context of harsh, threatening circumstances—whether natural disasters or attacks from outsiders—tend to develop cultures that are generally tighter, that is, more internally synchronized, rule bound, and punitive toward deviance.[38]

In sum, highly complex and volatile problems cause us to feel more anxious, think in more simplistic terms, make worse decisions, trust fewer people, prefer hostile leaders, close ranks, and prepare for battle. This is exactly what we are seeing in many of the trends in Pew polling over the past several years.

Our research has found that this *collapse of complexity* promotes more intractable conflict.[39] Two decades of research in our Difficult Conversation Labs in New York and Germany has found that when encounters between people with strong opposing views on complex, morally polarizing issues—abortion, free speech versus hate speech on college campuses, or Donald Trump—collapse and become cognitively, emotionally, and behaviorally more simplistic, participants get stuck, resulting in angry stalemates in which participants typically refuse to work with the other person in the future. This has been a particularly robust and central finding in our research: more simplistic, one-dimensional processing of complex problems leads to (and are fed by) more intractable conflicts. At some point, these processes of oversimplification, certainty, and contempt become self-organizing within and between people and groups and become impervious to outside attempts to alter them. This makes them more likely to become intractable attractors.

HOW CLOUD PROBLEMS BECOME ATTRACTORS

Not all cloud problems become *attractors*, coherent patterns that draw us in and resist change. Clouds of gnats or of gas molecules, as fascinating as they may appear, do not necessarily coalesce into attractor patterns. The same is true for some complex human groups. You could have a thousand people out on the Great Lawn in Central Park in New York City on a sunny day, but because most of them are doing their own thing (juggling, sunning, napping, picnicking, or smoking weed), they never form any particular patterns that stabilize. They look much like the gnats. We call these *loosely coupled systems.*

Attractors emerge from cloudlike dynamics when the many elements that compose them become more tightly linked and aligned. This is what we see when many different elements of hurricanes—low air pressure, warm sea-surface temperatures, moist ocean air, light westerly tropical winds, thunderstorm activity, the rotation of the storm, sparse land mass in its path, and so on—interact over time and combine to form to a major hurricane. Or when the many factors that can affect a marriage - unkind gestures, irritating habits, major indiscretions, spiteful in-laws, envious friends - coalesce in a manner that pulls the couple apart emotionally until they find themselves in a loveless relationship. When different factors begin to reinforce one another in consistent ways, the patterns they form become extremely hard to change because they result in attractor patterns, and then the laws about how they change, change. Attractors operate according to a very different set of laws than the standard cause-and-effect change principles with which we are most familiar. Understanding these laws is the key to changing seemingly unchangeable patterns.

In the next chapter, I offer a bit more of the backstory on this thing we call attractors: what they are, where they come from, and how we get stuck in them. Then I describe how they can, in fact, change, and how understanding their strange, underlying laws can help us better navigate and leverage these changes.

3

ATTRACTED TO CONFLICT

What happens when a constellation of initially unrelated beliefs, attitudes, action tendencies, norms, and symbols coalesce around a conflict into strong, toxic, attractor dynamics that become increasingly inescapable? Well, this can happen.

PLUNGING INTO THE CHASM OF ABRAHAM*

In 2019, I attended a meeting in Germany of a group of high-level players in the arena of international peace and conflict that had a rather remarkable ending. The purpose of the meeting was to share new ideas for a special issue of a policy journal on peace processes—pretty standard academic stuff. It was an invited group of former UN envoys, diplomats, think tank policy makers, and academics. Our task was to write about the "relevance gap" between the increasing complexity and chaos of the emerging challenges in the Middle East and the rather stagnant and increasingly ineffectual approaches to peace still offered by

* According to the book of Genesis, Abraham left Mesopotamia because God called on him to found a new nation in Canaan, which was situated in the territory of the southern Levant that today encompasses Israel, the West Bank and Gaza, Jordan, and the southern portions of Syria and Lebanon.

most of the international community. Although I was interested in the topic, I expected a rather uneventful several days of too much coffee and bakery goods and an assortment of long-winded speakers offering their standard critiques and solutions. The meeting mostly met my expectations.

Until the afternoon of the final day.

The meeting had been set up so that each of us would present our paper, and then one of the presiding dignitaries would offer commentary on our work. One of the final sessions on the last day involved the cochair of the meeting, a highly experienced Israeli negotiation expert, presenting his paper. It was a fine paper—a bit abstract and convoluted, but nothing offensive or out of the ordinary.

Then the respondent, a former Dutch ambassador, offered his comments. He began by saying something along these lines: "Given that the focus of the special issue will be on the Middle East, and that you, an Israeli, will be a coeditor, I suspect that the journal may receive some additional scrutiny." As he attempted to continue his remarks, the Israeli cochair raised his arms into the air and asked loudly, "Pardon me! What are you saying?"

The room tensed (or maybe just awakened). The Dutch ambassador paused for a brief moment, and then quietly reiterated what he had just said.

To which the Israeli replied pointedly, "But what are you saying?"

The ambassador, clearly taken aback, stammered somewhat and then attempted to clarify what he was saying: "I was only suggesting that given the focus of the journal . . ."

The Israeli immediately jumped in: "I have *never* been treated this way professionally. In all my decades of work in this field, no one has *ever* insinuated that I was in any way biased or unable to . . ."

"I did not say that," insisted the ambassador.

"That is *exactly* what you just said to me! Exactly. Is it not?" The cochair looked around the room to the rest of us, seeking support. We remained still.

The ambassador continued, "I was only raising the point . . ."

"I get your point!" the cochair bellowed. "I know exactly what you are saying, and I demand an apology! I cannot continue with this session without an apology!"

At this point, the other co-chair, an eminent scholar in the field, spoke up and said, "Now that's enough. Enough of this foolishness."

"I will absolutely not apologize for something I didn't say," the Dutchman cried. "I did not say anything about you being biased and will not apologize."

At this point, the Israeli started to dramatically, demonstrably pack up his belongings from the table before him as if he were preparing to exit.

Then things got really interesting. This was a room full of world class peacemakers—envoys and mediators who had helped to negotiate some of the most dangerous, intractable disputes imaginable. And here, one at a time, sort of like at a Quaker meeting, these dignitaries began to pipe up and try their hand at de-escalating the situation and finding a way out. It was quite a showcase of talent, skill, and artistry. Each one would chime in with new questions to consider, new ways of framing what was happening, new appeals to collegiality and professionalism, or new ideas for proposals that might be acceptable to the disputants. (I kept thinking, god, I wish I had this on tape!) None of this seemed to have much impact on either of the two disputants, who were now both visibly seething.

Someone then suggested that we simply proceed with the meeting as planned, to which the Israeli responded by packing up even louder and faster.

Here, I must emphasize that I have been an academic and a mediator in the field of peace and conflict studies for more than twenty-five years and have attended countless meetings just like this one—countless dull, predictable, talking head meetings—and I had *never* seen anything erupt and get derailed like this. One beautiful bit of irony is that an hour earlier one of the participants had presented an excellent paper on the power of identity issues causing stalemates in Middle East conflicts—and here we all were in the midst of one unfolding, and we were helpless. It was amazing. All of our inspired attempts at resolution fell flat.

Of course, this conflict was not really about meeting decorum or professional respect. It was a dispute that unfortunately, inadvertently, but not unsurprisingly touched the third rail of the Israeli-Palestinian conflict, and it dragged all of us into its more than one-hundred-year quagmire. Despite the formal academic culture of the meeting venue, the many good-faith attempts of experienced peacemakers, and the professional consequences of such an outburst for the disputants themselves, the lure of the underlying conflict attractor landscape prevailed.

Both the Israeli negotiator and the Dutch ambassador eventually stormed out of the meeting. The Israeli coeditor ultimately resigned from the project and broke off contact with the group (a highly consequential decision). Such is the power inherent in conflict attractors. Some of them are quite simply larger and stronger than our best-known strategies for working our way out of them.

THE PRIMORDIAL SEA OF ATTRACTORS

The idea of attractors was spawned in two worlds at about the same time: theoretically in psychology and methodologically in the world of complexity science. The idea emerged conceptually out of Gestalt psychology in the 1930s through the work of Kurt Lewin, a brilliant young scientist who developed *topological psychology*,[1] an idea that explained human motivation and action as the result of our experiences of the possibilities and constraints presented by our own psychosocial landscape. Complexity science, a branch of applied mathematics, identified attractors when using mathematics and differential equations to track and visualize patterns that emerge when plotting data over time. The origins of complexity science are a bit murky, having sprung from some combination of chaos theory, general systems theory, dynamical systems theory, and cybernetics.[2] Today the field is organized around the interdisciplinary study of complex systems, those cloudy systems—like our superstorm of polarization—that have many interacting parts and, as a result, are highly dynamic, multidimensional, and unpredictable.

AN ATTRACTOR IS BORN

When a group of very different cloudlike elements—such as a diverse group of people with divergent beliefs, attitudes, and preferences—align together and feed off one another to move the group in a consistent direction over time, an attractor is born. This is exactly what we are seeing from Pew polling in the marked increase in ideological consistency within both political parties today—a collapse of opinions across ten different issues into two simplistic tribal mindsets that become highly attractive, constraining, and resistant to change.

Attractors are simply patterns that form over time in some systems (such as in brains, bodies, relationships, groups, communities, nations, and galaxies) and resist change. Think of the relative stability of the pecking order dynamics of siblings in most families, or of the entrenched forms of racial segregation that have gripped Milwaukee, Philadelphia, Atlanta, and Buffalo, New York, for decades despite many good-faith efforts to change them, or of the seemingly intransigent oppositional voting patterns of Democrats and Republicans in the U.S. Congress over the last fifty years.[3] These strong, enduring patterns resist change.

Technically, attractors are "a state or pattern of changes toward which a system evolves over time and to which it returns if perturbed."[4] These patterns of thinking, feeling, behaving, and socially clustering develop through the interactions of the complex constellation of elements that influence the pattern. Attractors tend to be change resistant because they are determined by multiple factors; the factors are interconnected and reinforce one another; and these elements are always shifting and changing even though their general pattern remains stable. In other words, the *stability* and *durability* of attractor patterns of siblings, cities, and senators are not determined by any one thing but rather by the *dynamic flow* of the many different influences among the multitude of factors that constitute their systems.

Attractors are everywhere. In life, attractor dynamics account for strong, change resistant attitudes (e.g., more enduring progressive/liberal mindsets), habits (e.g., addictions or stringent exercise regimens), relationship patterns (both caring and abusive relations), and chronic patterns of discrimination, poverty, illness, violence, and well-being in communities.

In science, attractors have been increasingly advanced to explain and predict a wide range of complex processes that settle into patterns, from stem cell specialization in biology and pathological brain oscillations in neuroscience to national political alignments during WWII and the gravitational anomaly known as the Great Attractor in space, which is reportedly thousands of times more massive than the Milky Way.[5] Social scientists have employed the attractor perspective to investigate everything from how our self-concepts and patterns of social judgment become stable to enduring phases of happiness in marital relations and the rise and fall of public opinion and political transitions in societies.[6] Over the past two decades, my colleagues and I have applied attractor models to understand and address longer-term patterns of both conflictual and peaceful social relations in dyads, groups, communities, and nations.[7]

Attractors are not necessarily good nor bad, they are simply facts. Attractors are just as likely to result in robust, healthy, and functional patterns in our life (e.g., achieving a satisfying work-life balance) as they are to result in miserable and toxic patterns (desperate, exhausting workaholism) or even neutral and mundane patterns (work phases that feel inconsequential but tolerable).

Most scientists find *energy* to be the core of attractor dynamics. All physical and social systems have a finite amount of energy at their disposal.* In social systems, what we attend to, how we process information, how we feel, and whether or not we respond to changes in situations both affect and are affected by our energy resources. One of the main reasons attractors draw us into their grip is because they are *lower-energy states*. We are always seeking easier paths in life, and because attractors require less energy, we are more likely to fall into and remain in these much easier states. This is why it's so difficult for people to change their diet or exercise regimen or to really break free of a toxic family relationship or a destructive work pattern; it's hard to summon the energy required to change a deeply set pattern or habit. Particularly in situations of conflict, when our anxiety increases (which can be exhausting), we often welcome the comfort, familiarity, and ease of sliding into one of our more automatic attractor patterns.

On top of this, when engaged in a particularly complex conflict, attractors also satisfy two basic psychological motives. First, *attractors provide us with a coherent understanding of the conflict*, including the character of the in-group (usually good) and the out-group (most likely bad), the nature of the relationship with the antagonistic party, the history of the conflict, and the legitimacy of claims made by each party. Such clarity of meaning can feel essential when facing highly divergent realities such as in our current Divided States of America.

Second, *attractors provide a stable platform for action*, enabling disputants in a conflict to respond decisively to changes in circumstances or to an action initiated by the other side. As one of the Boston dialogue leaders said, "When you are involved in a political movement like we are, we are focused on mobilizing the troops, and the way you do that is we paint things in the starkest possible terms so that people are moved to act, so they know what to do." Clarity of meaning and purpose are not trivial things, especially for disputants engaged in exhaustingly complicated conflicts.

---

* This is a core assumption of a foundational law of physics, the law of the conservation of energy. Physicists view this law as generalizable throughout the universe.

CONFLICT IN THE LAND OF ATTRACTORS

One way to think about how attractors affect our conflicts is to envision how our past experiences form psychological landscapes for our lives. When we encounter others—friends, family members, coworkers, even to some degree strangers—we experience them in the context of these landscapes.[8] Some of this terrain is serene and easily navigable—with broad attractors for congenial relations and only small patches of negativity—whereas other parts are trickier and more treacherous to traverse.

Figure 3.1 illustrates a simple landscape for a situation with two attractors, A (for Awesome) and B (for Bad). The two valleys represent distinct attractors: A represents the potential in the situation for you to experience more positive dynamics and B represents the potential for more destructive conflict. The ball represents the current state of the system—what's happing right now (currently slightly negative but with the potential to get worse fast). Due to the effects of gravity (or energy minimization), the ball will roll down the nearest hill and come to rest at the bottom of the valley.

Every attractor has two basic characteristics: width and depth. The *width* of each valley represents the reach of the attractor—the range of circumstances that will evolve down into the base of the attractor. An attractor with a wide basin "attracts" a broad range of conditions, including information and events that seem unrelated or inconsistent with the attractor (such as when a simple, friendly gesture offered by a member of an opposing team is viewed with suspicion as a ploy to lower your defenses). Conflict attractors widen when antagonism from an ongoing dispute spreads into more and more mundane aspects of life ("I refuse to buy ice cream there anymore because the owner is clearly a Trump hater.").[9] In contrast, a narrower basin only "attracts" us within a smaller range of states and thus is limited to a particular set of conditions ("I *only* argue with my brother

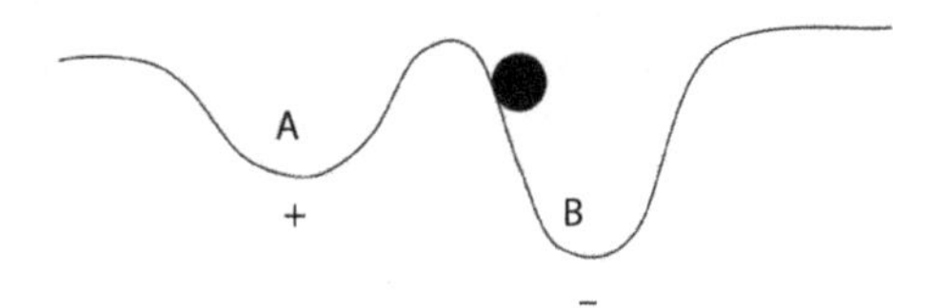

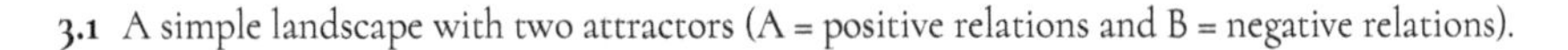
3.1 A simple landscape with two attractors (A = positive relations and B = negative relations).

when he brings up his ridiculous take on immigration; otherwise we get along fine."). In figure 3.1, the basin of attraction for Attractor A is somewhat wider than that for Attractor B.

An attractor's *depth* represents the strength of its resistance to change. It is difficult to dislodge people and groups from a deep (strong) attractor, even when they are being shaken by powerful external influences. Think of how hard it is to ween an elderly relative off the more opinionated celebrity commentators on FOX News or MSNBC; they are simply in too deep. Relatively weak influences, however, can more readily dislodge us from a shallow attractor. Note that Attractor B is deeper than Attractor A, so it would be more difficult for its attraction to be weakened by an external influence.

For illustration, consider a day in the life of a current U.S. senator. When the senator goes to work each day, she enters and must navigate an attractor landscape for partisan relations (figure 3.2). Her job is dependent on navigating this landscape as effectively as possible—within her party and between parties—to get things done for her constituents, our country, and her career. The particular landscape she will encounter on any given day took a long time to form, and it was formed to some degree before she was elected to office. It was shaped by a combination of forces such as the historical norms and procedures of the Senate; the current political climate; her individual relationships with the other members; her own individual tenure, status, gender, race, temperament, and skills;

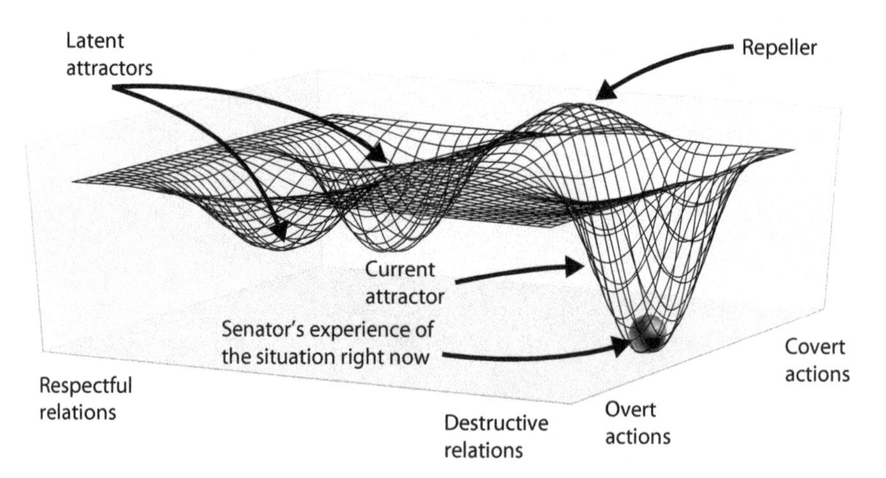

3.2 An attractor landscape for partisan relations in the U.S. Senate.

the focus of the work that day; and other factors. Regardless of the forces in play today, this is the territory she must either navigate or seek to transform to get things done.

The conflict landscape before our senator presents a variety of hills and valleys. Just like a physical landscape, it is a lot easier to walk downhill than uphill, so our senator will be much more inclined to move downhill and settle into the basin of the nearest valley. These valleys are called *attractors* because they are the patterns we are most disposed to be drawn into and in which we will tend to remain. They represent the stronger, more automatic, and incentivized habits, norms, mindsets, and behavioral scripts that have developed for our senator over time, and she will tend to slip into them as she navigates through her day—her more automatic reactions to her peers and surroundings. And the wider and deeper these valleys, the more likely it is that she will descend into them and remain there. This is exactly what we would expect to see if we were to measure how a staunch conservative senator tends to react when confronted in the hallway daily by liberal journalists, or how a more progressive senator responds whenever she is chastised publicly on the chamber floor by a pugnacious Majority Leader from across the aisle. If measured over time, these patterns would appear as deep, contentious, conflict valleys/attractors. However, due to Senate norms, these attractors are likely to be of a more covert or passive-aggressive nature, as depicted in the figure.*

Of course, our senator is likely to have more than one conflict attractor in her workplace landscape that draws her in (most of us do). This is called *multistability*. One may represent warm, respectful thoughts, feelings, and actions when in this professional space, such as when she is in dispute with a member of her own party over a piece of legislation, or even a member of the opposition with whom she has a friendly history (yes, a few still exist). Other attractors may represent more hostile, infuriating, and contentious experiences and interactions (e.g., the steep, negative pattern with the Majority Leader), or even more bland, neutral

---

* It is important to emphasize that attractors are *low energy states*, which means that they are relatively easy to fall into and to maintain and are much more difficult to get out of or to significantly alter—even when they are difficult or noxious states. Think of how hard it is to change the established dynamics between adult siblings within most nuclear families, even when they are toxic. Doing so takes concerted energy, will, persistence, support, and sometimes a serious shock to the system.

encounters (such as with members that she has little interaction or history). Together these represent the different *potentials* this setting holds for drawing our senator into very different experiences, reactions, and encounters. Of course, the wider and deeper any particular attractor valley becomes—whether of a more positive, neutral or negative nature—the more likely it is to determine her reactions to events.

This is an important point. The fact that most of us have more than one conflict attractor affecting us in our different personal and professional situations means that we often have the potential to respond to disputes that come up in very different ways. This contradicts most deterministic "personality" explanations of conflict behavior, and it accounts for the fact that some days we are much more cantankerous and others more congenial, even when dealing with the same person. Or that some days we seem to bounce back and forth between the two patterns, depending on whom we are disputing. Whenever we are in the grip of one attractor (positive, negative, or neutral), it is said to be our *current attractor*—the one that is shaping our experiences and responses right now. And, critically, the more time we spend in the valley of an attractor, the deeper and stronger it will tend to become because our experience of the pattern is being reinforced within and around us.

However, our other attractors are also still there, at the ready, and can take over our thoughts, feelings, and actions at any point in time. They are called *latent attractors*, the potential states that could capture our experience when circumstances change. Sometimes even a small comment or incident can tip us into a very different attractor and therefore a very different experience and set of responses. This is exactly what happened at the end of our "peace" meeting in Germany—we were drawn into a powerful latent attractor. This Jekyll and Hyde scenario is most likely to occur when the current state of the conflict is near a tipping point on our landscape between two attractors. We see this when there is a tense ceasefire between warring lovers that reignites into battle, or when a drawn-out conflict between battle-weary siblings collapses into playful, peaceful chatter. These changes are often dramatic because we are moving between two qualitatively different attractors. It is critical to remember, however, that when a shift occurs from one attractor to another, *it does not mean that the latent attractor is gone*. It simply means that, for now, it is hidden. Conditions can change again and bring latent attractors back to life. This is why it is so important to understand (and, ultimately, affect) the particular configuration of the underlying landscapes that we must navigate in our lives, and the relative strength and pull of each attractor. In essence, they represent our more likely tendencies, options, and scenarios for future relations.

Our conflict landscapes have one more important characteristic: *repellers*. They are the opposite of attractors. Our landscapes are usually surrounded by hills that represent the regions less-traveled in our lives. The peaks of the hills on our landscapes are called repellers because we rarely approach them, and if we do, we never stay there long because it requires too much energy. Repellers are regions that are either too demanding to reach or too unstable to sustain. We are drawn downhill, away from them, into someplace in which it is easier to settle. Repellers represent the various sociocultural taboos or more extreme emotional or behavioral responses that we are highly unlikely to evidence (such as our senator engaging in a public, curse-filled, emotional rant or initiating a fistfight on the chamber floor—not impossible but highly unlikely). These are the out-of-bounds limits to our experiences and reactions in a particular setting—the unimaginable (which, of course, can change). They also can be the source for important course corrections when our interactions start to go off the rails.

INTRACTABLE LANDSCAPES

How do attractor landscapes lead to intractable forms of polarization? It's simple—they become too simple.

Here's a thought experiment. Let's say someone you have never seen before walks into a diner and sits down at the counter on a stool next to you, and as he does so he spreads out and his arm touches your arm slightly (figure 3.3). A small matter. You could respond to this interaction in myriad ways—at this point you have many options because your conflict landscape for strangers in this restaurant is highly undeveloped. Sure, you bring your own baggage to this party—personality quirks, moods, temperament, your current level of exhaustion, and so on—but the situation itself is imposing few constraints on you other than standard protocol for diner decorum.

On this day this initial encounter triggers a minor irritation, in you, particularly because the guy keeps his arm up against yours and doesn't seem to notice.

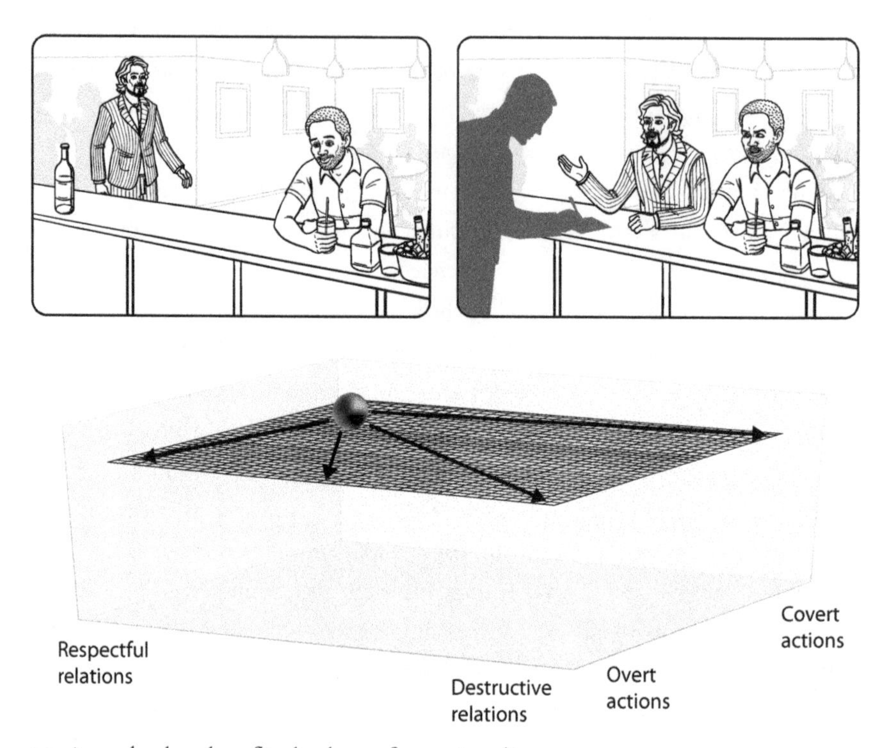

3.3 An undeveloped conflict landscape for you in a diner.

Seated there, you start wondering what his deal is, and your thoughts begin to center on this initial annoyance. You start to make connections in your mind with other things you notice about him, like what he's wearing (an expensive pinstriped suit), how he treats the waitress (not nice), what he orders (an egg-white omelet and strained juice with no pits), and the fact that he is *still* touching your arm. A slight pattern (valley) begins to form in your thinking and feeling as separate negative thoughts and sentiments about this guy begin to reinforce each other (figure 3.4). As a result, your negative judgments of him become harsher, and your sense of him becomes increasingly undifferentiated, organized around your initial irritation. In other words, your pattern of experience of him starts to simplify: He's a jerk!

Eventually, you communicate your agitation through your body language, audible sighs, and the facial expressions you can't hide, which initiates similar negative processes in him. At this moment, the two nascent systems of conflict

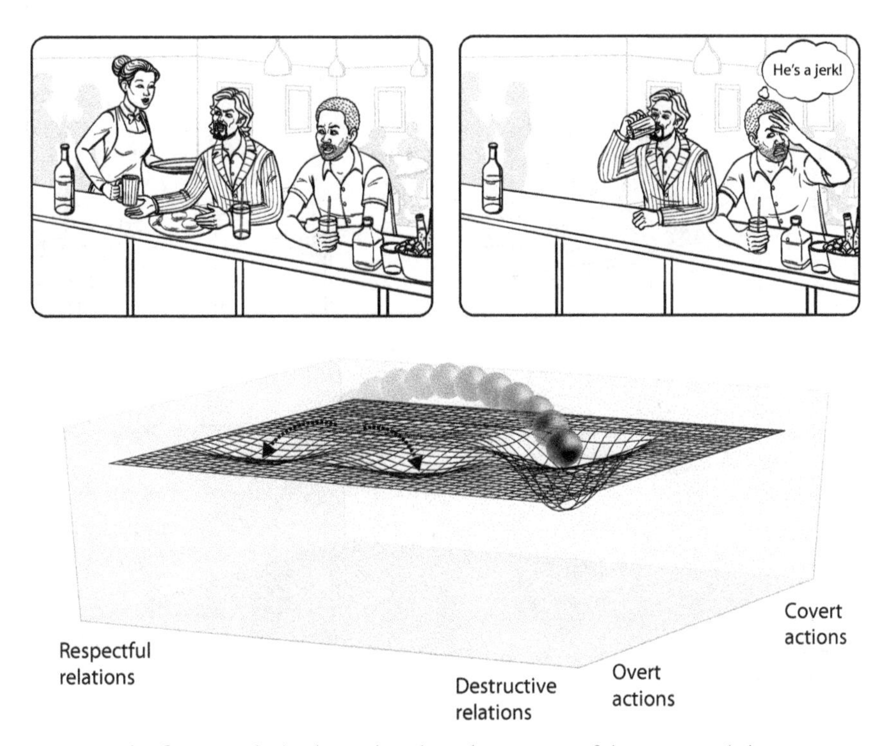

3.4 A grudge forms on the landscape based on observations of the stranger's behavior.

existing within the two individuals—you and expensive-suit guy—start to reinforce each other and reduce the possibility for positive interaction between you. And you haven't even spoken yet. Nevertheless, your mutual conflict landscape is now taking shape, with one growing attractor for negative interactions (figure 3.5). The thoughts, feelings, and behaviors of both of you are being processed within the structure of the conflict, which is now affecting your interpersonal interactions.

As luck would have it, you soon discover that the suit guy has recently moved into your neighborhood, and he begins to frequent your favorite eatery. He continues to evidence his clumsy, arrogant behavior, and you become evermore overt in how you communicate your dislike of him. As both of you start to seek support by recruiting others (your friends, waitresses, the manager, other regulars, etc.) to your side, the conflict spreads to the group level, where it is sustained by the chatter *within* each of your allied groups (few things bring more solidarity to

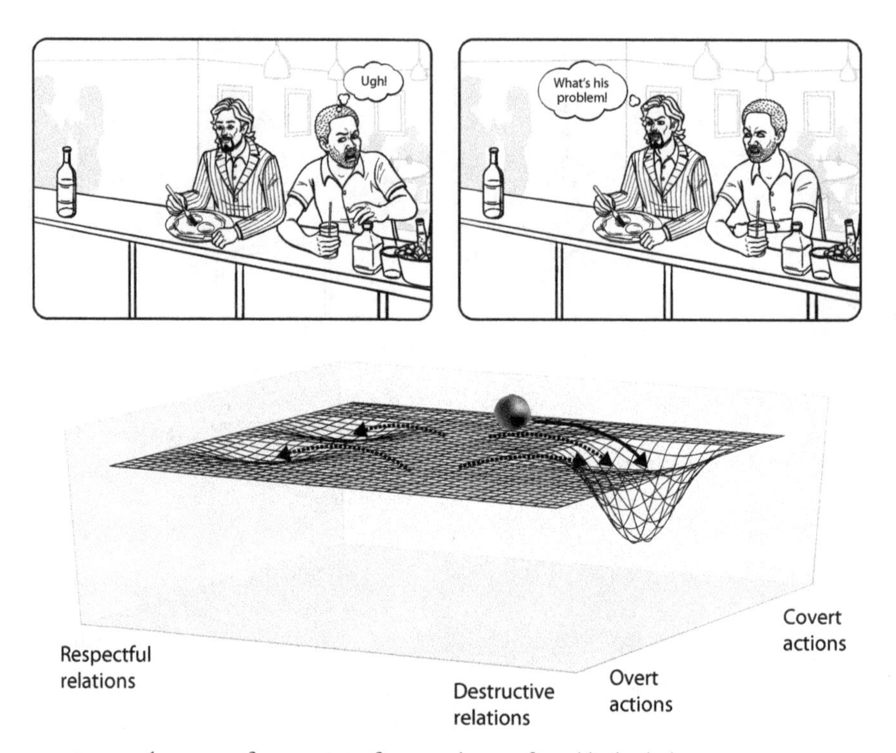

3.5 A mutual attractor for negativity forms and is reinforced by both diners.

a group than a common enemy—check out figure 3.6). The conflict attractor has now expanded, and the sustainability of the conflict increases because even if one of you two tire of the tension and try to disengage from it, others in either group of allies might now perpetuate it. As the conflict endures and spreads, more overt hostilities between members of the groups become increasingly likely. The conflict is now permeating the climate of the restaurant/community, thereby further reducing the odds of positive interactions between the opposing groups. What started out as a mundane interaction has now taken on significant meaning. At some point, the multitude of people, grievances, and events that perpetuate the tensions render fruitless any attempts to ignore or resolve the conflict. Intractability has begun to set in.

If the diner conflict persists over time, it could affect the identities of the group members (I am *your* friend and therefore *not* his!). If it also happens to touch on other meaningful or salient identity conflicts, such as tensions over

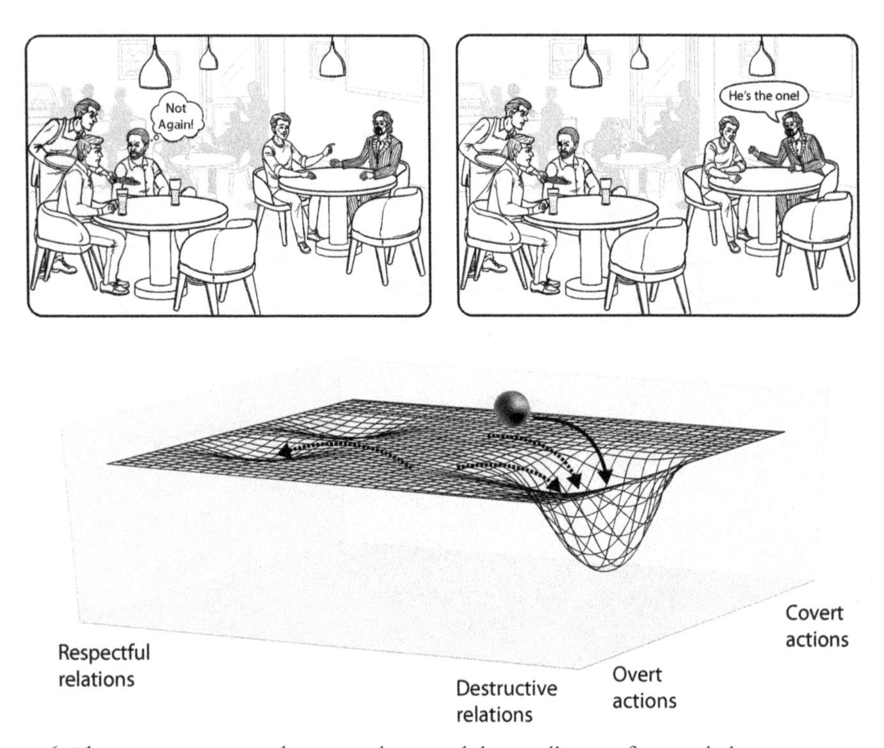

3.6 The negativity is spreading toward intractability as allies reinforce each diner.

political, racial, religious, class, or sexual orientation groups, then the landscape of the conflict could quickly become much deeper and broader. In other words, if you are a loyal Republican (or Christian or FOX News devotee) and he is a fervent Democrat (or Muslim or fan of *The Nation* magazine), the stakes and investment in the conflict for each group rise considerably (figure 3.7). At this stage, the conflict becomes embedded in the deeper cultural-political dynamics of the society, acquiring a new means of maintenance and contagion. Anyone entering the local community now is likely to adopt a position on the conflict. People who have never even had contact with the suit guy and his posse are nonetheless unlikely to form positive or even neutral relationships with them. In this way, the conflict begins to be passed on through group socialization processes.

At this point, many of the originally distinct processes necessary for the functioning of healthy communities become principally organized around the one-dimensional structure of the conflict. Like the Sharks and the Jets from *West Side*

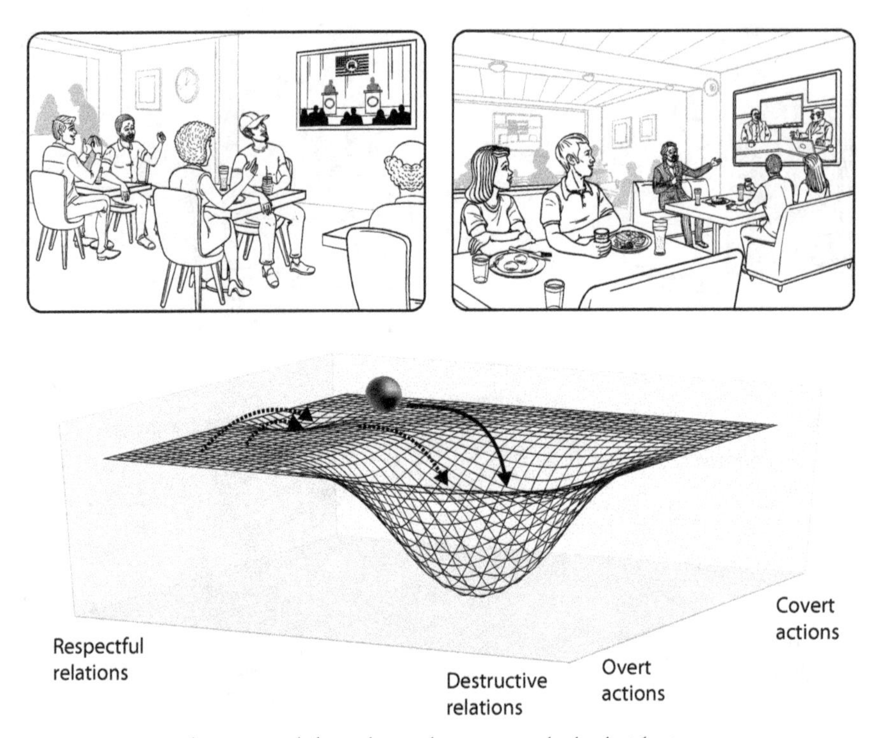

3.7 A storm is picking up, and the stakes and investment by both sides increases.

Story, or the Palestinian refugees and the settlers living in the West Bank, the conflict overtakes a growing number of social, economic, and political processes—where to eat, who to date, and who to trust—focusing them all on a single issue within the conflict (sound familiar?). The richness and multidimensionality of all the processes occurring in any healthy community become entrained in the deep structure of the conflict, leaving virtually no opportunity for positive interactions. Our conflict landscape now looks like figure 3.8.

In this terrain, virtually all intergroup encounters are likely to lead to destructive conflict. Why? Three reasons. First, no matter what happens next in the context of this landscape—even random events and mundane gestures from the other camp—the gravitational pull for destructive relations is such that things will likely go south.

Second, at this point the conflict attractor dynamics are *fractal*, or repeated at many levels.[10] This means that the simplistic, threatening, us-versus-them

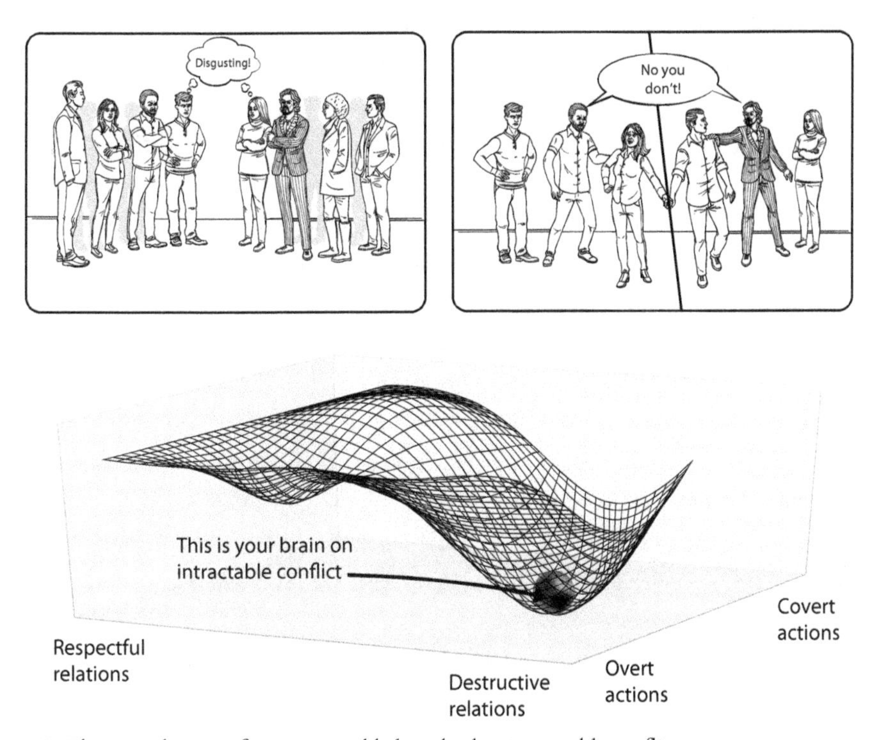

3.8 The near absence of positivity is likely to lead to intractable conflict.

patterns that have formed in the structures of our brains are now aligned with similar patterns within the psychological experiences (thoughts, feelings, and attitudes) of ourselves, our in-group and the out-group, which line up with the normative structure of social interactions that occur within our group and between our groups, which are in turn largely in sync with our local community leaders' rhetoric and ethos, which are also aligned with broader cultural symbols, celebrations, and messages that reinforce the same patterns within us, in our groups, and in our communities. No matter where on the food chain you slice it, you reveal the same simplistic pattern of us-versus-them enmity and division. These are the various elements of the deep structure of attractors.

Third, the *power of negativity* is extraordinary. One of the more robust findings from psychological research over the past few decades has been that bad is stronger than good.[11] That is, negative experiences and events have much more impact on us than positive ones, and negative information is processed more thoroughly and remembered much longer than positive information. Therefore, negative impressions and stereotypes are quicker to form and more resistant to disconfirmation than good ones. This accounts for the particularly robust mobilizing power of out-group threats and negative partisanship on political dynamics. When the awfulness and evil of the other party is salient and seen as defining, and especially when politicians and pretentious pundits repeat this ominous tale with great frequency, it becomes increasingly difficult to escape its pull. When this kind of menacing, ultracoherent, multilevel pattern has captured a conflict dynamic, it can be extremely hard to fix.

Research strongly supports this conclusion.[12] When deep and wide negative attractors have captured the dynamics of an encounter, relationship, family, community, or nation, many of our best, good-faith attempts to work them out directly—through discussion, negotiation, mediation, or other normally fruitful problem-solving techniques—usually fail. In fact, oftentimes, these attempts only make matters worse. They further agitate, frustrate, and exhaust already tense and angry disputants.

Can attractor landscapes for highly divisive, intractable conflicts ever change? Yes. But not how you would think.

BREAKING THE LAWS OF CHANGE

The study of attractors and complex systems has led to the identification of a set of what I call *crude laws** about how these systems change, which go against most of our standard assumptions about linear cause-and-effect change processes (e.g., If I increase X, I will see a proportional change in Y.). These laws have particular relevance for understanding how cloudy problems such as our current state of affairs can change.

Crude Law 1. *Attractors are highly sensitive to even slight differences in their early, initial conditions.* Attractors are often quite responsive to differences in their starting conditions, but only early on in their formation. Like

---

* This term was coined by Morton Deutsch. A crude law is a scientific observation of a phenomenon that is often but not necessarily always true.

a newborn infant, the first line of a new novel, or the first meeting of a business startup, the initial moments are formative and often highly determining of the eventual path taken. This is because first choices can constrain what seems logical or feasible for subsequent moves, and once the system is on track, it will tend to stay on track. This is due to the presence of *reinforcing feedback* (also known as positive feedback), in which the environment becomes increasingly supportive of choices consistent with earlier ones. So the beginnings of new systems are critically important, both in terms of their susceptibility to change and in terms of the consequences of early choices for their future trajectories. This can have major implications for the founding of new groups and initiatives or for significant resets undertaken within relationships and communities.

Crude Law 2. *Complex systems tend to move toward coherence and integration.* Due to the processes of reinforcing feedback, most complex systems (including our minds, personalities, relationships, and groups) are inclined to move toward states of increased consistency and coherence. This is the basic mechanism responsible for what I referred to as the consistency principle in chapter 2, and for development of any attractor. It is also why any random assortment of people who find themselves thrown together on a deserted island—as in *The Lord of the Flies*[13]—or at a street protest or political convention, tend to come together to develop group rules and norms and even penalties to encourage integration and predictability. This inclination for coherence is natural and mostly functional until the system reaches a state of hypercoherence, which can become pathological.

Crude Law 3. *Attractors can become highly impervious to outside influences.* When attractors become particularly deep and wide and begin to dominate the landscape, they fervently resist change. This is due to a process known as *self-organization*. Think of this as being similar to the behavior of a cult such as Heaven's Gate or Scientology. These cults have a set of beliefs, values, practices, norms, and incentives that keep their members in line and make them highly resistant to outsiders' attempts to change their ways. These are the deep structural processes that serve to maintain the system in its current state. If members stray, others in the group will shame or sanction them (or worse) to return them to conformity. At some point, these internal processes dictate the life of the group, so much so that they no longer require top-down leadership to drive behavior. Although I hesitate to call Republicans and Democrats cultlike, there are clearly parallels today, especially with the more extreme zealots and true believers on either side. What this suggests is that sustained change may be best instigated from *within* the parties.

Crude Law 4. *Significant shocks to strong attractors can destabilize their deep structure and ready them for change.* Scientists in a variety of fields have identified the critical role major disturbances play in bringing about dramatic changes in strong patterns in physical and social systems. Research on something known as *punctuated equilibrium* has found that significant shocks—from either external or internal sources—are often a necessary, albeit insufficient, condition for bringing about transformational change in these patterns.[14] For example, studies on international conflicts that become stuck in decades of enmity have found that between 75 and 90 percent of them end within ten years of a major political shock.[15] These jolts sufficiently destabilize communities, nations, or regions such that they trigger a variety of basic structural adjustments over time that—across some threshold—lead to major shifts from conflict to peace. The good news for the United States is that we have recently been living through a profoundly destabilizing series of shocks—from the radically unorthodox nature of the Trump presidency to a global pandemic and worldwide derailment of our social and economic structures. So the time is ripe for deep relandscaping.

Crude Law 5. *Highly complex systems are often significantly affected by changes to their most simple, basic rules of interaction.* At the heart of most complex systems—be they relationships, political parties, or nations—are the basic rules that guide and shape the interactions of their elements. In social systems, these are often implicit, unarticulated rules that members have been socialized to follow and have typically internalized, such as "Do unto others as you would have them do unto you," "An eye for an eye and a tooth for a tooth," and "Thou shalt not kill." In politics, these rules can include "The stakes are too high—win at all costs" or "The ends always justify the means." These rules, when followed and enacted innumerable times by members of a community, bubble up into normative patterns and expectations that shape entire cultures. This process is known as *emergence*. When the basic rules of our politics are altered in some significant manner, they can eventually have an inordinate effect on the climate and quality of our dominant attractor patterns.

Crude Law 6. *The effects of some changes to complex systems are obvious and immediate, whereas others may occur that are invisible or delayed but are nevertheless consequential.* Attractor landscapes can evidence four basic types of change: (1) changes in the *current state* of the system (such as a rapid shift from peaceful to violent protesting in a community); (2) changes in the current *manifest attractor* (e.g., increases in the number of instigators, norms, and incentives that encouraged the violence); (3) changes in *latent attractors* (such as degrading of the activists, norms, and incentives that promote nonviolent protests); and (4) changes in repellers for the situations (changes in what the protestors and police consider acceptable versus taboo behavior for a protest). Changes to the current state are the most immediate and apparent, and changes to the underlying structure of the landscape usually happen more slowly and subtly, but they eventually may be of even more consequence. Think of this like changes to an ocean. Storms, high winds, and extreme temperatures will affect the surface of the ocean in ways that are immediately clear and evident. Other forces, such as industrial waste, tectonic shifts in the ocean floor, or the death of large coral reefs may be less observable or immediate, but ultimately they can affect the health and viability of the ocean. The same holds true for complex social systems. Some attempts to change the current levels of tension in a community may be direct and apparent, whereas others may be less so and take considerable time to become apparent.

Crude Law 7. *Significant changes introduced to tightly coupled complex systems almost always result in unintended consequences.* Introducing changes to cloudy problems inevitably invites surprises, some good and some bad, due to how their effects unfold in nonlinear systems. We try to engage more frequently and politely with a neighbor who holds opposing political views from ours, only to become further alienated from one another. Television news networks try to promote bipartisan discourse by bringing in pundits from both sides of the political spectrum on their shows, which results in tensions and snarky remarks between the commentators and further polarization of the populace. The election of an African American to the U.S. presidency sparks speculation of a post-racial society, only to usher in an era of emboldened white supremacy across the country. In other words, the well-intentioned actions of people, groups, and institutions in complex systems almost always have effects that are unanticipated, unintended, or unwelcomed. They should be expected.

These seven laws of nonlinearity represent change of a different color. Although even more mundane problems may at times evidence some of these odd change dynamics, the more complex and tightly coupled the system of elements affecting the problem (e.g., the more strongly they affect one other), the more likely the system will begin to evidence attractor dynamics and operate according to these laws. Understanding and anticipating them can provide us with new insights into how change comes about in the life of highly polarizing attractors.

The following chapters of the book, on how to change the unchangeable, will show you how.

4

THINK DIFFERENT* — CHANGE YOUR THEORY OF CHANGE

Given the seemingly impenetrable structures at work in highly polarizing conflict landscapes, and their odd reactions to our good-faith attempts to address them, how might we go about realizing positive change?

THE TIME

In 2018, I was interviewed by a journalist for the popular German newspaper, *Die Zeit* (*The Time*), who was reporting on a major initiative his paper was heading up called "My Country Talks."[1] This was an attempt by media organizations around the world to bridge increasingly hostile political divides by matching people with opposing attitudes on thorny issues through an online survey and then encouraging them to meet on their own for a face-to-face encounter over coffee or beer.

---

* This is not a typo but rather is the title of Apple's *Think Different* advertising campaign, circa 1997. "Here's to the crazy ones. The misfits. The rebels. The troublemakers. The round pegs in the square holes. The ones who see things differently. They're not fond of rules. And they have no respect for the status quo. You can quote them, disagree with them, glorify or vilify them. About the only thing you can't do is ignore them. Because they change things. They push the human race forward. While some may see them as the crazy ones, we see genius. Because the people who are crazy enough to think they can change the world, are the ones who do." Steve Jobs, "Think Different," *Apple Computers*, http://www.thecrazyones.it/spot-en.html.

The reporter had been tracking polarization in the United States and elsewhere and had asked to participate in our Difficult Conversations Lab at Columbia University to learn more about the science on polarization. While providing some context for our interview, he shared this account of one partisan encounter.[2]

On November 9, 2016, the day after Donald Trump was elected president, the reporter flew to the United States. He sought out, met, and befriended two American men, separately: an ex-military Trump supporter who lived in Pennsylvania and an anti-Trump yoga teacher residing in Brooklyn, New York. The journalist followed and reported on both men over the next year. During that time, he said he grew quite close with them both and came to respect and enjoy them. He described both men as "very, very nice people . . . gentle and engaged with their communities." They both supported gay marriage and a woman's right to choose, however the Trump supporter was a very strong Tea Party conservative. The yoga teacher was eager to meet and speak with Trump supporters, believing that he could change their minds if he could sit down and speak with them one-on-one, but he was having a hard time finding someone to meet within his own community. The journalist eventually invited both men to come together to meet in New York City. He said he felt a bit anxious about it, but what's the worst that could happen?

In 2017, the three men sat down together for breakfast in a hotel restaurant in Manhattan, and after chatting for a bit went for a walk in Central Park. They talked about their kids, careers, yoga, and other aspects of their personal lives. They also broached politics, discussing the challenges of health care and Trump's propensity to lie. At the end of the meeting, they agreed to get back together the next evening to continue the conversation. The reporter said he got a sense that, as he had expected, they got along well and had a great deal in common.

The next day the Trump supporter got tickets to see a Brooklyn Nets basketball game, so the others went along as well. Afterward they went to a nearby restaurant to talk. The second meeting started off well, but after about twenty minutes the journalist broached the topic of Colin Kaepernick's NFL "kneeling" protests. A former NFL quarterback, Kaepernick had sparked a protest movement among professional athletes in 2016 by choosing to kneel rather than stand during the playing of the National Anthem at sporting events as a sign of support for the Black Lives Matter movement. As a former Marine who had lost close friends in combat while defending American interests abroad, the man from

Pennsylvania had strong feelings about Kaepernick's public refusal to stand for our National Anthem. He said he had fought for everyone's right to protest but that he had found what Kaepernick did shameful and unacceptable.

At this point, the yoga teacher "flipped out," told the Marine that his argument was inane, and then "the F-bombs started flying." This issue seemed to unleash deep resentments held by the yoga teacher, who had been thrown out of his own home by his father, an ex-military man. Within a few minutes, the encounter escalated to a threatening point, and the yoga teacher stormed out of the restaurant. Despite the journalist's repeated attempts to reconnect the two men, this ended his good-faith attempt to bridge the divide (figure 4.1).

These types of well-intentioned disasters are happening much more frequently today as various people and groups try to address our deepening political and cultural divides. Initiatives like Etgar 36, a national touring summer camp where youth are asked to confront challenging issues across the political spectrum;[3] America in One Room, a grand experiment in face-to-face deliberative democracy;[4] Better Angels and Crossing Party Lines, nonprofits that bring partisan citizens together for respectful discourse;[5] and Make America Dinner Again, which hosts small dinners for cross-political conversations,[6] are just a few of the thousands of groups working across the United States today to mend our fences.[7] These encounters are typically based on *intergroup contact theory*, an

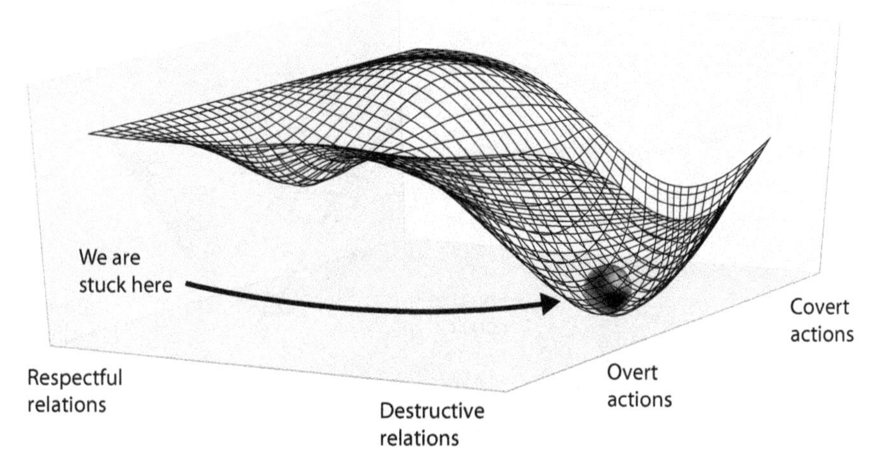

4.1 A landscape for intractable polarization.

approach to quelling intergroup strife by bringing disputants together to meet face-to-face, which was originally developed by social psychologist Gordon Allport in the 1950s.[8]

Some of these interpartisan encounters go quite well and show positive changes in political attitudes and relationships, especially when the discussants hold more moderate positions and the programs provide well-trained facilitation.[9] But these days their effects are often slight or fleeting, or worse yet, as in the case of the German journalist, they go sour and participants end up feeling even more outraged and alienated from the other side. A recent Pew Research Center study found that a majority of both Republicans and Democrats reported feeling they had less in common with members of the opposite party after speaking directly with them about politics, and was experienced as "stressful and frustrating," particularly by liberal Democrats.[10]

Why?

Because trying to fix a difficult *conflict* over political differences that arises in the *context* of a deeply contentious bio-psycho-socio-cultural dynamic is like trying to push a large boulder out of the valley of a deep attractor (figure 4.2). With great effort, you may make some initial progress dislodging the boulder, but the forces of gravity in the situation are so great that the likelihood of sustained change is low. Relax for one moment and the boulder will roll back to its basin, probably directly over you.

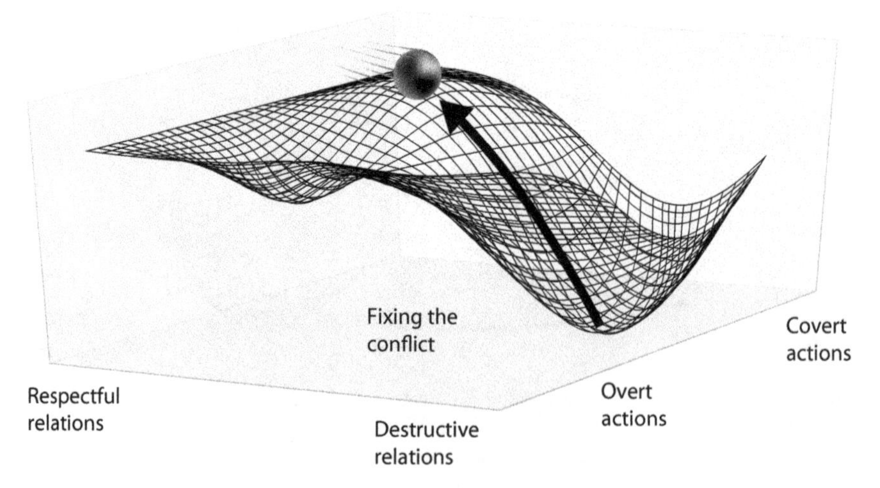

4.2 Fixing the conflict will not address the intractability of the divisions.

Remember, attractors become broader and deeper *over time* through the influences of a wide range of interacting and often nonrational factors: our relationship histories, emotional attachments to certain identity groups, implicit biases, a tendency to pay attention to information that confirms our existing beliefs, and more. When attempting to address toxic polarization, we are rarely confronting an isolated issue or a disagreement over facts. Rather, we are facing off against everything that underlies why the issue matters so much in the first place.

Nevertheless, this is how most of us tend to respond to difficult conflicts that erupt in our lives—we try to deal with the problem right in front of us. In fact, it's exactly how most of the international peace experts responded to the standoff at our meeting in Germany. Of course, it is a logical and reasonable reaction, and it usually works.

But this strategy does not work with attractor-induced conflicts. Talking across the divide might help to temporarily de-escalate tensions or improve understanding, but it will take considerable energy, vigilance, and persistence—and odds are high that something will occur to send the boulder right back down into the ease and comfort of the attractor. The more times this happens, the deeper and stronger the attractor becomes. Focusing on the current dispute is not futile, and may be necessary in the short-term, but it is not a solution to our more deep-seated divisions. It is at best a Band-Aid.

What can change these seemingly unchangeable divisions? It begins with changing your theory of change.

YOUR THEORY OF HOW TO CHANGE POLARIZING CONFLICT

Everyone has a theory of change about conflict, although most of us are unaware of them. A *theory of change* is simply a set of beliefs and assumptions about how change unfolds in the world and how to bring it about.[11] We learn these theories quite young, mostly through experience and observation of others, but they are also shaped significantly by our formal education and our cultural and religious upbringing. Cognitive science has shown that these theories often become physically present in the neural circuitry of our brains, which can result in a total disregard for information that contradicts them.[12] However, because they are often so fundamental to our understanding of reality—and of change-related concepts such as time, causality, and human nature—we rarely reflect on or articulate them (except in some philosophy or physics courses). We simply see them as fact.

I once had the honor of interviewing seventeen experts who specialized in working to bring disputants together across difficult, protracted divides, and I asked each of them to share with me their underlying theory of change.[13] They were all highly skilled at shepherding constructive change processes between disputants in conflictual relationships and in communities, and I was interested in hearing how they understood what they did and how they went about doing it. Most of them had never before stopped to articulate how they thought about change.

One of the experts was George J. Mitchell, a former United States senator (and Senate Majority Leader) and state judge from Maine who had been quite active in international peace processes for years, including the multiyear process of brokering the Good Friday Peace Agreement in Northern Ireland. Senator Mitchell began our interview by informing me that he didn't have a theory of change and that he didn't find theories very useful. This was an awkward moment. However, he then launched into an hours-long account of his theory. He said that he went into every conflict situation he was working in anew—with few preconceived notions about the conflict or the disputants or the process—and that he let the facts on the ground shape his understanding and approach. What he essentially described to me, in great detail, was a very well-developed, antitheoretical, bottom-up contingency theory of change, which he applied wherever he worked.

The problem, of course, with failing to recognize our underlying theory of change is that it can limit or trap us—particularly if the theory is rigidly adhered to or is based on erroneous assumptions that do not fit every situation. Such consequences are well documented in research I and others have conducted on *implicit theories*: the unarticulated assumptions and beliefs that we hold about aspects of ourselves, others, and the world around us that shape how we engage with the world.[14] These unarticulated theories have been shown to affect everything from how we approach learning new tasks and problem solving[15] to how we take on leadership roles,[16] engage in romantic relationships,[17] resolve conflict,[18] and experience emotions.[19]

Our understanding of how to address any conflict often depends on the specifics of the situation (so is data-driven), but it is also *always* influenced by the values, assumptions, and beliefs we bring to our understanding (so is also theory-driven), whether we acknowledge it or not.* This is particularly true when the situations we face are difficult to comprehend because they are vast, complex, volatile, and replete with contradictory information. The implicit theories of change we employ to address conflicts can differ dramatically across people and groups, but most of these theories share some combination of the following components: (a) a *metaphor* for the problem, (b) an *analytic framework* for diagnosing it, (c) a *North Star* or positive state toward which change is oriented, (d) a means of *intervention* on how and when to get there, and (e) the *role* played by change agents.[20]

In the course I teach at Columbia University on theory and research in conflict resolution, I begin each term by asking my students to articulate their (usually implicit) theory of conflict and change through a sequence of automatic writing tasks. I ask them to put pen to paper (which most of them no longer bring to class!) and to write quickly, for five minutes, without thinking, editing, or stopping, on a series of topics such as "What is the essential nature of conflict?" and "How can conflicts be changed for the better?" I then ask them to work with a partner in class to analyze their writing and to try to identify and discuss the underlying beliefs and assumptions they hold about conflict, change, and how they are related. Both the writing task and unpacking their previously unarticulated assumptions about conflict and change are often rather eye-opening for my students.

Although the students in my courses come from all around the globe, their implicit theories of conflict and change tend to be similar; they hold an overwhelmingly negative view of conflict as a problem or pathology to contain or cure, and their theories of change mostly reflect Western scientific assumptions of a linear, cause-and-effect nature (e.g., If I do X, then Y will happen.). This is understandable because the field of conflict resolution and most of the research, practical methods, and publications out there echo this same thinking. As a result, my students commonly view change in conflict as coming about through direct confrontation or coercion (fight) or recommend avoiding it altogether to

---

* Here's a trivial example. I once dated a woman for a short time who was a fervent believer in astrology and often understood our disagreements and spats as being brought on by past or current astrological configurations, such as "my Saturn moon rising." I never quite knew how to respond to these interpretations. Her strong astrological theory-driven approach to making sense of our relationship (and life in general) often collided head on with my more psychological theory-driven approach, which contributed significantly to our brief time as a couple.

circumvent harm (flight). But when asked *how conflicts can be changed for the better*, the dominant story of change they tell goes something like this: just fix it.

THEORY A: FIXING CONFLICT CLOCKS

When a conflict is triggered, goes bad, and stays bad, it means that something in our understanding, transactions, relationships, organizations, or communities is broken and needs repair. The good news is "we can fix it." Generally speaking, we have the knowledge, attitudes, and skills to find the problem and solve it—or at least to find someone else sufficiently well-equipped to do so on our behalf. Unless we can get away with unilaterally imposing our preferred solution to the conflict, or simply avoiding it altogether, we typically attend to our conflicts by sitting down and talking it out with the others involved (a classic, Western psychotherapeutic remedy). This allows us to take apart Popper's clock, identify the broken parts—misunderstandings, unintentional slights, hidden or unexpressed grievances, or other missteps or misgivings—and directly address them through apology, reparation, persuasion, debate, negotiation, mediation, or other forms of problem solving.

The conflict clock theory privileges *direct, reasonable, rational action* to fix what is broken and views *powerful emotions as something of a derailer*. When they arise, it's best to pause or "go to the balcony" and wait for these emotions to pass before proceeding to resolve the conflict.[21] It also has clear objectives: de-escalate the situation, fix the conflict (reach an agreement), and return to normal. The broken part raised tensions and impaired what was a good relationship or community dynamic, so you simply want to get back to where you were. The best way to do that is to *identify* the obstacles between where you are and where you want to be and *address them*. Once you isolate the broken parts and the obstacles to fixing them, you can grab your tools and repair them because you—the disputant, negotiator, or mediator—have the power, will, and capacity to fix it (what in cultural psychology is called a *mastery orientation* to problem solving). Yes, sometimes our conflicts require major repair jobs and may need to be "benched" (brought into extended mediation, arbitration, or litigation), but we have seen most of these problems before and know how to fix them. So let's get to it.

The conflict clock theory is commonly understood. I suspect it is how most of the readers of this book think about addressing most conflicts (fight, flight, or fix). I know it is how most of the field of negotiation, mediation, and conflict resolution views how to change conflict because I have now edited three editions of the fifty-six-chapter textbook *The Handbook of Conflict Resolution: Theory and Practice*, which is filled with variations of this theory of change. And this is how it should be. For the vast majority of cases, which I elsewhere estimated to be about 95 percent of the conflicts we face in our lives, it works.[22] The fix helps to address or resolve a majority of our conflicts.

However, if you dig a bit deeper into the conflict clock theory, you begin to see that this theory is based on a set of assumptions about change rooted mostly in Western culture and (Newtonian) scientific analysis that can limit its applicability. Namely, it emphasizes individual agency, economic rationality[23] (privileging efficiency), and direct processes of bringing about linear change. This thinking works well with clock conflicts: briefer episodes of conflict or anomalies in relationships that can be effectively identified, isolated, repaired, and resolved. This is simply not the case with much cloudier, more attractive conflicts.

THINKING DIFFERENT ABOUT CLOUDY CONFLICTS

About twenty years ago, I brought together a diverse team of academics and peacemakers to try to think differently about why some conflicts escalate, polarize, and become stuck in destructive patterns highly resistant to change. After years of studying pieces of these conflicts in my lab (the effects of toxic emotions such as humiliation,[24] us-versus-them identity formation,[25] and motives that encourage warring disputants to negotiate[26]), I began to seek a more comprehensive understanding of the intractability of these much cloudier problems. It was this team, which included three of the leading complexity science–informed psychologists, Andrzej Nowak, Robin Vallacher, and Lan Bui-Wrzosinska, and astrophysicist Larry Liebovitch, among others,* who together began to view these types of conflicts differently—not as games to win or clocks to fix but rather as conflicts arising from attractor dynamics. Employing the tools and methods of complexity science—in particular *dynamical systems theory*, a school of thought coming out of applied mathematics—provided new, highly original and practical

---

* The full team included Andrzej Nowak, Robin Vallacher, Lan Bui-Wrzosinska, Larry Liebovitch, Andrea Bartoli, Naira Musallam, Katharina Kugler and Peter T. Coleman.

insights about how cloudy conflicts of all types, from interpersonal to political to international, change and resist change.[27] This approach opened up a host of new ideas, metaphors, methods, and practices for understanding and working with more intractable patterns of polarizing conflicts.

The early theoretical work of our team on intractable attractors led to a series of empirical studies, including case studies, experimental research, and computer simulations, that ultimately led to the creation of the Difficult Conversations Lab at Columbia University,[28] where we began to study encounters over divisive moral conflicts. The design of this lab enabled us to "capture" the underlying attractor dynamics of conversations over polarizing issues, which allowed us to better understand different aspects of them, such as when they go well and when they go terribly wrong. This approach offered an alternative way of *thinking* and *working* with highly complex and intractable problems and taught us a great deal about the peculiar manner in which they do and do not change (figure 4.3).

Fixing Conflict	Radical Relandscaping (R^2)
Metaphor • Clock-like mechanical problems **Values/Assumptions** • Based on *Western* cultural values like having *mastery over* the environment, *individual* agency, *linear* forms of cause and effect, and aimed at *short-term impacts* **Objective** • Deescalate tension, reach agreement on issues/outcomes, fix the conflict, and return the situation to the status quo **Defining the problem** • In mechanistic, atomistic terms through analysis, essentialization of the *conflict* and a focus on presenting issues **The process** • Learn what is broken and fix it by isolating the core problem and overcoming obstacles to change through direct, rational, efficient processes focused on central, high-impact targets using persuasion and influence. Make a plan and stay the course **The role** • Expert problem-solver, go-to fixer.	**Metaphor** • Cloudy, dynamic attractor landscapes **Values/Assumptions** • Based on *Eastern* cultural values like being in *harmony with* the environment, *collective* agency, *nonlinear* forms of emergence and catastrophic change, and seeking *longer-term* sustainable *change* **Objective** • Leverage tension and instability, alter the *pattern* of interactions, and transform the structure of the attractor landscape **Defining the problem** • In systemic, dynamic terms through complexity visualization of the *context* and identification of latent traps and potential **The process** • Learn how the system is changing and work *with* trends in the situation by enabling existing solutions, working upstream away from the problem, diversifying actions, and using radical listening, dialogue and discovery, with an expectation to fail, adapt and learn over time **The role** • Facilitative solution-locator, change catalyst.

4.3 Two theories of how to change divisive conflicts.

THEORY B: RADICAL RELANDSCAPING (R^2)

When tense, complicated conflicts persist, become entrenched, spread into many parts of your life, and resist all good-faith efforts to work them out, it becomes necessary to think and respond to them in radically different ways. Instead of focusing on analyzing and identifying the broken pieces of the conflict in order to fix them, it may be helpful to shift your focus *from figure to ground*. That is, from probing the current presenting *conflict* to understanding and addressing the many forces in the past and present *context* that are giving rise to it. I call this *radical relandscaping or* R^2.

Martin Luther King Jr. once said, "True compassion is more than flinging a coin to a beggar; it comes to see that an edifice which produces beggars needs restructuring."[29] Intractable forms of harmful polarization require that their edifice be restructured. This, of course, is no small feat. It essentially requires moving from a more familiar point of view (seeing the figure of the presenting conflict) to another more complex and demanding one (identifying and comprehending the structural forces shaping the landscape that is feeding the conflict). Fortunately, we face fewer problems of these types. But when we do, they require a new mindset, new skills, and something of a leap of faith. They require what George Herbert Mead called *systemic wisdom*, or the ability to understand the complex nature of the context that gives rise to more enduring conflicts and the capacity to work with the forces and trends within the context to support the rise of more constructive patterns.[30]

Let me say that again. Addressing chronic patterns of political division requires the ability to understand the nature of the *context* that gives rise to these conflicts and the capacity to work with the *flow of forces* within the context to support the rise of more constructive patterns.

This is a fundamentally different theory of change for conflict. Rather than fight, flee, or fix the conflict, it recommends working with the *flow* of the (self-organizing) situation to realize sustained change. Rooted more in Eastern philosophy and values, which tend to emphasize the *power of situations* and *collective action* over individual agency,[31] it offers a less direct, multicausal, nonlinear view of some types of change. This perspective recognizes that direct action in cloudy, unpredictable situations often misfires. Rather than proposing a mastery approach to directly intervening with such divisions, this theory recommends a *harmony orientation*,[32] working *with* existing trends, movements, programs, and other inherent sources of energy and political will in the environment. Thus the aims are less immediate and proximal (fixing conflicts) and more long-term and distal (radical relandscaping), such as qualitatively changing the relational patterns of disputants and transforming the attractor landscapes of groups in conflict—over time.

PRINCIPLE 1: THINK DIFFERENT—CHANGE YOUR THEORY OF CHANGE

Radical relandscaping requires taking the time to acquire a more comprehensive, holistic view of the constellation of factors perpetuating the conflict—as well as the many less obvious avenues for change. This necessitates developing an understanding of how complex systems do and do not change (the seven Crude Laws) and, in particular, the importance of leveraging *destabilizing shocks* and establishing constructive *initial conditions* for promoting new or resetting old conflict dynamics. It also recommends beginning by identifying what is already working within the conflict system (family, community, etc.) to both mitigate destructive relations and to promote more positive ones. This approach may require circumventing the core presenting problems, which are often too polarizing to affect constructively, and addressing some of the upstream drivers of the conflict that might elicit less resistance. It also emphasizes the central importance in more entrenched conflicts of the emotional context of relationships involved, and of carefully resetting their course. Finally, it recognizes the inevitability and value of setbacks and failure as a means for learning more about the underlying rules of the system, and for adapting effectively.

This type of cloudlike thinking about changing contexts is much less common or familiar in the field of conflict resolution than the clock approach, but it has significantly influenced related areas including some forms of family systems therapy,[33] models of organizational development,[34] and more macro, complexity science-informed approaches to peacebuilding, humanitarian assistance and development in the international arena.[35] However, it is currently notably absent from most approaches to addressing political polarization.

Radical relandscaping is focused on the long game. There are no quick fixes to complex, deeply embedded disputes, but they are not impossible to solve if approached wisely.

Principle 1: Think Different—Change Your Theory of Change

Given the recalcitrant nature of some of the deeper divisions we struggle with in our lives, it may at times be best to back off from our mostly futile attempts to fight, flee, or fix them and instead learn to think differently about them. Changing our understanding of these problems from clocklike to cloudlike is the first step. Although radical relandscaping is unfamiliar to many, it is a way of thinking and responding to problems that is both rooted in rich cultural traditions and informed by the scientific study of physics, complexity, and psychology. Yes, it requires a significant change in focus from the conflict to the context, and a change in our sense of agency from the power of individual agents like ourselves to the power of working *with* the forces inherent to the situation. But when we are lost in landscapes of enmity, radical relandscaping can offer a way out.

But here's the truth—today we need options. There is no one best way to respond to the variety of minor disputes, major disagreements, and conflict disasters that arise in our lives. The vast majority of conflicts in life will respond favorably to clock fixes: like simply talking it out. But as Karl Popper warned us, we need to be careful to use clock tools when fixing clock problems and cloud methods for cloudier problems. Most of us are much more familiar and comfortable with our steady clock tools. And research suggests that they are likely to be embedded in the neurological structures in our brains, so switching modes will be no small matter. But when facing a more than fifty-year trend of increasing political and cultural enmity, clock fixes just won't do.

PRACTICE: MOVE FROM THEORY TO PRACTICE

I have been studying, teaching, and writing about complex, acrimonious, intractable conflicts for more than twenty-five years. When students take my courses, or read my books and papers on the research we have conducted, they often get *very* excited about the eye-opening possibilities that dynamical systems theory (DST) and attractor dynamics offer for addressing the more wicked problems they face. Early on, these born-again DST students would come into my office and proclaim their devotion to the DST approach and inform me that they planned to go back home (to Israel, Palestine, Nigeria, Korea, Colombia, and so on) and use DST to address some of the cloudiest, most difficult conflicts on earth.

When asked exactly how they planned to employ DST in their work, they would usually offer vague notions of their plans: "You know, I'll use DST to rethink everything about the conflict—how to understand it, who to work with, and what exactly to do!" When pushed further for specifics, I would get the same kind of animated generalizations.

Although their enthusiasm was heartening, it gave me pause. I often felt like we were sending these students off half-cocked, with energy and innovative ideas from science, but with few practical, concrete, specifics about what they might do when they really got down to work—how they might translate the ideas into useful practices.

In response to this, my much more practical colleagues, Josh Fisher and Nick Redding, began to work with me to develop a coherent set of DST-informed modes of practice that could help our students apply the ideas of attractors and repellers and nonlinear complex systems in concrete ways.[36] We initially developed this set of practices for work we did for the Internal Justice System of the World Bank Group, and then we developed them more fully for a course we offered. This approach informs the remainder of this book. Grounded in the most robust findings from research on complexity science and change, it describes what you, an exhausted human being stuck in a vortex of pain and polarization, can do in your life and your community to find a way out. Put simply, we recommend that you take the time to *reset*, *bolster and break*, *complicate*, *move*, and *adapt* (Figure 4.4).

The logic of these five modes of practice is straightforward. First, given the extraordinary set of forces we are facing that are pitting us against one another and the pervasive, often infuriating power of the resulting attractor landscape, it assumes that a significant *reset* is usually warranted. A reset is a pause in time when we might rethink and recalibrate our approach and our contributions to the pattern that we seek to change. Resets can serve to keep matters from getting worse in the short run and to point us in a new direction for the future. They are

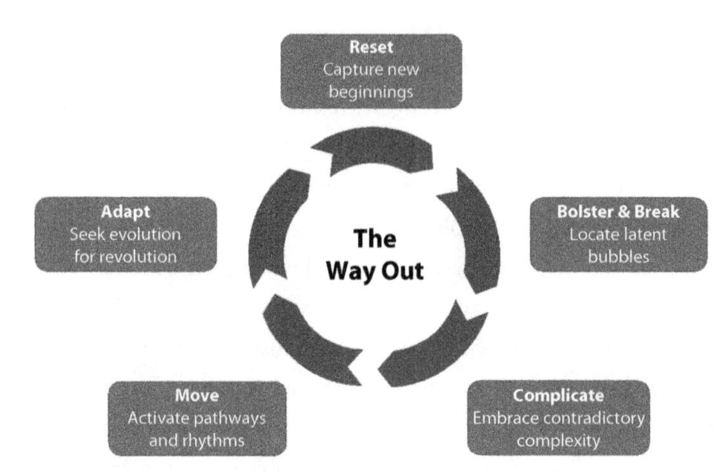

4.4 Five modes of practice for radical relandscaping (R^2).

often instigated by dramatic or otherwise extraordinary *shocks* or *ruptures* to the status quo of our lives: a horrible altercation that crossed a line, a health crisis, an accident, a scandal, or even just sheer exhaustion (such as the exhausted majority are experiencing today). I call this the *bombshell effect*. Resets may involve adjustments to our own emotional and motivational states, to how we think about a situation, to what we see as our intentions and objectives, and to what our next steps ought to be. They can be taken up by us alone but are best done jointly within a relationship, working group, organization, or an entire community. Given what we know about complex systems—particularly their *heightened sensitivity to initial conditions*, or the *butterfly effect*—we will want to take up any reset in a much more intentional and planful manner than usual to set us off down a better path. The actions outlined here illustrate how to enact the basic principle of *capture the power of new beginnings*, which is the focus of chapter 5.

After a sufficient reset, the next order of business is to locate what is already working. This practice is based on research findings that change-resistant problems are often most responsive to *positive deviance* or *bright spots*, existing remedies that have already arisen and proven useful and sustainable within the context of the problem. Chapter 6 offers ideas and illustrations of how to begin to carefully identify, *bolster*, and support those propensities, people, processes, policies, and programs that are already working well in our relationships, networks, and communities—working to either prevent or mitigate more destructive patterns from escalating or to promote more healthy, constructive patterns. It is organized around the principle of *locate latent bubbles*, which is based on the finding that significant changes in our strongest (self-organizing) attitudes, habits, relationships, and norms often happen when "bubbles of new appear in a sea of old" or when "bubbles of old regain dominance in a sea of new."

However, the bubble principle also suggests that in order to sustain any positive change in our situation resulting from building on what is working, it is paramount that we also seek to actively reduce the attraction of our more (now latent) detrimental tendencies. Therefore, we must also find ways to *break down* or otherwise diminish the attraction of the more destructive dynamics that are driving us to mitigate the worst inclinations of our system. These practices emphasize the need to address these drivers upstream, away from the heat of the conflict, to minimize resistance. In addition, it stresses the importance of leveraging or expanding existing repellers or social taboos for engaging in more destructive political acts. This is the focus of the remainder of chapter 6.

The next mode of practice for relandscaping your life is to *complicate* it. This practice suggests that how we experience and comprehend the context of the problem(s) we are facing must become more nuanced. For our perception and understanding of events to even begin to resemble the degree of complexity of the constellation of challenges we are facing, we must understand the people involved, their groups, past events, the current issues, and our own role in the matter in this light. We need to achieve a more accurate understanding of our predicament and of our options for changing it, which have likely collapsed, becoming overly biased, constrained, and simplistic. It requires seeking out and coming to terms with some of the many contradictions in our own life, and it may involve adjusting not only how we think and feel about our situation but who we think with, what we listen and attend to, and how we go about envisioning the problem and the way out. Ultimately, this mode of activity entails zooming out on our understanding of the conflict to provide the context for us to then zoom in and reorient where and how we are addressing it. These practices will help you translate the principle of *embrace contradictory complexity* into action, which is the focus of chapter 7.

A fourth mode of practice that is key to finding the way out is to *move*. This mode is based on research findings that when stuck in a difficult pattern there is great value in movement—cognitive, emotional, and physical—in ways that can free up and resynchronize our experiences and relations and redirect attention from the static to the dynamic. For the vast majority of our existence, Homo sapiens moved together—we migrated, hunted, and gathered together in small groups. This was the context in which our brains developed their more sophisticated cognitive capacities.[37] Yet these days, when we try to work out our most wicked problems, we tend to sit down at a table across from the opposition—or worse yet at a computer—and talk it out. This works well enough with lessor disputes, but severely constrains our capacities to see, feel, think, and work our way out of thornier, problems that we have come to embody physically. Chapter 8 is organized around the principle of *activate novel pathways and rhythms*, which is based on neuroscience and social science research on the benefits of increasing plasticity, openness, and synchronization when attempting to find a way out of entrenched patterns.

The fifth mode of practice, which we have found to be particularly challenging for most people, especially when they are caught in highly emotional, anxiety-provoking conflicts that feel like they demand an immediate response, is the need to become more comfortable with settling in to play the *long game*.[38] Remember, at this point we are not trying to impose a specific type of change on our relationship or situation (as much as we might want to). We have tried this, repeatedly, and it seemed to have negligible effects or *unintended negative consequences*. Rather, we are trying to learn, better understand, and *adapt* to the major forces operating in the context, working with them to navigate and transform the landscape over time. This practice helps us realize the principle gleaned from complexity science, *seek evolution for revolution*, which cautions us to work incrementally, adaptively, and with humility to realize significant, sustainable change. It offers a few relevant tactics: take a *gamers approach* to change, or one in which we seek to fail as rapidly as possible in order to learn the underlying rules of the situation with which we are working; *start small*, or experiment with changes to small but potentially high-impact targets; and learn to *adapt* to failures and alter our approach, holding on to the vision of the change we seek but adjusting our tactics in response to what our failures are teaching us. This is the focus of chapter 9.

A few final notes on the R^2 approach. First, the five modes of practice presented here are not offered as a sequence, although resetting is often a prerequisite for this method. Sequences of steps assume linear, cause-and-effect types of change: do this, then this, then this will happen. We are now working with a system of interrelated problems with a distinct set of laws that evidence unfamiliar forms of nonlinear change (If X, then who knows *what* will happen!). These practices of resetting, bolstering and breaking, complicating, moving, and adapting are all useful modes of action for perceiving, navigating, and transforming these landscapes. Much like our distinct senses of hearing, seeing, smelling, tasting, and touching, which combine to enhance our overall perception and experience, these five modes of practice work best when used in concert. Rather than seeing them as steps, see them as tactics that work best together.

Second, the good news about seeking significant change to enduring patterns in complex sociopolitical situations is that there are many roads to Rome. Although sustained change to these patterns is hard won, unpredictable, and requires smart, persistent efforts and adaptation, their high degree of complexity also present many alternative pathways for destabilizing old patterns and identifying or seeding new ones. This is promising.

Finally, I hope it is crystal clear by now that the challenges many of us are facing today are bigger than any of us alone. To find and sustain a way out requires more than merely a willingness and commitment to change ourselves—to increase our own awareness and understanding. In addition, we must also locate *constructive containers*—or what Morrie Schwartz, the hero of *Tuesdays with Morrie*, called micro-cultures. These are the other people, families, groups, and institutions in our world that are also committed to enacting the principles and practices shared in this book in service of finding a way out. These can be essential sources of inspiration, guidance, and support for our journey—as well as evidence that there is, in fact, a way out. Without them, we will surely tumble back down into the temporary but toxic comfort of our deepest attractors.

So let's get to it.

5

RESET—CAPTURE THE POWER OF NEW BEGINNINGS

THE STARTING LINE

Several years ago, an older, white professor colleague of mine made an off-hand comment during the first faculty meeting of the year that caused such a firestorm that the sheer quantity of responses to it online overloaded and shut down the entire email system at the college. My colleague claimed afterward that he had intended his comment as a joke, but when he referred to an "endangered species of white, male professors" at the college, it struck a nerve and ended up escalating racial and gender tensions and rattling the newly arrived, mostly white college administration for the remainder of the year. In fact, many of the eventual outcomes of the resulting maelstrom were long overdue, constructive, and fair. But it was also clear that no one in the meeting that morning had intended to have that conversation, and few if any of us were prepared to navigate it effectively. Consequently, it went sideways, sparked months of hostile recriminations and resentment, and my colleague's reputation never fully recovered.

Two weeks after the initial faculty meeting, I (a relatively young, white, newly hired, pretenured, male, assistant professor) was asked by the president of the college to chair a task force to address the many grievances about harassment, bias, and discrimination at the college that had been voiced in response to the incident. This presented me with a serious dilemma. On one hand, I had just been hired as a conflict resolution specialist with an expressed interest in promoting causes of social justice. I had also written to the president after the "joke" incident and recommended he view the current crisis of his administration as an opportunity to achieve substantive reform. On the other hand, I was an untenured, white, male rookie being asked by a brand new white male president to head up a process to address problems of gender and racial discrimination and exclusion at the college. As one senior African American professor said to my face, "Who the hell are you to do this work?" I was panicked.

After several sleepless nights, I agreed to take on the chair of the initiative under several conditions. First, I asked that the task force be comprised of representatives from all the major stakeholder groups at the college—students, faculty, staff, union employees, and management—who would be selected by their peers. Second, I requested that we be able to appoint a cochair for the process—a person of color chosen by consensus by the entire committee. Third, I insisted—in the face of some resistance from the president—that several of the most angry, outspoken members of the college who had given voice to grievances on race and gender bias be invited to join the task force. Finally, I asked that the task force be given enough resources and time—meeting weekly over several months—to produce a meaningful set of recommendations and that the final report be shared in full with the entire community.

The president of the college eventually agreed to these requests, and my experiences in that task force over those next several hot summer months were some of the most daunting, demanding, uncomfortable, humbling, and ultimately satisfying moments of my career. Our group's hard work together, shepherded by clear guidelines and careful cofacilitation, eventually made a significant positive difference at the college. This included changing the college's mission statement to incorporate diversity and justice objectives; reforming hiring, evaluation, and grievance policies and procedures; and establishing an office, staff, and budget line for a vice president of diversity. The effects of our work were robust and remain evident today.

This story of how two divergent conversations about explosive issues—both triggered by the same catastrophic incident—went down two very distinct paths, raises a host of questions about how to and how not to approach such loaded topics. But allow me to draw your attention to two particularly important facets—how one got started, and how the other reset. These new beginnings are the focus of this chapter (figure 5.1).

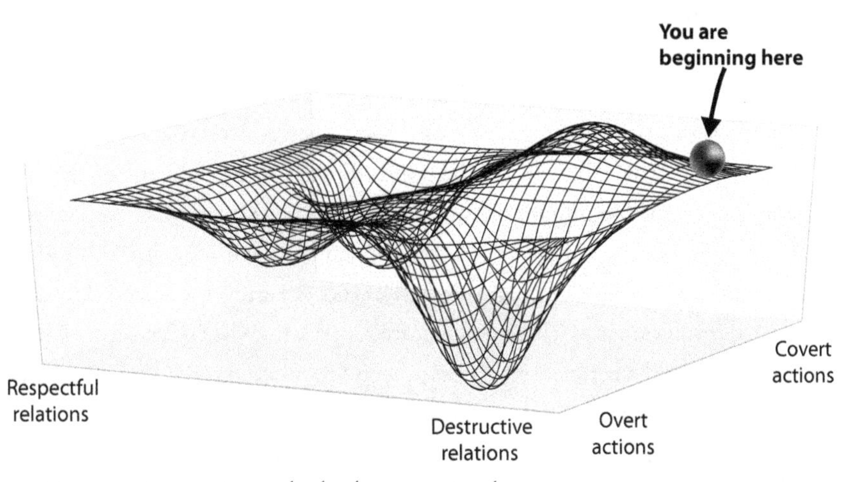

5.1 How we initiate action in this landscape is critical.

PRINCIPLE 2: RESET—CAPTURE THE POWER OF NEW BEGINNINGS

Every day in Alcoholics Anonymous meetings and other self-help groups across the globe, people stand up and publicly tell their desperate personal stories of falling into a painfully uncontrollable addiction, hitting bottom, being confronted by alarmed family members or friends, and then reaching out to AA (often with the support of a sponsor) to begin the long journey of trying to reset their life. Many addicts "slip" and backslide into substance abuse, but many also persevere, and some return to AA once they again hit bottom. Central to this moment of reset is the need for individuals to recognize and admit their problem, to surrender to the fact that it is much mightier than they are alone, and then to commit to changing the "persons, places, and things" in their life that draw them back into substance abuse.

Sound familiar?

Of course, I am not suggesting that we are all addicts (although we could all benefit from taking a hard look at the amount of time we spend online or otherwise consuming or contributing to partisan media), but there are clear parallels between the biopsychosocial trap of substance abuse addiction and the current, toxic, us-versus-them attractor dynamics infiltrating our lives. And *the way out* of addiction almost always begins with a significant and intentional reset.

In fact, history shows us that the way out of many pathological states began with a reset. In 1948, the nation of Costa Rica emerged from the bloodiest civil war in its history, which had cost thousands of lives, to become one of the only nations in the world to intentionally decide to disband their military and redirect national resources toward education, health, and the environment.[1] This radical reset took place because its president, Jose Figueres Ferrer, the former leader of the armed revolutionaries, chose to advocate for peacefulness. Today Costa Rica is ranked as one of the happiest and most peaceful nations on earth, and it has been referred to as "a model in terms of the development of a culture of peace."[2]

Or consider our Boston case. After the horrific shooting in Brookline, intentional resets were declared at the state level by the governor of Massachusetts and by the Catholic Church, calling for a moratorium on protests and talks between the two camps. In addition, six community leaders agreed to reset by engaging in a process that was a radical departure from the status quo of their past relations across the divide.

Closer to home, it is highly likely that many of you have at times come to a place in your life when you were acutely unhappy in love, miserable at work, or otherwise fed up with the status quo and looking for a radical change. This is clearly what the 86 percent of exhausted Americans are experiencing today.

Principle 2: Reset—Capture the Power of New Beginnings

This principle, based on the research on nonlinear change summarized in Crude Laws 4 (destabilizing shocks) and 1 (initial conditions), tells the story of how opportunities for resets in chronically divisive relationships and communities often follow two very different but sometimes related scenarios—one triggered by the *bombshell effect* and the other by the *butterfly effect.* Both can lead to dramatic changes in the status quo, and both can also be quite challenging to navigate.

Whether trying to escape individual-level addictive patterns, community-level traps of vitriol, or the strong pull to return to violence after a brutal civil war, resets are often the first step toward sustainable course corrections.

THE BOMBSHELL EFFECT

I hope it is abundantly clear by now that meaningful change in polarization dynamics situated within intractable landscapes is exceptionally hard to realize. Nevertheless, studies have shown that these enduring patterns often become more susceptible to change after some type of major shock destabilizes them.[3] This is what pioneering social psychologist Kurt Lewin described in the 1940s as the necessary initial phase of *unfreezing* in many change scenarios.[4] Although most families, organizations, communities, and nations change gradually over time through tinkering and adaptation, significant qualitative changes in how they function are primarily the result of dramatic jolts to the status quo. Change of this nature is thought to require a disassembly and reorientation of what is known as their *deep structure*, the assumptions, values, and incentives that determine our most basic decision-making processes.[5]

For example, consider the role of shock in the Boston abortion case. The polarizing pro-life/pro-choice attractor landscape in which much of the Boston community was trapped during the 1980s and 1990s had been forming and festering for decades. Many good-faith attempts to change the dynamics had been tried and seemed to have had little lasting impact. Then, in 1994, there was a devastating shock to the status quo in the form of a homicidal shooting spree at two women's health clinics in the area. In the immediate aftermath of the violence, several overt changes were made with regard to security policies and procedures, but there seemed to be little movement in addressing the underlying forces that created the conditions for the violence in the first place. Years later, in 2001, when the six community leaders came out publicly to share the story of their covert dialogue process, things seemed to change considerably.

Similar delayed, shock-induced change scenarios have been documented in situations involving long-term conflicts in the international arena. Significant political shocks at the interstate level can result from myriad events: civil wars, significant changes in international power relations, coup d'états, independence movements, natural catastrophes, or major transitions to autocracy or democracy. In a study of 850 enduring interstate conflicts that occurred between 1816 and 1992, between 75 and 90 percent were found to have ended *within a ten-year period* following at least one major destabilizing shock.[6] These were more than forty-year-long rivalries, many involving repeated incidents of violence or open warfare, that changed course dramatically toward peace within ten years of a major traumatic event.

The implications of this shock scenario for changing course on American polarization are significant. To illustrate, let's look at the political dynamics displayed in figure 5.2, which shows voting patterns in the U.S. Congress over 136 years.[7] The early phase of the graph shows that high levels of congressional polarization (indicated by higher lines on the graph) after the end of the U.S. Civil War in 1865 lasted, understandably, for quite some time. But then, around 1924, something strange happened—we started to see a precipitous decline in this form of polarization.

It is logical to wonder what happened in 1924 to bring about such a change. But if you look further back to 1914, you will see the onset of World War I—an unprecedented political shock that radically destabilized the world order—as well as the Spanish flu, which hit in 1918 and killed fifty million people across the globe. About a decade later, we see the beginning of a significant depolarization trend in our Congress, followed by decades of much improved bipartisan problem solving in Washington. This is what the research on these types of shocks tell us—their effects often take several years to coalesce and crystallize.

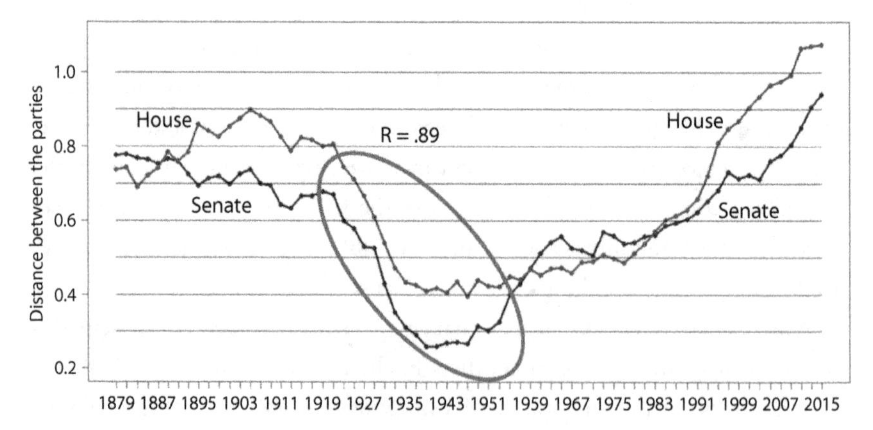

5.2 Decades of functional bipartisanship in the U.S. congress from 1924–1955.

Scholars refer to this delayed, nonlinear change scenario as *punctuated equilibrium* (see Crude Law 4), and it has been documented in many fields of scientific endeavor, including biology,[8] human and organizational development,[9] and the advancement of science more generally.[10] Punctuated equilibrium was first identified by two paleobiologists, Niles Eldredge and Stephen Jay Gould, who proposed it as a major revision to Darwinian theory on adaptation and evolution. From the study of fossil records, they observed that new species often formed, not gradually, as Darwin had originally claimed, but through *speciation*, that is, when small but critical genetic changes occurred that caused them to branch off sharply from a persisting parental stock, resulting in a fundamentally different species.[11] In other words, through discontinuous change.

Subsequent studies have uncovered similar patterns of abrupt change in a variety of systems. Scientists have found that complex systems typically stabilize at an equilibrium (a state of rest or balance due to the equal action of opposing forces). Small, incremental change is common thereafter, but a serious puncture in the status quo is often necessary to trigger a sequence of events leading to radical change. Hundreds of studies conducted in areas as diverse as changes in business markets, iconic branding, artificial intelligence, same-sex marriage policy, and team dynamics have demonstrated the validity and utility of this nonlinear model of change.[12]

For example, one study investigating organizational change found that a large majority of organizational *transformations* occurring in the U.S. computer industry could be attributed to rapid and discontinuous change resulting from ruptures over most or all domains of organizational activity. Although incremental changes in strategies, structures, and power distributions were more common, the researchers found that they were much less likely to produce fundamental transformations in these businesses.[13] We experienced this at my college too. After years of tinkering at the margins on institutional diversity and antidiscrimination efforts, it took a catastrophe to kick us into a new era. So shocks can get it done.

In organizations and communities, significant ruptures can result from public scandals involving leaders (e.g., Bill Clinton, Bill Cosby, and Bill O'Reilly) or institutions (e.g., Enron, the Catholic Church, and the National Security Agency), catastrophic "acts of god" (severe weather, fire, earthquakes, etc.) or significant acts of violence (mass shootings, terrorism, suicides), all of which create conditions conducive to serious scrutiny, reflection, reform, and realignment.

These breaks in "business as usual" are often painful and difficult and are initially met with great resistance, but eventually people, relationships, and communities begin to reexamine the status quo and to seek alternative patterns.

In the personal realm, major bombshells can come from a loss of employment, a personal scandal, the death of a loved one, or a health crisis. In addition, being forced to confront significant contradictions within our basic organizing beliefs (religious, ideological, ontological, or political convictions) can result in *disorienting dilemmas*, which tend to lead people and groups to consider radically new ways of seeing the world.[14]

Ironically, this particular change scenario provides a glimmer of hope for us today. However you feel about the forty-fifth president of the United States, Donald J. Trump (my hope is that about half of you favor him and the rest don't), most people would agree that he has shocked our system. The way Trump took up campaigning, politics, governing, use of the media, and foreign affairs was unprecedented in its violation of standard norms of presidential behavior, and this constituted an extraordinary shock to the American experiment. Some of the first-order effects of these shocks are predictable, but most of the second- and third-order effects are unforeseeable. Suffice it to say that the consequences of Trump's presidency are highly destabilizing.*

Adding to the considerable chaos caused by the unorthodoxy of the Trump presidency, we are living through a deadly global pandemic, the subsequent derailment of our basic social and economic foundations, and a historically large and consequential era of protest and civil unrest regarding racial injustice. The exact impact of these events is unknowable, but they will destabilize us profoundly.

However, it is paramount that I emphasize one critical feature of the bombshell effect. Significant shocks to people and societies can break in different

---

* Comedian John Mulaney has this to say about the Trump presidency:

> It's like there's a horse loose in a hospital. Like, I think everything is going to be OK, but I have no idea what's gonna happen next. And, like, none of you know either. We've all never not known together. . . . On the news they try to get people, they're like, "We have a man here who once saw a bird in an airport," and we're like "Get the hell outta here! This is a horse in a hospital!"

You can watch Mulaney's standup special, "John Mulaney: Kid Gorgeous at Radio City," on Netflix and access this "horse in a hospital" bit on YouTube at https://www.youtube.com/watch?v=JhkZMxgPxXU.

directions–encourage radical forms of positive change, further intransigence, or even make things terribly worse. For instance, precisely ten years after 9/11 and the U.S. military incursions into Afghanistan and Iraq (major shocks to the region and the world), Tunisia and others nations in the Middle East and North African (MENA) region erupted into a series of revolutions that today, in the case of Tunisia, offer the potential for a constructive shift from an authoritarian regime to more democratic rule. However, despite temporary shifts in the political dynamics of other states in the region, such as Egypt, Syria, and Mali, these states either returned to the previous attractor pattern of hardline military rule shortly after revolution or descended into bloody chaos.

These more destructive outcomes in the MENA region are consistent with the rest of the story of the aforementioned effects of shocks on international conflict. Not only do these shocks precede the end of most enduring interstate rivalries, but they also appear to *instigate* about 95 percent of the more harmful, protracted conflicts between nations, which also have been found to *begin* within ten years of a shock.[15] This suggests that the effects of bombshells, which can take months or years to become evident, do not ensure radical or constructive change. They must, therefore, be considered a near necessary but insufficient condition when working to reshape intractable attractors.

In fact, returning to political polarization and my favorite graph on historical trends (last time–I promise), note the considerable uptick in U.S. congressional polarization that began around 1979 (figure 5.3). This turn of events is often attributed to Ronald Reagan's conservative revolution of the early 1980s, which brought about major changes in the GOP. However, it also happened to occur about a decade after the U.S. experienced a period of considerable upheaval, including several political assassinations (John F. Kennedy, Robert Kennedy, Malcolm X, and Martin Luther King Jr.), a highly unpopular war (Vietnam), and a full-out antiestablishment (countercultural) social movement. This turning point, in fact, marks the onset of the path of division we are stuck on today.

In sum, dramatic shocks can reunite warring groups and bring renewed solidarity, have no visible impact whatsoever, or trigger new divisions that endure for decades. Given our current levels of instability, now is the time to begin to bolster old or to create new constructive attractors for our cultural and political discourse. Of course, the ten-trillion-dollar question is, "What does it take to tip us in this direction?"

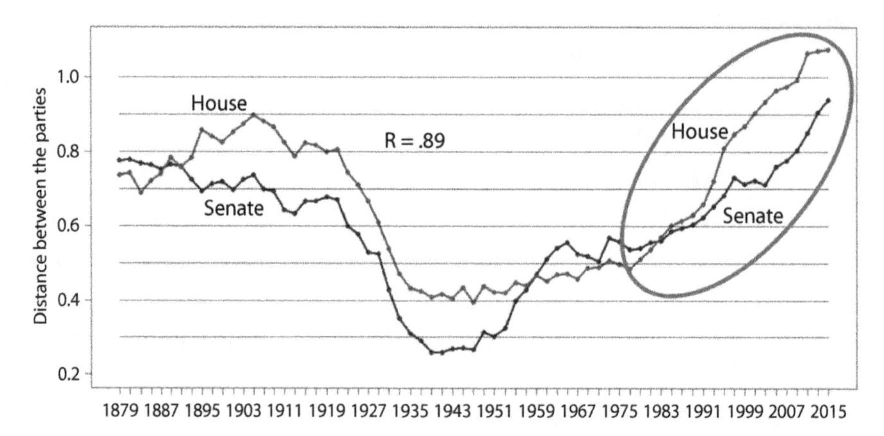

5.3 A tipping point into escalating polarization in the U.S. congress from 1979–2015.

PRACTICE—DIGGING DEEP

The research on punctuated equilibrium offers a few pathways for realizing desired changes in the wake of disruptive shocks, and they all pass through modifications in our *deep structure*.[16] In her groundbreaking 1991 paper on revolutionary change, Connie Gersick defines deep structure as "the set of fundamental 'choices' a system has made of (1) the basic parts into which its units will be organized and (2) the basic activity patterns that will maintain its existence." A bit obtuse, but she later clarified it this way:

> I argued that the heart of the Punctuated Equilibrium paradigm is the idea that complex systems are held together by a highly durable underlying order, or deep structure. The deep structure is what confines change during equilibrium periods to variations on an enduring theme—and it is also what disassembles, reconfigures, and enforces wholesale transformation during revolutionary punctuations.[17]

For our purposes, deep structure is synonymous with our attractor landscapes, although the latter is inherently more dynamic.[18]

But what does this mean exactly? Given the fractal nature of intractable landscapes described in chapter 1 (similar patterns repeated and reinforced across levels from our brains to our societies), it probably makes more sense to speak of deep *structures*, although the manner in which they align and fuel each other is also key. In either case, it is important to think of the need for change at multiple levels.

No, this does not mean that every component of our super storm of polarization must be altered to realize change. But it does mean that sustained change will most likely have multiple determinants up to some threshold that triggers a reverse in dynamics in which more vicious cycles become virtuous cycles within and between us, promoting healthier political relations. How can this happen? Gersick offers three potential pathways: through strangers, new species, and synchronization.

THE STRANGER—TOP-DOWN OUTSIDER CATALYSTS

A common pathway from entrenched problems through instability to positive change is what I call the *stranger story*. This tends to play out in systems—families, businesses, communities, and so on—that are somehow chronically failing and in distress. Although leaders and other stakeholders within these communities may try diligently to address these failures, they often misunderstand them or have strong vested interests in the status quo. They tend to keep doing more of what they usually do to address the problems, thus making them worse.

Then, out of the darkness, comes the stranger. The pain and suffering caused by the failures of the system have somehow managed to get the attention of this outsider, and in the stranger rides. The stranger comes from a foreign place and is unsocialized (and unincentivized) to the ways of the system and so is able to see the problems differently and identify new and novel solutions. With sufficient charisma, energy, ambition, and enthusiasm, the stranger can make the case for revolutionary structural change and mobilize large segments of the community to join together in making changes. Because the former leaders and bureaucrats often remain stuck in their old ways, the new leader sees the need to clean house and start over from scratch. Gersick writes, "It is then the newcomer's explicit task to break the old deep structure and establish a new one."[19] From this radical change arises a new era.

Sound familiar? It should. This scenario has a long legacy in American mythology ("Shane, come back!"[20]), the history of science, American business, and in

U.S. politics. Thomas Kuhn characterized the onset of scientific revolutions as the result of outsiders or newcomers to a field who can see the failures of the old paradigm and lack investment in the status quo.[21] In a study of U.S. tech companies, researchers found that a vast majority of the revolutionary changes that took place in them occurred as a result of discontinuous change brought on by the combination of an external shock in the industry coupled with the recruitment of a new, outsider CEO.[22] Strangers are more inclined to break stuff and get it done.

It could also be argued that the rise of both Donald Trump and Bernie Sanders followed this course. A significant shock to the United States in the form of the 2008 financial crisis caused great pain to many but was handled in a standard manner (big bank bailouts with little accountability), which set the stage for two charismatic outsiders (a reality TV businessman from Queens and a Jewish socialist from Brooklyn) to enter presidential politics, mobilize millions of aggrieved followers, and make a case for radical change. Once elected, Trump cleaned house, shattered presidential norms and procedures, and set to work to remake the U.S. government and the Republican Party to fit his new paradigm.

This is one way that radical change could again unfold—in the form of another unsocialized (but ideally prosocial) outsider coming in, taking the reins of leadership, offering a compelling vision of unity and solidarity for the United States and the planet, and then shepherding us back together. This would likely require someone with the moral stature and political acumen of an Abraham Lincoln, Mahatma Gandhi, Eleanor Roosevelt, Martin Luther King Jr., or Nelson Mandela. This is the main limitation of the stranger story—it requires that an extraordinary leader emerge who just happens to be right for the times.

THE NEW SPECIES—BOTTOM-UP INSIDER CATALYSTS

Another avenue for realizing substantive change out of chaos is through the *new species story*. These pathways often emerge spontaneously because of the tumultuous nature of the status quo, when new ideas, practices, leaders, or groups rise from the turmoil and form entirely new and different entities. This is the process of *speciation* that the paleobiologists Eldredge and Gould observed in the study of fossils, when small genetic changes occurred that caused species to branch off sharply from their parental stock, resulting in a fundamentally different species. In sociopolitical systems, these highly original groups and movements arise from a failing system to meet the challenges of the day—examples include the Tea Party movement in 2009, the Occupy movement in 2011, and the Black Lives Matter movement in 2013.

Take for example, Hope in the Cities, a nonprofit group that works to deepen interracial trust, reflection, dialogue, and action across the United States. It first formed in Richmond, Virginia, the former seat of the Confederacy where as many as 300,000 kidnapped African people were sold to plantations, a place that continues to grapple with the legacies of its past. In 1993, Hope in the Cities branched off from its parent group, the Oxford Group, founded in 1927 to link personal change to social transformation, and offered Richmond "intentional interventions in inter-racial facilitation and dialogue that have become models for individuals, communities and organizations across the world."[23] The combination of the historical context from which Hope arose, the resonant need for the services it offers, and their eclectic approach involving patience, persistence, personal responsibility, and adaptability has allowed the organization to thrive and grow.

Hundreds, if not thousands, of groups and organizations like Hope have sprung up across the country today in response to specific crises or challenges, and they actively work to support dialogue and to mobilize action to bridge divides.[24] Some work at the local community level to help Americans come together and build common understanding; others focus on mitigating polarization within influence sectors such as in journalism, social media, education, and governance. These groups often provide the guidance and support necessary to navigate difficult political conversations and to build bipartisan alliances. But more important, they help participants move beyond dialogue to build politically diverse teams that together are better positioned to take on some of the many structural incentives driving our divisions. *This step is critical to substantive change.* We will never talk our way out of this landscape; talk must lead to action and structural change.

However, when the initiating crisis ebbs, a common challenge for these groups is being able to sustain the financial and human resources necessary to continue or to scale their work. Many of them are temporary initiatives, and we all end up losing out on their support and local insight. In addition, when people try to build bridges in the context of deeply divided societies—particularly when they start to be effective and draw attention—they often face mounting resistance, obstruction, and even violence, often from both sides of the fissure. This happens regularly to peacemakers in Israel-Palestine, Syria, South Sudan, and Colombia, and it is not uncommon in the United States today. If these groups happen to offer a radically new approach—especially if it is highly effective—they can face considerable resistance from others working on these issues, who may see them as a threat to their own viability. Sustainability and scale are considerable challenges for these bottom-up catalysts.

GETTING IN SYNC—MIDDLE-OUT JOINT CATALYSTS

The third radical change scenario offered by Gersick is characterized less by unilateral heroic deeds of outsiders or the urgent concerns of insiders and more by close coordination between internal stakeholders and external change agents. I call it the *synchronization story*. Here local members of a failing system who have a particularly nuanced understanding of the specific challenges they are facing, as well as the more promising remedies, lack the resources, confidence, or vision to mobilize and realize them. Therefore, they will sometimes welcome outsiders into a collaborative process that is centered on local understanding and initiative but is supported and brought to scale through the value added by outsiders. Together, through adaptive problem solving and persistence, they are able to jointly realize radical change. Such strategic inside-outside partnerships have been quite effective in realizing transformative solutions to a variety of chronic challenges such as urban poverty and violence,[25] child protection,[26] health and conservation,[27] and peacebuilding.[28]

Insiders and outsiders could work together today to help to reunite us. These partnerships could capitalize on the current instability by helping to connect, support, and scale the many bridging groups currently working on their own. Gaining a more comprehensive sense of the large and robust ecology of groups and organizations addressing polarization could help to bolster a greater sense of purpose and efficacy in this work. And increasing the profile of this heretofore nascent movement may embolden more of the exhausted majority of Americans to join in common cause. Supporting a series of developmental communities of practice in different sectors (e.g., journalism, tech, education, and governance) could attract the resources and influence needed to take on the vested interests who are benefiting from our divisions.

In 2019, I began work on a new project with a nonprofit to do just this. Launched by Tim Shriver, former chair of the Special Olympics, *Unite* is a national initiative to promote unity and solidarity across differences.[29] Over the past year, we have begun identifying and networking with many U.S.-based organizations, large and small, that are working on depolarization. We are beginning to map the ecosystem of this movement, which will enable us to better connect these groups and to conduct a strategic analysis to locate gaps, redundancies, complementarities, and opportunities to cooperate and achieve economies of scale. Our goal is simple: to nurture and support the ecology of bipartisan solidarity in the United States that is ready to emerge.

The moral of the bombshell scenario is one of potential with caution. These days bring an extraordinary opportunity for our nation to reset, change course, and realize a more practical, functional, and hopeful era. They also present a dire warning of the dangers ahead if we fail to act.

Now let's turn to a discussion of new beginnings of another sort.

THE BUTTERFLY EFFECT

One of the more interesting findings from the study of attractor dynamics in complex systems is their heightened *sensitivity to even small differences* in their initial conditions—how they begin (Crude Law 1 on initial conditions). This phenomenon, coined the *butterfly effect*, was discovered accidentally by meteorologist Edward Lorenz, who found that even tiny variations in the initial values of variables he plugged into his computer weather models resulted in predicting dramatically divergent weather patterns. Small initial differences (e.g., rounding down from 0.506127 to 0.506) eventually resulted in extremely different outcomes.[30]

For our purposes, sensitivity to beginning conditions means that how new encounters, conversations, relationships, groups, businesses, or communities are initiated (or are intentionally reset) often has profound implications for differences in the paths they follow. Recall how my colleague's casual remark about endangered white men kicked the entire state of the college into a strong hostile attractor dynamic on race and gender discrimination in the United States—one with a long, fraught history—that almost immediately captured the minds, hearts, and actions of many. In contrast, the task force faced similar hard and painful issues, but we had the opportunity to reset, and to do so with sufficient thoughtfulness, intentionality, and care. The task force was not easy (I lost seven pounds due to worry and anxiety that summer), but we were able to establish a much more constructive process that enabled us to sit in the fire of heated exchanges over our differences, tolerate them, learn from them, and then address significant problems in the institution.

Research from several dynamical systems conflict labs across the country has come to the same conclusion: What happens at the onset of a conflictual encounter is critical. Studies conducted around the world—including John Gottman's research on marital conflict and divorce in his Love Lab, Barbara Fredrickson's research on human emotions in her Positive Emotions and Psychophysiology Lab at UNC Chapel Hill, and our team's research on polarizing moral disputes at Columbia University and at our sister lab at the Ludwig-Maximillian University in Munich, Germany—have shown consistently that what goes on in the first few minutes of conflictual encounters often has a significant impact on everything that follows.

For example, our research has shown that the emotional experiences and the tone of disputants that arises in the first few minutes of discussions over divisive sociopolitical issues often sets the course for the emotional climate of the remainder of the session. In fact, the initial emotions of the disputants, whether positive or negative, often only become stronger.

John Gottman found similar effects in his research on marital conflict. The emotional state individual members of married couples came into the lab with significantly shaped the emotional tone of their sessions.[31] Other researchers have found that even mild and fleeting positive feelings early in an encounter can produce large benefits over the long run.[32] Research by Barbara Fredrickson, for example, has shown that evidence of positivity with participants during early assessments in her lab predicted increases in well-being several weeks later.[33]

Beyond emotions, our initial decisions and actions in social encounters are also thought to be particularly influential because they often characterize subsequent choices as appropriate or inappropriate. For instance, groups in conflict often choose, to some extent, their group boundaries (who is in versus who is out), allies, moral norms, leaders, and preferred methods of conflict engagement. Their initial choices on these matters, whether automatic, reactive, or considered, substantially affect the nature of the conflict dynamic that unfolds. Research in our lab found that mediators working with protracted conflicts face a similar set of highly consequential choices upon entry to the conflict.[34] Decisions regarding who to speak with, how to engage with disputants, how long to remain engaged, and how high to set the aspirations for agreement can be critical in shaping the patterns of peace and conflict that emerge over time.

This is consistent with other research on nonlinear systems that shows a similar sensitivity to initial conditions. My astrophysicist colleague, Larry Liebovitch, created a mathematical model of two entities (people, groups, nations) in conflict to investigate how more intractable conflicts evolve over time.[35] The model was run through a computer simulation in which the two "disputants" would block and obstruct each other at every interaction—emulating an intractable stalemate (you know, like what we see in Congress daily). Then slight variations to the settings of the variables were introduced and the simulations were run over long periods of time to see what could be learned. Liebovitch, too, found that even extremely small differences in the initial conditions of the emotions of the conflicting disputants (e.g., a positive emotion of 1.0 versus 1.001 out of 4.0) eventually made a profound difference in the emotional experiences of the parties.

This is exactly what Laura Chasin and Susan Podziba had learned from their work with divided communities in Boston: new beginnings matter. When they convened the Boston dialogue in the early 1990s, they intentionally set up the encounter in a manner to increase the odds that it could work. They carefully designed and vetted their proposed dialogue process with members of both the pro-life and pro-choice communities, intentionally framed the initiative for the potential participants in a manner that reduced resistance, and structured and facilitated the process with vigilance and care. They did everything they could to set the group off on a journey that would eventually bring them and their respective communities to a better place.

This all suggests that the effects of slight differences in conditions at the onset of a conflictual encounter—such as the initial attitudes of disputants or framing the process or even the physical configuration of the room—can lead to dramatic differences in the dynamics as the discussion progresses.

Next I break down the implications of the butterfly effect on how to prepare for potentially difficult encounters across our tribal divides.

PRACTICE: PREPARE FOR DIFFICULT ENCOUNTERS

The principle of sensitivity to initial conditions has major implications for reflecting on how to prepare to engage with others over issues that are potentially polarizing, whether in the context of a new encounter or a long relationship. Research has taught us about the power of intentionally leveraging several different aspects of opening conditions to get more difficult encounters off to a more promising start. Remember, in the world of complex systems and attractors, *there is no one right way* to prepare; rather, several options can help. Here are some of the more consequential.

The Power of Our Initial Assumptions

Consider, first, the power of our assumptions. For most of human history, people did not believe in change.[36] Fact is, early on in our history, not much did change from year to year, so people simply didn't give it much thought. Then came the scientific revolution, and with it the notion that things and people could change and be changed for the better. Nevertheless, many things don't appear to change, at least not visibly or rapidly enough to be noticed, so it is easy to be lulled into the belief that some things, and some people, don't *really* ever change. Add to this the fact that we are today in the midst of a more than fifty-year pattern of increasing political obstructionism from "those fanatics" on the other side (no matter which side you are on), and you understand why some of us believe that our *situation* and *those people* will never change.[37]

This difference in the assumptions people hold about whether people and groups can and do change has been the focus of a great deal of research.[38] Some of us tend to believe that people are inherently stubborn and immutable and consequently will never really change. When we harbor this mindset, we are more likely to disengage from conflict (why bother?) or to approach it much more competitively and confrontationally (why not?) and, as a result, perform less well in negotiations.[39] This assumption also makes us prone to harboring more stereotypical judgments of members of out-groups and to be more punitive and retaliatory toward them for perceived wrongdoing.

Other people are more inclined to believe that people, groups, and situations are more dynamic and mutable and can, and often do, change.[40] Assuming this tends to open disputants to engaging with the other side, seeing more common ground in conflict, and persisting longer in conflict management processes. As a result, these individuals tend to generate more flexible, creative, and original solutions to their conflicts. Harboring the simple belief that people, groups, and situations *might* change makes it conceivable to see and realize possible solutions to problems where others see inevitable dead ends.

These findings have been supported by research on some of the most polarizing intractable conflicts, including the conflict in Israel-Palestine. One study found that when Israelis assume that Palestinians will never really change (they only studied Israelis), they tend to disengage from the conflict, give up, and cling to the status quo, and so things are much less likely to change. However, when Israelis believe that Palestinians sometimes can change, they are much more likely to work to bring that about. Harboring a change mindset also leads to lower levels of intergroup hatred and anxiety and more willingness to interact or compromise with members of out-groups.[41]

Allow me to illustrate one implication of these different assumptions for eventually establishing very different conflict landscapes in your own life. A close colleague of mine, Andrea Bartoli, is a world-renowned peacemaker and is affiliated with a Roman Catholic organization called the Community of Sant'Egidio. This group works tirelessly to help the poor in more than seventy countries around the globe, and when invited, they will at times become carefully, quietly involved in conflict resolution and peace processes in some of the more notoriously dangerous regions of the world.

One of the strategies that the community employs in their peacemaking work is to simply reach out, often persistently, to some of the most violent, vilified, and despised groups active in international conflict, including the Janjaweed in Sudan and Chad and Al-Qaeda in Asia and the Middle East. Bartoli tells me that in the past the community has been known to attempt to contact individuals (e.g., Osama Bin-Laden and the leadership of the Janjaweed) repeatedly, month after month, even when their previous attempts received no response or a threatening reaction. They often just call, leave a message, and then call again the next month.

"Why?" you may ask. Their rationale is simple, "Why not?" If there is a chance, no matter how small, that they could open a channel of communication with these groups that could lead to even a slight reduction in terror and bloodshed, then why not? They recognize that they, unlike many government and UN officials, are in a position to do this because there are less severe consequences for the community for associating with known war criminals and terrorists than there are for official government leaders doing so. So they try and try again. The impact this modest group has had in slowly building trust and eventually transforming some of the most entrenched conflicts of our time is legendary.

The main point here is this: A founding assumption of the community is clear—change, even with terribly violent organized militia groups, is possible. Does it always happen? No. Is it easy to bring about? Rarely. But can it happen? Yes it can.

And here is a bit of hopeful news. Recent research suggests that our implicit assumptions about change can, in fact, be changed (yes, this is a pun *and* a scientific finding). Results from a series of studies in places struggling with more intractable conflicts such as in the Middle East and Cyprus have shown that when disputants are introduced to a more dynamic, mutable way of thinking about a conflict and its disputing parties (such as through reading a *Psychology Today* article that frames conflict as changing), positive things can happen. Shifting mindsets from fixed to changeable has been shown to lead to decreased feelings of anxiety and hatred for out-groups and increased support for engaging with the other side and offering compromises. These effects are particularly strong when people are exposed to a member of the out-group who claims that peace and progress are possible. When these studies were conducted with younger adolescents, the effects of the change showed lasting effects months later.[42]

What do monthly calls to the Janjaweed and promoting peace in the Middle East have to do with you and your politically recalcitrant dental hygienist who insists on plying you with his propaganda while your mouth is occupied? Well, a lot. If we don't believe in the potential for change, where does that leave us? If they really are ignorant and recalcitrant and will never change, then that is that—we have no options. But if there is some chance that they (and we) can change, then we are at the starting line. If the Community of Sant'Egidio can manage to do this with Al-Qaeda, perhaps you can manage to do this with your brother-in-law or office suite mate. As Nelson Mandela once quipped, "It always seems impossible until it's done."

The point I wish to stress here is not only that change is often possible but that something as small as differences in this single assumption—in how we think about the potential for change in our world—can have a profound influence on the types of attractor landscapes we shape and encounter in our lives. Despite the fact that our landscapes are comprised of a highly complex set of factors interacting with each other in strange ways, our choices and actions can and do influence them, *especially during new beginnings*.

The Focus of Our Intentions

These days many of us find ourselves unwittingly wandering into conversations with neighbors or acquaintances across the political divide, with good enough intentions, only to find ourselves lost in a minefield of rage and resentment (it happened to me recently in the elevator of the building where I live). This makes some sense because research has found that about 95 percent of our everyday behavior is automatic, with only 5 percent attributable to conscious, intentional processes.[43] Most of us are rarely paying close attention to what we are saying or doing or to the potential impact it might have. We are mostly operating on automatic pilot.

In *Thinking Fast and Slow*, psychologist Daniel Kahneman describes research on a dual-process model of cognition that provides compelling evidence of the power of our intentions.[44] Decades of research has shown that what Kahneman refers to as our System 1 cognitive processes—our more rapid, automatic, default forms of judgment and response—rule most of our behavior, and this brings both benefits and costs. The benefits are that it is a much easier and efficient form of processing and decision making, which is essential in our increasingly complicated modern world. However, System 1 is also particularly susceptible to errors and forms of bias in cognitive processing because it is often not attuned to the subtle situational differences and changing conditions that we face.

Fortunately, Kahneman's research has also documented how, under certain conditions, we can and do switch to System 2 processing—our more intentional, systematic, but demanding type of information processing that is typically less susceptible to bias, more accurate, and brings fewer unintended negative consequences. This is the type of decision-making process that kicks in when we realize that we are facing a more risky or otherwise consequential set of choices that must be weighed more judiciously.* In summary, System 1 is easier but more problematic when the stakes are high, whereas System 2 is harder work and therefore is less commonly employed.

This is exactly what appeared to befall my elderly professor colleague when he stepped unwittingly into the minefield of race and gender discrimination. Whatever his implicit or explicit attitudes on the matters, it became eminently clear that he had no intention to trigger the angst and backlash he did, and that he soon regretted it. I have heard many such stories from friends and colleagues of late about similar missteps in business meetings, coffee shops, classes, and even at the gym that end in animosity and regret. They are increasingly difficult to avoid in the current political riptide of our landscape.

My experience as a conflict mediator has taught me that, a majority of the time, people don't really know what they want from a conflictual encounter—even when they recognize that they are in one. They know they feel angry or hurt or somehow aggrieved and want to lash out, but exactly what they hope to get out of the encounter with the other is often quite fuzzy. Of course, this is fine when these spats happen within our family or with friends over trivial matters. But under the current conditions of hyperpolarization in the United States, it is best to be more vigilant and more prepared.

Clarifying your intentions beforehand can help. Although how we actually behave in the face of conflict is affected by a wide variety of factors—our attitudes, norms, and personality—our intentions have consistently been found to have a large effect on what we actually do (about a .53 correlation, which is considerable).[45]

Of course, if your intention in such encounters is to *challenge* someone, escalate matters, and show that person who's right, by all means have at it. However, if your intention is to not make matters worse, or even to try to better understand—to learn something about the other side's concerns and the complex problems you are both facing—then you need to *intentionally* choose to take another path entirely. These distinct objectives—prevailing in an argument

* This is exactly the type of thinking I spent most of my summer as cochair of the diversity and discrimination committee locked in—one reason I lost so much weight.

versus avoiding harm versus learning or mending fences—engage very different processes in our brains and dynamics in our social encounters. However, when conversations begin as a challenge, debate, or direct assault, their sensitivity to initial conditions make them very hard to rewind, de-escalate, and reverse course.

When possible, clarify your intentions.[46]

The Force of Our Emotional Reservoirs

When I first began working in psychology in the late 1980s, I held a position as a mental health associate in an adolescent psychiatric, drug and alcohol facility in New York City. The insurance and health care industries were undergoing dramatic changes, and the facility I worked at had to change as well. When I first arrived at the hospital, it had a strict policy of "no drugs, violence, or sex on the unit," and if the policy was violated, the patients involved were summarily expelled. But as insurance coverage dried up and the patient population dwindled, one day the policy was reversed. In fact, when the patients "acted out" violently, sexually, or otherwise on the unit, they would be kept in inpatient treatment for longer periods (yes, a morally questionable policy decision). As a result, the unit I worked on became a much tenser, more threatening, and sporadically violent environment, with a more troubled population of twelve- to twenty-eight-year-olds. It was in this environment that I learned the critical power of emotional reservoirs.

Being younger myself at the time (twenty-eight), my inclination was to immediately introduce myself and sit down with new patients that were admitted to the unit to get to know them. They were often afraid, intimidated, sick, or otherwise vulnerable, and it seemed to comfort them to speak with someone closer to their age. By establishing early, friendly, trust-worthy contact with these patients (especially the really large ones), I discovered that I was often able to more effectively intervene and de-escalate tense, hostile encounters with them that could erupt. On a few occasions, Special Weapons and Tactics (SWAT) police teams had to be called to the unit because patients barricaded themselves in their rooms and threatened violence. During these incidents, even the more aggressive, enraged patients found my presence at the front of these tense negotiations disarming—even disappointing (they *wanted* to lash out and fight)—because of the rapport we shared. These positive bonds made it much more difficult for them to escalate further and direct their hostilities my way.

Most techniques of conflict management offer recommendations for dealing with emotions like: "If you become emotional during conflict, wait until it passes before you act" or "Rise above your emotions and try to get a rational perspective on the situation." But in our current climate of in-group infatuation and out-group distain, our emotions and our emotional experiences of each other may be *the* central driver of conflict. Research on emotions and decision making with patients suffering from severe brain injuries has found that when people lose the capacity to experience emotions they also lose their ability to make important decisions.[47] This suggests that emotions are not only relevant to our perceptions, decisions, and actions in conflict but that they are *fundamental* to them.

One of the more important findings from our research in the Difficult Conversations Lab is that for people to be able to hear each other and learn from tense discussions over morally divisive issues they need to be able to establish some degree of rapport or positivity between one another. As I outlined at the beginning of this chapter, the earlier in our encounters that this happens, the more formative and determining it is. Positive emotions have been found to widen people's scope of attention, broaden behavioral repertoires, and increase intuition and creativity.[48] Over time, reservoirs of emotional positivity that accumulate in relationships can act as a buffer during heated conversations, making it easier for people to hear, empathize, and learn from the other side. Conversely, reservoirs of negativity prepare us for a quick descent into battle.[49]

This has two major implications: one for ourselves and one for our relationships. First, we are living in a particularly toxic time with record high levels of frustration, depression, suicide ideation, and anxiety. The constant exposure to negativity online, in the media, and in person accumulates in us and can make us more irritated and agitated. Most of us have learned to just white-knuckle through these emotions or to simply complain and perseverate about it with our like-minded peers (or aloud at the TV). But research suggests that neither of these responses prepares us well for mending fences.[50] In our research, we have found that people who are highly anxious and agitated are much more likely to be derailed by their own extreme behavioral reactions to conflict, becoming overly rigid, intellectualizing, or revealing, which results in lower levels of well-being and higher levels of negative emotions.[51]

Therefore, it is paramount to learn what you need to do to process and *move through* your more toxic emotions constructively. Learning to meditate, jog, dance, pray, sing, box, do yoga, go bowling, knit, go to church, walk in the forest, get a massage, seek counseling, cry it out, or do primal scream therapy can sometimes help. Regardless of how you go about it, it is critical to recognize the toll toxic emotions may take on your mental and physical health. Take sufficient care of yourself to avoid burning bridges and perhaps build a few. Consider this a necessary warm-up exercise before the big game.

Second, as I came to learn working with more volatile patients, it is often immensely helpful to lay the positive emotional groundwork for future encounters (and be mindful of how negative reservoirs can set traps for us). There are many ways to do this. One of the methods psychologist John Gottman employs with couples stuck in a difficult conflict is to assign positivity exercises.[52] Gottman instructs one partner in the estranged couple the task of noticing ten positive things the other partner does over a week. This tends to both elicit positive acts from one partner and make them more salient and noticeable to the other. By reminding both partners of this potential in their relationship, this exercise triggers and reinforces the positive attractor latent in their dynamic. Of course, this method assumes that parties are willing and able to engage in the task, which may not be the case. Nevertheless, simple initiatives like this can go a long way toward increasing positivity in an otherwise challenging relationship.

The Impact of Unfamiliar Framing

Most of the more obstinate conflicts we face in life have been bothering us for quite some time and have likely been mostly unresponsive to good-faith attempts to work them out. As a result, many people in these types of conflicts feel burnt out, frustrated, and hesitant to try anything to help. Many Americans are feeling this way today. We know from the recent study "Hidden Tribes" that the exhausted majority are not only fed up with our current state of dysfunction but are also wary of touching the stove again. They fear agreeing to meet and speak with people across the divide and ending up even more frustrated and disillusioned.[53]

Research on *framing* could prove useful here. Over the past few decades, cognitive scientists have determined that people are particularly susceptible to framing effects, how new ideas or proposals are framed linguistically. Framing is a decision-making strategy in which the language used to describe options greatly influences the decision maker's choice.

Classic research by Amos Tversky and Daniel Kahneman has shown the powerful effects of positive versus negative semantic framing on decision making.[54] In one study using a *disease task* (where participants were asked to "imagine that the United States is preparing for the outbreak of an unusual Asian disease expected to kill six hundred people), participants in the *positive frame condition* were asked to make a medical treatment choice (from more to less risky) based on a description of how many lives they could save (two hundred of the six hundred people would be saved). In the *negative frame condition*, participants made the same treatment choice based on a description of how many lives would be lost even if treated (four hundred of the six hundred people would die). Participants were consistently found to be more likely to respond to the negative loss framing of the situation by choosing a riskier treatment option than they were when situations were framed positively in terms of saving lives. In general, we are more motivated by frames that suggest we can reduce or mitigate harm than by frames that suggest we can make gains or have a positive effect.

Many of my more experienced practitioner colleagues working with conflicts in polarized communities use framing intentionally, and not only with regard to losses and gains. For example, Laura Chasin, who directed the Public Conversations Project (PCP), once described to me how she would initially frame the possibility of new encounters between members of highly divided groups by first clarifying what she was *not* asking the participants to do. She would say that she was *not* asking them to negotiate or to participate in some type of mediation process in which they would be asked to reach an agreement on an issue or sign a document. She would say that she was also *not* asking them to like, love, or forgive the people on the other side. She would stress that what she *was* asking them to do was participate in a process that was quite different from anything they had been involved in previously. She would inform them that they would be kept safe (often these processes begin covertly in secret locations), that the process would be carefully facilitated, and that there were absolutely no expectations that they would come to an agreement on the issues or have to share their conversation with others.

Chasin and others like her found that framing the encounters as *different* from the participants' prior experiences and expectations was key to their efficacy. This framing (and the fact that these processes were different) helped overcome some of the participants' resistance from feeling burnt out by the same tired old machinations, and the unfamiliar but safe nature of the new process opened them up to eventually moving beyond the old thinking-feeling-behaving dynamics that had become so ingrained and impossible to escape. These dialogue sessions, run by PCP and other similar organizations, are not easy, nor are they always successful. But framing them in a way that helps shift motives, expectations, and habits—especially at the outset—is another useful lever for shifting dynamics.

The Leverage of Choosing Time and Place

When I first started teaching a course at the United Nations in New York in the late 1990s, I was immediately struck by something odd—the furniture in most of the meeting rooms was bolted down. The rooms were all set up in large circles or long rectangles, with big tables in the middle and chairs secured to the floor. There very well might have been a good reason for designing the UN that way. Perhaps it was to avoid the throwing of chairs or stealing of furniture, or simply to provide a foundational sense of security. But in teaching conflict resolution courses there, I learned that these structures often proved to be problematic. The fact that it was so difficult to move people and groups around into different configurations to facilitate different types of educational experiences and human interactions was both challenging to instructors and (just maybe) a simple metaphor for some of the deeper structural problems lurking at the UN. Such is the power of place.

If you think for a moment of the different times and places where you were when difficult conflicts in your life went very badly, and when and where you were when they went pretty well, you may start to see a pattern. Destructive conflicts are much more likely to happen when we are tired, fatigued, highly emotional, anxious, alienated, intoxicated, physically overheated, vulnerable, or just generally unhinged. (My colleague from *Die Zeit*, who attempted to bring together two men from opposite sides of the Trump divide, shared with me his regret that he agreed to hold their second meeting late at night, after a basketball game, and after they all had a few beers.) Problems are also more likely to happen in locations where people feel unsafe or otherwise insecure; in places that are unfamiliar, noisy, filthy, crowded, or otherwise uncomfortable or threatening; when people feel they have been set up or are at a disadvantage; or in situations that are highly constrained or controlled.

These are insights that many conflict engagement professionals understand quite well, and we all can learn from them. Time and place are typically decided intentionally or even negotiated beforehand by representatives. Even the Jets and the Sharks in *West Side Story* knew enough to hold a prefight war council to jointly decide on time and place (and weapons) for their rumble.

Time and place are also often used intentionally to gain advantage. Any condition that is likely to distract, flummox, disorient, or slightly irritate one's opponent in a negotiation can be advantageous when careful attention to detail is required (one reason surprise is often an effective tactic[55]). But these tactics are risky and can backfire, so most professionals seek locations for difficult encounters where all parties can feel secure. That's why sites like Camp David in Maryland, The Fafo Institute in Oslo, Norway, and the YMCA in West Jerusalem have become famous. They are all sites that have proven conducive to safe and serious negotiations over very difficult matters.

This chapter is meant to help you get started. Opportunities for leveraging destabilizing shocks and initial conditions to transform difficult landscapes come in many different flavors. The stranger, new species and synchronization stories offer a few comprehensive strategies to consider. At a more micro level, being mindful of how our *assumptions* about situations can reset their course, how our *intentions* matter, how the *emotional reservoirs* we set can serve or derail us, and how our *framing* and *settings* for encounters can determine their path are all options. Consider and use them wisely. Locate groups and organizations in your community that are already seeking like-minded resets and new beginnings; they can provide you with essential sources of inspiration, guidance, and support for these steps. I turn to this topic in chapter 6.

6

BOLSTER AND BREAK—LOCATE LATENT BUBBLES

THE WISDOM OF THE BODY

In August 1964, the acclaimed American political journalist Norman Cousins was diagnosed with a mysterious, crippling illness and informed by his doctors that it was irreversible and probably fatal.[1] He was hospitalized in critical condition with a fever and found it increasingly difficult to move his neck, arms, hands, fingers, and legs. After conducting a series of tests, the physicians were completely stymied, and they gave him a one in five hundred chance of recovery.

Having recently returned from a long, arduous business trip to the Soviet Union, Cousins eventually deduced that he had heavy-metal poisoning from being exposed to high quantities of diesel exhaust fumes while there. Given the extreme stress of the trip, he thought his immune system was probably compromised to the point that it was unable to fight the toxins. During his stay in the hospital, Cousins's condition worsened. His joint and spinal pain became extreme, gravel-like nodules appeared under his skin, and his jaws began to lock, indicating the systemic nature of the disease. It was misery.

Mercifully, Cousins's will to live was exceptional. Even as his health deteriorated and the hospital staff seemed to lose hope, he began problem solving with his own physician and friend of twenty years, William Hitzig. Reasoning that his trip had left his endocrine system exhausted, in particular his adrenal glands, they began identifying strategies for bolstering his immune system to fight the toxins.[2] Eventually, they landed on two strategies: getting out of the hospital and getting off his current medications.

By this point Cousins had observed, as the old joke goes, that the hospital is no place for sick people. Being subjected to multiple blood draws daily, a "promiscuous use of X-ray equipment," poor nutrition, less than sanitary conditions, and sleep deprivation due to the privileging of hospital routines over patients' needs for rest was further taxing his immune system, which seemed completely antithetical to his recovery. Furthermore, the hospital physicians had been plying Cousins with painkillers, including high doses of aspirin (twenty-six tablets a day), phenylbutazone (twelve tablets a day), as well as codeine, colchicine, and sleeping pills—many of which levied a heavy tax on the adrenal glands, yet another form of immune system suppression.[3] With Hitzig's support, Cousins made plans to check himself out of the hospital and into a quiet hotel (at one-third the price), and he committed to getting off all pain medications as soon as possible.

But what about the pain? Cousins wrote that "the bones in my spine and practically every joint in my body felt as though I had been run over by a truck." And this was *with* painkillers. What would it be like without them? In a word—unbearable—unless they could find other less poisonous means of pain management.

The hypothesized source of his depleted endocrine system was prolonged states of negativity due to stress, frustration, anger, fatigue, and so on, and Cousins began to wonder about the healing potential of positivity. He later wrote, "If negative emotions produce negative chemical changes in the body, wouldn't the positive emotions produce positive chemical changes? Is it possible that love, hope, faith, laughter, confidence, and the will to live have therapeutic value?"

They decided to try laughter.

Cousins's friend, Alan Funt, was the producer of a popular hidden camera TV show called *Candid Camera*, and he sent Cousins some films from his show along with a projector. The distressed patient began to watch zany episodes of the show and some old Marx brothers movies, and it seemed to help. He later wrote, "I made the joyous discovery that ten minutes of genuine belly laughter had an anesthetic effect and would give me at least two hours of pain-free sleep."

Through trial and error with a few potential immune system bolstering regimens (e.g., massive doses of vitamin C), in time Cousins recovered from his death sentence of an illness, although it remained unclear exactly why and how. Some combination of allowing his body to heal in a quiet place with good nutrition, sanitation, and support; reducing the toxic intake of his medications and substituting them with laughter and positivity; and partnering with his doctor in a way that gave him a solid sense of efficacy and hope played a role. Cousins wrote, "I was incredibly fortunate to have as my doctor a man who knew that his biggest job was to encourage to the fullest the patient's will to live and to mobilize all the natural resources of body and mind to combat disease. . . . He was also wise enough to know that the art of healing is still a frontier profession."

This case illustrates the very different paths and consequences that promoting positive states and dismantling negative ones can take when seeking change. I hope the implications of this story for healing our current toxic body politic are somewhat self-evident. Here a group of "experts" was facing an unusual but potentially catastrophic case that defied diagnosis and was unresponsive to standard forms of treatment. In fact, their best, well-intentioned efforts to treat and care for the patient, such as hospitalization in the critical care unit and pain management with pharmaceuticals, backfired and did more harm than good. Ultimately, healing and recovery required the knowledge and insight of the patient himself, supported by a sage and humble physician friend, and together they carefully reconstructed the history and context of the illness and worked systematically *with the wisdom of the patient's body* to navigate a way out. This necessitated a clear recognition of the critical importance of the body's own capacities, through its immune system, to heal under the right conditions. It also required a willingness (and the hutzpah) to discard medical convention and to work adaptively *with* the patient and the patient's unique physiology to learn new ways to *bolster* his own strength and tolerance to *break down* the pathogens inflicting his system.

This process is akin to the approach to conflict engagement we have found to be uniquely effective in altering chronic, divisive patterns in social relations. How we should go about treating our damaged relationships and engaging with others over our political differences is often pretty straightforward—that is, until it isn't. It is usually effective to engage others with respect, intelligence, reliable information, honesty, and humor, if at all possible—just like we were taught in kindergarten. But given the minefield of attractors and repellers we are all navigating these days, these tactics often fail. The gravity of our conflict landscape is simply stronger than we are. This is when it can help to engage in ways that involve something of a reset and a capacity to work *with* the dynamics of the situation we face.

These situations are like encountering a strong riptide at the beach. When we get caught in a riptide, our instinct is to save ourselves by swimming as fast as we can directly back toward the shore. But doing so places us right in the middle of the rip current, which will only drive us farther out to sea and in time exhaust our energy. So long! However, if you understand how the system of currents that create riptides work, you'll know how to work with the power of these situations. You'll know to swim parallel to the shore (which is in fact swimming *with* parts of the tide) until you are sufficiently out of the pull of the current, and only then swim back to shore. In other words, you'll know how to leverage the forces of the rip current itself to produce your desired result—survival.

Now that you recognize that fixing the problem directly isn't going to work, perhaps it's time to consider how you might actively *engage with the context of the problem*—the conflict landscape or the broader set of forces currently affecting it—which can offer you a different way to address the conflict. There are three ways to actively reshape a highly divisive conflict landscape.*

First, you can try to build a new attractor. That is, you can reset, start anew, and begin to grow or develop an alternative attractor pattern (mindset, habits, interaction patterns, norms, and so on) for a more nuanced, tolerant, constructive relationship, network, or community. This is not impossible, but it often takes considerable time, discipline, and perseverance and is, of course, unpredictable.

Second, you can attempt to bolster and build on more positive, functional, latent attractors. This involves locating and working with existing *bright spots*[4] or cases of *positive deviance*[5]—processes that are already working in your situation—to capitalize on their effectiveness. That is, you can carefully identify, support, and possibly *bolster* those propensities, people, processes, policies, and programs that are already working well in your relationships, networks, and communities and serve either to prevent or mitigate more destructive patterns from escalating *or* to promote more healthy, constructive patterns (these may be some of the "new species" discussed in chapter 4). Think of these as agents of your communal immune system that may be ripe for encouraging, boosting, or scaling up.

---

* Of course, if you can jump ship—get out of a toxic relationship or group without significant negative consequences—I recommend you consider it. But if not, read on.

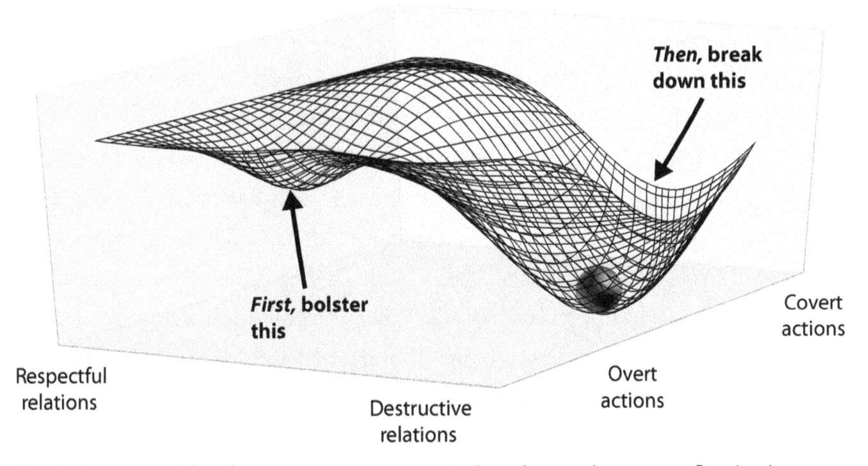

6.1 Bolstering and breaking are two ways to actively reshape a divisive conflict landscape.

Third, you can identify and go about *breaking down* or otherwise diminishing the attraction of the more destructive propensities, people, and so on that are feeding the current toxic attractor and working in concert to trap and drive you (and them) to perpetuate the conflict. A specific understanding of the deep structures that are driving these attractors can be used to "reverse engineer" them. This presents a different way to address the conflict, working from the outside in (or *circumventing the conflict*), but this strategy is best utilized *after* mobilizing those forces inherent to the situation that are already effectively serving the same purpose.

The principles and practices of *bolstering* and *breaking* are the focus of this chapter.

PRINCIPLE 3: BOLSTER AND BREAK—LOCATE LATENT BUBBLES

One of the more provocative things we have learned in recent years from research on changing people's more important, self-defining beliefs and attitudes is that you usually can't—at least not directly. Less important attitudes, such as how you feel about blue cheese or escargot, can shift slowly over time, but not the more defining ones. Our more central, cherished attitudes do not seem to change incrementally, a little at a time. But they can change dramatically, from one extreme to another.[6]

Typically, when others challenge our views on important issues that we hold firmly (such as our views of the successes and failures of the Obama administration), their attempts to persuade us with facts and figures end up reinforcing our original attitudes or pushing us out to even further extremes—not in their intended direction. But strong attitudes can evidence what complexity scientists call "threshold-effect changes" (see Crude Law 4). When we are exposed to information contradicting our attitudes, that information—even if we ignore, discount, or deny it—can seep into our thinking and accumulate over time until it crosses some threshold. Then people radically reverse their views. So nothing much changes until everything changes.

For example, from 1956 to 1975, David Horowitz was an extremely provocative left-wing peacenik who worked for the Bertrand Russell Peace Foundation, was a devout Marxist, an outspoken voice of the New Left, and editor of the radical antiwar *Ramparts Magazine*. In the late 1970s, Horowitz completely reversed course, rejecting progressivism and becoming a staunch supporter of and agitator for more right-wing values and policies. For instance, in 2001, during Black History month, a movement emerged on American college campuses advocating reparations to American Blacks for their accumulated, generational, and systematic economic disadvantages and the corresponding advantages for whites caused by slavery, Jim Crow policies, and residential and educational segregation. Horowitz responded to this movement by attempting to place full-page ads in fifty-two college newspapers titled, "Ten Reasons Why Reparations for Slavery Is a Bad Idea—and Racist Too." In it, he argued that not only have there been sufficient reparations made to Blacks through affirmative action and welfare but that Blacks owe Christian whites reparations for their role in ending slavery in this country.[7] Today Horowitz is often described as a "conservative provocateur."[8]

Dramatic jumps from one extreme attitudinal position to another on self-defining issues are surprisingly common. Such reversals and have been documented with former skinheads turned tolerance trainers,[9] peace activists turned violent militants,[10] and religious zealots turned atheists.[11] How and why do such dramatic shifts in attitudes come about?

Bubbles.

Research from a dynamical systems perspective suggests that significant, rapid changes in strong attitudes, relationships, groups, and communities often happen when "bubbles of new appear in a sea of old" or when "bubbles of old regain dominance in a sea of new."[12] This view, known appropriately as *bubble theory*, likens significant and dramatic psychosocial change processes to the basic dynamics underlying rapid change in physical systems, which evidence something called a *phase transition*—essentially movement between two attractors.

For instance, water is seen as undergoing a phase transition from liquid to gas when it is heated, reaches its boiling point, and turns into steam. When water starts to boil, bubbles of steam begin to appear in the water, and for a period of time the water evidences two types of states simultaneously—liquid and gas, the old and the new—until the water evaporates fully into steam, transitioning completely from one state to the next.

Similarly, rapid social and attitudinal change processes often occur when bubbles of a new idea, attitude, relationship, or custom appear in a sea of the traditional status quo. As a new attitude catches on, it can accumulate and spread to more and more people and groups, eventually replacing the old attitude in representing the status quo within a group. We have seen this recently with changing attitudes regarding the "mainstream media" on the political right (even though distrust of the media has long flourished on the left). During times of polarization, when our own community's attitudes start to move in more extreme directions, our old, more tolerant attitudes of the out-group fall out of favor or are openly shunned within our groups, and we are less likely to express them or even admit to harboring them. However, these old attitudes do not vanish, they simply retreat to more isolated corners of our minds and communities. Here they can form isolated *clusters* of beliefs, remaining isolated and hidden until conditions change and they regain acceptance or prominence. These have now become latent attractors for alternative ways of feeling, thinking, and acting in reference to the out-group.

Think about this for a moment. This proposition suggests that for highly important matters in our life, like our feelings, attitudes, and beliefs about our family, friends, political party, country, and god, we don't hold a single strong view but are more likely to hold two (or more) views simultaneously. One view (attractor) determines our current conscious experiences of the matter, but others hold the potential for experiencing and responding to it in fundamentally contrary or otherwise different ways. This explains David Horowitz's radical jump to the right, or the dramatic changes in attitudes of the Boston pro-life and pro-choice leaders for those on the other side. It also explains the recent rapid transition from more covert forms of modern racism in American society to more explicit forms of overt white supremacy and racism. Bubbles.

This bubble change scenario, which is simply another way to characterize the simultaneous coexistence of current and latent attractors (Crude Law 6), has two major implications for becoming unstuck from the toxic status quo of our relations. First, it suggests that political attitudes and relations from a bygone era—perhaps a kinder, gentler, more functional one—may still be present somewhere within ourselves, our relationships, our leaders, and our communities, if we know to look for them. Second, it suggests that if or when a tense, divisive conflict de-escalates and relations improve, the *potential* for regressing or returning to past levels of enmity (or worse) remains—unless we know how to block and dismantle them. This suggests that in times of de-escalation, with the ascendance

Principle 3: Bolster and Break—Locate Latent Bubbles

When we find ourselves stuck in a hostile, divisive encounter, relationship, or community dynamic that feels immoveable and unresponsive to our best-faith efforts to work it out, one potential way out of these traps is to work *with* the dynamics of the current situation by finding existing bubbles (formerly prevalent tendencies, people, relationships, groups, and so on) and transitioning back to them. These alternative, counter current cultural bubbles may be difficult to locate at first, but they are typically there and can be informative and provide opportunities to join with others in common cause. These bubbles take different forms, but two types are most relevant to our concerns: those that evidence healthier, more constructive social patterns and those that might draw us back into more hostile relations. The remainder of this chapter describes how to build up the former and break down the latter.

of more constructive forms of political engagement, we need to double down on preventing and mitigating more destructive forms of interaction and discourse from resurfacing.

PRACTICE: BOLSTER—BUILD ON WHAT WORKS

As Norman Cousins learned quickly while struggling to survive in the hospital in 1964, it is vitally important *to bolster the inherent healing properties* of a person's system before you attack its disease. Cousins's own robust life force, and his capacity to remain hopeful and optimistic in the face of terrible agony and impossible odds, was foundational to his survival and recovery.

This finding has been supported by sound clinical research across levels. In a classic thirty-year study republished recently in the prestigious *Proceedings of the National Academy of Science*, researchers reported that the most optimistic men and women they studied (those who held high expectations that good things would happen or believed that the future would be favorable because they could control important outcomes), evidenced 50 to 70 percent greater odds of living to eighty-five years old and had an 11 to 15 percent longer life span compared to the members of the least optimistic groups.[13] Our own levels of positivity, hope, and optimism for a better future offer us a place to start.

The same holds true for the importance of a high baseline for positivity and optimism in many conflict-ridden relationships, a finding John Gottman and his team have seen in their work with distressed married couples. Their approach, what Gottman calls the sound relationship house theory, is based on the view that the foundation of a sound home is "the friendship and positive affect system."[14] Through the study of thousands of couples over decades, his team found that the basis for effective repair of a relationship rife with conflict is first to resurface old and then encourage new experiences of positivity in the relationship. To this end, Gottman employs exercises in his sessions such as building love maps (encouraging asking open-ended questions of one's partner's inner world), sharing fondness and admiration (instructing couples to notice and express mutual appreciation), and turning toward instead of away (responding positively to one's partner's bid to connect) to "put money in their emotional bank account that gets built over time."[15] Without rebuilding a formerly positive relational foundation, Gottman has found that marriages typically collapse into enmity and are 97 percent more likely to end in divorce or worse (perpetual marital misery).

Communities often benefit from positive pockets of self-healing potential as well. When the Public Conversations Projects (PCP, now called Essential Partners) is invited to work with communities deeply divided over issues such as immigration, gay rights, or gun control, Laura Chasin states that they always *begin* by identifying the community's existing "networks of effective action." These are the people and groups within otherwise polarized communities who are still open and able to speak and work constructively with those on the other side of the divide. Chasin would quietly seek them out and work carefully to provide them with the support they needed to sustain or enhance their impact. This is akin to bolstering the existing immune system of a community, those agents already working to reduce hostilities and keep constructive conversations flowing.

When it came time to start a clandestine dialogue process in the Boston abortion case, the PCP had already been working in the community for some time to facilitate dialogues and train facilitators to bridge the increasingly tense pro-life/pro-choice divide. After the women's clinic shooting incident in Brookline, Laura and the PCP already had access to a network of leaders and activists on both sides of the issue to whom they could reach out to begin a process of designing and vetting a new approach to working together after the violence. Active bubbles to connect with were already in place.

Research in societies mired in protracted conflicts has also found these existing "islands of agreement" instrumental for peacebuilding.[16] Many of these communities evidence pockets of more conciliatory citizens working quietly together across divides to address shared needs and to improve relations. They may be merchant groups, clergy, sports associations, or women and youth groups, who have somehow found a way to *hold the middle*—to resist the pull toward the extreme poles and remain in relationship with those on the other side. These are bubbles of functionality in seas of hate and dysfunction, which can be found in places as diverse as the conflict zones in Kashmir, Israel, and South Sudan and in smaller communities with religious groups bitterly divided over LGBTQ+ policies and extended families in the grip of a nasty divorce. These individuals and groups represent the functional middle, a source of great hope and promise in difficult times.

Because these more conciliatory individuals and groups often arise from *within* the community, having managed to survive and navigate the adverse conditions of the conflict, they stand a better chance of affecting positive change and enduring.[17] Identifying and working with existing groups in a community first—rather than bringing in outside intervenors—is akin to promoting health and healing with individual patients by bolstering the antibodies in their physical bodies. Of course, the more we support and the longer we engage with these groups, and the more members and resources they attract, the stronger their attraction and resilience becomes. They are like the intrepid seedlings that rise through the ashes of cataclysmic forest fires to offer the promise of new life.

NEVERTHELESS, IT IS OFTEN HARD TO DO

Here's one caveat. Finding and supporting what is already working to improve relations or prevent violence in a tribal, high-conflict setting is no small matter. Typically, doing so faces four significant challenges, which I call the fit, fear, friend, and fixer problems.

- **The Fit Problem**. When we find ourselves stuck in a destructive relationship that enrages us and frustrates our best attempts to be civil and work things out, the last thing we are usually interested in doing is looking for the good. This has been documented in decades of research on the relative fit of preventive (avoiding harm) versus promotive (seeking nurturance) motivational orientations, wherein negative experiences of high conflict tend to focus us more on lashing out or preventing short-term harm than on promoting ideal, positive states.[18] When the super attraction of contempt and blame of them has captured us, it just feels wrong to turn our attention to finding positive solutions.
- **The Fear Problem**. We know very little about finding positive solutions to polarized conflicts because how to do so is rarely studied. When scholars study and write about polarization today, they overwhelming focus on the problem, "Why are we polarized?"[19] They are keen on analyzing and diagnosing the illness because they assume this will be sufficient to inform remedies. This is a pervasive tendency in all of

science—humans tend to prioritize the study of the things we fear.[20] But as John Gottman discovered after fifteen years of studying the conditions that predict divorce in marriage, the opposite of the conditions that predict divorce did not predict thriving marriages. In fact, his team needed to study flourishing couples for another ten years before their predictions became clear.[21] In other words, *good* and *bad* aren't opposites; they are distinct experiences that involve different processes. Decreasing the bad is not the same thing as increasing the good. Similar processes have been found in the study of preventing war versus promoting peace—the factors that prevent war are fundamentally different from those that promote and sustain peace. And we know much less about the latter,[22] so the road map to bright spots is usually much less clear.

- **The Friend Problem**. When tight groups have formed around us-versus-them tribal conflicts, deviating from the in-group in any way—thinking differently, expressing opposition to your group's attitudes and beliefs, or (god forbid) fraternizing with members of the out-group—can lead to harsh forms of in-group shunning and sanctioning.[23] At a time in our history when social isolation and alienation are incredibly high due to increased fracturing of nuclear families, declines in organized religion, distrust in public institutions, and online addiction, the political and cultural affiliations we do hold tend to become much dearer to us.[24] In this context, the consequences of seeking countercultural solutions or constructive alternatives to the mandated "good group member" actions can be extremely costly.
- **The Fixer Problem**. Those of us working on reducing political polarization (clergy, academics, journalists, and other do-gooders) are often looked upon as experts in what we do—which feels so great! However, feeding our egos tends to foster in us some degree of what has been termed a "savior complex," or a taste for being viewed as the go-to fixer. When we decide to think and work differently—to identify and bolster what is already healthy and functional within a relationship or community—we must relinquish the fixer role and learn to give credit and attention to the inherent mechanisms for positive efficacy already operating in the situation. This is hard for many of us. In fact, the research on leveraging positive deviance in organizations has found that

the difficulties experts have with relinquishing the fixer role is one of the biggest obstacles to the success of these initiatives.[25] Jerry Sternin, one of the pioneers of positive deviance, put it this way:

> The biggest challenge is for leaders to relinquish their power to enable others to find their own solutions. It's difficult for a doctor or a school principal—whose whole self-image is, "I'm the person who fixes things, who has the solutions"—to relinquish that power and to really believe that they, the folk people, have the solutions. It's more of getting people who need to support the project to change their role and be willing to trade in their power for a different kind of power. . . . Her job is to create the space in which the community itself discovers their own solution.[26]

Despite these obstacles, many people can and do find and leverage what is already working. Here's how (figure 6.2).

Ask Different

In the late 1990s, while researching five decades of Hindu-Muslim communal violence in India, Ashutosh Varshney, a young Harvard professor, noticed something odd. Gazing at a map of India, he noted that the vast majority of incidents of

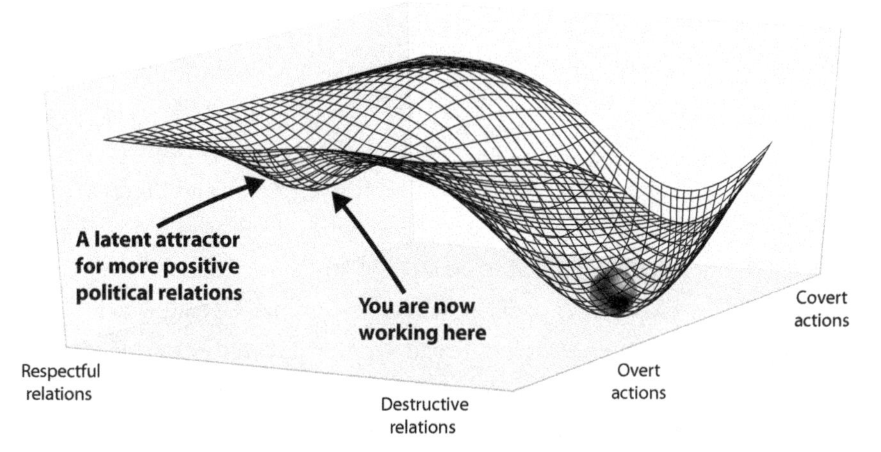

6.2 First build on what works—positive deviance.

ethnic violence between Hindus and Muslims in India were located in a handful of urban cities that were home to only about 5 percent of the total population. Somehow, despite rising Hindu-Muslim tensions, 95 percent of country had managed to remain relatively peaceful and nonviolent while this small sliver of the urban populace faced enduring patterns of ethnic violence. Scholars had been studying these violent cities for years and had learned a good deal, but they were still stymied as to the main drivers of the violence. Varshney realized that the missing piece in their understanding of this puzzle was peace—scholars had not been studying the more peaceful areas as comparisons. He concluded, "In short, until we study ethnic peace, we will not be able to have a good theory of ethnic conflict."[27]

Due largely to the fear problem, most disputants, mediators, academics, consultants, and other problem solvers working to address polarization tend to focus first and foremost on the problems (perhaps we need to coin an alternative label to problem solver, perhaps, *solution locater*). When addressing highly urgent or threatening situations in acutely polarized societies, focusing on the problem is particularly common. Focusing away from the problem in these cases can seem frivolous and absurd (due to the fit problem). As a result, we tend to learn much less about what works in these settings, and this imbalance directly reflects the questions we tend to ask and not ask.

As research in the field of appreciative inquiry has documented—a strengths-based approach to leadership development and organizational change—the questions we ask when seeking change not only shape our understanding of the challenges (and opportunities) we face but also determine our expectations and sense of hope and possibility for the future.[28] Merely asking "Why doesn't our polarization get worse than it is?," "How do some families and communities manage tense political divisions more effectively than others?," or "What provides a sense of hope, optimism, and even cross-party unity in my community today?" can orient us toward the more constructive people, places, and things. Asking "Where are the islands of agreement or the networks of effective action that are holding things together in this situation today?" or "What taboos exist regarding open hostilities and violence in this situation (such as those operating in places of worship, around children, in hospitals, and so on) that should be protected, highlighted, or leveraged?" is information that is typically ignored in standard forms of conflict analysis. However, this kind of information can help reveal aspects of the immune system that are already operating to mitigate the conflict.

So, ask different.

Circumvent the Conflict

Some of the more effective social-entrepreneur groups working to address divisions do so by intentionally operating away from the heat of conflict. *Ashoka* is a well-established, nonprofit organization that supports local change makers around the world.[29] Typically, they visit war-torn, marginalized, or otherwise struggling communities to identify effective, existing local change agents and initiatives (aka positive deviants), vet them carefully, and then offer to support them for several years. These individuals and groups often benefit from the right types of support (usually quiet, confidential, unconditional, and longer-term support) to enhance or scale up their impact.

In 2010, my colleagues Ryszard Praszkier (of Ashoka), Andrzej Nowak, and I published a study on Ashoka fellows titled "Social Entrepreneurs and Constructive Change: The Wisdom of Circumventing Conflict."[30] We documented how some of these fellows operate in contexts of conflicts that are highly polarized and seemingly unsolvable "by building on positive attractors outside the field of influence of the destructive conflict attractors." They do so by intentionally avoiding addressing the more polarizing issues in the conflict (typically, they avoid even characterizing their work as peacebuilding) and focusing instead on initiatives that address the "upstream" drivers of tensions (for example, building communal outhouses in Brazilian *favelas* or slums) that eventually help to mitigate the conflict. The authors write of the approach, "Through subsequent positive experiences, they introduce constructive change outside of the field of conflict in a manner that modifies the societal balance based on higher levels of trust and tendencies to cooperate. Through this strategy, they make conflict less relevant and less salient."[31]

Circumventing the epicenter of the presenting conflict and working on the peripheral drivers of the polarization is another tactic.

Don't Do It Yourself

The pull to try unilaterally to solve our current addiction to hyperpolarization is often great and irresistible for many of us (aka, the fixer problem). The reason not to do so should be clear by now—it is highly likely to fail. When the more automatic or compulsive behaviors of a community are organized around an us-versus-them conflict and reinforced by friends, family, community, leaders, and the media, getting them to change can seem virtually impossible.

Unless *they* want to change. As positive deviance advocate Jerry Sternin points out:

> People whose behavior needs to change are the ones who discover the solution that already exists within their system. For that reason, you don't get the best practice push back. "Best practices" evokes the immune system rejection response to a foreign body . . . to outsiders coming in and saying, "Hey, look at the answer here." . . . With PD [positive deviance] the solution and the host in a sense share the same DNA, so you don't get that push back or rejection.[32]

However, when community members observe or interact with others in their group who are enacting a change that people feel that they themselves need to make, it can mobilize shifts in ensconced habits. Sternin's approach to promoting positive deviance, which he defines as "an uncommon practice that confers advantage to the people who practice it compared with the rest of the community,"[33] encourages the "deviants" themselves to interact directly with others in their communities.

For example, when Sternin was working in Vietnam to address malnutrition in rural communities, he first identified a few local children who were better nourished than others and studied the cooking practices of their mothers. Once he unearthed their solution (the mothers caught small crabs and shrimp while working in the rice patty fields and brought them home to add to their family's rice meals), Sternin was eager to spread the word. But he had learned not to simply tell the other mothers what to do: "Don't teach new knowledge—encourage new behavior." So he asked some of the deviant mothers to invite groups of other women into their homes where they would together cook and prepare food for their families—not teaching but merely cooking together. As a result, malnutrition rates dropped between 65 percent and 85 percent in their villages over two years.

So, don't just do it—help establish the conditions that enable others to learn to do it with and for themselves.

Connect the Dots

Once you are asking different questions and learning more about the functional aspects of your situation, it can help to begin to connect the dots between them.

In 2015, our peace and conflict group at Columbia University was asked by the Fragility, Conflict and Violence unit of the World Bank to conduct some complexity mapping workshops in Colombia related to its decades long war and, at the time, its ongoing and highly troubled peace processes. Rather than focus the workshop on the obstacles peacemakers were facing, we agreed to convene a group of local community-based organizations (CBOs) who were already working effectively across the nation on issues related to reconciling differences between the warring parties. Over several days in May of that year, we gathered together members of a dozen CBOs of varied sizes and histories in Bogota for a systems mapping workshop.[34]

As you might imagine, the mapping process with the CBOs was both simple and complex. It was simple in that it involved a rather straightforward procedure of the groups working alone within their organizations and then together in mixed groups to (1) specify the positive end state they were working to promote (e.g., promoting healing and reintegration of ex-soldiers into communities), (2) list all the current activities that were helping to achieve this end state, (3) list the obstacles that existed to promoting the positive state, and then (4) draw maps of how all of these elements affected one another and the positive end state. The complexity of the process emerged in the highly nuanced and sometimes disagreement-filled conversations that resulted.

A variety of benefits are often derived from these complexity mapping activities. In Bogota, it was useful for members of the CBOs to surface and discuss their very different views on the nature of the problems and solutions they sought—differences that existed both within their own organization and between different agencies. It was immensely helpful for the groups to begin to articulate the many different drivers of the violence in the system and to acknowledge the many remedies for addressing these drivers. By drawing connections and mapping their understanding of all of this, the participants were eventually able to see redundancies in their shared work and significant and consequential gaps in both geographic areas and thematic drivers that were being neglected. These organizations, which had often been in competition with each other for funding, began to coalesce as a network of actors in a common cause. This group had both a clearer sense of the road ahead and a greater feeling of solidarity and efficacy—critical elements for success when working under such dire conditions.

So, connecting the positive deviants within a community is another way to begin to realize and help scale up their impact.

Find Resonance

Some community-centered change makers try to identify new sources of *resonance*, existing pockets of shared needs or interests in groups and communities that can provide a resource for mobilizing new initiatives.[35] For example, my colleague Danny Burns, who works on development challenges with some of the most marginalized communities in conflict zones around the world, typically begins his work by scouting for local resonance.[36] His team hires and works jointly with local people, oftentimes for several months or years, to gain a nuanced understanding of the realities on the ground. They will then convene a series of conversations with a multitude of members of the community with the primary objective of answering the question, "Where is the energy here?" They mine the stories of members of the community to uncover common clusters of underlying needs and aspirations that might be able to unite and mobilize troubled communities in service of collective goals.

Of course, resonance can be leveraged for constructive or destructive purposes, depending on the direction of the group's shared interests (e.g., a community mobilized to address joblessness versus an angry mob wanting payback against an out-group). This also assumes that there are unmet needs shared within a divided community of sufficient interest to bring people together in joint action. Sometimes, however, simply identifying and raising awareness of shared goals or concerns in a group are sufficient to activate mobilization. Doing so may also trigger a process of local problem solving that takes on a life of its own, with the group beginning to address new problems in the community as they emerge.

So, even in the absence of existing bright spots, identifying resonance is a tactic for building on the energy and political will that is already there for establishing new ones.

Handle with Care

Alas, even positive deviance can have negative consequences. When working within the context of heated topics, distressed relationships, divided communities, or warring groups, it is all too easy to trigger unintended harm. For example, the development and use of new crisis-mapping technologies like Ushahidi allows local people to capture images of illegal activities, such as government intimidation and suppression of voters during an election. In Kenya, Ushahidi was initially lauded as a citizen-based check on abusive power. However, it was soon discovered that such technologies can also be used to track users and expose them to further harm and intimidation.[37]

In polarized contexts, simply identifying our more effective conciliators can expose them to risks and retribution. They may be seen by some as negative deviants or traitors and targeted accordingly. For example, my colleague Maria Hadjipavlou is an academic, a feminist, and a Cypriot peace activist who has worked tirelessly for decades in the divided nation of Cyprus to promote Greek-Cypriot and Turkish-Cypriot understanding. As a result of this work, she has received numerous threats and suffered alienation from both sides of her island nation.

Unfortunately, there are too many examples of this today on both sides of the American political spectrum. In fact, it is often the case that peacemakers, aid workers, and other do-gooders working in potentially dangerous contexts of destructive conflict and violence choose to lay low or suspend their activities during particularly tense times to avoid exposing themselves, their colleagues, or their families to harm.[38] When trying to bolster what is working, it is critical to take care not to break it—be particularly vigilant to *do no harm*. This begins by being mindful of the potential unintended consequences of these actions (Crude Law 7).

I want to emphasize the good news here. You are typically not alone in desiring better days and often do not need to start from scratch. Not only is more than 86 percent of our population sick and tired of being sick and tired, but families, groups, and organizations in your local community are currently working hard and modeling how to effectively bridge our divides. Your first best move is to find them.

PRACTICE: BREAK—WEAKEN THE WORST

To sustain any positive change in our situation resulting from building on what is working, the bubble principle suggests that it is paramount to reduce the

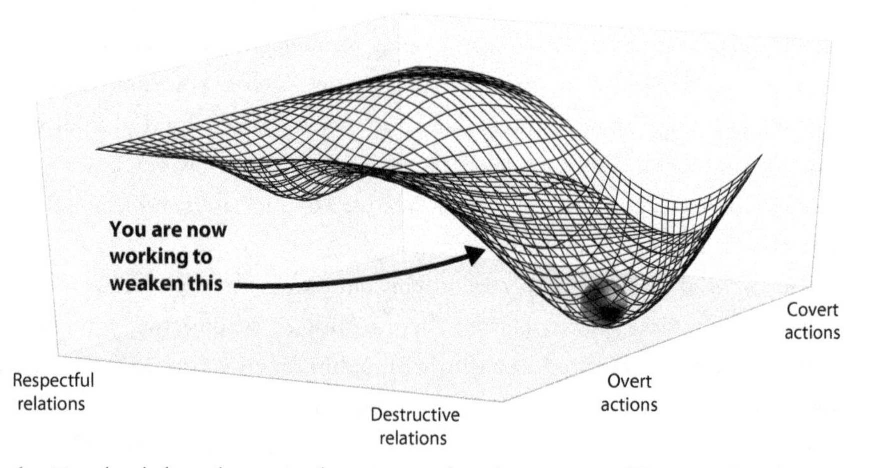

6.3 Next, break down destructive dynamics to reduce the attraction of detrimental tendencies.

attraction of our more (now latent) detrimental tendencies. In other words, we must also *break down* or otherwise diminishing the lure of the more destructive dynamics driving us (figure 6.3). To reduce the worst inclinations of our system and dismantle destructive attractors, we must focus on the three R's: ruptures, resistance, and repellers.

Ride Shock Waves (Ruptures)

The bombshell effect described in chapter 4 is one of the best possible sources of pressure for weakening the deep structures constituting the attractors driving our divisions, but leveraging its effects requires some understanding of nonlinear change (particularly Crude Law 4). As a reminder, research on punctuated equilibrium has found that incremental changes in tightly coupled systems are much less likely to produce fundamental transformations and that significant jolts to the status quo are typically necessary.[39] However, these forces can show different types of positive and negative effects, and they often take months or years to become evident. They must, therefore, be considered a near necessary but insufficient condition.

Perhaps it's best to think of the effects of significant ruptures to the status quo as *shock waves*. These are large pressure waves produced by actions such as explosions, lightning, or supersonic jets traveling faster than the speed of sound. These waves can be highly destructive because they vibrate out from the area around the point of explosion through an extremely hard and fast wave, causing things that the wave touches to vibrate and sometimes to explode. The pressures from the shock wave perturbs structures, which affect other structures, and so on, until their downstream effects become evident. It is under these unstable conditions that charismatic outside strangers, promising new species, or synchronized projects between local stakeholders and outside agents arise, some of which may take aim at changing the primary drivers of our divisions.

For instance, Donald Trump's victory in the 2016 U.S. presidential election produced an astonishing shock wave in the United States and around the world (most polls predicted a 70 to 99 percent chance of a Hillary Clinton win the night of the election).[40] The news of Trump's triumph against all odds sent shock waves through a majority of homes and sectors across the nation, one of which was the media. The hyperpoliticization of much of the mainstream media in the United States had played a key role in Trump's election, and it has continued to exacerbate our ongoing crisis of division.[41] Nevertheless, the media, with a few exceptions, simply doubled down into their tribal political camps after the election.

In 2015, Annafi Wahed, born and raised a New Yorker, left her well-paying job in the private sector and set out to campaign door-to-door for Hillary Clinton in New Hampshire. In a Zoom call with me this year, she described her amazement when she discovered that the more conservative folks she was trying to reach in these communities lived in a completely parallel universe to her own. The talking points given her by the Clinton campaign to appeal to conservative voters had absolutely no resonance with these folks, who spent much of their time watching FOX News or listening to Rush Limbaugh. Every attempt she made to speak to the issues that most likely concerned these voters—affordable health care, decent jobs, functional public schools, you name it—were met with blank stares because the facts and figures they had at hand were completely different from her own.

After the election, Wahed left the world of business and politics to found her own online media platform called The Flip Side,[42] which vets and tracks well-informed news on the right and the left and reports daily on central issues from across the spectrum. The goal of this initiative is to help bridge the increasing divides between liberals and conservatives by providing thoughtful perspectives on different sides of important issues to increase the opportunity for common understanding. Other bridge-building media initiatives have also sprung up in the context of our current information schism, including Solution Journalism's Complicating the Narrative project, the Aspen Institute's Weave Social Fabric Project, the Storycorps initiative One Small Step, BBC's project on Crossing Divides, Tim Shriver's call to Unite,[43] and many more. These are examples of the more promising second- and third-wave effects that can arise from major shocks to help mitigate the drivers of extreme polarization.

Reduce Resistance

In the 1940s, Kurt Lewin, one of the first physics-informed psychologists, offered us two basic methods for bringing about change in social systems: increase forces driving change in the desired direction or diminish opposing forces that resist the change.[44] Typically, increasing driving forces such as threats and physical force, offering positive incentives, or applying moral or social pressure tend to increase pressure on people and groups.[45] Of course, increasing the level of tension in our current high-stress state will likely be accompanied, as Lewin suggested, by "greater fatigue, higher aggressiveness, higher emotionality, and lower constructiveness." This is quite risky in such a divided society. Therefore, it might be prudent to give serious consideration to an alternative method of promoting change—address some of the main obstacles resisting change—thereby facilitating movement while lowering tension.

The relative effects of removing resistance versus driving change for promoting better outcomes has been supported by research in many areas, including clinical psychology, organizational development, and international affairs.[46] We conducted one such study in the lab at Columbia University, comparing the effects of increasing drive-inducing versus reducing change-resisting forces in interventions to address a long-standing, heated racial conflict in a school between a white, European American principal and an African American teacher.[47] The study found that interventions we developed that reduced participants' obstacles to change (such as a perceived lack of alternatives to escalation, a sense of distrust, a sense of hopelessness, and a lack of constructive problem-solving skills) were much more effective at increasing positive movement than those aimed at driving change (such as demands from authorities, threats of consequences, and offers of incentives). In fact, reducing resistance and therefore pressure resulted in participants feeling significantly less angry, indignant, and stuck and feeling more positive, hopeful, and relieved. Notably, these participants also took more personal responsibility for the conflict (a particularly hopeful finding) and reported more peaceful and less coercive behavioral intentions regarding how they planned to proceed in the relationship.

Returning to the abortion dialogue in Boston, reducing resistance played an important role in its success. Rather than pressure, incentivize, or coerce the participants, the process was quite effective in removing obstacles to change that were cognitively based (extreme degrees of distrust and stereotypical misperceptions), feeling-based (rage, disgust, fear of violence, and retaliation), behaviorally based (lack of effective anger management and conflict-resolving skills), motivationally based (seeing little value or purpose in engaging), and environmentally based (the vast schisms between the two camps in the broader community). The careful, vigilant support offered by Laura, Susan, and the PCP staff before, during, and after the dialogues helped ensure physical and psychological safety, a reduction in the automatic use of hostile rhetoric, complete confidentiality, clear and respectful forms of communication, and sufficient time for the process to run its course.

One particularly promising approach to reducing disputants' resistance to change in the context of deep-rooted polarization is through the use of exaggeration of their closely held attitudes. In a series of innovative field studies conducted in the context of an especially tense phase of the Israeli-Palestinian conflict, researchers found that *paradoxical thinking interventions* were fruitful for mitigating more hostile, extreme attitudes.[48] The authors hypothesized that in these contexts attacking core conflict-supporting beliefs directly would backfire but that presenting these beliefs in their most extreme versions could serve to unfreeze proponents blind adherence to them. For their studies, the researchers developed a YouTube-based video campaign called "The Conflict," which shared ideas consistent with the more extreme conflict-supporting societal beliefs but amplified them by extrapolating absurd conclusions from them. Here is an example they shared:

> One video-clip dealt with the shared societal belief that the Israeli army is the most moral army in the world. . . . The clip started with the message "Without

it, we would never be moral." Then for approximately 20 seconds different pictures portraying Israeli soldiers helping Palestinians were presented, while an instrumental version of "What a Wonderful World," made famous by Louis Armstrong, was played. The video-clip ended with the message "In order to be moral, we probably need the conflict." Importantly, this, and all other video-clips did not refute the core conflict-supporting beliefs, but rather amplified them to extrapolate an absurd conclusion (i.e., that because of these beliefs, Israelis really need the conflict to continue).

The effects of these interventions were impressive. The study found that Israeli's exposed to the campaign immediately reported a shift away from their conflict-supporting attitudes, an increase in conciliatory attitudes toward Palestinians, and a loosening of their positions on sensitive issues such as the evacuation of Jewish settlements in the West Bank. These effects were reassessed a year later and seemed to have held. Even more surprising was that the campaign was found to influence voting patterns in the 2013 Israeli general elections, with participants of the study exposed to the paradoxical thinking campaign reporting that they tended to vote "for more dovish parties which advocated a peaceful resolution to the conflict"—a remarkable illustration of the power of resistance reduction.

Responding to those we hold in contempt with threats, pressure, confrontation, or attack often *feels right* (the fit problem) for most of us, but in protracted conflicts, these behaviors tend to reinforce the destructive dynamics between us and are likely to do little to change the status quo. If so, it may serve to consider changing course. This may sound counterintuitive and simply *feel wrong* under these conditions, but changing course may offer a way out if handled effectively.

Reinforce Repellers—Turn to Taboos

If riding shock waves or reducing resistance does not appear to make enough difference in the pull of the us-versus-them attractor, it may be time to turn to taboos; that is, to draw attention to the importance or violation and degradation of critical social, cultural, or religious taboos, norms, and values. Fortunately, most communities (even those ruled by despots or organized crime figures) have laws, norms, or other prohibitions against some forms of destructive behavior, establishing what we call *repellers* in complexity parlance. In fact, archeological research has found that communal taboos against direct violence and other hostile acts have existed for the bulk of human history and were a central feature of our prehistoric nomadic hunter-gatherer ancestors.[49] Indeed, a key characteristic of most peaceful societies today is the presence of taboos against aggression and violence.[50] In fact, it was the breaking of this taboo—the horrific acts of violence in Boston—and the need to reduce the chances it would ever happen again that became the galvanizing force, the superordinate goal, that initially brought the leaders—the enemies—together in dialogue.

When taboos are broken, they present both an immediate and a longer-term danger to the survival of relationships and communities. Broken taboos can degrade or change important standards, which may unravel the very fabric of a home, community, or nation. We see this almost daily in the deterioration of civil forms of political discourse in our state houses and in our media. Drawing attention to such violations, and to their potentially dire consequences, is one way to reinforce the importance of such repellers, strengthen their repulsion, and thereby constrain more destructive attractors.

For those of us living in many Western democracies today, this has become an urgent matter. In a survey conducted in 2019, 85 percent of Americans said that political debate in the country had become more negative and less respectful, and 73 percent felt that elected officials should avoid using heated language because it could encourage violence.[51] The taboos and norms that have emerged over generations to shape how we work together in public office and in the public square, as flawed as they may be, have usually enabled us to address the challenges of the day without deteriorating too far into toxic relations and violence. When they deteriorate, we will follow.

Remember, the wider an attractor, the more likely and easily it is to fall into it. Reinforcing the taboos associated with more extreme forms of rhetoric and action can serve to narrow these gravity wells. Of course, drawing attention to these violations is most effective when it arises from voices *within* the community, within the in-group, because it is then less susceptible to being ignored or deflected or seen as a political ploy. Most of us have an innate sense that without such guardrails in our lives and communities we are soon lost.

This last section focused on the need for weakening the attraction of the broadest and deepest cultural pattern operating in the situation of us versus them. Once caught in polarizing traps, our instincts and tendencies are to fight and obstruct *them* at every turn, which is fine if it is truly necessary and works well enough in your life. But when it doesn't, it is critical to find alternative ways to change the nature of the relationship or situation. The primary objective is to weaken the us-versus-them attractor and decrease the odds it will continue to rule relations, and to increase the odds that another more benign attractor will replace it.

7
COMPLICATE—EMBRACE CONTRADICTORY COMPLEXITY

NO DOUBT

Megan Phelps-Roper was born into a world of moral certitude. As the granddaughter of Fred Phelps, the founder of the Westboro Baptist Church community in Topeka Kansas, her entire life and worldview had been shaped by the doctrine of her church. Westboro is a fundamentalist Christian ministry known for its use of inflammatory hate speech and provocative protest, especially against LGBTQ+ people, Catholics, Orthodox Christians, atheists, Muslims, Jews, Romani people, U.S. soldiers, and politicians (if you search "God Hates Fags" on the internet, Google takes you to Westboro's main website). It was founded on the essential beliefs of her grandfather, a civil rights attorney and minister, who viewed all harms that came to human beings as the result of God punishing us for having "bankrupt values" and tolerating gay people.*

Phelps-Roper was an active, cherished, charismatic young leader of the community, picketing daily and pioneering the use of social media in the ministry's activism. She would appear often on the *Howard Stern Show*, speaking for

---

* Some of this account was gathered by personal communication with Megan Phelps-Roper during an interview she conducted with me at my office at Columbia University in 2015.

her community. She described their views in an open letter she penned in a blog post:

> In a city in a state in the center of a country lives a group of people who believe they are the center of the universe; they know Right and Wrong, and they are Right. They work hard and go to school and get married and have kids who they take to church and teach that continually protesting the lives, deaths, and daily activities of The World is the only genuine statement of compassion that a God-loving human can sincerely make. As parents, they are attentive and engaged, and the children learn their lessons well. This is my framework.[1]

In an email I later received from Phelps-Roper, she elaborated further on her community's worldview:

> The protesting began in 1991, when I was five, and I grew up absolutely believing the ideology I was inculcated with from the time I was old enough to understand words: that God hated and utterly detested most of mankind; that I needed to separate myself from the world in order to avoid His wrath; and that it was my non-delegable duty to warn the world every single day that they were headed for eternity in Hell—and that this warning was the manifestation of Jesus' command to "love thy neighbor."

Then, in 2012 when Phelps-Roper was twenty-seven, everything changed. Ironically, through her activist engagement with community outsiders on social media, she was made aware of a significant contradiction between something written in Romans 9, a passage on *mercy* in the New Testament of the Bible, and the scornful protest activities for which her community had become notorious. Initially her friends denied and discounted the discrepancy, claiming that the elders could easily explain it away. However, when her father validated this basic inconsistency between their scripture and their deeds, Phelps-Roper claims that the clarity and certainty of her highly dichotomized good-versus-evil life began to unravel. Afterward, she claimed that she would daily, even hourly, encounter another contradiction and then another, which shook her to her core. Within six months, she and her younger sister left the community and were subsequently shunned and excommunicated by the remainder of her family and friends. She described this process of undoing in a 2017 TED talk:

> My friends on Twitter took the time to understand Westboro's doctrines, and in doing so, they were able to find inconsistencies I'd missed my entire life. Why did we advocate the death penalty for gays when Jesus said, "Let he who is without sin cast the first stone?" How could we claim to love our neighbor while at the same time praying for God to destroy them? The truth is that the care shown to me by these strangers on the internet was itself a contradiction. It was growing evidence that people on the other side were not the demons I'd been led to believe.[2]

And then she offered this:

> This has been at the front of my mind lately, because I can't help but see in our public discourse so many of the same destructive impulses that ruled my former church. We celebrate tolerance and diversity more than at any other time in memory, and still we grow more and more divided. We want good things—justice, equality, freedom, dignity, prosperity—but the path we've chosen looks so much like the one I walked away from four years ago. . . . Compromise is anathema. We even target people on our own side when they dare to question the party line. This path has brought us cruel sniping, deepening polarization, and even outbreaks of violence. I remember this path. It will not take us where we want to go.

Phelps-Roper's story illustrates the extraordinary power of certainty, dichotomous thinking, and oversimplification for capturing our understanding of the world, and the equally consequential power of contradiction and complexity for correcting it. Under conditions of heightened polarization and contempt, certainty rules. Our research in the Difficult Conversations Lab has found that this is exactly when increasing complexity is paramount.

ENHANCING CONTRADICTORY COMPLEXITY TO RECONFIGURE CONFLICT LANDSCAPES

Principle 4: Embrace Contradictory Complexity

Our human tendency to prematurely oversimplify the more daunting, contentious challenges we face, as well as our understanding of the people and groups involved, is legendary. This is a normal, logical response to having to make decisions in a highly complicated and rapidly changing environment, and the pressure to do so increases considerably under conditions of heightened uncertainty and threat.[3] As our world becomes increasingly more complex and unpredictable,

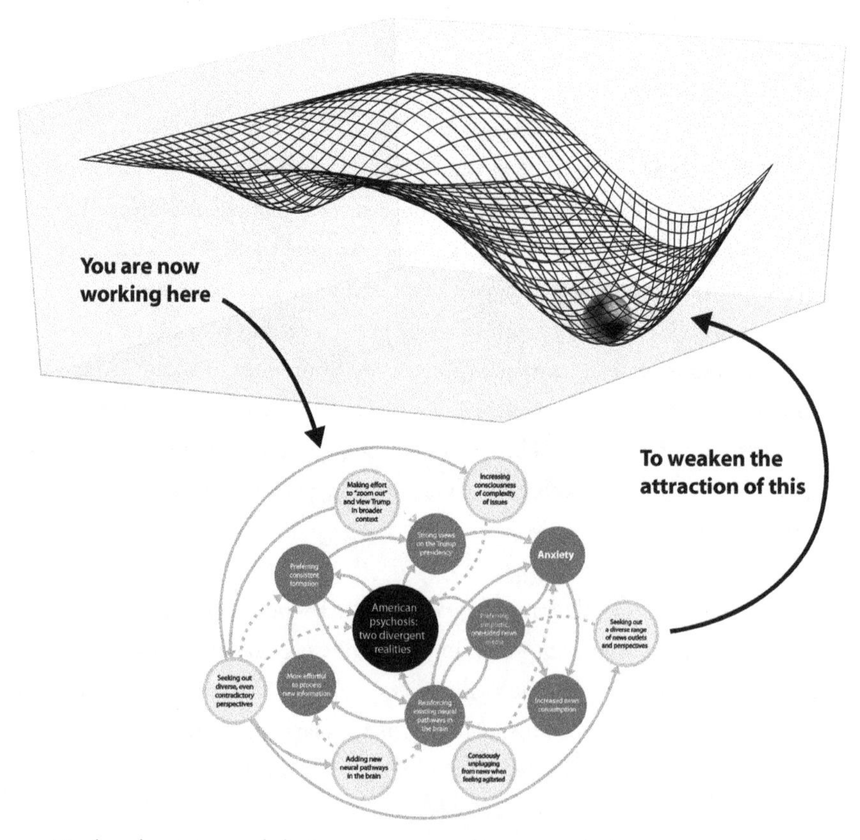

7.1 Weaken the vicious cycle by increasing contradictory complexity.

our sense of it will tend to become narrower and more simplistic. This is what I referred to previously as the *big collapse*, and it is a recipe for disaster.

In chapter 2, I argued that the intransigence of our decades-long trend of escalating polarization is not due to any one cause but rather is the result of many different influences fueling and feeding each other, establishing *vicious cycles*, that, in turn, are fed by other divisive dynamics forming *vicious cyclones* that can connect across individual, community, and national levels to create *superstorms of polarization*. This extraordinary degree of complexity and dynamism is what leads to the emergence of some of the strongest change-resistant attractors.

It also presents various pathways out of them.

There are, in fact, two fundamentally different types of complexity dynamics, with one type promoting more intractable forms of polarization and the other preventing or mitigating them. The first type—let's call it *consistent complexity*—has been the principle focus of this book thus far (figure 7.2). It involves those constellations of factors that align together and reinforce each other and therefore pull us mostly in the same direction (often against or away from opponent groups), eventually leading us to highly simplistic, ultracoherent views of us,

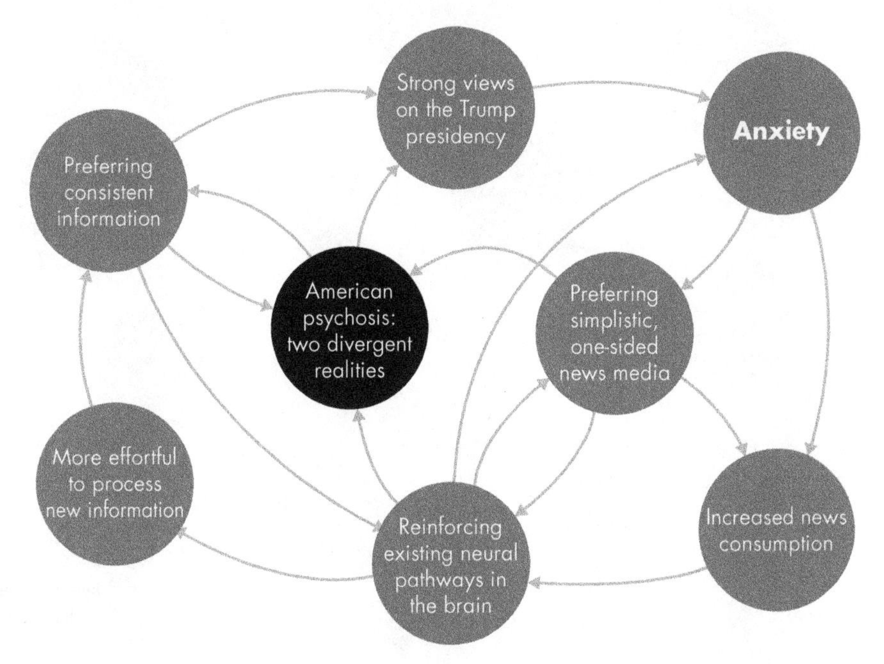

7.2 Reinforcing components of a vicious cycle.

them, and the issues. This is what Sartre described regarding the Nazis in 1944, and it is where too many of us seem to be headed today.

The second type of complexity, labeled *contradictory complexity*, entails constellations of factors that may be just as highly numerous and complicated but that contain more internal contradictions—inherent checks and balances—that tend to inhibit each other and therefore are less polarizing and escalating, instead promoting more balanced (and often more accurate) views of us, them, and the issues. In other words, rather than living in the maelstrom of figure 7.2 we might find more solace inhabiting figure 7.3.

In figure 7.3, the lighter-shaded factors in the outer circle (e.g., seeking out a more diverse range of credible conversations and news outlets or unplugging from news reports altogether) are pushing back and mitigating against the

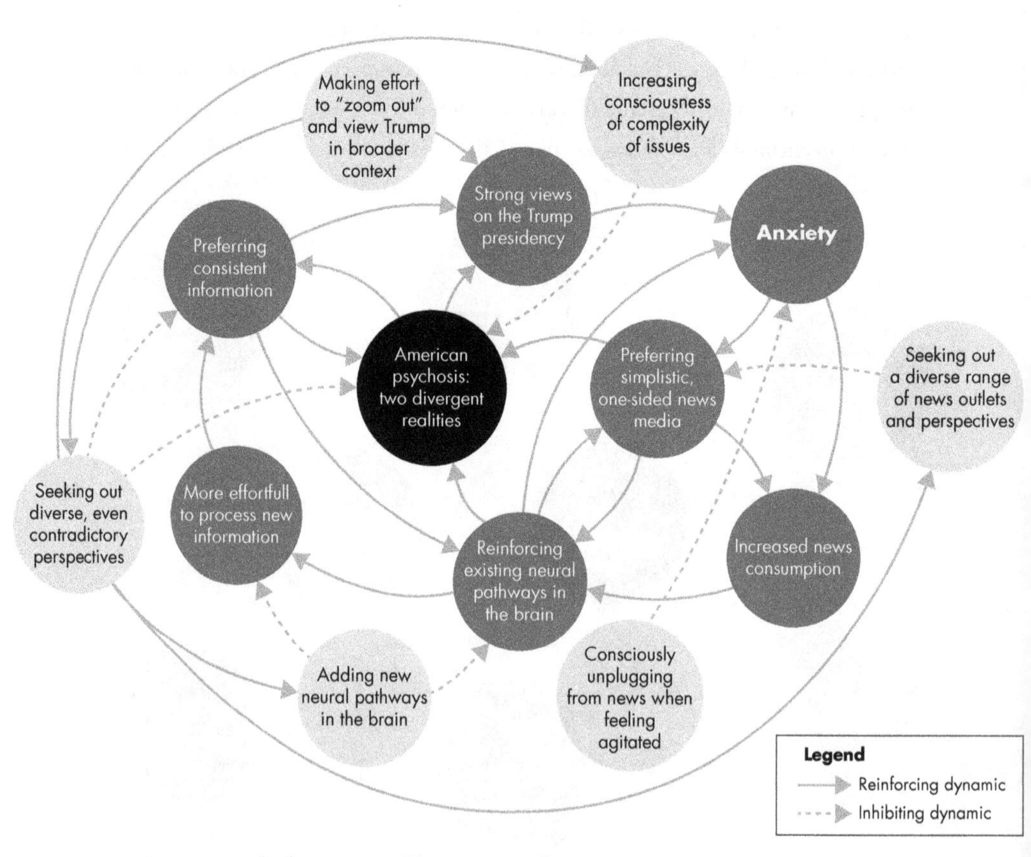

7.3 A vicious cycle showing possible mitigating forces.

dynamics of anxiety, certainty, and oversimplification that would otherwise prevail in their absence. These checks block and reduce the tendency of the system to escalate and gather strength (dotted lines indicate inhibiting forces). This is exactly the experience of the world Phelps-Roper came to discover—a world more complicated and replete with internal contradictions, which forced her to question the underlying roots of what she believed. Typically, the stronger and deeper the attractor, the more likely it is that the *consistent* rather than the *contradictory* type of complexity rules.

To illustrate, consider the different types of worldviews of the abortion issue that were prevalent within the pro-life and pro-choice camps in Boston in the 1990s. One perspective clearly viewed abortion as a sin and a crime, not unlike murder, and believed that those who choose to commit this sin, or to support those who did, were also sinners—perhaps even fundamentally evil people—and that they therefore needed to be stopped by (almost) any means possible. This included through acts of public shaming, lawsuits, protests, prayer, and the use of chilling rhetoric and gruesome images that exposed the evilness of their deeds. This worldview on abortion was woven deeply into all-encompassing beliefs about God, religion, evil, heaven, and hell. This point of view on abortion was certain, solid, and hermetically sealed by scripture. No room for doubt.

An alternative perspective prevalent within the pro-choice camp at the time viewed abortion as an excruciatingly difficult, highly personal decision regarding pregnancy that *must* be left up to the pregnant woman to decide. This worldview saw the right to choose as both a legal right under current law and a basic human right, and the group believed that to relinquish this right was yet another step down a slippery slope toward men regaining complete control over women's bodies and lives. Pro-choice advocates viewed pro-life religious zealots as being out of touch with contemporary reality and being used as pawns by patriarchal institutions such as the Catholic Church to control women (similar to characters in the *Handmaidens Tale*). This view was enshrined in *Roe v. Wade*, a landmark Supreme Court decision that found that the U.S. Constitution guaranteed protection of a pregnant woman's right to choose to have an abortion. Simple. Case closed.

These clearly divergent worldviews on abortion were highly complex, evoking a host of values, attitudes, and beliefs within individuals; norms, narratives, and rules within groups; and institutions and structures within the broader society (particularly religious and legal institutions). Nevertheless, each worldview was organized around one simple story, a highly coherent form of logic: abortion is a sin or abortion is a right. Neither left much room for doubt or questioning.

Now let's consider the alternative views on the abortion issue that emerged from both camps after a well-facilitated, six-year clandestine dialogue process. As I mentioned previously, some aspects of the attitudes of the women in each camp remained the same or, in fact, became even more polarized—particularly with regard to the religious tragedy associated with the issue and the vital importance of women maintaining legal control of their bodies.

At the same time, the views from both camps also became much more complicated. The profound respect, care, and love that grew between the women during their time together radically changed how they saw the members of the other camp—not just the leaders with whom they met but much of their membership as well. The personal stories shared and heard on both sides also expanded and complicated the leaders' understandings of the *many* issues involved with abortions (moral, legal, psychological, health-related, family, spiritual, and so on) and of the sometimes unintended consequences of their own activism. Each camp also began to recognize some of the contradictions inherent in their own position, which had been extremely difficult to attend to previously. In summary, their experiences of the issues, the others, and their own side became much more nuanced, much less one-sided, and therefore less closed, defensive, and destructive. Some would also suggest that the views of the two camps became more accurate, realistic, and reasonable and oriented the leaders down very different pathways in both their personal and professional lives. Such is the power of more contradictory or balanced forms of complexity for mitigating runaway polarization.

Evidence from the Difficult Conversations Lab

The value of contradictory complexity for stemming the seductive riptide of us versus them is one of the more robust findings from our research in the Difficult Conversations Lab (DCL). In our lab, we study the conditions under which conversations over politically polarizing issues such as abortion, climate change, and the Trump presidency get stuck in heated contention or the conversations go well enough—despite important moral differences—that the participants are willing and interested in continuing them. Over the past several years, we have run hundreds of these conflicting groups and have studied a variety of different conditions and processes that seem to affect the constructive versus destructive direction they take. The most significant finding to date has been on the power of contradictory complexity for mitigating escalation, polarization, and hostile stalemates.

To illustrate, lets return to the topic of how simple differences in the initial framing of conversations can lead to big differences in their outcomes. In one study, conducted by my colleague Katharina Kugler in her DCL at the Ludwig Maximilian University of Munich, Germany, we looked at how differences in the complexity of how difficult conversations are *framed* would affect how they unfolded.[4] This was an experiment with two different conditions. In the low-complexity condition, we presented information on the issue to be discussed (abortion, punishment for pedophiles, free speech versus hate speech) in a clear pro-versus-con manner. The two sides of the issue were described and presented as opposing views. In the high-complexity condition, the same *content* on the issues was presented as a complex set of challenges related to the focal issue. That was it—simple differences in the way the same information was framed and presented to the discussants.

The effects of the study were powerful. When compared with the low-complexity (pro-con) condition, the high-complexity (multiple issues) condition resulted in the participants

Feeling significantly more positive emotions and fewer negative emotions during the encounter;

Thinking about the issues in more nuanced and sophisticated ways at the completion of the discussion;

Behaving in ways that were more open, respectful, obliging, and ultimately identifying and focusing on things they both had in common during the talk; which ultimately

Resulted in their group's enhanced abilities to reach a consensus; generate better, more politically sophisticated joint statements; and leave the session reporting more cooperative, satisfying feelings about the encounter and a willingness to meet and speak with the other participant again in the future.

That's right, reframing how the information on the issue was presented at the outset of the conversation affected how the participants felt, thought, acted, and ultimately viewed future encounters. Increasing the degree of complexity of how information was delivered to a more highly nuanced set of dilemmas and trade-offs (contradictory complexity—you know, like so much of our life) made a huge difference.

Why? When information on hot emotional topics is presented as pro versus con, we attend more carefully to the information that supports our position (*selective perception* and *confirmation bias*) and ignore or discount the other side of the argument—mostly because we find consistency more comforting under these conditions.[5] However, when the information is presented as more complicated, multidimensional, and interlinked—as a series of dilemmas and trade-offs—it is much harder to ignore the contradictory information. This promotes a more balanced understanding of the issues.

This is a central point. So much of our society today is built on idolizing pro-versus-con arguments, which are rooted in the belief that presenting both sides of an issue on television, debating two positions on a topic in class, or arguing both sides of a legal case is the best pathway to the truth. But here's some breaking news: Most of the issues over which we are divided today—immigration, health care, climate change, education, good governance—*have more than two sides.* These are all highly complex, multidimensional matters that are often intertwined with other issues and present us with challenging dilemmas and trade-offs. Yet many of the traditions of our educational, media, and legal systems are organized around the pro-versus-con model. This is, of course, quite superior to presenting only one-sided propaganda on an issue. However, suffice it to say that the increasingly complex problems that we are facing today—which include the toxic quagmire we are in currently—cannot be understood from only two sides. Our approach to comprehending our world must reflect the increasing complexities inherent to it.

Evidence Across Levels

The benefits of contradictory forms of high complexity for promoting more constructive social relations has been found in research that scales across levels. The degree of complexity in how we think, feel, and act; with whom we socialize, work, live, and network; and how we structure our homes, schools, workplaces, and communities have all been found to have significant implications for how we respond to the conflict in our lives. Here are just a few illustrations:

Integrative complexity: *How we think about new problems.* Decades of research on integrative complexity—the cognitive tendency to break new problems down into component parts (differentiation) and then put them back together again to gain a coherent understanding of the whole problem (integration)—has shown that using more complex cognitive rules to analyze information has positive implications for the degree of effectiveness of decision making, outcome forecasting, and tendencies to respond in more constructive, conciliatory, ways to conflict.[6]

Political complexity: *How we make political decisions.* Research has also found that more complex, holistic ways of thinking about political conflicts pay important dividends. In a study of forty-six politicians in Poland, researchers found that those who thought about political challenges in a more concrete, sequential, or linear (cause-and-effect) manner tended to evidence more competitive, contentious attitudes when facing political conflict. In contrast, those who possessed more complex, systemic ways of thinking about these challenges (could differentiate distinct perspectives on a problem and see beyond their own point of view) tended to display less confrontational and more cooperative or compromising behaviors, even after experiencing an emotional attack from their opponents.[7]

Emotional complexity: *Our capacity to tolerate contradictory feelings.* Research from our DCL, as well as John Gottman's Love Lab studying marital conflict and Barbara Frederickson's Positive Emotions and Psychophysiology Lab, has consistently found that higher levels of emotional complexity, or the capacity to experience diverse and contradictory emotions—especially when they evidence a high positivity-to-negativity ratio—is associated with healthier, more long-lasting relationships, more productive work/strategy teams, higher levels of human flourishing, and more constructive approaches to important moral conflicts.[8]

Behavioral complexity: *Our ability to take a stand <u>and</u> listen.* Behavioral complexity is defined as the array of oppositional behaviors that people employ.[9] Two opposing behaviors relevant to conflict include acts of *inquiring* (exploring the other's positions, interests, and needs) and acts of *advocating* (advocating for one's own positions, interests, and needs). In our research on moral conflict, we have found, unsurprisingly, that advocacy behaviors were much more prevalent than inquiry behaviors overall. However, we also found that more constructive discussions over moral differences were characterized by more balanced ratios of inquiry-to-advocacy behaviors and more openness to the other person's thoughts and ideas than were those resulting in more intractability.[10]

Social identity complexity: *How our group affiliations fit together.* The degree to which people see themselves as members of groups that are *contradictory and do not overlap* (higher complexity) rather than groups that are more *aligned and consistent* (lower complexity) have been found to predict more tolerance of out-groups and more openness in general.[11] In other words, a liberal, pro-choice, pro–gay rights individual would have much lower social identity complexity (more consistency) than an openly gay, conservative, NRA supporter (higher internal contradiction). In this case, the liberal would tend to show less tolerance for out-groups than the conservative. Our internal levels of contradictory complexity matter.

Group complexity and contradiction: *How to reduce groupthink.* Tight-knit groups, particularly identity groups who feel threatened or under attack from an out-group, tend to struggle with the challenge of chronic consensus-seeking in their decision-making processes, something called *groupthink.*[12] This typically occurs within groups when the desire for harmony or conformity is characterized by the suppression of dissent, resulting in suboptimal decision-making processes and outcomes. An effective remedy to this type of hyperconsensus is conflict and contradiction. This is sometimes done by designating *devil's advocates* or critical evaluators of decisions within the group, or by modeling, encouraging, or otherwise rewarding dissent and constructive in-group disagreement.

Social network complexity: *The diversity of our community.* When people are exposed to more diverse networks of outsiders, their brains are forced to process more complex and unexpected types of information, and they become better at producing complex and unexpected information themselves.[13] People with more diversified social networks have also been found to be more tolerant of out-groups and more supportive of policies helpful to them. They tend to have more positive out-group experiences, share more interests with people outside their own groups, and be more informed about the contributions of out-group members and the problems they face. Finally, people with smaller, more cohesive networks have been found to evidence poorer communication and reasoning skills about politics, culminating in a lower quality of policy-relevant thinking and are more resistant to attitude change than people within networks made up of others with a range of views.[14]

Structural complexity: *The likelihood of cooperative contact with out-groups in my community.* Decades of anthropological research has demonstrated that societies differ in the degree to which they are organized in ways that groups are insulated from versus integrated with one another. Some societies are organized in nested groups (low complexity) where members of distinct ethnic or political groups tend to work, play, study, and socialize with members of their own group and have little collaborative, equal-status contact with members of other groups. Other societies are organized through a prevalence of crosscutting structures (high complexity), including integrated business associations, trade unions, professional groups, political parties, and sports clubs. These higher-complexity community structures have been identified as one of the most effective ways of making intergroup conflict more manageable, nonviolent, and tractable.[15]

The effects of contradictory forms of complexity can also become fractal, that is, repeated at many levels. If you recall the discussion of intractable attractors in chapter 3, I suggested that one of the drivers of intractable polarization is the fact that the simple us-versus-them patterns that form in the structures of our brains can align with similar patterns within and between our groups, communities,

Principle 4: Complicate—Embrace Contradictory Complexity

We can do a lot to create conditions in which we are less susceptible to the seduction of certainty, oversimplification, and vilification of others; we can intentionally complicate our lives. Research across levels of human experience has demonstrated the critical importance of introducing higher levels of contradictory complexity to constructive conflict, especially when situations become more taxing, stressful, and threatening. Increasing complexity, by more intentionally choosing what we read, watch, and listen to, and joining groups, projects, and teams with more diverse others, can help us navigate and transform intractable attractors. So go ahead, get complicated.

and with broader cultural symbols, which in turn reinforce the same patterns within us. What the findings on contradictory complexity tell us is that complexity can operate as a counterbalance in much the same way. Thinking, feeling, or behaving in more complex ways contributes to and is reinforced by living, working, and socializing in more complex groups, networks, institutions, and cultures. All of this can help to establish an ecosystem in which most forms of intergroup conflict are much less likely to become overly contentious, chronic, or dangerous.

PRACTICE: GET COMPLICATED

Contradictory complexity is a big idea. Whether it is how we think, feel, or behave; how we view or choose our own group identities; how we approach group decision making and social networking; or how our organizations and societies are structured, the degree of contradictory-versus-consistent complexity in our lives matters. Particularly when we are stuck in a difficult, long-term conflict. Conflict intensifies our natural desire for tribalism, consistency, and coherence, which can become dysfunctional during prolonged conflicts.[16] Developing more complex patterns of thinking, feeling, acting, and social organizing can mitigate this, resulting in more constructive responses to conflict.

As the research on complexity suggests, there are a variety of experiences and pathways we can take to help increase our own capacities to think, feel, and act in more balanced ways—and to fend off the urge to prematurely oversimplify and vilify others in difficult conflicts. Here are a few ways to cultivate contradictory complexity.

Acknowledge Your Own Contradictions

Decades of research on *cognitive dissonance* (no, not the crust/metal band from Minneapolis but "the state of discomfort felt when two or more modes of thought contradict each other"[17]) has shown that most Americans really hate to contradict themselves.[18] We absolutely despise being seen as acting in a way that is inconsistent with our more important values (Hypocrite!) or having to change our public stance on a moral or political issue (Flip-flopper!). Doing so brings a sense of confusion that triggers feelings of noxious anxiety. In fact, brain research has shown that the higher the level of uncertainty people experience when making decisions, the greater the electrical activity in their amygdala—the notorious fear region of the brain.[19] When people discover that they have contradicted themselves or have been tricked into doing so by an undergraduate sophomore in a psychology experiment, they will often go to great lengths to deny, discount, or otherwise justify the discrepancy. It just feels bad, wrong, and noxious to be inconsistent.

But, of course, we all contradict ourselves often. In fact, many philosophical and cultural traditions assume that the world revolves around dialectical tensions derived from our most basic contradictions: good versus evil or war versus peace.[20] As William Blake wrote, "Without contraries [there] is no progression. Attraction and repulsion, reason and energy, love and hate, are necessary to human existence."[21] How many devoted married people who have vowed before their god and community to be monogamous ultimately violate their vows? Even Saint Augustine, considered by many to be the champion of moral certainty, devoted many pages of his book *Confessions* to acknowledging his own sinful ways. These opposing tendencies and acts are seen as the primary sources of our personal, social, and societal development. Unless you live in a puritan bubble in an isolated community with no external sources of information and you and your comrades have completely internalized the values and norms of your group, you can't help but feel, think, and behave in contradictory ways.

In the context of a highly polarized political conflict, it is exponentially more difficult and more consequential to admit to our own internal discrepancies and inconsistencies regarding the accepted attitudes and feelings for the adversary. During wartime, people are often shunned, jailed, or shot for even considering aiding, consorting, or collaborating with the enemy. Similar mechanisms are employed when tensions arise between competing cliques in high school, or diehard fans of sports teams, or, ethnic or political adversaries. The in-group sanctioning and out-group vilification that so often follow escalating tensions can become so constraining or threatening that our capacity to harbor divergent thoughts regarding the out-group collapses. We put any kind or conciliatory thoughts of members of the other group out of mind.

However, it is exactly in this type of context that recognizing and tolerating our own internal contradictions (self-complexity) is crucial. This was the bitter truth that Megan Phelps-Roper had to come to terms with—acknowledging her own value-behavior inconsistencies as well as those of her family and religious community. These inconsistencies can be very difficult to identify let alone accept or discuss with others, but research suggests that doing so can provide an adjustment that matters.

For example, the research on *social identity complexity* has found that people who acknowledge that they are a member of contradictory groups (more highly complex identities) are more accepting and open to members of out-groups than those who only identify with groups that are more aligned and consistent (lower complexity identities).[22] Why? People who live with internal contradictions (e.g., being an openly gay *and* highly religious evangelical Christian) become more accustomed to tolerating differences and contradictions, have more practice taking the perspective of different sides on such issues, and may learn to reconcile or hold both identities without having to deny or choose one over the other. These experiences tend to promote more tolerance and acceptance of out-groups.

In fact, just thinking about all the possible discrete identity categories that people can be placed in can lead to a significant reduction in biased judgments of out-groups.[23] Participants in these experiments were asked to list as many possible group categories as they could that people use to define themselves before being asked to rate members of their in-group and an out-group on a performance task. The researchers found that simply increasing awareness of the many possible group categories with which people can identify—what they called *categorical complexity*—decreased the incidence of intergroup bias and in-group favoritism.

Decades of related empirical research on people's *tolerance for ambiguity* (as well as *tolerance for uncertainty*) has found that people who are more able to accept and not become destabilized by uncertain, inconsistent, or otherwise ambiguous situations and information are generally happier and healthier, cope more effectively with major changes, and are better able to make high-quality complex decisions.[24] Ambiguity tolerance has also been found to be associated with more solution-oriented (as opposed to confrontational) conflict management processes.[25]

To be clear, consistency, certainty, and coherence of thought in relation to ourselves is not a bad thing. In fact, some degree of orderliness and stability in our self-concept is considered foundational to our mental health.[26] However, when our self-certainty begins to blind us to the inherent contradictions within us all and to the ambivalences we feel about our political peers (in-group) and opponents, then a correction is warranted. So go ahead, contradict yourself.

Learn to Think with the Best of *Them*

Although we tend to believe that our thinking takes place within our heads and brains, the fact is that we mostly think *with* other people.[27] This is what has transpired in the context of our families, friendships, kitchens, barbershops, schools, movie theaters, libraries, places of worship, street corners, chatrooms, and workplaces since we were born. Some of this cothinking is conscious and deliberate, but most of it is automatic and unconscious. In philosophy and psychology this is called *symbolic interactionism* or the *social construction of meaning*—the constant linguistic, symbolic, and interactive processes by which we jointly make sense of the world around us and our roles in it.[28] In college, we just called it *hanging out*.

As creatures of habit in a highly polarized era, most of us tend to follow the rule, "move toward similar others and away from different." We are automatically inclined to surround ourselves with and therefore think with similar others who share "congenial information" versus "uncongenial information"—simply because it is easier and more comforting.[29]

Be honest, how often do you *choose* to hang out with people who hold strong opposing views from yours on political matters? Think of the last several parties or social events you attended (family gatherings don't count; we usually don't choose our family). Was a diversity of opinions represented? In fact, were any dissenting political opinions voiced? Unless you are an outlier, this is a highly unlikely scenario in the United States today. Most of us tend to close ranks and prefer to listen to those we mostly agree with during such tense times (it just feels so good!). This tendency to move toward the similar is intensified by the internet sorting algorithms employed today by many of the major technology platforms that automatically direct us to news, information, and opinion content that is complementary to our own. This all serves to significantly reduce the nuance and accuracy of our understanding of complicated issues.

One check on this echo-chamber effect is to actively choose to think and learn with *different* people; that is, intentionally choose to hear from people across the divide. No, it does not mean that you need to tune into the nut jobs on talk radio and cable TV that spout nonsense and conspiracy theories.[30] But it does suggest that there is much to gain from seeking out the best representatives of people you disagree with and thinking through complex issues (although not necessarily agreeing) with them.

Our lab research on conversations over hot topics supports this; difficult dialogues with thoughtful, reasonable people who hold opposing opinions make us smarter. In our studies, the groups that were able to have more nuanced and constructive conversations over their moral differences were consistently able to generate joint statements that offered more sophisticated and reasonable analyses and positions. Philip Tetlock's research goes even further, finding that people with more diverse networks (who also are able to disagree without being disagreeable) more effectively anticipate and forecast future outcomes (out to about eighteen months) because their understanding of complex issues and trends is much more accurate. He calls them *superforcasters*.[31] But to achieve this in our lives, we must learn to "move toward different others and away from similar." So, if you are interested in gaining a more accurate understanding of a particular issue, learn to seek out the best thought leaders on the other side.

Complicate the Problem

After publication of *The Five Percent: Finding Solutions to Seemingly Impossible Conflicts*, I received an invitation to conduct a workshop with the League of American Orchestras, a North American service organization with seven hundred orchestras as members. They were meeting to discuss a set of long-term industry concerns that had culminated in a seemingly intractable labor-management conflict at the Detroit Symphony Orchestra. At some point, the dispute had turned ugly, with death threats and acts of violence. Yes, you heard me right—death threats over an orchestra dispute.

I agreed to the workshop, and after introducing some of the main ideas from the book (conflict, complexity, intractability) to the participants, I engaged the group of twenty or so leaders of symphonies in a mapping exercise of the *context of their conflicts*. A few members of the Detroit group were there, and I invited them to work with me before the whole group to model the mapping process. At first, the Detroit team's sense of the problem was crystal clear—the leadership and membership of the musician's union, the American Federation of Musicians, "were thugs and criminals who should be rounded up and arrested." That would put an end to it.

I asked the group to do three things. First, generate a list of the economic, cultural, political, and industry-related problems they thought might somehow be related to the tensions at the symphony. Second, get up from their seats and start drawing on a large flipchart how each of the problems they had listed were related to (a) the bitterness of the negotiations and (b) to each of the other problems on the map. Within half an hour, the Detroit team had generated an immensely complicated map that included everything from the general decline of unions in the United States and Detroit's history of violence, to the economic collapse of 2008, and to the role of social media in fanning the flames of antagonism.

This map gave the Detroit group pause. Clearly, the tactics of some members of the union leadership were infuriating, incendiary, and probably illegal. But they were not the cause of the intransigence of the problem and crisis that both management and labor were facing. The mapping process provided this critical context and opened the conversation considerably.

This kind of complexity mapping has become increasingly useful for envisioning and addressing complex problems in organizations, communities, nations, and in the international arena. Developed originally by Magoroh Maruyama, best known for his work in cybernetics, mapping is useful for identifying the many factors and dynamics that serve to escalate, de-escalate, and stabilize destructive patterns of conflict and polarization.[32] These maps not only allow us to capture the multiple sources of complex problems but also help us identify hidden causes and broader patterns that are unrecognizable by other means.

The mapping process can take many different forms, but it typically begins by identifying the *focus of interest*—the central phenomenon we wish to comprehend (polarization, violence, solidarity, etc.).[33] Next, the *core dynamics* are identified, the factors and relationships most closely associated with the increase or decrease of the problem. After this, the maps can be built out further to help participants see the broader set of factors that are affecting the patterns. These visuals can be generated alone by individuals, jointly in relationships, and at broader group or community levels. They often help spark meaningful conversations between stakeholders and can offer new insights and opportunities for intervention. When employed by experts, these maps can help generate new questions for data gathering, organize available knowledge in more integrative ways, and act as a diagnostic tool to identify potential gaps in current policy approaches.

With problem-context mapping, the goal is not necessarily to get it right. The goal at this point is to complicate matters; to reintroduce a sense of nuance into the understanding of the conflict. When people engage in the process of mapping, especially in a diverse group of stakeholders, they are challenged to look beyond the factors that are most obvious to them. A broader picture begins to emerge as each individual contributes to a process that leads to a shared understanding of the context of the problem that, in turn, opens new avenues for change.[34]

Complexity mapping often results in extremely complicated images of a problem, so it is important to offer strategies for eventually focusing and prioritizing. For instance, the ecologist Eric Berlow recommends eventually focusing on factors that are *local* and *actionable* and can feasibly be addressed.[35] Another strategy is to look at each of the factors in the map and take stock of how many other factors are connected to them. Elements that have fewer connections may be easier to change, whereas those that influence many other elements may have more impact on changing the overall patterns. This is essentially applying a process of *integrative complexity* to your visualization of the problem you face, breaking problems down into component parts and then putting them back together again to gain a coherent understanding of how to address them.

But here is one caveat. At the heart of much of what we've discussed so far regarding contradictory complexity is that it can be a double-edged sword. If the understanding of a conflict has become overly simplistic and polarized, reintroducing some degree of nuance into its comprehension is critical. But adding too much complexity can easily make an already complicated situation seem overwhelming, even immobilizing, resulting in the opposite of groupthink—something called *polythink*, in which the plurality of viewpoints impairs decision making.[36] Or it can lead to increased resistance and an even stronger push to oversimplify and choose sides. The ultimate goal of such exercises is to identify simplicity informed by complexity.[37] As the statesman and playwright Vaclav Havel once wrote, "Simple answers which lie on this side of life's complexities are cheap. However, simple truths which exist beyond this complexity, and are illuminated by it, are worthy of a lifetime's commitment."

Complicate the Conversation

How we choose to communicate and discuss problems with those in the other camp will have profound effects on everything else: our understanding, our relationships on both sides of the dispute, and the direction and duration of the conflict. So the question is: Should we dialogue or debate?

The term *dialogue* is often used to describe how people try to work out their differences. But, in fact, most Americans debate by default—mostly because we are highly socialized to debate through learning it in schools, watching legal proceedings, or seeing debates in political campaigns. It also often feels like a more fitting response when tensions run high—a chance to intellectually confront and defeat the other. But there is a big difference between dialogue and debate.

Debate involves a more closed, strategic, instrumental form of persuasion and influence aimed at scoring points and winning an argument. It involves making a solid case for your original position, then listening attentively to the other side to identify flaws in their logic or evidence that you can cite to bolster your own. It also often involves spewing as much information for as long as possible to wear down your adversary.

Dialogue is the opposite. It involves significantly more opening, sharing, discovery, and learning. When in dialogue, participants often learn new information about themselves, the others involved, and the issues under discussion. It often involves a careful (or carefully facilitated) process in which the disputants share personal or otherwise meaningful stories about their own experiences regarding the issue in dispute. They are typically asked to speak one at a time and not to interrupt each other, although each disputant many have several opportunities to speak. However, no cross-examination or interrogation of one another is allowed. The participants are instructed to speak as honestly and personally as possible and to listen carefully to each other.

The power of dialogue comes from two simple sources: *hearing others* and *being heard.* Emile Bruneau, a neuroscientist who has lived and worked in conflict zones around the world, conducted some lab experiments on dialogue that yielded surprising results.[38] He studied the effects of dialogues on changing attitudes toward the "other" in members of four groups involved in different ideological conflicts: Mexican immigrants and white Americans in Arizona and

Israelis and Palestinians in the Middle East. The participants were all assigned to either (a) write about the difficulties of life in their society—to be shared with others (what he called perspective-giving), or (b) accurately summarize the statement of the first person (perspective-taking). The surprising effects Bruneau found were based on power differences between the groups. Positive changes in attitudes toward the out-group were greater for Mexican immigrants and Palestinians (lower-power disputants in these contexts) after perspective-*giving* (being heard), and for white Americans and Israelis (higher-power) after perspective-*taking* (listening and hearing the other). The effects of dialogue differed based on real power asymmetries. This, of course, makes sense, given that members of lower-power groups have been found to usually attend much more carefully to the words and actions of those in authority, whereas those with higher power attend less to low-power others. And frankly, they are just more used to being listened to by others.[39]

Dialogue is the type of process that was employed in Boston over abortion. The leaders were organized around hearing each other and being heard, which led to considerable discovery and insight. Nevertheless, dialogue is mostly misunderstood and underutilized in the hypercompetitive, litigious context of the United States.

When seeking to understand and engage with people who think and feel in direct opposition to you today, it is critical to *begin* with a process of listening and learning through dialogue.

Complicate the Narratives

In early 2018, I was approached by Amanda Ripley, a journalist on a mission to discover what psychology and conflict resolution had to offer the world of journalism regarding mitigating polarization. Ripley was in the process of visiting and interviewing researchers and mediators working in this area, and ultimately visited our Difficult Conversations Lab as a participant, in addition to interviewing me and my staff and students over several sessions.

After months of research, Ripley published "Complicating the Narrative" on *Solutions Journalism Network*, "an independent, non-profit organization that advocates for an evidence-based mode of reporting on the responses to social problems."[40] The article soon went viral, being tweeted out around the world by

David Brooks and Nicholas Kristoff of the *New York Times* and Krista Tippett of National Public Radio. In her article, Ripley offered journalists the following advice:

> The lesson for journalists (or anyone) working amidst intractable conflict: complicate the narrative. First, complexity leads to a fuller, more accurate story. Secondly, it boosts the odds that your work will matter—particularly if it is about a polarizing issue. When people encounter complexity, they become more curious and less closed off to new information. They listen, in other words.
>
> There are many ways to complicate the narrative. . . . But the main idea is to feature nuance, contradiction and ambiguity wherever you can find it. This does not mean calling advocates for both sides and quoting both; that is simplicity, and it usually backfires in the midst of conflict. "Just providing the other side will only move people further away," Coleman says. Nor does it mean creating a moral equivalence between neo-Nazis and their opponents. That is just simplicity in a cheap suit. Complicating the narrative means finding and including the details that don't fit the narrative—on purpose.
>
> The idea is to *revive complexity in a time of false simplicity*. . . . Usually, reporters do the opposite. We cut the quotes that don't fit our narrative. Or our editor cuts them for us. We look for coherence, which is tidy—and natural. The problem is that, in a time of high conflict, coherence is bad journalism, bordering on malpractice.

Ripley went on to recommend six practices for reporters that have utility for anyone trying to swim upstream against the current pull of division. Among them she suggests that we amplify contradictions (as we have been discussing), widen the lens (what I refer to as zooming out to comprehend the complex context of the conflict), and counter confirmation bias (the tendency to select belief-confirming information). Ripley's work eventually resulted in a more comprehensive initiative on how to more effectively report on intractable conflict.[41]

Given the profound role media plays today in directing (and distracting) our limited attention and shaping our political and cultural priorities, it is incumbent on all of us to intentionally seek out and accustom ourselves and our families to the types of media that follow Ripley's prescriptions and offer more nuanced views of events unfolding in our increasingly complex world.[42] National Public Radio (NPR), the Public Broadcasting Service (PBS), and the British Broadcasting Corporation (BBC) are *less* influenced by corporate sponsors, the profit motive, and related trends toward the "entertainmentization" of the media and are much more likely to embrace these standards of reporting. In addition, journalistic organizations such as The Flipside, which curates more than thirty news sources daily to present "the most thoughtful and informed perspectives on major issues," and AllSides, a group that uses media-bias ratings to offer what they describe as "balanced news, perspectives and issues across the political spectrum,"[43] are working to provide a more nuanced media landscape. Regardless of where you turn, the onus is clearly on us these days to strive to complicate the stories of our time.

Complicate Your Community

In the 1990s, Speaker of the House Newt Gingrich eliminated a basic structure from Washington political life that had served as a civilizing force in our government for more than a century: *crosscutting ties*. As part of his campaign to secure permanent Republican control of the government, Gingrich changed the workweek in Congress from five days to three.[44] He argued that this would allow his Republican colleagues to live in their home state and raise more money, but it also kept the members of his caucus from fraternizing with politicians on the other side.

Prior to this time, most lawmakers had homes in Washington, D.C., and their families socialized on weekends. What Speaker Gingrich did, wittingly or not, was to sever the bonds that are formed on the playgrounds, in schools, on little league teams, and at places of worship, where families from different parties grow up together. Through these encounters, members of Congress often became more moderate as they and their families befriended members on the other side. Today few members of Congress live in Washington, D.C. Instead they share an apartment with other members of their own party or sleep in their offices. The effect on cross-party relationships has been toxic.

Now, the fact that a Democrat's six-year-old shares the same crummy T-ball uniform as the child of a Republican is a small matter indeed. But when these experiences are multiplied over the thousands of interactions that people have with their neighbors when living in the same community, something emerges that is bigger than their sum total: trust. This is the sense of confident positive expectations that people hold for others in situations entailing risk. Trust is the connective tissue that holds our communities and our body politic together and makes them more resilient to hardship. The type of trust that can grow between neighbors over time is particularly sturdy. When political decisions over scarce resources are made in a context devoid of trust, something else quickly fills the void: suspicion. This dynamic has derailed the ability of Congress to meet the needs of the people, resulting in only 25 percent of Americans having trust in Congress today.[45]

The research supporting the powerful positive effects of a prevalence of crosscutting structures in groups, organizations, and communities on the health of the community is strong and goes back decades.[46] This research has documented that when communities promote equal-status, cooperative contact and association between members of distinct ethnic, religious, and political groups through work, play, study, commerce, and other forms of interacting, their intergroup conflicts tend to be much more manageable, nonviolent, and resolvable. In other words, they are much less likely to escalate, polarize, and become chronic.

It may surprise you to learn that the United States is home to many politically tolerant communities today. In fact, *The Atlantic* recently published an interactive map and database that allows you to search all three thousand counties to locate the most and least politically tolerant ones in the nation. They call it the Geography of Partisan Prejudice.[47] (New York County, where I live, is ranked in the 81st percentile, which means that eighty-one out of every one hundred counties in the United States are *more politically tolerant* than mine. Ugh!) As you might suspect, those counties that are more politically tolerant today (much of North Carolina and Upstate New York) tend to have more mixed political marriages, families, places of worship, and other crosscutting features.

What does this mean for you and your community? First, look around a bit. Do you live in a politically and ethnically diverse building, neighborhood, or town? If so, does this lead to meaningful interactions and relationships with others across the current divide? If not, are there opportunities for you to push the limits of your community by choosing to shop, play sports, worship, go to a hair salon, or just visit more diverse nearby communities?

In this chapter, I have focused on one major idea–the power of *contradictory forms of complexity* for establishing the mindsets, relationships, conditions, and processes to better resist toxic forms of polarization. The many versions of the type of complexity outlined here offers you various tactics for seeing, feeling, and engaging with the other side differently. However, it is also true that these tactics can work in concert. It is a fact that a more politically heterogeneous environment increases the diversity of our social networks, of the media we tend to consume and discuss, of whom we tend to think and learn with, and ultimately of our own capacities and comfort with recognizing our own internal inconsistencies regarding our political preferences. When this all lines up, we can start to see the beginnings of the opposite of a vicious cycle–*a virtuous cycle*–and a better view of the way out.

8

MOVE—ACTIVATE NOVEL PATHWAYS AND RHYTHMS

BREAKING AWAY

Early one morning in 2006 my colleague, Andrea Bartoli, had an epiphany. A group of about forty of us who study intractable conflict had come together in a small remote village in Poland called Kazimierz, a historic haven for Jews in a predominantly Catholic region of the world.[1] The meeting was filled with days of poster sessions and presentations on technical, scientific studies of very trying conflicts. Fascinating, but a bit dry. On the third day, Bartoli, an accomplished peacemaker and devout Catholic who works tirelessly around the world to reduce deadly conflict, offered some highly emotional remarks—an account of a risky interfaith encounter that had occurred during the Nazi occupation of the local area that illustrated the profound power of compassion and forgiveness in the face of evil. That night, after a short fitful sleep, Bartoli sprung from his bed, grabbed his computer, and spent the remainder of the dawn drafting a PowerPoint presentation titled "Peace Is in the Movement."*

When I arrived at our meeting room that morning, I found Bartoli waiting for me and the other organizers in what I can only describe as a fit of euphoria.

* When I asked Andrea Bartoli to review this section, he answered by email with this: "Over the years, I became convinced that peace is not only in the movement but also a gift. It is a gift shared in relationships, given and received often as a surprise, when we are not afraid, hardened by the pain of trauma, and frozen by the anguish of the future."

Although we had planned a full agenda, he implored us to sit and listen to his revelation. He then launched into an hour-long presentation of his thesis (illustrated with clever, primitive slides), arguing that because highly contentious conflicts can become so constricting—in terms of what we are allowed to feel, imagine, aspire to, discuss, or make happen—they imprison us. In his words, high conflict becomes a place where we come to exist "in the frozen reality of high tensions," what I now refer to as the *big collapse*. Even contemplating reaching out to a member of the enemy in conflict zones such as Northern Ireland, Sri Lanka, or Mozambique in the 1980s was so likely to trigger the wrath of your own community that it became unthinkable. Under these circumstances, he concluded, *movement is the cure*. In other words, moments and deeds that allow the imagination to wander, doubts to surface, or aspirations to soar—or incidents that bring us to new places or expose us to fresh perspectives—can provide the release that people drowning in conflict come to so desperately crave. In these moments of movement, of liberation from the constraints of impossible conflicts, peace becomes possible. When Bartoli completed his feverish exposition, the room erupted in applause.

A few years later our team stumbled on a similar finding while running a computer simulation of a mathematical model of intractable community conflict.[2] A subgroup headed by Andrzej Nowak had been developing an algorithm that could model the most basic dynamics of societal conflicts that accumulate negativity and enmity over time, eventually resulting in deep divisions that resembled fortresses of opposition. We ran a type of computer simulation called *cellular automata*, which presents a checkerboard surface that looks like an urban neighborhood from one thousand feet up, and each of the squares represents people or households in the community. In figure 8.1, the slightly raised squares represent minor disputes growing over scarce resources—the small dots.

We ran the simulation under different conditions to see when conflicts in the community would get better and worse. Sometimes the disputes would remain minor and vanish over time. Other times, events would escalate in the community, and the conflicts would become very hostile, deep, and embedded, resulting in much more change-resistant conflicts that looked like figure 8.2.

This is a precarious conflict landscape. Here you see the growth of structures of deep-seated hostility and violence in some areas of the community (the raised sections that look like infected blemishes[3]), with pockets of relative peacefulness

8.1 Computer visualization of the onset of community conflict at an early stage.

8.2 Computer visualization of the emergence of intractable community conflict at a later stage.

in others (the flat, colorless sections). This model validated robust empirical findings from decades of previous research by Morton Deutsch, who found that intense competition between people or groups—if incentivized and left unchecked—would trigger a reinforcing feedback loop that would escalate and intensify to a point of mutual destruction.[4]

Cool visual, right?

Then we learned something new. These math models have a set of basic assumptions and rules built into them limiting how individual agents (squares) interact in their environment, which can drive or limit what happens during the simulation. Our team had somewhat arbitrarily set a rule stating that people *could not move* across the community (this simplified the dynamics of the initial model for us). When we changed that operating rule to allow mobility in the space, the tendencies toward intractable disputes disappeared—even when the agents needed to compete for scarce resources! If people could move away from tensions, they often did, and this reduced the self-perpetuating clustering of negativity in these fortress structures, allowing it to dissipate in time.

Bartoli was right! Peace *is* in the movement![5]

PRINCIPLE 5: ACTIVATE NEW PATHWAYS AND RHYTHMS

For nearly the entire history of our species, Homo sapiens walked about this earth together in small groups of hunter-gatherer foragers. We only began to stop and settle in place relatively recently (about ten thousand years ago). Evolutionary psychologists believe that our brains were largely shaped during this early era and that many of the difficulties we face in modern times are a direct result of our forager brains contending with the demands of modern society. One logical extension of this argument is the misfit between how we learned to solve problems while traversing the Sahel and how we try to do so today sitting in conference rooms.

The idea that certain types of movement, flow, and moving together with others can be conducive to more positive psychological states, cooperative social relations, and constructive forms of conflict resolution is well documented in research.[6] To break free of the constraints of our intractably polarizing landscape, the two most promising areas of study are *locomotion* and *synchronization*.

SHAKE IT OFF

Michelle LeBaron, a law professor at universities in Vancouver and Melbourne and an expert on cross-cultural conflict resolution, tells a story about a group of diplomats from around the world that she gathered near Dublin, Ireland, in 1993 to try to generate new ideas for addressing one of the most entrenched conflicts of our time, conflicts within and between Israelis and Palestinians in the Middle East.[7] A primary challenge for LeBaron and the other facilitators of this event was to figure out how to help this group move out of their well-worn ruts of thinking and working on the situation in the Middle East (deep attractors): their certainty, rigidity of attitudes, extreme frames, and limiting assumptions. For the first two days of the meeting, the process followed a standard (clocklike) problem-solving format, and the results were not impressive.

However, on the third day, the diplomats climbed aboard an old school bus for a planned visit to the sites of the "Troubles" in Belfast, Northern Ireland during a time before the Good Friday Agreement (i.e., when life there was particularly edgy). Jostled considerably by the bus ride, the participants began to relate to each other differently, more playfully. Throughout the day, they bounced from site to site across West Belfast—down the Falls Road on the Catholic side and the Shankill Road on the Protestant side, two places that saw the most sectarian violence. They participated in dialogues with Northern Irish disputants and peacemakers while visiting a few bicommunal projects on peacebuilding. As the day unfolded, the camaraderie within the group of diplomats appeared to blossom. Following a group meal in the evening, the bus headed back to Dublin, and the participants broke into song together in the darkness. LeBaron later wrote, "Only after this excursion did conversations enliven, originality emerge, and imaginative possibilities for shifting intractable conflict in Israel-Palestine begin to reveal themselves."[8]

The facilitators of the meeting were thrilled by the change among the participants but struggled to understand what had actually happened. Then something struck them. Human beings are physical entities, but when we bring disputants, diplomats, mediators, or other problem solvers together to work on thorny problems, we usually sit them down in a room and ask them to resolve, create, or otherwise find solutions to difficult and often deeply embodied problems. Perhaps ignoring or denying our physical and biological essence when we try to talk things out, innovate, or negotiate is a mistake. Maybe making physical changes—movement, jostling, visiting new projects, traveling to foreign places—can shake up and alter our chronic responses to problems, allowing and encouraging us to see, think, feel, and respond differently.

This is what we are beginning to learn from neuroscience.[9] One critical finding from research in this area is that the circuitry in our brains is much more pliable than we once thought. Research on neuroplasticity has shown that the brain can rewire itself much more rapidly than initially believed, usually in response to changes in external stimuli.

This neurological rewiring has implications for both intractability and the way out of it. As LeBaron writes,

> neuroplasticity reveals that neurons that fire together are wired together, and those that fire apart remain wired apart. Repeated instances of associated neurons firing in particular patterns creates pathways in the brain that become neural "superhighways," relegating the untraveled "back roads" of unfamiliar pairings to increasingly less accessibility and use.[10]

In today's turbulent times, the more time we spend consuming propagandistic news that pairs images of Republicans with pointy-booted fascists and Democrats with masked anarchists, the more we wire our brains for interpartisan war. But an intentional reset—the decision to wean ourselves off of pure opinion entertainment masquerading as news or *changes of a physical nature*—can increase our chances of altering old and activating new neural pathways. As LeBaron learned in Belfast that day, two promising physical techniques are through locomotion and synchronization.

Principle 5: Move—Activate Novel Pathways and Rhythms

When we find ourselves immobilized by the crushing constraints of a bitter political feud, get moving. Recent advances in neuroscience and social science research have documented the benefits of movement—cognitive, motivational, emotional, and physical—for increasing our neuroplasticity (brain flexibility) and openness to new experiences. To find a way out of entrenched patterns, both simple locomotion and synchronization with others can free us and rewire our experiences and relations in a manner that can lead to more creative and constructive patterns in our life. So get moving.

THE LOCOMOTION STORY

Two colleagues of mine, Tory Higgins (who was a member of my dissertation committee) and Christine Webb (a former student), have studied movement. Higgins is a renowned psychological theorist at Columbia University, who studies things like motivation and social cognition, but his work on self-regulation (how we control ourselves when pursuing goals) and the regulatory mode called *locomotion* is most relevant here.[11] Webb studies motivation and conflict resolution in both primates and humans (who have way too much in common) and, as a student, worked with me, Higgins, and Frans De Waal, a noted primatologist.[12]

Concerns about locomotion have a long history in psychology, beginning in the 1940s with the work of Kurt Lewin, a brilliant social psychologist whose thinking was influenced by trends in both Gestalt psychology and physics.* Lewin developed *field theory*, from which dynamical systems theory is descended, which views human behavior as the result of a complex constellation of influences.[13] Our psychological experience of this "field of influences" is called the *life space*,[14] and when we move through this space—cognitively, emotionally, or physically—it is called *locomotion*. As one psychologist wrote, "locomotion includes any kind of approach or withdrawal—even looking at a pretty object or away from an ugly one, or listening to liked music and avoiding disliked or uninteresting music."[15] Locomotion includes both physical and psychological movement.

Higgins studies locomotion as a basic human motive—the need or desire to move from one state to another, for example, from being cold to being warm. He often contrasts this with another basic motivation humans have for *assessment*, which is the need to stop and critically evaluate what we are doing (our goals) and how we could best achieve them (our strategies). His research has identified a variety of implications for whether we are *more* motivated to "Just do it" (get moving) or whether it is more important for us to "Do the right thing," that is, choose the best objective and course of action.[16]

---

* Kurt Lewin was a Jewish German intellectual who fled Nazi Germany and came to the United States; he was one of the founders of the subfield of social psychology. Lewin supervised the research of Mort Deutsch at MIT, who supervised my dissertation at Columbia University, so I like to think of Lewin as my intellectual grandfather.

Webb's dissertation connected the dots between movement and conflict. She was one of the first since Lewin to link locomotion and assessment motives with differences in conflict resolution.[17] Across a range of studies with both humans and primates, Webb found that locomotion was good for conflict resolution. Whether she measured people's individual preference to locomote (move) versus assess (evaluate) or experimentally induced them, higher levels of motivation to move from here to there, rather than to stop and critically evaluate options, increased the likelihood that people would resolve their interpersonal conflicts and report more eagerness to rectify ongoing disputes.

Webb found similar results with primates (thirty-one adult and adolescent chimpanzees, *Pan troglodytes*).[18] Data was collected in a series of controlled observation sessions over several years, with researchers recording all occurrences of chimpanzee antagonistic interactions (tugs, brusque rushes, trampling, biting, grunt-barking, shrill-barking, fighting, crouching, shrink/flinching, or bared-teeth screaming—just as seen on Capitol Hill) and affiliative interactions (kisses, embraces, grooming, touch, finger/hand in mouth, play, and mounting—less common in public on Capitol Hill). Webb found that the chimps evidencing more locomotion behaviors (a general tendency to quickly initiate movement from state to state), had higher rates of reconciliation with other chimps (showing affiliative behaviors), and did so more rapidly after an antagonistic encounter. So even locomotor primates prefer peace.

Why does this matter? In the human conflict resolution world, mediators, negotiators, and diplomats of all stripes—as well as parents, teachers, managers, and other dispute resolvers—tend to spend the vast majority of their time (95 percent?) going deep into the analysis of our problems and assessment of our solutions and very little time moving—cognitively or physically—forward. Of course, going deep into the specifics of our problems and options is important and useful. But Webb's research consistently found that a *predominance* of interest in locomotion over assessment was best for promoting readiness and a willingness to resolve conflicts, reconcile, and move on.

Our research in the Difficult Conversations Lab has yielded similar findings. We have found that the capacity for *emotional locomotion* helps us navigate stormier conflicts.[19] Our use of a "mouse tracking" method[20] for measuring disputants' emotional experiences over the course of the discussions has enabled us to track their more positive and more negative feelings, and when they switch back and forth. We have found that the conversations between disputants who locomote more between their emotional attractors—as measured by the ratio of time they spend feeling good versus bad—consistently predicts less intractability. Groups that have a higher ratio of positive to negative emotional experiences during the talks—and therefore evidence more switching—show less intractability, better outcomes, and increased willingness to keep the conversation going.[21]

Evidence for the value of locomotion also extends to an aspect of our research called *conflict adaptivity*, the capacity to use different resolution strategies in different types of conflict situations in a manner fitting and effective within the situational differences.[22] This body of research (described in *Making Conflict Work: Harnessing the Power of Disagreement*) has demonstrated the critical importance of *strategic locomotion*, the cognitive and behavioral flexibility necessary to effectively respond to changing circumstances in conflict. Given that the essential nature of most of our relationships and conflicts are fluid, changing from moment to moment or day to day, our capacity to read important changes in situations (like major shifts in power relations or in our dependence on other people) and to employ resolution strategies that work better in those situations pays great dividends.

Research by others has also demonstrated the positive effects of physical locomotion on cognitive flexibility and creativity, two critical components of constructive conflict resolution, particularly in high conflicts when cognitive schemas tend to become frozen.[23] For instance, across four experiments, researchers found that physical movement (walking) increased participants' creativity scores on a test of divergent thinking (more open, creative association) by 81 percent and on convergent thinking (closing in on a best choice) by 23 percent, both of which are necessary for innovative problem solving.[24] These effects were particularly strong when people moved outdoors. Moderate physical activity has also been shown to increase positive affect[25] and cognitive control and focus in people's ability not just to attend to relevant information but also to disregard irrelevant information.[26]

Taken together, these findings add considerable support to Andrea Bartoli's experientially grounded insight that locomotion matters in freeing us from the restrictive confines of conflict. How do we translate the idea of motivational, emotional, strategic, and physical locomotion into action? That is the topic of the next section.

PRACTICE: GET MOVING!

There are a multitude of ways to leverage the insights from research on locomotion to begin to loosen the grip of polarization on you and your community. Here are a few tactics, small and large.

MoveOn.You

The most straightforward application derived from locomotion research is the value of getting up and moving for freeing up your feeling and thinking. Going for a walk, exercising, building something, gardening, playing catch, and running have all been shown to help shift our mind out of deep ruts and at times liberate us from dysphoric rumination and other types of adverse emotional traps. This seems to be what transpired among the diplomats in Belfast. Moving outside in nonurban spaces has been shown to have the most revitalizing and reparative effects, helping us reorient to the flow of change that is the natural state of our life (our brains evolved in the open plains, not in the context of static, squared-off rooms).[27] When you feel particularly stuck—in a terrible mood, hateful thought pattern, or painful relationship dynamic—just do it! As Kierkegaard once wrote, "I have walked myself into my best thoughts and I know of no thought so burdensome that one cannot walk away from it."

Forward Framing

Most dispute resolution processes, whether formal or informal, spend an inordinate amount of time deeply examine grievances, frustrations, and other problems at hand. This makes sense because it is likely that those very things brought you there in the first place. But the research on locomotion versus assessment seems to indicate that this is a good recipe for getting even more stuck. Starting off in this critical mode will likely set the tone and trajectory for the remaining process (see new beginnings discussion in chapter 3). So here's a novel idea; how about starting with a discussion of where you all ideally want to go? What is the best-case scenario for you and the other disputants if you are able to work your way through the current tensions? Where do you hope you will all end up?

Elise Boulding, one of the founding pioneers of the field of peace and conflict studies, developed a method for working with conflicting groups that begins by locomoting to the future.[28] The method first came about in the late 1970s as Boulding began to realize that peace activists working to bring about a nonviolent world often had no idea how a world in which armies had disappeared would function. How could they work to bring about something they could not even see in their imaginations? She developed a process called *future imaging*, asking participants to envision their situation thirty years into the future when they would find themselves living together peacefully with members of the out-group. She would walk them through exercises that encouraged imaginative exploration of "how things worked" in that future before asking them to look back to the present and imagine how all the peaceableness had come about. The workshop culminated with personal commitments to actions in the present to help bring about the future participants had pictured.

Some of the experiments on the effects of locomotion versus assessment also do something like this to "prime" or ready participants for either a movement focus or an evaluative one.[29] For assessment, participants are asked to reflect on questions like "think of some occasion in which you compared yourself with other people" or "think of some occasion in which you critiqued work done by others or yourself." For locomotion, participants are asked to "think of a time when you finished one project and could not wait long before you started a new one" or "think of a time when you felt excited just before you were about to reach a goal."

Rather than beginning a hard conversation or mediation with "tell me about your conflict and about what an idiot this guy is and why he makes your life so miserable," try taking another tack. Perhaps something like this: "In a while, we are going to talk about all the problems and tensions that brought you here. But first, it would be really helpful to know that if this conversation went really well and you both left here feeling proud of yourselves and satisfied with what came of this and with an increased sense of respect for one another, what might that look like? What would the best possible result of this process look like?" Alternatively, if the disputants have been in a family, friend, or work relationship and have a long history, begin by exploring past solutions: "Please think of a time in the past when you had difficulties with one another but somehow found a way to talk them out or get past them. Has that ever happened? If so, please share with me how it transpired and how you were able to move through it."

These small but hopeful "nudge" tactics are not going to make deep problems go away. But they might encourage us to dip our foot back into a latent positive attractor for the relationship that we haven't visited for a while and remember or imagine that it is possible. If done early in the session, these thoughts can help to trigger the disputants needs and desires to move on and move through this difficult patch.

Seeing and Feeling the Flow

As hard as it is for most of us to get our heads around the high degree of complexity of our political divisions (recall our superstorm of polarization), it is just as difficult to make sense of their temporal dynamics—how their many elements interact to affect how they flow, develop, settle into patterns, and change over time.[30] Yet this is critical to understanding them (which is what the seven crude laws of nonlinear change are all about). Remember that the deep structures of attractor landscapes are not made up solely of the distinct elements of assumptions, values, rules, and norms. These structures are also largely determined by the flow of influence between the elements—how these different aspects align and feed or constrain each other over time.

In chapter 6, I discussed the value of complexity mapping for reintroducing nuance into understanding our more wicked problems and increasing the cognitive complexity of the disputants with regard to the context of their conflict. Mapping techniques can also help us begin to better see and understand the flow of some of the cycles that are affecting our divisions. Sketching how certain elements are increasing each other (e.g., when spikes in our anxiety increase our political news intake, which further heightens our anxiety) or decreasing each other (such as when listening to thoughtful speakers from the other side of the aisle discuss their views of contested issues lessens your animosity for the other group and increases the odds you will seek out their opinions again) can help us locate levers for change.

Beyond the cognitive benefits of mapping, I want to highlight the fact that the *physical* nature of joint mapping—of getting up with markers and whiteboard or flipcharts and together discussing and sketching an understanding of the problem set—can also change the conflict dynamic. Typically, we ask disputants to sit in chairs on either side of a table and talk through conflicts. This makes it much more likely that each disputant sees the other side as the problem—thus personalizing it. With mapping, disputants are tasked with cocreating their shared understanding of a complex set of elements that feed the problem by physically drawing key factors and connecting the dots on a surface in front of them. This process promotes both synchronization and collaboration through moving together,[31] allowing the disputants to externalize the problem onto the flipchart or wall, thereby decreasing personalization. We have found that these joint action mapping processes can be game changers when groups are mired in a state of mutual contempt.[32] Try it!

Finally, seeing dynamics is believing. One of the most powerful benefits of employing computer simulations and visualizations to help us understand complex polarization dynamics is that they allow us to see how they evolve over time. Tools like cellular automata or other visualization tools or games can help us understand the strange ways complex systems do and do not change in time.*

Traveling Strange

In the mid-1800s, Mark Twain traveled across Europe, eventually publishing an autobiographical account of his experiences in *Innocents Abroad*. In it, he remarked on the potential impact of such journeys for building our trust in humankind. He wrote, "Travel is fatal to prejudice, bigotry, and narrow-mindedness, and many of our people need it sorely on these accounts. Broad, wholesome, charitable views of men and things cannot be acquired by vegetating in one little corner of the earth all one's lifetime."

The positive effects of foreign travel on people's openness to experience and tolerance for difference has long been a truism, but little research had been done on this until quite recently. One project looked at the effects of studying abroad on changes in students' personalities and found that it was associated with increases in two of the "Big Five" personality traits—openness to experience and agreeableness—and a decrease in a third trait, neuroticism.[33] A second project found even more evidence for the specific effects of locomotion during travel. Over five studies, the authors found that the effect of "breadth of foreign travel" (number of countries traveled) but not the depth of experiences (amount of time spent traveling) produced greater levels of generalized trust.[34] This is an

* See https://www.washingtonpost.com/news/wonk/wp/2015/04/23/a-stunning-visualization-of-our-divided-congress/. Also, go to https://ncase.me/ to play with a series of fun visualization games displaying nonlinear change.

important finding because the effects of more extensive forms of travel not only improve travelers' attitudes toward the people they visit but also seems to generalize to a more comprehensive sense of trust in humans. All of these foreign travel-induced effects—increased openness, agreeableness and trust, and decreased neuroticism—make for more effective and constructive conflict resolution.

So how far out is the notion of red-blue student and citizen exchanges, or travel packages to the foreign territories and cultures of urban versus rural America? Not so much. The nonprofit group Etgar 36 currently does just this with American teens.[35] Their mission is to develop the political voices of American youth by taking them on journeys across the country and exposing them to different cultures, ideas, and methods of argumentation. To date more than eighteen thousand adults and teens have "gotten on the bus." Might this be a blueprint for moving America forward?

Mandating Locomotion

When Botswana first achieved independence from the British in 1966, they were worried.[36] Having watched other African nations recently emerge from colonialist rule (Mali, Congo, and Nigeria), many of them finding that their new borders had been sketched out on the back of a cocktail napkin by the former colonial powers, they feared the worst. These haphazard renderings of their new boundaries often cut through long-established ethnic territories and forced different groups together that were less than friendly with each other. Too often this resulted in deadly ethnic clashes and civil wars.

The same was essentially true for Botswana. The new configuration of lands put together by their former rulers included some twenty different tribes[37] (a term used for these groups by the Botswanans), many with different languages and traditions, including the Kalanga in the north, the Bakwena south of the Kalahari Desert, and the Bangwato in the center. This made the new leadership very nervous. What could they possibly do to try to head off what seemed like inevitable ethnic violence?

They did three things. First, they decided to only teach English and Setswana in the schools to establish common channels of communications between the groups. Second, they offered a parcel of land to anyone who requested it, with the stipulation that whatever existed or was discovered beneath the surface of the land belonged to everyone (i.e., the government). This helped to mitigate tensions over scarce resources such as diamond reserves. Third, and most critical, they implemented a mandatory policy of *employment location transfers* for all civil servants—doctors, teachers, engineers, and public administrators—which made up the largest percentage of the workforce in the country. Every few years, these workers would be reassigned to other regions of the nation. They would need to pull up stakes, move, take on a new position, and settle into a new community, typically with a different dominant tribe. In other words, they were forced to move and mix with strangers.

The policy of location transfers does have its downsides. It is often experienced as inconvenient and frustrating, and for a while it actually split families up—although this aspect of the initiative has been changed. On the upside, this policy has been heralded as one of the main reasons Botswana has been able to avoid ethnic violence and establish one of Africa's least corrupt, most prosperous, and best functioning democracies. The intentional mixing of civil servants in and out of different historically tribal areas seems to have provided sufficient levels of meaningful intergroup contact and cross-ethnic bonding to make ethnic violence much less likely.

Implementing a similar labor policy or law seems farfetched in the United States today, but the idea is solid. If we get serious about resetting our partisan divide and establishing a more unified and functional democracy, how might we institutionalize a more fluid set of social structures that encourages partisan, racial, and ethnic mixing?

One way would be to modify and support the CORPS Act (Cultivating Opportunity and Response to the Pandemic Through Service Act), a bipartisan bill recently before Congress that is jointly sponsored by senators Chris Coons (D-DE) and Roger Wicker (R-MS). The bill proposes doubling the number of AmeriCorps positions this year to 150,000, providing a total of 600,000 opportunities for unemployed youth to assist struggling communities. The initiative could stipulate the need for these workers to travel across our political divide and serve communities in areas quite different from their own, moving from urban to rural and from rural to urban. Building in practices of locomotion would be less demanding than the Botswana transfer policy, but it could begin to reintroduce the interpartisan contact currently missing in the United States.

Locomoting of all types clearly helps to open us and mitigate our more selfish, tribal, and ethnocentric tendencies. One type of motion—joint synchrony—has been found to be particularly useful for moving us forward together.

THE SYNCHRONIZATION STORY

Two of the most original and innovative researchers I have ever had the honor of working with are Robin Vallacher and Andrzej Nowak. Since Kurt Lewin, they have been the two people most responsible for bringing the considerable insights and breakthroughs from physics, applied mathematics, and complexity science to the world of psychology—and to my world of peace and conflict studies. Both social psychologists, they are close colleagues who have worked together productively for decades and whose work has been highly influential across a variety of disciplines, including business, technology, sports, and the arts. They also have one of the strangest working rituals of any team of scientists I know.

Their work day often goes something like this. After massive amounts of coffee (Nowak was at sixteen cups a day at one point), they meet in the late morning in one of their offices at Florida Atlantic University in Boca Raton to begin or resume work on some lofty project. Vallacher, an inspired writer, is soon sitting at a desk with his computer while Nowak prowls around the room or lays down on the floor of the office, speaking aloud and spinning long, often meandering life-meets-science narratives. On occasion Nowak dozes off for a bit, but Vallacher continues typing unabated. Together their team makes progress in this manner until their energy or insight lags, or until they find themselves stymied by a problem in their work. Then they head out for a walk.

Once outside, these scientists wander around campus or town, chatting about their lives and trying out different takes on the work problem at hand. At different points in the conversation, Nowak will stop and exclaim something along the lines of "That's it! Brilliant!" Vallacher, who is deeply steeped in the details of a vast body of psychological literature, will often push the issue and challenge the solution that emerged. And so they continue on in their journey until they both reach a shared understanding of a solution to their conundrum that feels right. Then they grab more coffee and head back to one of their offices to start the cycle again. It should come as no surprise to learn that Vallacher and Nowak have studied and mathematically modeled synchronization extensively.[38]

Synchronization is simply the operation or activity of two or more things at the same time or rate. Clocks, computers, engines, and factory lines are often synchronized. *Interactional synchrony* is defined as coordinated movement during a social interaction that is matched in form (style) and time (rhythm).[39] Dancers, emergency room medical teams, orchestras, restaurant kitchen staff, and Olympic synchronized swim teams all need to get in sync to function effectively. So do lovers, fencers, parents and infants, tennis partners, and negotiators. These groups often need to coordinate their actions, but the better ones eventually move in sync. These phases of people moving together in time and space have proven to have considerable influence on how the individuals involved think, feel, and behave, and on success in their relationships, outcomes, and capacities to work out their differences.

Research has shown that interactional synchrony is good for many aspects of effective conflict management. For instance, it has been shown to increase interpersonal affiliation, connectedness, self-disclosure, and rapport with others.[40] In fact, one study showed that experimentally inducing experiences of synchrony (through enacting finger-tapping communication tasks in pairs) increased interpersonal empathy in both autistic and nonautistic subjects.[41] Neuroimaging studies have also shown that synchronizing with others activates regions of the brain related to self-other information processing, which has been shown to be associated with increased concerns for a partner's outcomes.[42] This has led to considerable research on *mirror neurons*, which are the synaptic connections in our brain that fire when we act and when we observe someone else performing the same action.[43] These are believed to be the underlying neural mechanisms responsible for our basic experiences of empathy.

Synchronization between disputants was one of the more intriguing findings from our studies of difficult conversations.[44] When dyads had conversations over moral differences that went well, we found that these pairs evidenced higher levels of *emotional synchronization* (feeling similar emotions at similar times) than pairs that resulted in negative outcomes. It was interesting that the emotions of the more contentious pairs were not negatively correlated—such as feeling the opposite of each other—they were simply uncorrelated, out of sync. This finding is consistent with those of other conflict lab studies that have found similar differences of *emotional synchrony and inertia*, or decoupling of emotions, evident in happy versus unhappily married couples,[45] and top-performing versus subpar work teams.[46]

Most relevant to our focus, however, is the finding that *physically moving in sync* with others has been shown to enhance cooperation, prosocial behavior, and the ability to achieve joint goals, and it also increases our compassion and helping behavior.[47] One study showed that walking in sync with a group of people made them more willing to make personal sacrifices that benefited the group.[48] In fact, some of the effects of synchrony on cooperation and helping have been evident in research with participants as young as four years old and infants![49]

The relationship between synchrony and conflict is a bit trickier. Studies have found that strangers who meet and launch into debate or argumentation automatically experience less synchrony—much like the more contentious dyads in our Difficult Conversations Lab.[50] Furthermore, face-to-face negotiations have been found to impair cooperative behavior and induce the tendency to use pressure and domination tactics, such as staring down the opponent.[51] However, these studies were all conducted with the participants seated.

Things start to look better for synchrony and conflict once people get up and start moving together. When people walk side by side, they often develop greater attentional synchrony, or attention to the same things at the same time, which can help shift their perspectives from egocentric and selfish to allocentric and shared—something found to also increase cooperation.[52] In fact, research in evolutionary biology has found that physical synchrony between people promotes heightened endorphin release within them, which enhances group bonding.[53]

Research on getting up and moving together has shown positive and robust effects on some aspects of conflict management (matched emotions, positive rapport, bonding, shared concerns, and so on). However, research on the direct effects of synchrony on conflict has, to my knowledge, not yet been conducted. Nevertheless, these findings strongly suggest that moving together could help to create the conditions for dislodging groups from deep divisions.

PRACTICE: GET IN SYNC

When you go walking with a group of people or hit a tennis ball with a partner or ride bikes adjacent to each other, it is quite easy to synchronize. In fact, studies have shown that if instructed to move out of sync with a partner while walking or swinging your legs together when seated next to each other, it is quite hard to remain out of sync. We are somehow pulled back into parallel movement.[54] Getting in sync with someone is tapping into our natural inclination to be in rhythm with adjacent others, whether we like it or not. Here are a few illustrations of how this tactic might be used to alter the dynamics of our conflicts.

A Walk in the Woods

In the late summer of 1982, two nuclear arms negotiators, American Paul H. Nitze and Soviet Yuli A. Kvitsinsky, left a formal session on arms control talks in Geneva and took a private, unofficial walk in a wooded area outside the city.[55] Walking along a path in this more serene setting, they were eventually able to achieve a breakthrough in a stalemate in the talks.[56] This informal practice of strolling in nature has begun to be integrated to some degree in other types of dispute resolution and peacebuilding, particularly those that require deeper thinking, healing, and repair.[57] Unfortunately, this simple adjustment is sorely underutilized.

Nevertheless, the combined findings from the studies on both locomotion and synchronization strongly indicate that you should make a good-faith effort to incorporate walking into your conflict management portfolio whenever possible. Whether it involves tensions with a sibling, schoolmate, or senator, the potential benefits from walking together–particularly when moving smoothly, in nature, and side by side–have been shown repeatedly to help trigger synchrony and deliver various individual, interpersonal, and group benefits. A recent study found that even walking alone, before engaging in a tense encounter, can help to mitigate the negative feelings and perceptions that often accompany such alienating encounters.[58] So what, really, do you have to lose? As it is written in the Bible: "Can two walk together, except they be agreed?"

Cooking Together for Peace

I once spoke on a panel with a mediation colleague of mine who claimed she never practiced mediation without preparing food together. An African American and highly accomplished dispute resolution professional, Janice Tudy-Jackson said that the first, most powerful mediator she had ever experienced was her grandmother (the family matriarch) who took it upon herself to mend every torn or broken fence in the family. She was formidable. When a problem would arise within the ranks of their large family, her grandmother would call the affected subgroup together, and they would all help prepare a feast before sitting down and listening to the issues under contention. Tudy-Jackson said that the tight sense of community that comes with collectively preparing a meal has continued to be a staple in her work, especially with her more difficult, protracted cases.

Others have followed in this grandmother's footsteps. Conflict Café and Conflict Kitchen are both initiatives that show how food can unite and inform.[59] Many involve chefs and cuisine from war-torn countries in an attempt to destigmatize how Americans view these lands. With a dozen chapters across the country, Make America Dinner Again is a direct attempt to unite reds and blues in the United States by inviting people to shared potluck meals and sit together and dine to build understanding and move forward together. These usually small dinners feature respectful conversation, guided activities, and delicious food shared among six to ten guests who have differing political viewpoints and "America's best interests at heart."[60]

Imagine the unifying potential of countless other synchronizing activities: gathering across partisan lines to repair or build homes for indigent families, running in a 5K event together to raise funds for COVID-19 affected families, or volunteering in mixed-partisan groups to bolster the resources for teachers and administrators in struggling schools. Can you identify a community need that will encourage people to get up and work physically together and help trigger the virtuous psychosocial cycles that can come from it?

A Walk in the World

One of the most striking and ambitious examples of transporting synchronized peacebuilding is an initiative called Abraham's Path.[61] Founded in 2006 by William Ury, coauthor of *Getting to Yes*, it is a project aimed at building unity in one of the most historically divisive places on earth—the Middle East. The project researched and established a walking trail and cultural route across ten nations in the region that retrace the steps of the historic journey of the family of Abraham, the common patriarch of the Abrahamic religions—including Judaism, Christianity, and Islam—and considered by many to be one of the most important sources of common heritage of all these groups. The path runs from Abraham's birthplace in Urfa in southeastern Turkey to the site of his tomb in Hebron in the West Bank of Palestine.

The idea for the project is both simple and inspired—to encourage humans from around the world (in particular Jews, Muslims, and Christians) to walk the path of Abraham shoulder to shoulder with others in mixed groups, experience the extraordinary hospitality of the many families, groups, and cultures along the way, and in doing so break down stereotypes and other barriers to peace and bring positive attention and economic development to the region. The trails connect 134 different communities across 1,204 kilometers (750 miles) of trail, and attracts approximately seven thousand pilgrims (synchronized locomotors) a year. It has also inspired other multidenominational walks between mosques, churches, and synagogues throughout cities across the globe, including in the United States.

The connection to addressing our current political divide is straightforward. One could fund and organize bipartisan groups to travel together to Abraham's Path and walk and learn together. I could also imagine a Jane Addams, Abraham Lincoln, or Martin Luther King Jr. walk that celebrated the life and legacy of our own American legends and sources of national unity.

A Unity March for America

Finally, the many benefits of synchrony and locomotion could be harnessed and combined with the purposefulness and greater sense of belonging that many Americans might experience from a National Unity March for America. This could entail one national march in Washington, D.C. or thousands of local marches around the country aimed at bringing red and blue Americans together in motion in support of solidarity through synchrony. One recent study found that when members of different out-groups simply walk together—even without having direct contact or speaking with one another—it leads to significant reductions in both explicit and implicit prejudice and stereotyping toward members of the out-groups (both the specific out-groups and out-groups in general).[62] Such is the transformative power of shared movement.

This chapter is meant to get you moving. The positive effects of locomotion and synchronization for connecting people and groups are clearly evident. They provide a set of unusual levers and activities for prying open your mind and experience, and that of others around you, in service of building momentum for all of us finding a way out.

9
ADAPT—SEEK EVOLUTION FOR REVOLUTION

THE LOGIC OF FAILURE

Imagine that you are the prime minister of Israel chairing a lively meeting of foreign dignitaries when you are handed an urgent memo by your aide that reads: "A Palestinian suicide bomber just detonated an explosive packet with ball bearings aboard a Jerusalem bus . . . 18 are dead, including children . . . more than 100 are injured. . . . Israeli officials are reacting with fury and frustration . . . responsibility claimed by members of the Islamic Jihad."

Visibly shaken, your aide then whispers to you, "Prime minister, we await your orders."

This is how it begins.

In a computer lab located in a sublevel basement at World Bank Group headquarters in Washington, D.C., twenty of the bank's more experienced lawyers, managers, and economists have been facing this decision and inadvertently escalating violence and triggering catastrophic war in the Middle East. One by one, the computer monitors of each of these peace and conflict resolution specialists light up with explosions or flash warnings of other forms of humanitarian disaster. The frustration in the room is palpable as these usually competent, well-intentioned leaders make decisions and commit to actions in the region that typically lead to increased misery and suffering of Israeli and Palestinian civilians and ultimately result in their own political demise. At some point, these decision makers begin to spring from their computer monitors, one by one, and exit the lab, visibly agitated. One exclaims, "This is impossible."

These twenty individuals were involved in a series of studies we conducted on decision making in tense, complex, high-risk environments. In the studies, participants played a "microworld" game called PeaceMaker, a compelling, user-friendly simulation designed to replicate the extraordinary challenges of decision making in the context of the ongoing Israeli-Palestinian conflict.[1] The players are asked to take the role of the Israeli prime minister or Palestinian president and to work toward de-escalating and resolving the conflict in a forty-five-minute session. The game begins with news of the bombing, and the participants must then choose how to respond in the situation, selecting from seventy-six possible decisions that fall under the categories of *security*, *political*, and *infrastructure/aid*. They are given no indication of which decision is most appropriate, although their stated objective is to try to increase both their Palestinian and Israeli public "approval scores" simultaneously to stabilize the region (if either score goes too low, war breaks out and the game is eventually terminated).

When we first began using PeaceMaker for our research, I asked the members of my lab—some of the best and brightest graduate students at Columbia University—to try it out. Their results were surprising.

> "I went to war in under five minutes" confessed Kyong, my lab coordinator who held a master's degree in international relations.
>
> "You made it five minutes?!," shouted Regina, a psychology PhD student. "The game shut me out after two minutes!"
>
> "It made me crazy," admitted Chris, a master's student in conflict resolution and former COO of a family business. "After the bombing, I just panicked and sent in the military. It went downhill from there."

These responses are typical of those of the hundreds of participants in our studies. Despite the fact that we eventually set the game to its lowest level of challenge, and that these were all individuals with considerable experience and expertise in constructive conflict management and peacemaking, the complex nature of the game left them stymied.

> I felt really lost in this situation. It felt impossible to know how to have a positive impact.

No, the PeaceMaker game is *not* impossible to play. In fact, a handful of participants in our trials did rather well their first time through the game, and others learned to navigate it fairly quickly. But the majority of intelligent, well-meaning do-gooders in our research wreaked havoc on the simulated people in the region. Even after several attempts at playing the game, the logic behind it eluded many, and the virtual carnage continued.

Unfortunately, these results are common and are typical for similar types of studies run with complex simulations in other domains, such as business, education, development, and government in which individuals face volatile, unpredictable, multifaceted problems. They also hold for studies of *actual* decision making under conditions of complexity, opacity, and uncertainty—*even when experts are involved*. Researchers across several studies found that under circumstances in which the relations between decisions and outcomes in a system are unclear, experts are no more effective at decision making than novices. The noted psychologist Philip Tetlock found this in a study with 284 expert political and economic forecasters from media, academia, government, and prominent international organizations.[2] He found that even the most successful experts were only able to predict about 20 percent of the outcomes across a range of complex domestic (U.S.) and world affairs. Tetlock concluded, "the average forecaster was roughly as accurate as a dart throwing chimpanzee."

Why were my doctoral students and the other experts so bad at navigating these cloudy problems? Of course, it's complicated. But one critical factor is *how* they tended to think about affecting change in these situations, and particularly their capacities to learn from their inevitable mistakes, adjust, and play the long game. In other words, how *adaptive* they were in response to failure.

THE E^4 VORTEX

One of the things we have learned consistently from decades of research on decision making is that humans are pretty bad at it. The more complex the problem, and the further out in time we attempt to make judgments, the worse we fare. This has been well-documented by cognitive scientists the likes of Jerome S. Bruner in the 1940s, James G. March and Herbert A. Simon in the 1950s, Daniel Kahneman and Amos Tversky starting in the 1970s, and more recently Dietrich Dörner and Phillip E. Tetlock. These scholars and hordes of others spent their careers documenting the various flavors of errors, biases, shortcuts, and just plain follies most of us seem destined to succumb to when solving problems.[3]

The short backstory on *why* we humans are such crummy decision makers comes down to what I call the *E^4vortex*: the tyranny of efficiency, existence, esteem, and environment to the fourth power. *Efficiency* stands for the fact that although Homo sapiens have impressive brains when compared to most other earthly creatures, our equipment is old, having mostly developed during our early hunter-gatherer days in Africa, and slow, so we have a hard time keeping up with the increasing pace of the times. As a result, we are hardwired to take cognitive short-cuts much of the time to improve the efficiency of our processing, which skews the information we receive. On top of this, we also have a hard time processing and remembering even this limited amount of information.

Existence speaks to the simple fact that humans have a terribly hard time thinking about, planning for, or responding to situations that do not exist. When we face new, unexpected events, outcomes, or consequences that we have never seen before, or even entertained, we don't know what to do. Before 9/11, few of us ever imagined that a jet airplane with a fuselage full of fuel could be weaponized into a missile with the capacity to take down a ninety-four-story building. Our capacity to envision and respond to it—even though a scenario for it was provided in an intelligence briefing to our top decision makers months before—proved to be an insurmountable challenge.[4] In this way, we are captives of our current reality.

Esteem points to the fact supported by much research that when choosing between our need to feel positive about ourselves (self-esteem) and our groups (collective self-esteem and belonging) and our needs for accurate information about the decisions we face, we will almost always choose feeling good over accuracy.[5] Our emotional and affiliation needs typically trump the truth.

Finally, *environment* is simply shorthand for the multitude of situational demands—complexity, volatility, opacity, unfamiliarity, time pressure, threat, extreme physical conditions, and so on—that stress and impair our already challenged cognitive capacities. The more of these conditions and the more extreme they are—a common occurrence today—the worse off we are. When the effects of efficiency × existence × esteem × environment (E^4) are interacting and multiplying the effects of one another, watch out! We're lucky if we can decide which shoes to wear in the morning.

BUMBLING IN BAMBERG

Some of the most important research relevant to our challenges and capacities to make effective decisions when facing cloud problems comes from the German psychologist, Dietrich Dörner, out of his lab in the Institute of Theoretical Psychology at the Otto-Friedrich University in Bamberg.[6] For decades, Dörner studied decision making in complex environments involving computer-based "simulated communities" that he created, such as a fictional West African village (Tanaland) or a small British township (Greenvale). Typically, he would bring research participants into his lab, inform them that they would have ample resources and complete authority over the inhabitants of the communities, and then task them with promoting the well-being of the population and the surrounding region. The participants were instructed that they could essentially do anything without opposition–impose hunting regulations, fertilize fields, irrigate, electrify villages, improve medical care, introduce birth control, and so on–at six different time intervals over the course of the simulation. Dörner would then observe the participants' decision-making processes over a period of twenty years in the life of the computer simulation–years went by in minutes but took approximately two hours in the lab.

A typical lab scenario with Tanaland, the simulated African village, would go like this. Participants would first review information about the situation in the community, which included conditions such as drought, infestations of various creatures, poor medical care, and a declining population. He or she would then set out to improve life in Tanaland by, for example, increasing the food supply with new tractors, fertilization, and irrigation and setting up vaccination programs and medical clinics to improve medical care. As a result, the food supply in Tanaland would improve, and over time the number of children would grow and the number of deaths decline. Life expectancy increased; problem solved. Except that long about the eighty-eighth month of the one-hundred-twenty-month experiment, the population would suddenly grow exponentially and outrun the food supply, which would trigger an irreversible famine that would eventually kill off the community's livestock, deplete its water table, and lead to a stark increase in the mortality rate of the local people. In other words, a catastrophe.

These types of outcomes were pretty standard in Dörner's research. Existing problems would be "solved" by participants with insufficient consideration given to the *unintended consequences* the solutions might create, which would then sneak up on the decision makers and undermine the community. This, unfortunately, is not an anomaly in the development and peacebuilding worlds. Rather, it is the age-old story of well-intentioned "fixes that failed."[7]

Dörner's program of research found that most decision makers working on cloudy problems typically commit a standard set of decision-making errors:

- They act without sufficient prior analysis of the situation, or with insufficient clarification and prioritization of their goals.
- They fail to anticipate the side effects or long-term repercussions of their actions.
- They assume that the absence of immediately obvious negative effects means their measures have worked (Surprise!).
- They let overinvolvement in pet subprojects blind them to emerging needs and other important changes on the ground.
- They become prone to cynical reactions like blaming the victims or their collaborators once their best attempts at solutions repeatedly fail.

Ouch. But it gets worse.

GOING BALLISTIC

One of the major traps that Dörner observed the problem solvers falling into when their decisions backfired was what he termed "ballistic behavior," or what many of us call doubling-down on the same bad solution.

For example, in a study similar to the Tanaland case, teams of people were asked to promote community well-being by distributing development aid over a twenty-year period to a (simulated) region in Africa, and to track its effects on the local people, the Dagus. In this simulation, a crisis would occur at the ten-year mark when a neighboring state would boldly occupy and lay claim to about 30 percent of the Dagus's territory. In addition to the usual measures, the researchers tracked how often the participants "controlled" their interventions or inquired about how effective they had been in their previous trials.

The results were scary. First, even before the crisis broke, participants only requested information on the efficacy of their past interventions 30 to 50 percent of the time. The majority of time they would just implement a strategy repeatedly and let it ride without questioning it. But once the crisis hit, controlled inquires dropped to less than 10 percent, which means that more than 90 percent of the time participants were making unexamined (ballistic) decisions and never looking back.

Equally as scary was the consistent tendency for participants to respond to the "crisis" in this humanitarian development simulation with extreme, morally questionable responses. The researcher conducting the study described them this way:

> Decisions to purchase weapons and to provide military training to a population with no previous military experience were reached with relative unanimity. To raise funds for these additional expenses, the participants then decided they needed a major increase in yields from both field crops and from cattle raising. And to this end they radically increased the use of fertilizers and pesticides and drew more heavily on the groundwater supply. Conscription of some of the male population meant a reduction in the workforce, and participants tried to compensate by demanding more work from the remaining workers and especially from women and children. And this measure was frequently accompanied by food rationing.

Of course, a crisis such as an occupation of territory in a nation we are trying to help would challenge the best of us. But these were decision makers working on a *development aid scenario*, who uniformly reacted to the crisis by deciding to prepare this pastoral, seminomadic community for war, which often triggered a vicious, runaway, antidevelopment cycle.

After the simulation, when participants were asked to rate each of the actions they took by the degree to which they "deviated from the participant's moral and ethical standards," the results were staggering. The moral deviations jumped from relatively few during the precrisis phase to many in response to the crisis. This is not a surprising finding for a group of humans thrust into the E^4 vortex. But, again, their assigned mission was *to promote the well-being of the people and the region*, but their reactions led to the exact opposite.

What can we learn from this (so far depressing) research on decision making in complex environments? First, it offers a vivid example of Crude Law 7, the fact that the well-intentioned actions of people, groups, and institutions in complex systems almost always have effects that are unanticipated or unintended. In these studies, Dörner's lab participants, much like my PhD students and my journalist colleague from *Die Zeit*, were trying their best to be helpful, but often they did so in a manner that backfired and made matters worse. As Dörner cautions,

> It is far from clear whether "good intentions plus stupidity" or "evil intentions plus intelligence" have wrought more harm in the world. People with good intentions usually have few qualms about pursuing their goals. As a result, incompetence that would have otherwise remained harmless often becomes dangerous, especially as incompetent people with good intentions rarely suffer the qualms of conscience that sometimes inhibit the doings of competent people with bad intentions. The conviction that our intentions are unquestionably good may sanctify the most questionable means.[8]

Alas, the research suggests that we often, through no intentional fault of our own, contribute to making bad cloud problems worse.

Second, the studies suggest that the considerable challenges we face to effective decision making in cloudy situations seem to just get worse over time. As our proclivities to make bad decisions mingle with the other malignant dynamics of the situations we face (furious emotions, exacerbating interactions, unexpected negative outcomes, etc.), we tend to double-down on the same bad decisions time and again, and the worse things become, the less likely we are to reflect on or revise our responses. This appears to have been acutely evident in the Trump administration's disastrously incompetent respond to the COVID-19 pandemic. On top of this, when a crisis hits, we also tend to drift away from our usual moral standards and employ more contentious and extreme tactics—a great recipe for making matters horrific.

Dörner sums it up,

> What kind of psychology do we find here? We find a tendency under time pressure, to apply overdoses of established measures. We find an inability to think in terms of nonlinear networks of causation—an inability, that is, to properly assess the side effects and repercussions of one's behavior. We find an inadequate understanding of exponential development, an inability to see that a process that develops exponentially will, once it has begun, race to its conclusion with incredible speed. These are all mistakes of cognition.[9]

Third, this research illustrates how confusing causes and effects can be in cloudy situations (Crude Law 6). Typically, we do X to achieve Y, but not here. When Dörner's participants increased the food supply and the quality of medical care in Tanaland, they saw a decrease in the mortality rate. But the game continued, and few foresaw that these new conditions would set off a slow motion, population growth time bomb that would throw the entire ecosystem into disarray. When Bastian Berbner, the *Die Zeit* reporter, brought the Trump foes together, they initially seemed to get along fine, much as he had anticipated. But late the second night, when they became comfortable enough with one another to get real, their pent up outrage spewed. When my students increased security measures after a violent incident in East Jerusalem, they didn't imagine that it would further fuel an underground insurgency that would erupt into worse violence down the road.

These types of delayed, nonlinear effects are both hard to predict and are to be expected when intervening in complex systems. Cloud problems are not finite problems but are *infinite problems*.[10] Unlike clock problems that tend to have more consistent rules and a beginning, middle, and end, these problems are ongoing, evolving relationships or situations with changing conditions and shifting rules and dynamics that require different types of responses. They require adaptation.

PRINCIPLE 6: ADAPT—SEEK EVOLUTION FOR REVOLUTION

This principle highlights one of the most important considerations when attempting to radically change an enduring pattern in our life: *time*. Let's remember our objective in these efforts—to find a way out of the sociopolitical quagmire we are stuck in that is satisfying and sustainable. Not only where we have been able to navigate through the more difficult moments, the hills and valleys of our landscape, but where we have reshaped their contours. Yes, we are probably eager to see an end to this toxic phase of our life. And yes, what we are seeking is a revolution of sorts, a complete turnaround or change in our deeper patterns of thinking, feeling, relating, and living.[11] But *how* we go about doing this is paramount. Some changes to conflict-filled relationships, such as lowering the current level of tension, are more immediately evident and achievable. But transforming the attractor landscape of the relationship in which we are experiencing the conflict takes time, persistence, and adaptation.

We live in an age of mounting impatience and immediate gratification and often expect quick fixes to the problems we face. When we are anxious, it can feel intolerable to have to wait. But building or rebuilding positivity and trust across significant ruptures takes considerable time. Many pundits today recommend that people just get together across our divides and talk it out. This will allow us to see that those on the other side are human too. But decades of research on the power of the *negativity effect*[12] and on the challenges of significant *relational repair*[13] tell us that this only works when the right conditions have been established. These conditions begin with allowing *sufficient time* for such encounters to

Principle 6: Adapt—Seek Evolution for Revolution

Addressing the immediate source of tension in a conflict—especially when it is heated or violent—typically gets most of our attention and resources. However, we have found that these effects are often short-lived with cloudy problems. In addition, the attractors driving and containing the tension are usually overlooked, and they change on a completely different time scale. Affecting sustained positive change in the nature of the relationships involved in enduring disputes entails responding to the current situation in a way that is mindful of both the immediate impact and the (perhaps unintended) consequences of today's actions for tomorrow relations.

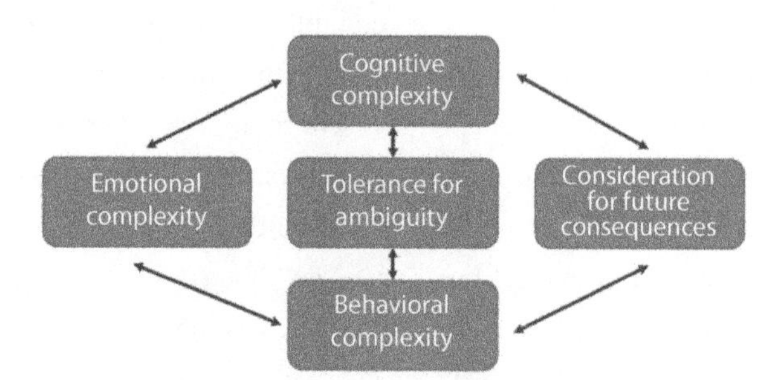

9.1 Five competencies for adapting to complex, long-term problems.

have a positive impact on the underlying scaffolding of the relationship. My German journalist colleague was very well-intentioned in his efforts to build bridges across the Trump chasm, but the idea that this could be done in a meeting or two was naive at best.

Adjusting our aspirations, expectations, and approach to be more consistent with how change processes unfold in complex situations with a long, difficult history is a muscle that can be retrained. Recognizing this fact can take some of the pressure off trying to force change, but change will take patience and perspective. Fortunately, the findings from our studies on decision making in these environments, combined with those of Dietrich Dörner, Phillip Tetlock, and others, have revealed some basic underlying competencies and tactics that are associated with better navigation of and adaptation to such cloudy, unpredictable conflicts (figure 9.1).

PRACTICE: ENHANCE YOUR ADAPTIVE COMPETENCIES

Our research involving the PeaceMaker simulation studied the effects of five basic competencies associated with more constructive responses to complex problems: tolerance for ambiguity, cognitive, emotional, and behavioral complexity, and consideration of future consequences (table 9.1).[14] We assessed participants on these aptitudes through standardized survey measures before they played the simulation in which they acted as political leaders working to navigate the complexities of the Israeli-Palestinian conflict to bring about a peaceful resolution.

9.1 Five complex adaptive competencies

Tolerance for Ambiguity	The ability to respond to unfamiliar, complex, uncertain, or otherwise ambiguous situations without becoming destabilized. More specifically, the degree to which people are comfortable with and even desire ambiguity.
Research has found tolerance for ambiguity related to:	• Being more effective in facilitating organizational change • Using more solution-oriented conflict management styles • Achieving more positive outcomes in negotiations • Prolonging conflicts less
Cognitive/Integrative Complexity	*Cognitive complexity* is the ability to differentiate among the multiple perspectives and sources of information in a situation.
	Integrative complexity is the ability to first differentiate, then integrate the information in a manner that informs decisions.
Research has found cognitive/integrative complexity related to:	• Increased leader success in highly turbulent environments • Successful revolutionary leadership • Greater likelihood of reaching mutually beneficial compromise agreements • Successful diplomatic communications • Employing cooperative tactics during negotiations
Emotional Complexity	The ability to experience and tolerate a broad range of positive and negative emotions simultaneously, and to differentiate subtle distinctions within specific categories of emotions. Emotional complexity also refers to the extent to which individuals can identify a range of positive and negative emotions in others.
Research has found emotional complexity related to:	• More work engagement • Increased creativity • More effectively leading organizational change • Engaging in more constructive conflict processes that have better outcomes
Behavioral Complexity	The capacity to employ a broad array of contrasting behaviors, integrating multiple, sometimes contrasting roles. This refers to both an individual's ability to identify a range of different roles required to engage effectively with complex systems and their ability to adaptively enact behaviors that fit different demands at different times.

(*continued*)

9.1 *(continued)*	
Research has found behavioral complexity related to:	• Leaders who are more likely to meet organizational demands • Higher evaluations of effectiveness on performance measures • More constructive conflict dynamics
Consideration for Future Consequences	The extent to which an individual considers future outcomes in the present moment, and the extent to which their current behaviors are shaped by awareness of potential consequences of their actions. The ability to balance short-term demands with long-term vision.
Research found consideration for future consequences related to:	• Lower aggression, more prosocial behaviors, increased academic achievement, and increased behaviors related to concern for the environment • Tendencies toward transformational leadership such as providing vision, setting high expectations, and adaptively providing support, scanning the environment more frequently to identify factors relevant to future outcomes, and developing more creative solutions to abstract problems • Propensities to choose more cooperative intergroup engagement strategies

Working with the designers of PeaceMaker at Carnegie-Mellon University, we were able to adjust their program to measure aspects of *how* participants played the game as well as how they scored. We found these five adaptive competencies to be significantly associated with more effectively navigating the challenges presented in the simulated Israeli-Palestinian conflict. Specifically, those who scored higher in *tolerance for ambiguity* (the ability to respond to ambiguous situations without becoming destabilized) made more decisions that enhanced trust between the disputing parties, made fewer decisions to increase only their own power or diminish the other's side's power or to obstruct the other's goal pursuits, and had a lower gap between Israeli and Palestinian approval scores (resulting in a lower likelihood of war).

People with higher levels of *cognitive complexity* (the ability to differentiate among multiple perspectives and sources of information) were able to enhance communications between the parties, were less likely to take violent action, and were more likely to employ multiple approaches to improving the situation rather than sticking to one approach. This strategy is associated with more efficacy in addressing complex problems. Participants with more *emotional complexity* (the ability to experience and tolerate a broad range of positive and negative emotions simultaneously) tended to identify a broader set of actors involved in the conflict, relied less on drastic measures that would result in longer-term negative impacts, and were generally more successful in navigating the game. Higher scores on *behavioral complexity* (the capacity to employ a broad array of necessary but contrasting behaviors) resulted in more communication enhancing decisions and more balanced scores between Israelis and Palestinians (lower likelihood of violent conflict). Those players who scored higher on *consideration for future consequences* tended to take more time between decisions and took less violent action during the initial ten turns of the game.

Finally, those higher in a combination of cognitive complexity, emotional complexity, and tolerance for ambiguity were found to employ more constructive actions throughout the simulation when compared to those lower in these competencies. Overall, these individuals focused their actions more on enhancing communication, building trust, coordinating efforts, and responding to the other party's (Palestinian or Israeli) needs. The findings suggest that these are some of the building blocks or skills that can be developed for increasing our capacity to navigate situations of tense, enduring conflict.

The lesson: when possible, get complicated, patient, and future oriented.[15]

PRACTICE: PLAN TO FAIL AND LEARN

Given the prevalence of imprecision and cloudiness in our world, Karl Popper argued that we must be careful to view our solutions to cloudy problems critically and vigorously, and to seek out and correct our inevitable errors. He quotes the physicist John Archibald Wheeler who said, "Our whole problem is to make the mistakes as fast as possible." This problem is solved by consciously adopting a perpetually critical attitude. Popper writes: "This, I believe, is the highest form so far of the rational attitude, or of rationality."[16]

Okay, but no one likes to fail. However, operating in the context of chronic, cloudy problems is in fact synonymous with failure. The question is not how to avoid failure in these cases but how to learn from it most effectively and with the fewest negative consequences. Here we turn to Carol Dweck, who knows a lot about failure. Dweck is professor of psychology at Stanford University (and another member of my dissertation committee) and has studied the vital role failure plays in learning and problem solving for decades, including the negative consequences of trying to avoid it. Early in her career, Dweck studied how children thought about intelligence.[17] In a series of groundbreaking studies, she identified a basic difference in children's unarticulated assumptions—or implicit theories—about intelligence. Some saw intelligence as a trait that people were born with—as an entity or a gift—something that you either had or you didn't (these children she referred to as "entity theorists," or those with "fixed mindsets"). Other's viewed intelligence as something that could be developed and nurtured incrementally and increased over time through effort and experience (these children she referred to as "incremental theorists," or those with "growth mindsets"). This difference had profound implications for how students would view failure and take up new problems.

When children view intelligence as a fixed trait, they tend to approach new problems with what Dweck called a *performance orientation*; they try to perform their best right out of the gate to demonstrate their intelligence. When children view intelligence as something they can grow and develop, they are significantly more inclined to approach new problems with a *mastery* or *learning orientation*; through trial and error they focus on learning as much about the problem as fast as possible so they can master it. Learning-oriented students tend to fare much worse when solving new problems in the short run, but they learn much more and master the problem more often than performance-oriented students. Obviously, the more complex the problem, the more likely it is that a learning approach will promote success and avert disaster. This finding has been supported by decades of research.[18]

Learning-oriented individuals focus more on increasing their competence and self-improvement, and tend to persist more and exert more effort in the face of difficult challenges than performers. Studies suggest that learners experience more difficult tasks as an opportunity to push their limits and grow their competencies, whereas performers experience them as dead-ends, indicating the limits of their intelligence.[19] It is important to note that this research began with a focus on the learning-performance distinction as a personality or person-centered variable, but it has also been shown through research and educational practices to be something that can be fostered and developed in people.[20]

One learning tactic is *failing smart.* Experienced computer gamers approach new game simulations in a manner very distinct from the rest of us. Rather than attempting to win the game (such as a performer would do), they attempt to fail at the game—as often and as quickly as possible—to better understand the underlying rules that are defining the game. In business and government, this often involves trial-testing new solutions or launching pilot projects, expecting failures as a means of learning how a system reacts to the test. This needs to be done with great caution in the context of social situations, but with a sound understanding of how nonlinear systems operate, we can learn to expect that our initiatives are likely to have strange effects: no effect whatsoever, no lasting effect, delayed effects, counterintuitive effects, and so on. Understanding this promotes humility and the need to be more vigilant and adaptive.

What might this look like in the context of working through a particularly stuck and troubled relationship or community dynamic? In the 1990s, Geoffrey Canada set out to stem the tide of urban violence in Harlem to "save" young black and brown youth from an epidemic of premature death and imprisonment. To accomplish this, he established a program for young people in the community that combined martial arts with conflict resolution training to provide youth with more self-discipline, a sense of security, and constructive negotiation and problem-solving skills. Two years after launching the program, Canada realized that it was a failure. He had been able to help a few individual adolescents here and there, but the vast majority were pulled back into a life of drugs and gangs and violence.

At this point Canada regrouped. Having now spent several years living and working in the Harlem community and getting to know the conditions on the ground more intimately, he realized that he had not sufficiently understood the immense complexity and power of the dropout, drug, violence, poverty landscape of the Harlem community in the 1990s. Initially he had believed that by providing individual youth with enough care, attention, and nonviolent problem-solving skills, they would thrive. He now realized that his good-faith attempt to address the problem of violence head on—by training the youth directly—could not begin to alter in any significant way the complex destructive dynamics that captured their lives. So he radically changed course.

Canada then launched the Harlem Children's Zone (HCZ), a revolutionary social experiment that combines educational, social, and medical services for children and families from birth through college that is woven into an interlocking web of support for an entire neighborhood. Recognizing the tightly linked nature of many urban problems that combine to constitute vicious cycles of desperation and violence, he and others in the HCZ began to work systemically within a one-block, then a twenty-four-, a sixty-, and ultimately a ninety-seven-block radius of the Harlem community to offer a comprehensive set of services. Parenting classes, school programs from pre-K through grade 12, college preparation programs, career counseling, community centers, legal and tax services for families, fitness programs and medical resources, and beyond were provided to help the most at-risk children thrive. This work involves a great deal of perseverance, adaptation, and resourcefulness on the part of the HCZ staff.

The story of Canada's involvement with urban school violence in Harlem is, in many ways, a story of trying different strategies and tactics, learning from success and failure, and adapting accordingly—even when adaptation meant wholesale changes in their approach. This is an example of an unusually ambitious, comprehensive, systemic approach to working upstream at the "margins" rather than directly targeting a problem (youth violence). Clearly, the pathways to efficacy for such strategies are tricky and often unknown, which makes it all the more important to work with them in highly adaptive, systemic, fail-smart ways.

PRACTICE: GET SMALL

Crude Law five on changing complex systems is based on the finding that patterns are sometimes significantly altered by changes to their most simple, basic rules of interaction. These often appear as small or even insignificant rules such as "Take a deep breath before you react to another's behavior in conflict," or "In an argument, try to identify some part of your opponent's logic that you feel is valid." Adopting small rule changes can lead to important, emergent changes over time.

John Gottman works with this idea in his Love Lab through *proximal change experiments*.[21] The goals are much smaller than those for traditional couples' therapy. The proximal goals are to change specific aspects of a couple's interaction patterns, such as how they enter or begin a conflict discussion or how they respond to their spouse's initial attempts at communication. The researchers then observe the effects of small adjustments on subsequent discussions between the couple and may use this information to reinforce the value of the change. By changing one smaller component of the system, the couple and their counselor can experiment with potential levers for improving the system, learning more about how the relationship responds to each adjustment over time. For a couple in distress, Gottman's group found that a brief intervention focusing initially on improving their friendship significantly reduced future negativity. Rather than committing to a lengthy and involved series of therapeutic interventions with an indeterminate outcome, couples were able to see small positive changes after just one session. Although the goals of these interventions are typically more modest, they are informed by knowledge of complex systems (such as the power of initial conditions and emergence) and target potentially significant "small" adjustments.

In one study conducted by Julia Babcock and colleagues at the University of Houston, the effects of proximal experiments on men with a history of intimate partner violence (IPV) were investigated. The researchers studied two conflict encounters between the men and their partners and explored whether small interventions aimed at instructing the men to substitute their immediate negative responses in conflicts with a more neutral one or encouraging men to find the "kernel of truth" of their female partner's argument with which they can agree could teach compromise and how to de-escalate an argument. Both the IPV men and their partners showed greater decreases in aggressive feelings in both skills-training conditions than IPV men in a time-out (control) condition.

The objective in proximal change experiments is to identify, test, and then make small adjustments to aspects of dysfunctional social interaction patterns that hold the potential to trigger a cascading process resulting in inhibiting a vicious and initiating a virtuous cycle. Like pushing the first domino in a chain of dominos, the first step is small but it can lead to broader-scale effects.[22] If even slight progress can be made, it will tend to instill positive emotions, motivation, and perceptions, and the more frequently people experience a sense of progress, the more likely they are to be inspired to endure over the long run.[23] The ultimate goal is to further reinforce or integrate a positive attractor into the relational system.

PRACTICE: ADAPT WITH A DISTANT VISION

The considerable research on decision making in the context of cloudy problems conducted in our lab, as well as in the labs of Dörner, Tetlock and others, suggests the value of a process of *adaptive decision making*, which is less familiar to most of us. Simply making more careful, systematic decisions (which is a highly uncommon experience itself) is a good start, and research now offers some specific recommendations for actions that have been shown to be especially fruitful in these more opaque contexts (figure 9.2).

Think and reflect critically on your own thinking, with guidance from these principles. Dörner's research found that people who were instructed to simply think

Standard Decision Making	Adaptive Decision Making
• Don't bother thinking about your thinking, what's the point – just do it!	• Think and reflect critically on your own thinking, with guidance from these principles.
• Set clear goals and objectives that are attainable and measurable.	• Identify your North star – a vision for the direction you hope to travel toward – to help navigate the journey.
• Focus – Don't get too distracted with too many different types of information on decisions.	• Seek out divergent sources of information on the problem and feedback on your ideas.
• Make many decisions early on in the analysis phase and then stay the course.	• Make many decisions, and then make more decisions over time to continually adapt.
• Keep it simple: Find the best action to take to achieve your goal and get on with it. First things first.	• Act in more complex ways: Take various actions to achieve the same goal.
• Address the squeaky wheels – the first aspects of the problem that arise.	• Identify where the real sources of the problems lie and address them first.
• Generate hypotheses about the effects of your actions and then apply them immediately.	• Generate hypotheses about the effects of your actions and then test them out before applying them.
• Take events at face value, sometimes their causes are quite simple.	• Ask more *why* questions to understand the causal network driving the problem.
• If you encounter a particularly difficult aspect of the problem, move on to other aspects.	• Remain focused on addressing the most difficult problems by trying various tactics to attend to them.
• Be ad hoc – allow yourself to follow the most currently salient events.	• Structure your behavior as much as possible, prioritize your actions if possible.

9.2 Models for standard and adaptive decision making.

about their decision-making processes—to reflect on their experiences in thinking about solving their more complex problems at each stage—were significantly better problem solvers. When they later trained people in systems' concepts (such as positive and negative feedback loops and nonlinear change), they found some slight effects but posited that the training simply boosted "verbal intelligence," giving participants a new language and terminology for unpacking their reflections. Ultimately, they found that some combination of training and reflection served the decision makers best. So reflect critically on your own decision-making processes, and make efforts to modify them as needed.

Identify your North Star—a vision for the direction you hope to travel toward—to help navigate your nonlinear journey. Problem solvers facing complex, daunting challenges (like resetting their lives!) benefit from spending sufficient time gaining an understanding of what it is they ultimately hope to achieve and the steps necessary to move in that direction. Because focused problem solving alone is never enough when dealing with cloudy situations, we have to learn to focus on how to influence the future of the system that gives rise to the problem. This entails learning to identify a *guiding star* (a goal that is a navigational tool to help you constantly adapt) by asking, "What is the broader relational or community change I would like to see in the long run?" Your ultimate end goal should be defined in terms of a healthier system (e.g., less toxicity in my day, relationship, life).

Seek out divergent (complex) sources of information on the problem and feedback on your ideas. One of the more interesting findings from Philip Tetlock's research on the Good Judgment Project,[24] created with the Central Intelligence Agency to identify superior forecasters of future events, was the quality of the networks that the superforcasters evidenced. These exceptional decision makers tended to have developed broad networks of intelligent friends and colleagues who held opinions and views that were very divergent from their own. These contrary individuals proved to be important sources of corrective feedback when trying to make forward forecasts—both in terms of shaping a more nuanced understanding of the details of the challenges and in anticipating the probabilities of consequences of certain choices.

Make many decisions, and then make more decisions over time to continually adapt. Both Dörner's research and our studies on the PeaceMaker simulation found that the most effective decision makers in complex contexts not only tended to assess a situation and set a course, but they continually adapted and adjusted their decisions, staying open to feedback to reconsider and alter their course as needed. They were found to make more, not fewer, decisions as their plans unfolded over time. They also actively investigated the *why* behind events, the causal links that made up the networks of causation in their community. In other words, they discovered more possibilities for enhancing the system's well-being as the situation evolved.

Act in more complex ways, taking various actions to achieve the same goal. The better decision makers in many of these studies seemed to understand that the multitude of problems they were addressing were closely linked with other problems and that their actions would have multiple effects. Therefore, they tended to take a wider variety of actions when attempting to achieve one goal ("I'll increase revenues in Greenvale by creating new jobs, investing in product development, and advertising."). This was in contrast to those who introduced fixes that failed and typically made one decision per goal ("I'll raise taxes in Greenvale to raise revenues.").

Identify where the real sources of the problems lie and stay focused on addressing them first, albeit indirectly. The superior decision makers also took time to gather enough information to determine the *central* problems that needed to be addressed. They did not jump into action prematurely or simply focus on the problems they *could* solve just because doing so felt good. They also remained focused on addressing the most difficult problems by trying various tactics to attend to them. Ineffective decision makers were easily distracted and diverted; they shifted from problem to problem as each arose. Effective decision makers did not develop a single-minded preoccupation with one solution. If the feedback data informed them that a solution was too costly or ineffective, they altered their approach.

Generate hypotheses about the effects of your actions and then test them before applying them. Like Gottman's use of proximal change experiments, effective decision makers tested their solutions in pilot projects and assessed their effects before committing too deeply to them. This was in contrast to those who tended to jump into actions and caused harm.

Structure your behavior as much as possible, and prioritize your actions if possible. Decision making in the face of highly unstructured infinite problems benefits from some modicum of imposed structure. Dörner found this. The best decision makers prioritize a sequence of actions: first A, then B, but don't forget C. However, they were also ready to make adjustments as the situation unfolded. Some balance of both structure and improvisation proved most effective.

This approach to addressing difficult problems is more open, complex, flexible, and tolerant of ambiguity. It requires more reflection on *how* we are thinking and solving problems, as well as a keen recognition that unexpected things will happen. We should be looking for them and ready to adjust as needed. It means recognizing that when feedback on the result of our actions comes in it is time to pay more attention, not less; to make more decisions, not fewer. It involves starting wisely, making corrections in midcourse, and learning from our mistakes. Because every situation is unique and circumstances are always changing, we must stay online in real time if we are going to effectively navigate these infinite problems, especially when we think they are solved. The best results, or the results that lead to more constructive engagement and more sustainable solutions over time, are those that result from a process of adaptation to the inevitable changes in the system. By increasing our underlying competencies, we can improve our capacity to respond in ways that enable stakeholders to engage in the process of learning how to adapt to new dynamics and maintain a new level of constructive dialogue and collaboration.

10

CONCLUSION

New Rules for *The Way Out*

We have covered a lot of ground together. We began with a focus on the problems we are facing—defining polarization, outlining some concerning trends we are facing today (e.g., American psychosis), describing the fifty or more theories that explain why we are so stuck here (and why each of them is a little bit right but mostly wrong). I then sketched how our superstorm of polarization connects the dots between many of the fifty theories, resulting in the *big collapse*, a chronic state of oversimplification of our thinking, feeling, and living that sucks us right into the same pattern. Then I shared the story of attractor landscapes—how they take shape from certain types of cloudy problems and how they can form into treacherous psychosocial territories (even in diners) that can trap and constrain us—and some of the weird ways that they sometimes can change.

Then we got down to business, walking through *what we can do in our lives today* to begin to find a way out of these cavernous traps. It starts with thinking differently about how things change—not as mechanical clocks, but as dynamic clouds. Then it involves taking a major reset—a pause in time when we can seriously reflect, regroup, and reform our ways. No small matter. The next best move we can make is to find and join in common cause the people and initiatives that are already working in our world—the efforts out there that seem to be helping others escape the enmity by building up patterns and breaking down old ones. I shared the science on how complicating our life, and moving through that complexity, can go a long way toward reshaping the contours of our conflicts in ways that bring better health, functioning, and well-being. Finally, I explained why this journey takes time. Despite our frustration and impatience with the status quo, approaching the way out as an ongoing process is key, even when we find ourselves struggling with an infinite game, which requires practice, failure, and adaptation.

Now that we have reached this summit together, I wish to leave you with two parting gifts. First is a guiding star of sorts, a taste of the kind of place where this work might lead us. And second are some tools for the remainder of your journey—a simple set of new rules gleaned from the pages of this book—to serve as guideposts to help you on your way.

WHAT DOES GETTING OUT REALLY LOOK LIKE TODAY?

Jefferson County, in the north country of New York state, up by Lake Ontario, is Trump country. Leaning conservative, with a third of its workers employed at nearby Fort Drum Army base, Jefferson went for Donald Trump by 20 percentage points in 2016 and almost 30 points in 2020.[1] It has also recently been dubbed one of the most politically tolerant counties in America.[2] That's right, one of the most politically tolerant.[3]

In an article written by my colleague Amanda Ripley in 2019, she tells a surprising story of openness in Watertown, New York, the seat of Jefferson County, and attempts to unearth the secrets of this most politically accepting of places.[4] These national rankings were based on an analysis conducted by *The Atlantic* in cooperation with the opinion-polling firm PredictWise. This study looked for differences in affective polarization in residents across the three thousand counties in the United States—and found them. Counties, and the states they inhabit, were found to differ significantly in the level of discomfort their constituents felt with the possibility of interpolitical marriage in their family and the degree to which they felt that members of the other political party were selfish and ignorant versus compassionate and patriotic.

Watertown rose to the top in tolerance, ranking in the highest 1 percent. Why? you ask. The answer is, of course, complex, in a particularly contradictory way. For instance, despite the fact that the number of mixed-political marriages have declined by 50 percent in the United States since 1973, in Watertown 25 percent of the marriages are mixed Republican and Democrat—compared with only 10 percent in less tolerant places. Research has shown that such marital odd-coupling (a true example of cross-cutting ties) leads to higher levels of tolerance and more politically diverse progeny, which bodes well for future generations of Watertownians. It is also a relatively small community of twenty-nine thousand residents, and the population tends to be younger and less educated but are inclined to live in politically mixed neighborhoods. Watertown has a substantial civic culture as well, with a local newspaper (that has an editor who describes his politics as "slightly fiscally conservative but otherwise wild-man liberal"—a poster child for social identity complexity), twenty-three houses of worship (including two temples and a mosque), two Rotary clubs, and a YMCA. All this adds up to a place where citizens in both political tribes get to know each other fairly well and understand that they need each other—even if just in case—creating an environment in which political screaming matches are scarce.

The town also holds an important political history. A century ago the Watertown city council took the bold step of excluding political parties from interfering in their local affairs, and as a result, the national R and D political monopolies and their donors hold little sway there. Locally elected officeholders tend to be from different parties, and their county board of legislators goes against the tide with Republicans and Democrats always meeting together as one board. This all appears to have helped to insulate the community from some of the more toxic effects of our national pull to the extreme poles.

And then there are the small things, like the Monday breakfasts. Local pastor Fred Garry describes himself as "one click above a communist," and he cooks and runs a politically mixed men's breakfast group on Monday mornings at the First Presbyterian Church. About a dozen guys show up and discuss books, life, and politics—and they keep coming back. Garry believes that the secret to their effectiveness is three things: (1) they meet face-to-face, (2) they share good, home-cooked food (his), and (3) they take their time with each other. "We talk about (issues) long enough until we realize what we don't know. Once you realize how much you don't know, the honest conversation comes out."

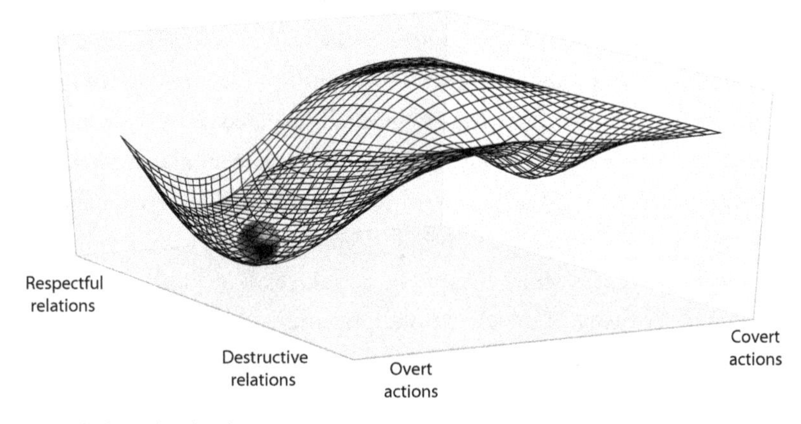

10.1 An ideal conflict landscape.

Despite the sturdy foundation provided by this type of mixing, recent years have put stress on the tolerant political tendencies of even this top-ranked community. The degrading effects of the normless vacuum of social media, the vitriol and dripping sarcasm of cable news, and the modeling of an openly contemptuous national political elite have begun to take their toll. This has led to an increasing tendency among some in Watertown to avoid speaking about politics in public.

Nevertheless, a majority of the townspeople in Watertown continue to engage with one another and maintain a close, functional, resilient community (figure 10.1). Despite the occasional tiffs and bruised egos, they interact frequently across the political divide in diners, sports fields, and schools. Although they may disagree fervently about politics, they express hate and vilify members of the other party much less than is typical today. These cross-party encounters reportedly do make people uncomfortable, but they seem to have become accustom to it, resulting in a more nuanced understanding of the issues and an open acceptance of those on the other side.

THE VIEW FROM WATERTOWN

This Is What Sustainable Political Tolerance Looks Like

What do we see here smack in the middle of Trump country? We see a place where people with complex identities live, work, and play with people of differing political views; where they come to know, marry, befriend, and depend on one another despite their differences; and where the citizens recognize that difficult conversations and meaningful relationships take time to navigate and nurture. We see a community that intentionally decided to reset a century ago, taking a courageous step to protect its local interests from major outside political influences. As a result, it is somewhat insulated from the national political forces driving our divisions, and people seem able to tolerate the discomfort of political differences while continuing to take care of local issues. In other words, we see evidence of the basic principles offered in this book: resets, complexity, moving on together, and positive deviance. We also see how these many positive forces work together to fuel *virtuous cycles* affecting ways of being, feeling, relating, and organizing homes and communities, resulting in more balanced, healthy, and functional lives. And we see that arriving at this place took—and continues to take—considerable time, intention, and adaptation.

Many of the other politically tolerant and peaceful places that our team at Columbia University has studied all over the world evidence similar conditions and historical turning points.[5] Seventy years ago Costa Rica survived a bloody internal civil war (an extreme political shock) to become one of the only nations in the world to intentionally decide to disband their military and redirect significant national resources toward education, health, and the environment.[6] At the time, they had the foresight to begin to teach tolerance in many of their schools as a way to grow more peaceable citizens. In 1997, Costa Rica passed a law that required peace education in all schools, which has been credited for developing the skills and knowledge that contribute to the country's robust culture of peace.[7] Despite being situated in a tough geopolitical neighborhood within one of the world's busiest drug-trafficking corridors today, Costa Rica is ranked as one of the happiest and most peaceful nations in the world.[8]

Or consider New Zealand, a nation of islands located in the southwestern Pacific, which was the last habitable land mass be discovered by humans. It is believed that its first inhabitants, now referred to as Māori, were sailors who migrated from East Polynesia in the thirteenth century; white European settlers arrived much later in the eighteenth century. In 1840, the British and more than five hundred Māori chiefs signed the Treaty of Waitangi, formalizing the Māori acceptance of British rule. The treaty stipulated that Europeans could settle there, but in exchange the Māori could maintain customs, land, and the traditional authority of chiefs. New Zealand is technically still a Dominion of the British Empire, but practically speaking the country is considered fully independent. It currently has a number of policies aimed to ensure inclusion, not only of indigenous populations but also of women and other minorities.[9] As a result, it frequently shows up among the top peace indices globally.[10]

Similar conditions can be found across the world in Canada, Japan, Botswana, across the Nordic nations (where the peaceful resolution of internal conflicts has been a legacy for more than two hundred years[11]), among the Aborigines of the Western Desert in Australia, the people of the Nilgiri Plateau in India, the Upper Xingu River Basin in Brazil, and everywhere else where peace reigns. In the United States, Yadkin County, North Carolina; McMullen County, Texas; and Millard County, Utah all rank in the top 1 percent in the nation for political tolerance.[12] Similar to Watertown, New York, these places also have a history of significant turning points, of intentional resets, and of having taken—and continue to take—considerable time, intention, and adaptation to manage and sustain their peacefulness.

Now let's bring this all home by focusing on how these conditions can translate into a set of new rules and actions to affect your life today.

THE FORMULA

My physics colleagues are very keen on taking fuzzy ideas such as empathy, complexity, movement and tolerance, and essentializing them in order to express them as specifically as possible in mathematical terms. In doing so, they feel that we learn a lot about our underlying assumptions and are then able to develop much cleaner, more predictive models.

So, let's add this up. Here is my sense of the most essential elements that the research summarized in this book has identified for escaping malignant relations captured by destructive, polarizing dynamics:

- **Crossing a motivational threshold.** Experiencing sufficient pain and a sense of possibility (a way out)—both within yourself and on the other side—when a mutually hurting stalemate and a mutually enticing opportunity combine, we feel sufficiently motivated to try the way out.

- **Resetting.** Taking advantage of significant destabilizing events to stop and pause in our life to recalibrate our approach, recognize our own contributions to the pattern that we seek to change, and begin to establish new initial conditions for a qualitatively different future.
- **Thinking different.** Seeing old problems in completely new ways. Recognizing that our standard ways of envisioning problems and problem solving are not only insufficient to address cloudy problems but often contribute to their perpetuation.
- **Bolstering and Breaking.** Learning to work *with* the self-organizing dynamics within ourselves, our relationships, and our communities to leverage the positive deviance inherent to them in order to bolster our more compassionate tendencies, virtuous cycles, and constructive attractors *and* break the negative, vicious, destructive patterns.
- **Complicating.** Increasing our contradictory complexity (promoting more balance, nuance, and accuracy) in our experiences, perceptions, analyses, encounters, and environments.
- **Moving.** Cognitively, emotionally, and physically locomoting in ways that free up and resynchronize our experiences and relations and redirect attention from the static to the dynamic.
- **Adapting.** Planning to fail and responding to the inevitable unintended consequences of our actions adaptively over time. Settling-in to address our infinite problems by making more decisions and taking more actions and adjustments while holding true to our guiding vision for a better future.
- **Connecting.** Joining with others in common cause. Identifying and reaching out to other people, families, groups, and institutions in our community that are also committed to enacting the principles and practices shared in this book in service of finding a way out that is robust, contagious, and sustainable.

These elements are of critical importance to transitioning to sustaining tolerant communities. This is what we can glean from scientific research and from the lives and experiences of Watertownians, Costa Ricans, and others living in both peaceful and divided societies. These are all factors that readily translate to a set of *new rules* for our sociopolitical behavior—for a new ethic of politics.

OVERRULING OUR DEEP RULES

In the 1940s, the visionary science fiction writer Isaac Asimov began work on his now classic series of *I Robot* stories, in which he foreshadowed the vital importance of our basic operating rules for the future of our species. In *Runaround*, Asimov introduced his now infamous Three Laws of Robotics:

1. A robot may not injure a human being or, through inaction, allow a human being to come to harm;
2. A robot must obey the orders given it by human beings except where such orders would conflict with the First Law; and
3. A robot must protect its own existence as long as such protection does not conflict with the First or Second Laws.

As the story goes, Speedy, a highly sophisticated robot sent to serve and protect a group of humans on a mission to Mercury, becomes trapped by the logic of these three rules when finding itself in unforeseen circumstances. This glitch in its programming ends up jeopardizing the lives of its human "Masters."

This work of fiction helped to establish an entire genre of literature involving technology behaving in dangerous ways as an unintended consequence of its basic rules. It also anticipated the profound significance of even slight changes in such rules for human health and safety in our current technology saturated world (with driverless cars, biosensors in our bodies, internet sorting algorithms, bots, computer viruses, artificial intelligence, and on and on). Perhaps most important, it offered an allegory for reflecting on how our own basic rules can come back to harm us (see Crude Law 5).

Since the dawn of civilization, humans have largely been ruled by rules. Rules-based cultures began taking hold in the eighteenth century, and today rules structure virtually every form of human action and interaction. The Golden Rule ("Do unto others as you would have them do unto you."), rules of ethics and etiquette,

Robert's Rules of Order, the Rule of Law, the Rules of War (Geneva Conventions), and most recently the public safety rules associated with preventing the spread of COVID-19 are just some of the many rules that guide and constrain us today.

Rules are essentially statements of principle or standards of behavior (If X, then Y.). They are the foundation for mathematics, physics, engineering, logic, language, grammar, music, and the coded algorithms that Google and Amazon use to sort us into groups of blue and red consumers. Generally, rules make our lives more predictable, safe, efficient, and stable, and often serve as practical guidelines for navigating our world. But rules can also be used to control, exclude, attack, undermine, exploit, and oppress.

Although our social rules can be derived from widely different sources like scripture, law, top-down decision makers and local cultural tradition, rules gleaned from science often offer the benefit of being empirically tested and refined through systematic research. In fact, many science-based rules that have become more automatic such as "*Wear seatbelts when in riding in cars*," "*Cover your mouth when you cough*," and "*Scrub your hands for two minutes before performing surgery . . . and count your sponges afterward*," have saved countless lives.

New rules, once set and accepted, typically become automatic, implicit guides for decision making and action and, when shared with others in a group, can bubble up into social norms or ethical mores and begin to shape culture. In other words, rules are the basic building blocks for establishing new patterns for what eventually become considered good and bad, right and wrong, and normal and deviant behavior in our communities. They are our decision-making DNA.

Some rules, however, matter more than others. Research on artificial intelligence has clarified that there is always a hierarchy of rules that differ in importance, scope, and influence in human groups. For example, there are more localized rules of social etiquette, such as "Don't talk with your mouth full," "Wear garments that cover your reproductive organs in public," and in Tibetan homes, "Sit quietly in front of the fire with your hosts after dinner and don't speak for hours at a time." More consequential and broadly shared safety rules include "Never shout 'Fire!' in a public auditorium," "Never point a loaded gun at anyone," and "Remain still when encountering a bear in the wild." Finally, our more basic and determining operating rules include "Avoid pain and seek pleasure," "Secure stability and order," "Move away from deadly predators," and "Protect your offspring." This last set are *deep rules*, the basic, unconscious, instinctual rules that tend to govern our lives. These rules have been established through evolutionary processes over the centuries and are shared widely in human and chimpanzee groups alike. They are rooted in our most basic needs for safety, reproduction, and survival.

Today, how each of us responds to the storm of polarization in our daily lives is significantly affected by our basic rules. When faced with a high degree of intergroup (red versus blue) threat, frustration, and enmity, most of us fall back on some of the deeper rules we have developed to cope with spikes of risk and uncertainty. Under these conditions, we automatically move to simplify, essentialize, close ranks, defend, blame, and attack. In other words, we move from relatively more open, curious, nuanced, and accessible modes of experience and action to more closed, certain, and defensive modes. We are virtually hardwired to do so.

These automatic *emergency rules* have been derived over eons from essential needs for security. They lead to dramatic differences in how we feel, perceive, think, act, and interact with others, and they usually serve us well.

However, these rules are meant to be followed *temporarily* in response to spikes in threat levels. They represent our emergency security mode and are accompanied by physiological changes in the brain leading to hormonal and neurotransmitter increases in acute stress responses. When the threat subsides, we are meant to return to more nuanced, open, and benevolent modes of functioning. We need both modes of operation equally—to aid both wolves struggling within us—but healthy social functioning thrives most in the open, nonacute stress mode.

Allow me to illustrate. One of the more ancient rules that we have been programmed through evolution to follow is, "Move toward similar others and away from different." For ages, this rule helped us to avoid harm by moving us away from potential threats from the unknown. Even brief exposure to images of members of out-groups triggers activity in the amygdala, the fear center of the brain.[13] But today it also inclines us to sort ourselves into tribes of similar others and makes us all the more susceptible to being intentionally divided, conquered, and controlled by political actors seeking power. When this rule becomes chronic, we see the tightening of our lives and factionalization of families, communities, and entire societies.

The same holds true for all four emergency rules. They all serve a purpose under extreme threat but result in physical, mental, and social pathologies when sustained or taken to extremes. Chronic simplification leads to premature judgment, stereotyping, misperception, dehumanization, and deficiencies in decision making. Sustained forms of closed information processing are associated with a range of psychosocial pathologies such as rigidity, dogmatism, and obsessive-compulsive disorders. Operating in a persistent defensive mode of attack, alienates, escalates conflict, and invites negative reciprocity from others—plus wreaking havoc on one's adrenal functioning. And, of course, behavioral reactions like these only add more fuel to our current raging storm of polarization.

NEW RULES FOR THE WAY OUT

Despite the fact that some of our more primitive instincts and rules ready us automatically for partisan battle and that our political climate is pulling us forcefully into this mode, we can *decide* intentionally to override these forces in ourselves and to show our children a different path.[14] For the individual, for *you*, this begins with understanding how some of these emergency rules of social interaction are contributing to keeping us trapped in dysfunctional us-versus-them patterns and identifying new rules that can offer you a way out (figure 10.2).

So, IF you are trapped in a toxic dynamic and feel helpless, fed up, and exhausted, and you desperately want to make a change, THEN:

GET READY

See—See the way out. Recognize that others from both sides of the divide are finding their way out of our trap. There is hope. Believe in change.

Stop—Take the time necessary for a significant reset to recalibrate, regroup, and begin again. Take enough time. This should be hard. Then carefully reset with an eye toward a better future.

Shift—Shift your habits of mind. Turn your attention from the conflict to the context, from the presenting problem to the constellation of forces driving the problem. Change your theory of change.

CHANGE COURSE

Spot—Spot positive deviance, or what is already working in your community to prevent or mitigate more destructive patterns from escalating and to promote more healthy, constructive patterns. Build on these seedlings of possibility.

Simplify—Simplify, but only *after* you sufficiently complicate your experience and understanding of the situation. Zoom out to zoom in.

Synchronize—Move forward together with others physically and psychologically in ways that free us and connect us with empathy, compassion, and new possibilities.

Settle-in—Settle-in for a long, circuitous journey that will require considerable attention, adaptation, and adjustment. Start small, fail smart, and keep your eyes on your guiding star.

Support—Find others in your world with whom you can connect, turn to for support, and join with in common cause. You are not alone—you are part of a powerful new movement.

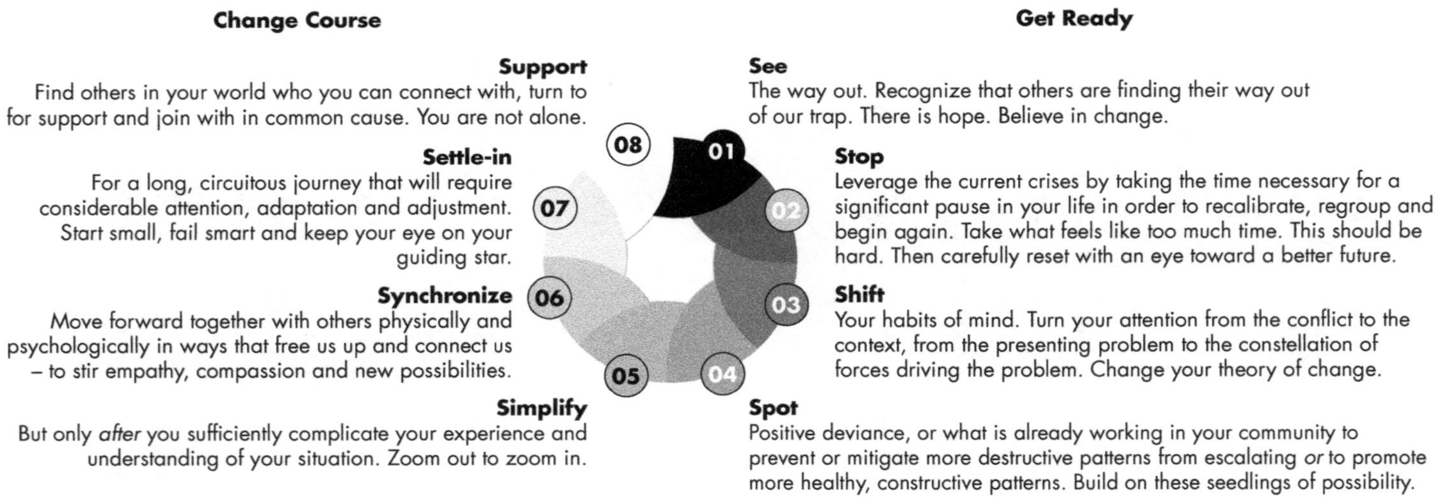

Get Ready

01 See
The way out. Recognize that others are finding their way out of our trap. There is hope. Believe in change.

02 Stop
Leverage the current crises by taking the time necessary for a significant pause in your life in order to recalibrate, regroup and begin again. Take what feels like too much time. This should be hard. Then carefully reset with an eye toward a better future.

03 Shift
Your habits of mind. Turn your attention from the conflict to the context, from the presenting problem to the constellation of forces driving the problem. Change your theory of change.

04 Spot
Positive deviance, or what is already working in your community to prevent or mitigate more destructive patterns from escalating *or* to promote more healthy, constructive patterns. Build on these seedlings of possibility.

Change Course

05 Simplify
But only *after* you sufficiently complicate your experience and understanding of your situation. Zoom out to zoom in.

06 Synchronize
Move forward together with others physically and psychologically in ways that free us up and connect us – to stir empathy, compassion and new possibilities.

07 Settle-in
For a long, circuitous journey that will require considerable attention, adaptation and adjustment. Start small, fail smart and keep your eye on your guiding star.

08 Support
Find others in your world who you can connect with, turn to for support and join with in common cause. You are not alone.

10.2 New Rules for *The Way Out*.

What does it look like when people choose, intentionally, to alter their behavioral reactions and swim against a strong cultural riptide like ours? It looks like the six Boston leaders who chose to jeopardize their own safety and careers to stop, shift, and settle-in for a difficult but transformational journey promoting nonviolent discourse and activism over abortion. It looks like the Task Force on Community and Diversity that convened at my college over that long, hot summer of 1999 to reset and begin a new trajectory toward a less discriminatory and more inclusive workplace. It looks like the countless Americans who are today choosing to take the time to participate in ongoing, well-facilitated political dialogue groups such as those run by Better Angels and Crossing Party Lines and then move into action to reform the structures driving our divisions. It looks like the members of the media who are today joining together in common cause to *complicate the narrative* and help to mitigate their own contributions to fostering an acutely polarized society. It looks like the Community of Sant'Egidio, who break international norms and attempt to communicate with some of the most violent militias in the world to find a glimmer of positive deviance in their ranks and support a way out. It looks like the nations of Mauritius, Costa Rica, Norway, and New Zealand, and the U.S. counties of Jefferson, New York; Yadkin, North Carolina; McMullen, Texas; and Millard, Utah that all chose to reset and today continue to work actively and adaptively to promote and sustain political tolerance in their homes and communities.

Or it looks like you, waking up tomorrow morning and deciding to join or create a new microculture in your home, workplace, or community that will help reduce the toxicity and hate in your life, begin to repair broken relationships, and start you on a new path. It looks exactly like that.

AFTERWORD

I prefaced this book on a personal note, and so I will conclude it. It has been a terrible, arduous, exhausting year. A crucible of sorts. There continues to be immeasurable pain, anxiety, and loss—grief and hardship the likes of which our nation has only seen in world wars and the Great Depression. The experiences I have had and the images I have seen—of thoroughly spent frontline workers, of empty main streets, school rooms, and baseball stadiums, of boarded up storefronts on Broadway, and of the hundreds of thousands of faces shared on the nightly news of those we have lost from COVID-19, the opioid epidemic, and at the hands of our own police—will never leave me.

Yet there has also been something remarkable about these days—being forced to stop, quarantine, stay in place, social distance, and wear surgical masks and gloves. Not being able to travel to see the ones we love, even the ones we don't, when they need us. Celebrating the selfless courage of the frontline workers by banging pots and pans at our windows every evening at 7 p.m. for months on end (Oh, the cacophony!). And losing access to many of the distractions and excuses that fill our automatic-pilot lives to the point that we are often left today to our own thoughts, worries, hopes and dreams, and to those of the precious few with whom we are fortunate to share our home.

This is a great reset—whether we choose to recognize it or not. For the rest of our lives, we will all mark this moment in time—did that happen before 2020 or after? Before our moment of instability[4] or after? This is what we typically see when communities are devastated by earthquakes or tsunamis—a clear demarcation in time, a potential turning point.

So, the question I leave you with is this: "What path will you choose now?" What new direction will you set off on today—for you, your family, and community—and what learning do you hope to look back on through these most astonishing of times? Our world is changing, rapidly and radically, all around us. What will you make of it?

At the end of his autobiography, Nelson Mandela, a man who lived his entire life—27 years of it in prison—on a daunting journey to overcome injustice in his country and help his nation find freedom and unity, wrote this:

> I have walked that long road to freedom. I have tried not to falter; I have made missteps along the way. But I have discovered the secret that after climbing a great hill, one only finds that there are many more hills to climb. I have taken a moment here to rest, to steal a view of the glorious vista that surrounds me, to look back on the distance I have come. But I can rest only for a moment, for with freedom comes responsibilities, and I dare not linger, for my long walk is not yet ended.[1]

I had planned to let Mandela's words complete this book. But then, on July 30, 2020, the day that the great nonviolent civil rights leader and U.S. congressman John Lewis was put to rest, his final message to us was printed in the *New York Times*. In it, he wrote:

> While my time here has now come to an end, I want you to know that in the last days and hours of my life you inspired me. You filled me with hope about the next chapter of the great American story when you used your power to make a difference in our society. Millions of people motivated simply by human compassion laid down the burdens of division. . . . Like so many young people today, I was searching for a way out, or some might say a way in. . . . When historians pick up their pens to write the story of the 21st century, let them say that it was your generation who laid down the heavy burdens of hate at last and that peace finally triumphed over violence, aggression and war. So I say to you, walk with the wind, brothers and sisters, and let the spirit of peace and the power of everlasting love be your guide.[2]

Words to move by.

APPENDIX A

TAKEAWAYS

CHAPTER 1: INTRODUCTION

- The United States is more polarized today than at any time in our history.
- The bad news is that the divide is deep, tribal and consequential—it has led to a strange form of *American Psychosis.*
- This is a first order problem. It is toxic and contagious and is making us unable to address the other existential problems we are currently facing (from COVID to Climate Change).
- However, our extreme forms of misery and instability bring a bit of good news, as they are a necessary condition for radical change.
- Now all we need is a vision for a way out.
- This book offers this vision.
- Boston, in the 1990s, offers a parable for what this might look like.

CHAPTER 2: WHY WE ARE STUCK

- Polarization is a natural response to being attracted to similar (positive) things and repulsed by different (strange), which can have benefits and consequences.

- There are several types of polarization that affect groups in the political realm, in particular *affective*, *ideological*, *political* and *perceptual*.
- America is evidencing 3 concerning polarization trends: (1) escalating polarization for 50-plus years, (2) acute levels of affective polarization and (3), a collapse and over-simplification of attitudes across the top 10 most divisive issues within parties.
- Despite what we are told, there are no single sovereign causes that account for these trends—rather it is how the different facets coalesce into vicious cycles, cyclones and superstorms.
- This can result in change-resistant forms of *toxic polarization*.
- These are what are known as cloud problems, which differ fundamentally from most (clock) problems we face in our lives.
- Humans hate highly complex problems—we recoil from them by collapsing our experience, understanding and reactions to them—which only exacerbate these problems.
- When cloud-like problems collapse, they can form attractors.

CHAPTER 3: ATTRACTED TO CONFLICT

- Attractors are born when a group of unrelated elements align and influence each other in ways that create coherent patterns.
- These patterns scaffold our experiences of the world.
- Attractors are essentially *low-energy states*—which means they are easy to fall into—but take great effort to escape and are used to explain change-resistant patterns in everything from cells to galaxies.
- Our experiences of different situations are shaped by our psychosocial landscapes for them, which are composed of different attractors and repellers from the past
- Attractor landscapes affect our experiences and responses to polarization and conflict—well beyond the issues in contention.
- Attractor landscapes can become intractable when they become self-organizing, hyper-coherent and simplistic—then all roads lead to pathological polarization.

- At this stage attractor dynamics are usually fractal—which means their us-vs-them patterns are repeated from our brains to our social interactions to our cultures.
- When this occurs, the laws for how things change, change.
- The Seven Crude Laws for Nonlinear Change explain how.

CHAPTER 4: THINK DIFFERENT

- Our best attempts to "fix" our more divisive, intractable conflicts often backfire or have little sustained effect. This is due to our focus on moving the boulder (the presenting conflict), not reshaping the hill (the underlying landscape).
- We all have implicit theories of how change happens—and of how to change our worst conflicts. The most prevalent theory is the *mechanical clock theory*—just fix it.
- An alternative but less familiar theory-of-change is *Radical Re-landscaping theory or R2*, which views change according to the *Seven Crude Laws for Nonlinear Change.*
- However changing our theory of change—especially one we have grown up with—is no small feat.
- So we have developed *five practices* to help you do so, which include *resetting*, *bolstering/breaking*, *complicating*, *moving* and *adapting* .
- These practices are not offered as a sequence, but rather as a set that can complement one another, and offer useful levers for finding the way out of toxic polarization.

CHAPTER 5: RESET

- The overwhelming attraction of the many forces working in concert to pull us apart suggests that real change in these dynamics will require a substantial reset.
- One way this happens is through *the bombshell effect*—when major shocks destabilize the *deep structures* of ourselves and our communities and ready us for radical change.

- Three scenarios have emerged for how these shocks can be leveraged to realize radical change—through restructuring by outside strangers, the spawning of entirely new insider species, and though careful synchronization between the two.
- Another way to reset is to capitalize on *the butterfly effect*, or the sensitivity to initial conditions of complex problems by prepping for difficult encounters in a way that leverages your first moves.
- This can be done by checking your assumptions about change, clarifying your intentions, building up the emotional reservoirs for positivity in relations, unexpected framing of encounters, and leveraging the power of time and place.

CHAPTER 6: BOLSTER AND BREAK

- When trapped in the riptide of a deeply polarized community, it is best to figure out how to work *with the flow of forces and energy* in the situation to find a way out.
- This is best achieved by identifying and building on *bright spots*—those people and programs that are already working effectively across divides.
- Tapping into these forms of *positive deviance* can be done by learning to inquire about them first, working away from the heat of conflict, learning to trust the insight and expertise within the community, connecting the dots between such groups, and doing so carefully as to not do harm.
- This can be challenging to do due to the *fit, fear, friend and fixer* problems.
- Beyond supporting what works, we also need to find ways to weaken our worst tendencies. This can be done by leveraging *ruptures*, reducing *resistance* to change, and increasing *repellers* (taboos).

CHAPTER 7: COMPLICATE

- Two types of complexity were outlined here—*consistent* and *contradictory*. The first is the main source of intransigence in our thinking, feeling and action, the second a remedy for it.

- Both forms of complexity can operate at different levels—from our brain structures, thinking and feeling to our family and community structures and international relations.
- Consistent forms of high complexity are often the source of vicious, runaway cycles of escalation, while contradictory forms often are able to keep escalation in check.
- The research clearly shows that contradictory complexity results in more constructive forms of conflict management—up to a point.
- There are a wide variety of ways to increase contradictory complexity in your world, from acknowledging your own internal contradictions and learning to think with smart people who differ politically from you, to increasing complexity in your problem analyses, political conversations, media choices and community groups.

CHAPTER 8: MOVE

- If agonizing, antagonizing conflicts result in *The Big Collapse* and leave you feeling trapped and confined in Us-v-Them, then perhaps you might consider *movement* as a remedy.
- Both empirical and anecdotal evidence suggests that movement can help us to break free of narrow, engrained patterns of thinking, feeling and behaving.
- Neuroscience research has found that our brains show much more plasticity and flexibility than previously thought, even well into adulthood. This suggests that certain types of movement can help us to shake off attitudes and positions that have actually come to be embodied in our neural structures.
- Most relevant, research has shown that movement is particularly conducive to increasing many aspects of constructive conflict, such as creativity, flexibility and positivity.
- We can integrate movement into our depolarizing practices, by introducing joint movement, mapping, traveling and interactive activities into them.

- And integrating moving together—side-by-side and ideally outside—has shown great promise for connecting disputants and helping to synchronize them in ways that promote more empathy, rapport and flexibility.

CHAPTER 9: ADAPT

- The strange and often exasperating outcomes we often see in response to our best attempts to solve complex problems—should be expected.
- When faced with these cloudy, crazy-making problems, we are thrust into their *E4 Vortex* due to pulls toward *efficiency, existence*, *esteem* and *environmental* demands, which are dizzying.
- But research on decision making in these contexts suggests that *how* we respond to them can make all the difference—and that playing the long game is key.
- Learning to respond adaptively to dynamic problems is critical. This often entails learning to fail smart and fast, and then making slight adjustments to your course of action.
- It also often involves testing small nudges to the system—slight shits in our thinking and approach that help us to test the waters and learn about the rules of the system.
- This chapter offers several *learnable competencies* that we have found to help us better navigate these environments—and they begin with learning how to learn (not perform) in the face of new problems.

CHAPTER 10: CONCLUDING

- We have traveled together from normal, healthy types of polarization to pathological, from mechanical theories of change to complex and nonlinear, and from standard approaches to problem solving to five modes of radical re-landscaping.
- The concluding chapter offers two final elements of The Way Out.

- First, it offers a North Star of sorts. A vision of what life looks like in today's more politically tolerant communities in The United States and around the world.
- Second, it distills the main actionable insights from the research shared in the book into a simple set of *New Rules for The Way Out*.
- That is, a sequence of eight "IF X, Then Y" behavioral rules to practice and follow when finding yourself trapped in a pathological pattern of polarization in your family, workplace, community or nation.
- These new rules do not offer a fixed recipe for depolarizing your life, but rather offer the ingredients for making such a change possible. The rest is up to you.

APPENDIX B

EXERCISES AND ASSESSMENTS BY CHAPTER

On the website for *The Way Out*, https://www.thewayoutofpolarization.com/resources-exercises, are a set of appendices and exercises that supplement each chapter. These are designed to help deepen your understanding of specific concepts introduced in the chapters in a variety of ways—by providing more elaborated examples of the ideas, by offering reflection questions to deepen your own thinking on concepts, by listing practices I recommend using to build your skills for navigating and transforming our polarized world, and by presenting self-assessments to help you learn more about your own orientations, assumptions, and competencies.

I encourage you to go to the website and read through the corresponding appendix as you finish each chapter. You may work through the exercises and questions right away, or just skim them and revisit them as you continue along in the book. But they are designed to be a "tool kit" to carry with you as you apply the lessons and new rules from this book.

Embedded in these exercises and prompts are tough questions without clear answers. Contemplating these issues will better prepare you to engage difficult divides thoughtfully, effectively, and sustainably.

NOTES

PREFACE: WHILE ROME BURNS

1. Douglas McGregor, *The Human Side of Enterprise* (New York: McGraw-Hill, 1960).
2. Mary P. Follett, *Creative Experience* (New York: Longmans, Green, 1924); Mary P. Follett, "Power," in *Dynamic Administration: The Collected Papers of Mary Parker Follett*, ed. Elliot M. Fox and Lyndall F. Urwick (London: Pitman, 1973), 66–87.

1. OUR CRISIS AND OPPORTUNITY

1. For more background on King Philip's War, see History.com Editors, "King Philip's War," November 13, 2019, https://www.history.com/topics/native-american-history/king-philips-war.
2. For a roundup of the New England Patriots' history of cheating scandals under head coach Bill Belichick, see Scott Davis, "The Patriots Are Once Again Embroiled in a Cheating Controversy," *Business Insider*, December 12, 2019, https://www.businessinsider.com/patriots-cheating-scandals-accusations-examples-2019-12.
3. Betsy Klein, "Trump's Invitation Leads Red Sox Players to Split Across Racial Lines," *CNN*, May 19, 2019, https://www.cnn.com/2019/05/09/politics/red-sox-white-house-cora-trump/index.html.
4. NFL.com, "Donald Trump on Kaepernick: Find Another Country," *NFL*, August 29, 2016, http://www.nfl.com/news/story/0ap3000000692256/article/donald-trump-on-kaepernick-find-another-country.
5. Alex Silverman, "Most Sports Fans Back Teams' White House Visits Under Trump Administration," *Morning Consult*, November 22, 2019, https://morningconsult.com/2019/11/22/most-sports-fans-back-teams-white-house-visits-under-trump-administration/. See also, Molly Olmstead, "Which Championship Teams Still Make White House Visits?," *Slate*,

May 9, 2019, https://slate.com/culture/2019/05/trump-white-house-visits-championship-teams-sports.html.

6. Nick Selbe, "Red Sox Back Up Torii Hunter's Claims of Racism in Boston," *Sports Illustrated*, June 10, 2020, https://www.si.com/mlb/2020/06/10/boston-red-sox-confirm-torii-hunter-racist-slurs-fenway-park.
7. Amanda Ripley, Rekha Tenjarla, and Angela Y. He, "The Geography of Partisan Prejudice," *The Atlantic*, March 4, 2019, https://www.theatlantic.com/politics/archive/2019/03/us-counties-vary-their-degree-partisan-prejudice/583072/.
8. Evidence from the American National Election Studies and national exit polls indicates that ideological polarization has increased dramatically since the 1970s among the mass public in the United States, as well as among political elites. These divisions are not confined to a small minority of activists; they involve a large segment of the public, and the deepest divisions are found among the most interested, informed, and active citizens. Alan I. Abramowitz and Kyle L. Saunders, "Is Polarization a Myth?," *Journal of Politics* 70, no. 2 (2008): 542–55.
9. In the months before the 2016 election, national polls conducted by the Pew Research Center showed that Democrats and Republicans held intensely negative emotions about people on the other side of the political divide. Needless to say, the election itself didn't diminish any of those feelings. Specifically, Pew found that the proportion of Republicans and Democrats who hold "very unfavorable" views of the opposite party had more than doubled since 1994, with 53 percent of Republicans harboring "very cold" feelings toward Democrats and 52 percent of Democrats feeling the same toward Republicans. Pew polling also found that majorities of highly politically engaged Republicans (62 percent) and Democrats (70 percent) reported that the other party makes them feel "afraid." Pew Research Center, "Partisanship and Political Animosity in 2016," June 22, 2016, https://www.pewresearch.org/politics/2016/06/22/partisanship-and-political-animosity-in-2016/. It is worth noting that similar "chilling" trends were found in a recent study on partisanship run out of our lab in 2019.
10. See Karen Gift and Thomas Gift, "Does Politics Influence Hiring? Evidence from a Randomized Experiment," *Political Behavior* 37, no. 3 (2015): 653–75, https://link.springer.com/article/10.1007/s11109-014-9286-0.
11. More in Common, an organization working to connect people across lines of division, points to what they call "the Perception Gap" as part of the problem. In a study conducted in late 2018 that sought to better understand the process driving polarization, they found that 55 percent of Republicans and Democrats say they think the opposing side holds extreme views, but in reality only about 30 percent in each party hold extreme views. Moreover, Republicans polled believe that 32 percent of Democrats are gay, lesbian, or bisexual (6 percent report they are), and Democrats estimated that 38 percent of Republicans make more than $250,000 a year (only 2 percent earn that much). This gap suggests that Americans have distorted views of each other that contribute to our divides. This study is worth reading in full and includes many other interesting findings: for example, the more news you consume, on average, the bigger your perception gap. David Yudkin, Stephen Hawkins, and Tim Dixon, "The Perception Gap: How False Impressions

are Pulling Americans Apart," *More in Common*, June 2019, https://perceptiongap.us/. A June 2020 analysis by another group found a similar perception gap, so it appears to persist. "American's Divided Mind: Understanding the Psychology That Drives Us Apart," *Beyond Conflict*, June 2020, https://beyondconflictint.org/americas-divided-mind/.

12. Partisans used to hold a mix of more traditionally liberal and more traditionally conservative positions on the main issues of the day, but today people are more and more holding views that strictly conform to the straight party line, what Pew calls "ideological consistency." See "The Shift in the American Public's Political Values: Political Polarization, 1994–2017," *Pew Research Center* October 20, 2017, https://www.people-press.org/interactives/political-polarization-.1994-2017/.
13. Nolan McCarty, Keith Poole, and Howard Rosenthal, *Polarized America: The Dance of Ideology and Unequal Riches* (Cambridge: MIT Press, 2006). See also Adam Boche, Jeffrey B. Lewis, Aaron Rudkin, and Luke Sonnet, "The New Voteview.com: Preserving and Continuing Keith Poole's Infrastructure for Scholars, Students, and Observers of Congress," *Public Choice* 176, no. 1 (2018): 17–32. In this extraordinary study, researchers pulled together website and database resources that document every vote in the U.S. Congress since 1879 (after the U.S. Civil War) and reveal the ups and downs of partisan voting and bipartisan polarization over that time. Check it out, and pay special attention to the fifty-plus-year trend we are stuck in!
14. Read the full *New York Times* op/ed following the February 5, 2019, State of the Union address. New York Times Editorial Board, "A Message of Unity from an Agent of Discord," *New York Times*, February 5, 2019, https://www.nytimes.com/2019/02/05/opinion/state-of-the-union-trump.html.
15. For the full description of psychosis, see National Institute of Mental Health, "What Is Psychosis?," accessed November 15, 2020, https://www.nimh.nih.gov/health/topics/schizophrenia/raise/what-is-psychosis.shtml.
16. "Stress in America 2020: Stress in the Time of COVID-19, *vol.* 2, *American Psychological Association*, June 2020, https://www.apa.org/news/press/releases/stress/2020/stress-in-america-covid-june.pdf.
17. Mohd. Razali Salleh, "Life Event, Stress and Illness," *Malaysian Journal of Medical Sciences* 15, no. 4 (October 2008): 9–18, https://www.ncbi.nlm.nih.gov/pmc/articles/PMC3341916/.
18. "Public Opinion Poll—Annual Meeting 2019," *American Psychiatric Association*, April 6–10, 2019, https://www.psychiatry.org/newsroom/apa-public-opinion-poll-annual-meeting-2019.
19. "Facts and Statistics," *Anxiety and Depression Association of America* accessed July 27, 2020, https://adaa.org/about-adaa/press-room/facts-statistics.
20. "Major Depression," *National Institute of Mental Health* accessed February 1, 2019, https://www.nimh.nih.gov/health/statistics/major-depression.shtml.
21. Mary E. Duffy, Jean M. Twenge, and Thomas E. Joiner, "Trends in Mood and Anxiety Symptoms and Suicide Related Outcomes Among U.S. Undergraduates, 2007–2018: Evidence from Two National Surveys," *Journal of Adolescent Health* 65, no. 5 (2019): 590–98.
22. See Holly Hedegaard, Sally C. Curtin, and Margaret Warner, "Increase in Suicide Mortality in the United States, 1999–2018," *National Center for Health Statistics* Data Brief, no. 362, April 2020, https://www.cdc.gov/nchs/data/databriefs/db362-h.pdf. Additionally, it

is worth highlighting that lesbian, gay, bisexual, transgender, and queer (LGBTQ) individuals have reported "higher levels of stress pertaining to sexual orientation rumination and daily experiences of harassment and discrimination" since the 2016 election, and women and people of color are reporting significantly higher levels of stress, anxiety, and depression, as reported in Kirsten A. Gonzalez, Johanna L. Ramirez, and M. Paz Galupo, "Increase in GLBTQ Minority Stress Following the 2016 U.S. Presidential Election," *Journal of GLBT Family Studies* 14, nos. 1–2 (2018): 130–51. See also, Masha Krupenkin, David Rothschild, Shawndra Hill, and Elad Ymo-Tov, "President Trump Stress Disorder: Partisanship, Ethnicity, and Expressive Reporting of Mental Distress After the 2016 Election," *SAGE Open* 9, no. 1 (March 2019): 1–14, https://journals.sagepub.com/doi/full/10.1177/2158244019830865.

23. American Psychological Association, "Stress in America 2020," 1.
24. Nathan P. Kalmoe and Lilliana Mason, "Most Americans Reject Partisan Violence, but There Is Still Cause for Concern," Democracy Fund Voter Study Group (blog), May 7, 2020, https://www.voterstudygroup.org/blog/has-american-partisanship-gone-too-far.
25. Tim Dixon, cofounder of More in Common, wrote about the unique moment we find ourselves in as polarization increases worldwide, and he offered some ideas about how to solve the crisis. Tim Dixon, "Here's How We Solve the Global Crisis of Tribalism and Democratic Decay" (paper presented at the World Economic Forum Annual Meeting, Davos, January 9, 2019), https://www.weforum.org/agenda/2019/01/can-globalization-tackle-tribalism-and-democratic-decay/.
26. For a comprehensive discussion of these conditions, see I. William Zartman, *Ripe for Resolution* (New York: Oxford University Press, 1989); I. William Zartman, "Ripeness: The Hurting Stalemate and Beyond," in *International Conflict Resolution After the Cold War*, ed. P. C. Stern and D. Druckman (Washington, DC: National Academy of Sciences, 2000); Peter T. Coleman, Antony G. Hacking, Mark A. Stover, Beth Fisher-Yoshida, and Andrzej Nowak, "Reconstructing Ripeness I: A Study of Constructive Engagement in Protracted Social Conflicts," *Conflict Resolution Quarterly* 26, no. 1 (2008): 3–42.
27. Connie J. G. Gersick, "Revolutionary Change Theories: A Multilevel Exploration of the Punctuated Equilibrium Paradigm," *Academy of Management Review* 16, no. 1 (1991): 10–36; Robin R. Vallacher and Daniel M. Wegner, "Action Identification Theory," in *Handbook of Theories in Social Psychology*, ed. P. A. M. Van Lange, A. W. Kruglanski, and E. T. Higgins (Thousand Oaks, CA: Sage, 2012), 327–48.
28. Paul F. Diehl and Gary Goertz, *War and Peace in International Rivalry* (Ann Arbor: University of Michigan Press, 2001).
29. Elaine Romanelli and Michael L. Tushman, "Organizational Transformation as Punctuated Equilibrium: An Empirical Test," *Academy of Management Journal* 37, no. 5 (1994): 1141–66.
30. See I. William Zartman, "Ripeness Revisited, the Push and Pull of Conflict Management," in *Negotiation and Conflict Management: Essays on Theory and Practice*, ed. I. William Zartman (London: Routledge, 2007). Diehl and Goertz, *War and Peace in International Rivalry*.
31. You can read more about the international work of More in Common on their website at https://www.moreincommon.com/. This organization focuses on piloting efforts to

bring people together across lines of difference and to promote narratives about what we have in common. They provide a great deal of research and thoughtful commentary about where we are, why, and what we can do about it.

32. For original reporting on the tragic shootings, see Fox Butterfield, "Insanity Drove a Man to Kill at 2 Clinics, Jury Told," *New York Times*, February 15, 1996, http://www.nytimes.com/1996/02/15/us/insanity-drove-a-man-to-kill-at-2-clinics-jury-is-told.html.
33. For a more detailed account of the Boston abortion dialogue process, see Susan L. Podziba, *Civic Fusion: Mediating Polarized Public Disputes* (Chicago: American Bar Association, 2013).
34. The women who participated in these groundbreaking talks collectively published an article about their experience. Anne Fowler, Nicki Nichols Gamble, Frances X. Hogan, Melissa Kogut, Madeline McCommish, and Barbara Thorp, "Talking with the Enemy," *Boston Globe*, January 28, 2001; full text available at https://www.feminist.com/resources/artspeech/genwom/talkingwith.html.
35. You can learn more about the dialogue process the pro-choice and pro-life leaders engaged in by watching "Pro-Choice and Pro-Life Leaders on Dialogue" (video), Women and Power 2005 Conference, VDAY and the Omega Institute, June 10, 2011, https://youtu.be/52Q9FV5eWKo.
36. It is important to emphasize that the leader dialogue initiative was only one component of the Public Conversation Project's broader strategy for depolarizing the climate surrounding the abortion controversy in the Greater Boston area. Other actions enacted simultaneously included a series of introductory abortion dialogues, a training program for pro-choice and pro-life facilitation teams, establishment of a network for "graduates" of the introductory dialogues interested in opportunities for sustained dialogue and collaboration, and distribution of their acclaimed *Abortion Dialogue Handbook*.
37. Mary Barton, "Reducing Angry Rhetoric Helped Abortion Dialogue," *National Catholic Reporter*, January 22, 2009, https://www.ncronline.org/news/reducing-angry-rhetoric-helped-abortion-dialogue.
38. For more expansive exploration of intractable conflict across a variety of contexts and from a range of perspectives, see Robin Vallacher, Peter T. Coleman, Andrzej Nowak, Lan Bui-Wrzosinska, Katharina Kugler, Andrea Bartoli, and Larry Liebovitch, *Attracted to Conflict: Dynamic Foundations of Malignant Social Relations* (Berlin: Springer, 2013). Peter T. Coleman, *The Five Percent: Finding Solutions to (Seemingly) Impossible Conflicts* (New York: Perseus Books, 2011).

2. WHY WE ARE STUCK

1. Sheera Frenkel, Nicholas Confessore, Cecilia Kang, Matthew Rosenberg, and Jack Nicas, "Delay, Deny and Deflect: How Facebook's Leaders Fought Through Crisis," *New York Times*, November 14, 2018, https://www.nytimes.com/2018/11/14/technology/facebook-data-russia-election-racism.html.
2. If you were following the news at all in late 2018, it was hard to miss coverage of Facebook's role as an unwitting tool in and platform for Russian attempts to influence the

U.S. election. For a refresher on what happened and Facebook's subsequent efforts to counteract "the disinformation, divisive messages, and false news" spread on the site, see Sheera Frenkel and Mike Isaac, "Facebook 'Better Prepared' to Fight Election Interference, Mark Zuckerberg Says," *New York Times*, September 13, 2018, https://www.nytimes.com/2018/09/13/technology/facebook-elections-mark-zuckerberg.html.

3. Perhaps less centrally on the radar of the American public was the role Facebook's platform played in other international conflicts. To learn more about how military officials in Myanmar utilized Facebook to systematically spread anti-Rohingya propaganda that fueled a genocidal purge of these Islamic minorities, see Paul Mozar, "A Genocide Incited on Facebook, with Posts from Myanmar's Military," *New York Times*, October 15, 2018, https://www.nytimes.com/2018/10/15/technology/myanmar-facebook-genocide.html.
4. Facebook also provided a platform for rapidly sharing inaccurate and panic-inducing news stories amid broader governmental instability and civil war in South Sudan. Justin Lynch's reporting for *Slate* has highlighted how the dissemination of untrue and sensational stories, propaganda, and hate speech has fueled violent ethnic conflict in South Sudan. See Justin Lynch, "In South Sudan, Fake News Has Deadly Consequences," *Slate*, June 9, 2017, https://slate.com/technology/2017/06/in-south-sudan-fake-news-has-deadly-consequences.html.
5. Lisa Schirch, "Peacebuilding Takes on Tech and Terror" (paper presented at the Building Sustainable Peace Conference, University of Notre Dame, Notre Dame, IN, November 7–10, 2019). Schirch further argued that the *attention economy* (based on the psychology of increasing addiction), combined with AI and algorithms built to maximize our use, and the business model of *surveillance capitalism* (where tech companies make money from collecting and selling our data) intentionally exploit vulnerabilities in our brains, societies, and institutions, resulting in a cascade of deleterious effects from social isolation and depression to polarization and violence.
6. Jean-Paul Sartre, "Paris Alive: The Republic of Silence," *The Atlantic* 174, no. 6 (December 1944): 39.
7. This originated in Gestalt psychology and, in particular, in the work of Kurt Lewin on field theory, Leon Festinger on cognitive dissonance, and Fritz Heider on the importance of sentiment balance in interpersonal relationships. It is an underlying motivational principle across psychology and in studies of consumer behavior today. See, for example, John T. Jost, Jack Glaser, Arie W. Kruglanski, and Frank J. Sulloway, "Political Conservatism as Motivated Social Cognition," *Psychological Bulletin* 129, no. 3 (2003): 339–75.
8. Edward S. Herman and Noam Chomsky offer a detailed accounting of the vast discrepancy in the number of column inches in the *Times* that are devoted to covering the United States–implicated world problems (fewer inches) versus non-U.S.-implicated problems (more), offering this as one example of the propagandistic nature of major media outlets. Edward S. Herman and Noam Chomsky, *Manufacturing Consent: The Political Economy of the Mass Media*, 3rd ed. (New York: Pantheon, 2002), 1:480.
9. See Aaron Bramson, Patrick Grim, Daniel J. Singer, William J. Berger, Graham Sack, Steven Fisher, Carissa Flocken, and Bennett Holman, "Understanding Polarization: Meanings, Measures, and Model Evaluation," *Philosophy of Science* 84, no. 1 (2017): 115–59.

10. Both affective and ideological polarization involve discrete intragroup and intergroup dynamics, such as *group polarization* effects (also known as *risky shift* effects) in which the attitudes of in-group members tend to shift together toward more extreme positions—or even begin to splinter into more extreme subgroups—and attitudes between groups that move either further away from (polarization) or closer toward (depolarization) each other. For a fuller account, see Jin Jung, Patrick Grim, Daniel J. Singer, Aaron Bramson, William J. Berger, Bennett Holman, and Karen Kovaka, "A Multidisciplinary Understanding of Polarization," *American Psychologist* 74, no. 3 (2019): 301–14.
11. A great deal of interesting empirical research looks at the ways political polarization is associated with other important phenomena. For instance, to read more about

    a. how political polarization is associated with aggressiveness and hostility toward out-groups, see De Agnieszka Golec De Zavala, Aleksandra Cislak, and Elzbieta Wesolowska, "Political Conservatism, Need for Cognitive Closure, and Intergroup Hostility," *Political Psychology* 31, no. 4 (2010): 521–41.
    b. how our tendencies to form ethnic group identifications fuel broader social conflicts, see Joan Esteban and Debraj Ray, "On the Salience of Ethnic Conflict," *American Economic Review* 98, no. 5 (2008): 2185–2202.
    c. how different types of political and social polarization increase the risk of violent conflict, see Joan Esteban and Gerald Schneider, "Polarization and Conflict: Theoretical and Empirical Issues," *Journal of Peace and Conflict* 45, no. 2 (2008): 131–41.
    d. how Democrats' and Republicans' increasing levels of reported dislike toward each other is largely independent of changing policy attitudes and is more likely related to negativity in campaigning, see Shanto Iyengar, Gaurav Sood, and Yphtach Lelkes, "Affect, Not Ideology: A Social Identity Perspective on Polarization," *Public Opinion Quarterly* 76, no. 3 (2012): 819.

12. "America's Divided Mind: Understanding the Psychology That Drives Us Apart," *Beyond Conflict* June 2020, https://beyondconflictint.org/americas-divided-mind/.
13. American Political Science Association's Committee on Political Parties, *Toward a More Responsible Two-Party System* (New York: Rinehart, 1950).
14. Feng Shi, Misha Teplitskiy, Eamon Duede, et al., "The Wisdom of Polarized Crowds," *Nature Human Behavior* 3 (March 2019): 329–36; Feng Shi, Misha Teplitskiy, Eamon Duede, and James A. Evans, "Are Politically Diverse Teams More Effective?," *Harvard Business Review*, July 15, 2019, https://hbr.org/2019/07/are-politically-diverse-teams-more-effective.
15. For more in-depth discussions of polarization today, see Pew Research Center, "Political Polarization" (website page), https://www.pewresearch.org/topics/political-polarization/; Ezra Klein, *Why We're Polarized* (New York: Simon and Schuster, 2020); Nolan McCarty, Keith T. Poole, and Howard Rosenthal, *Polarized America: The Dance of Ideology and Unequal Riches* (Cambridge, MA: MIT Press, 2006); Nolan McCarty, *Polarization: What Everyone Needs to Know* (Oxford: Oxford University Press, 2019).
16. Nolan McCarty, Keith T. Poole, and Howard Rosenthal, *Polarized America: The Dance of Ideology and Unequal Riches* (Cambridge, MA: MIT Press, 2006). I used updated data and ran the models out to 2018, and the trends continue unabated.

17. Alan I. Abramowitz and Kyle L. Saunders, "Is Polarization a Myth?," *Journal of Politics* 70, no. 2 (2008): 542–55.
18. This does not deny the fact that split ticket voting has all but disappeared and that independents tend to lean consistently in support of one party or the other. Nevertheless, self-reported party and ideological affiliations are flat.
19. In 2018, More in Common conducted a fascinating large-scale national survey that both confirmed the existence of increasing polarization in the United States and complicated the dimensionality of our polarization. The study identified seven "tribes" that are based on beliefs and attitudes distinct from political party affiliation. See Hidden Tribes, "The Hidden Tribes of America," *More in Common*, October 2018, https://hiddentribes.us.
20. In the last several years, polling conducted by Pew has given interesting insight into the nature and nuances of America's polarization, stating in a report from 2017 that "the partisan divide on political values grows even wider." Pew researchers provide robust data on both the specific policy divides and the negative emotional associations with partisan opponents. See Pew Research Center, "Partisan Animosity, Personal Politics, Views of Trump," October 5, 2017, https://www.people-press.org/2017/10/05/8-partisan-animosity-personal-politics-views-of-trump/.
21. In 1994, only 16 percent of Democrats and 17 percent of Republicans held very unfavorable views of the opposite party, whereas in 2017 those proportions rose to 44 percent and 45 percent, respectively. As of August 2017, 53 percent of Republicans had "very cold" feelings toward Democrats, and 52 percent of Democrats had "very cold" feelings toward Republicans. A recent study from our lab found that 87 percent of Democrats and 85 percent of Republicans view members of the other party as "more immoral," 85 percent of Democrats and 75 percent of Republicans view the other side as "more dishonest," and 96 percent of Democrats and 64 percent of Republicans rate the other party as "more close-minded."
22. See Alan I. Abramowitz and Steven W. Webster, "Negative Partisanship: Why Americans Dislike Parties but Behave Like Rabid Partisans," *Political Psychology* 39, no. 1 (2018): 119–35.
23. Blake M. Riek, Eric W. Mania, and Samuel L. Gaertner, "Intergroup Threat and Outgroup Attitudes: A Meta-Analytic Review," *Personality and Social Psychology Review* 10, no. 4 (2006): 336–53.
24. Pew's research on what they call "ideological consistency" provides critical insight into the difference between party loyalty and interest in specific policy issues. See Pew Research Center, "The Shift in the American Public's Political Values," October 20, 2017, https://www.people-press.org/interactives/political-polarization-1994-2017/.
25. Shelly Chaiken, Roger Giner-Sorolla, and Serena Chen, "Beyond Accuracy: Defense and Impression Motives in Heuristic and Systematic Information Processing," in *The Psychology of Action: Linking Cognition and Motivation to Behavior*, ed. Peter M. Goldwitzer and John A. Bargh (New York: Guilford, 1996), 553–87.
26. Matthew Gentzkow, "Polarization in 2016," Toulouse Network for Information Technology Whitepaper, March 2016, https://web.stanford.edu/~gentzkow/research/Polarization2016.pdf.

27. See John R. Hibbing, Kevin B. Smith, and John R. Alford, *Predisposed: Liberals, Conservatives, and the Biology of Political Differences* (New York: Routledge, 2013).
28. Jonathan Haidt and colleagues have been leading efforts to research what they call the "Five Moral Foundations"—or the five core moral values that all people have to some degree, but hold with different levels of priority. These moral values—identified as loyalty, authority, purity, care, and fairness—can help illuminate the differences in policy priorities and issues between liberals and conservatives. See MoralFoundations.org (webpage), https://moralfoundations.org/.
29. See John T. Jost, Jack Glaser, Arie W. Kruglanski, and Frank J. Sulloway, "Political Conservatism as Motivated Social Cognition," *Psychological Bulletin* 129, no. 3 (2003): 339–75; Karen Stenner, " 'Conservatism,' Context-Dependence, and Cognitive Incapacity," *Psychological Inquiry* 20, no. 2–3 (2009): 189–95.
30. One of the first to make this argument was Muzafer Sherif, *Common Predicament: Social Psychology of Intergroup Conflict and Cooperation* (Boston: Houghton Mifflin, 1966).
31. This search, conducted by Becca Bass, drew significantly from Piercarlo Valdesolo and Jesse Graham, eds. *Social Psychology of Political Polarization* (New York: Routledge, 2016).
32. Karl Popper, "Of Clouds and Clocks: An Approach to the Problem of Rationality and the Freedom of Man," in *Objective Knowledge: An Evolutionary Approach* (Oxford: Oxford University Press, 1972). The text of the lecture is available at http://www.the-rathouse.com/2011/Clouds-and-Clocks.html.
33. Reportedly, General Stanley McChrystal, who headed American and NATO forces in Afghanistan, was once shown a high-complexity PowerPoint mapping of U.S. military strategy on the ground to win the hearts and minds of the Afghani people, which looked like a large pile of spaghetti. McChrystal responded to the presentation by saying, "When we understand that slide, we'll have won the war." After which, the room erupted in laughter. Elisabeth Bumiller, "We Have Met the Enemy and He Is PowerPoint," *New York Times*, April 26, 2010, https://www.nytimes.com/2010/04/27/world/27powerpoint.html.
34. To learn more about how specific kinds of complex thinking drive different political actions, and specifically how complexity of thinking influences political violence and political success, see Lucian Gideon Conway III, Peter Suedfeld, and Philip E. Tetlock, "Integrative Complexity in Politics," in *The Oxford Handbook of Behavioral Science*, ed. Alex Mintz and Lesley Terris (Oxford: Oxford University Press, 2018).
35. In my lab at the Morton Deutsch International Center for Cooperation and Conflict Resolution at Teachers College, Columbia University, our team has been developing a "Conflict Anxiety Response Scale." Based on common coping strategies observed during Morton Deutsch's own experience as a couples' therapist, this scale seeks to help people identify their own adaptive and maladaptive responses to anxiety and conflict. In our pilot studies to date, we've consistently found that the more extreme people report being in their responses to conflict anxiety—the more avoidant or escalatory or harsh or controlling they tend to get—the more likely they are to report negative affect and the lower is their overall self-reported well-being. Peter T. Coleman and Anthea Chan, "How to Manage

COVID and Conflict in Our Homes and Workplaces," *Earth Institute* (blog), Columbia University, May 26, 2020, https://blogs.ei.columbia.edu/2020/05/26/covid-conflict-anxiety-survey/.

36. See Sean Westwood and Erik Peterson, "The Inseparability of Race and Partisanship in the United States," Political Behavior, 2020, https://doi.org/10.1007/s11109-020-09648-9.
37. See Jeff Greenberg, Sheldon Solomon, and Tom Pyszczynski, "Terror Management Theory of Self-Esteem and Cultural Worldviews: Empirical Assessments and Conceptual Refinements," in *Advances in Experimental Social Psychology*, ed. M. Zanna (San Diego, CA: Academic Press, 1997), 29:61–139; See also Mark J. Landau, Sheldon Solomon, Jeff Greenberg, Florette Cohen, Tom Pyszczynski, Jamie Arndt, Claude H. Miller, Daniel M. Ogilvie, and Alison Cook, "Deliver Us from Evil: The Effects of Mortality Salience and Reminders of 9/11 on Support for President George W. Bush," *Personality and Social Psychology Review* 30, no. 9 (2004): 1136–50.
38. See Michele J. Gelfand, *Rule Makers, Rule Breakers: How Tight and Loose Cultures Wire Our World* (New York: Scribner, 2018), https://www.michelegelfand.com/rule-makers-rule-breakers.
39. See Katharina G. Kugler and Peter T. Coleman, "Get Complicated: The Effects of Complexity on Conversations over Potentially Intractable Moral Conflicts," *Negotiation and Conflict Management Research* 13, no. 3 (July 2020): 211–30; Robin R. Vallacher, Peter T. Coleman, Andrzej Nowak, and Lan Bui-Wrzosinska, "Rethinking Intractable Conflict: The Perspective of Dynamical Systems," *American Psychologist* 65, no. 4 (2010): 262–78.

3. ATTRACTED TO CONFLICT

1. Kurt Lewin, *Principles of Topological Psychology*, trans. Grace M. Heider and Fritz Heider (New York: McGraw-Hill, 1936).
2. For a great map of the origins of complexity science, see Brian Castellani, "2018 Map of the Complexity Sciences," *Art and Science Factory*, February 9, 2018, https://www.art-sciencefactory.com/complexity-map_feb09.html.
3. Over decades-long careers, Keith T. Poole and Howard Rosenthal compiled an impressively robust collection of data on historical voting patterns in Congress. Visit their data archive at http://legacy.voteview.com.
4. This chapter provides an introductory overview of the concept of "attractors" and how this framework can help us better understand the seeming intractability of polarization in American society. For a deeper dive into the concept of attractors and the way dynamical systems theory can help us understand phenomena as diverse and complex as social relations, attitudes, social cognition, and interpersonal behaviors, see Robin Vallacher and Andrzej Nowak, eds., *Dynamical Systems in Social Psychology* (Cambridge, MA: Academic Press, 1994).
5. For more on attractor landscapes in a variety of disciplines, in:

   a. epigenetics, see Konrad Hochedlinger and Kathrin Plath, "Epigenetic Reprogramming and Induced Pluripotency," *Development* 136, no. 4 (2009): 509–23, https://pubmed.ncbi.nlm.nih.gov/19168672/; specifically represented in Figure 1:

The Developmental Potential and Epigenetic States of Cells at Different Stages of Development.

b. pathological brain oscillations, see Tomas Ros, Bernard J. Baars, Ruth Lanuis, and Patrick Vuilleumier, "Tuning Pathological Brain Oscillations with Neurofeedback: A Systems Neuroscience Framework," *Frontiers in Human Neuroscience* 8 (2014): 1–22, https://doi.org/10.3389/fnhum.2014.01008; specifically, see Figure 4.
c. political alignments in WWII, see Robert Axelrod and D. Scott Bennett, "A Landscape Theory of Aggregation," *British Journal of Political Science* 23, no. 2 (1993): 211–33, https://www.jstor.org/stable/194248.
d. gravitational anomalies in space, see John Huchra and Daniel Fabricant, "Voyage from the Great Attractor," *Center for Astrophysics at Harvard University*, 2009, https://www.cfa.harvard.edu/~dfabricant/huchra/seminar/attractor/.

6. For more comprehensive scholarly reviews of the literature on attractor dynamics in psychology, see Stephen J. Guastello, Matthijs Koopmans, and David Pincus, eds., *Chaos and Complexity in Psychology: The Theory of Nonlinear Dynamical Systems* (New York: Cambridge University Press, 2009). Robin R. Vallacher and Andrzej Nowak, eds., *Dynamical Systems in Social Psychology* (Cambridge, MA: Academic Press, 1994).
7. This chapter distills big concepts around complexity that in many ways represent my life's work and the life's work of many of my colleagues and peers. Some readers may be relieved by the abbreviated introduction, but for those who want to learn more—you're in luck! For more detail on my research on attractor landscapes and dynamical systems theory, I recommend the following works.

a. Peter T. Coleman, Lan Bui-Wrzosinska, Andrzej Nowak, and Robin Vallacher, "A Dynamical Systems Perspective on Peacemaking: Moving from a System of War Toward a System of Peace," in *Peacemaking: From Practice to Theory*, 2 vols., ed. Susan Allen-Nan, Zachariah Cherian Mampilly, and Andrea Bartoli (Santa Barbara, CA: ABC-CLIO, 2012), 637–50.
b. Peter T. Coleman, *The 5 percent: Finding Solutions to Seemingly Impossible Conflicts* (New York: Public Affairs, 2011).
c. Peter T. Coleman, Nicholas Redding, and Joshua Fisher, "Understanding Intractable Conflict," in *Negotiators Desk Reference*, ed. Andrea Schneider and Christopher Honeyman (Chicago: American Bar Association Books, 2017), 489–508.
d. Peter T. Coleman, Nicholas Redding, and Joshua Fisher, "Influencing Intractable Conflict," in *Negotiators Desk Reference*, ed. Andrea Schneider and Christopher Honeyman (Chicago: American Bar Association Books, 2017), 509–28.
e. Robin R. Vallacher, Peter T. Coleman, Andrzej Nowak, and Lan Bui-Wrzosinska, "Rethinking Intractable Conflict: The Perspective of Dynamical Systems," in *Conflict, Interdependence, and Justice: The Intellectual Legacy of Morton Deutsch*, ed. Peter T. Coleman (New York: Springer, 2011), 65–94.
f. Larry S. Liebovitch, Robin R. Vallacher, and J. Michaels, "Dynamics of Cooperation—Competition Interaction Models," *Peace and Conflict* 16, no. 2 (2010): 175–88.

g. Andrzej Nowak, Morton Deutsch, Wieslaw Bartkowski, and Sorin Solomon, "From Crude Law to Civil Relations: The Dynamics and Potential Resolution of Intractable Conflict," *Peace and Conflict* 16, no. 2 (2010): 189–209.
h. Robin R. Vallacher, Peter T. Coleman, Andrzej Nowak, and Lan Bui-Wroszink, "Rethinking Intractable Conflict: The Perspective of Dynamical Systems," *American Psychologist* 65, no. 4 (2010): 262–78.
i. Robin R. Vallacher, Peter T. Coleman, Andrzej Nowak, Lan Bui-Wrzosinska, Larry Liebovitch, Katharina Kugler, and Andrea Bartoli, *Attracted to Conflict: Dynamic Foundations of Destructive Social Relations* (New York: Springer, 2010).

8. Kurt Lewin referred to these psychological landscapes as our *life space*. Kurt Lewin, "Constructs in Field Theory," in *Resolving Social Conflicts and Field Theory in Social Science* (Washington, DC: American Psychological Association, 1943).
9. For more on how more difficult conflicts spread over time, see Naira Musallam, Peter T. Coleman, and Andrzej Nowak, "Understanding the Spread of Malignant Conflict: A Dynamical Systems Perspective," *Peace and Conflict: Journal of Peace Psychology* 16, no. 2 (2010): 127–51.
10. Joshua Fisher and Peter T. Coleman, "The Fractal Nature of Intractable Conflict: Implications for Sustainable Transformation," in *Overcoming Transforming Intractable Conflicts: New Approaches to Constructive Transformations*, ed. Miriam F. Elman, Catherine Gerard, Galia Golan, and Louis Kriesbert (London: Rowman and Littlefield International, 2019).
11. Roy F. Baumeister, Ellen Bratslavsky, Catrin Finkenauer, and Kathleen D. Vohs, "Bad Is Stronger Than Good," *Review of General Psychology* 5, no. 4 (2001): 323–70.
12. To explore how attractor patterns can be a helpful lens in a variety of contexts, I recommend these works:

a. for escalation and de-escalation of war and conflict: Paul F. Diehl and Gary Goertz, *War and Peace in International Rivalry* (Ann Arbor: University of Michigan Press, 2001).
b. for habits of leaders who are successful (and unsuccessful) in complex leadership contexts: Dietrich Dörner, *The Logic of Failure: Why Things Go Wrong and What We Can Do to Make Them Right* (Cambridge, MA: Perseus Press, 1996).
c. for how patterns of interactions and affect impact the quality and longevity of marriages over time: John M. Gottman, *Principia Amoris: The New Science of Love* (New York: Routledge, 2014); John M. Gottman, James D. Murray, Catherine C. Swanson, Rebecca Tyson, and Kristin R. Swanson, *The Mathematics of Marriage: Dynamic Non-Linear Models* (Cambridge, MA: MIT Press, 2002).
d. for conversations over highly divisive issues: Katharina G. Kugler, Peter T. Coleman, and Anna M. Fuchs, "Moral Conflict and Complexity: The Dynamics of Constructive Versus Destructive Discussions over Polarizing Issues" (paper presented at the International Association of Conflict Management 24th Annual Conference, Istanbul, Turkey, July 3–6, 2011), https://ssrn.com/abstract=1872654.

e. for creatively disrupting patterns of tension in communities: Ryszard Praszkier, Andrzej Nowak, and Peter T. Coleman, "Social Entrepreneurs and Constructive Change: The Wisdom of Circumventing Conflict," *Peace and Conflict: The Journal of Peace Psychology* 16, no. 2 (2010): 153–74.

13. Better yet, see Dutch historian Rutger Bregman's forthcoming nonfiction book about a group of shipwrecked boys from Tonga who joined together to create a much more positive, compassionate society. For some excerpts, see Rutger Bregman, "The Real Lord of the Flies: What Happened When Six Boys Were Shipwrecked for 15 Months," *The Guardian*, May 9, 2020, https://www.theguardian.com/books/2020/may/09/the-real-lord-of-the-flies-what-happened-when-six-boys-were-shipwrecked-for-15-months.
14. Connie J. G. Gersick, "Revolutionary Change Theories: A Multilevel Exploration of the Punctuated Equilibrium Paradigm," *Academy of Management Review* 16, no. 1 (1991): 10–36; Elaine Romanelli and Michael L. Tushman, "Organizational Transformation as Punctuated Equilibrium: An Empirical Test," *Academy of Management Journal* 37, no. 5 (1994): 1141–66.
15. Paul F. Diehl and Gary Goertz, *War and Peace in International Rivalry* (Ann Arbor: University of Michigan Press, 2011).

4. THINK DIFFERENT—CHANGE YOUR THEORY OF CHANGE

1. For more information on My Country Talks, visit the website at https://www.mycountrytalks.org/.
2. For original reporting on this encounter, see Bastian Berbner and Amrai Coen, "The Hunter and the Yogi," *Die Zeit*, December 6, 2017, https://www.zeit.de/2017/51/ein-jahr-donald-trump-waehler-stadt-provinz-erfahrung.
3. This cross-country travel program focused on teaching participants about the culture and history of the United States through firsthand exposure to important cities and sites, creating more well-informed and engaged citizens. For more information on Etgar 36, visit the website at https://www.etgar.org/.
4. Organized by the Center for Deliberative Democracy at Stanford University, Helena, by the People Productions, and NORC at University of Chicago, this gathering of more than five hundred representative American voters in 2019 met for a structured examination and discussion of key political issues and a discussion with political candidates. To learn more about America in One Room, visit the website at https://cdd.stanford.edu/2019/america-in-one-room/.
5. Better Angels uses lessons from family systems therapy to help structure and inform workshops, skills trainings, debates, and local membership groups with the goal of reducing political polarization across the United States. To learn more about Better Angels, visit the website at https://www.better-angels.org/our-story/. Crossing Party Lines offers an online toolkit of resources based on active listening practices and nonviolent communication that is designed to help people talk across political divides more constructively. To learn more, visit the website at http://www.crossingpartylines.net/.

6. Make America Dinner Again provides a guide for hosting intentional dinners with people with different political views. To find out if there is an active chapter in your city, visit the website at http://www.makeamericadinneragain.com/.
7. For a growing list of U.S.-based dialogue facilitation groups, visit the Morton Deutsch International Center for Cooperation and Conflict Resolution website at https://icccr.tc.columbia.edu/resources/dialogue-facilitation-organizations/. The Civic Health Project also has evolving efforts to organize a list of civic health organizations nationwide. For more information, visit the website at civichealthproject.org.
8. Gordon W. Allport, *The Nature of Prejudice* (Cambridge, MA: Addison-Wesley, 1954); to catch up on the decades of research on intergroup contact theory, see Loris Vezzali and Sofia Stathi, eds., *Intergroup Contact Theory: Recent Developments and Future Directions* (New York: Routledge, 2017).
9. See James Fishkin and Larry Diamond, "This Experiment Has Some Great News for Our Democracy," *New York Times*, October 2, 2019, https://www.nytimes.com/2019/10/02/opinion/america-one-room-experiment.html. This article offers a more in-depth description of the process and outcomes of the America in One Room event held in 2019, which gathered more than five hundred American voters for structured exploration and discussion of five key issue areas in current political debates.
10. "More Now Say It's 'Stressful' to Discuss Politics with People They Disagree With," Pew Research Center, November 5, 2018, https://www.people-press.org/2018/11/05/more-now-say-its-stressful-to-discuss-politics-with-people-they-disagree-with/.
11. Theories of change are also a specific type of methodology commonly used for planning, participation, and evaluation in companies, philanthropy, and not-for-profit and government sectors to promote change. For a more thorough explanation of theories of change, see Ann-Murray Brown, "What Is This Thing Called 'Theory of Change'?," *USAID Learning Lab*, March 18, 2016, https://usaidlearninglab.org/lab-notes/what-thing-called-theory-change.
12. For an exploration of how the metaphors we use to characterize nations help rationalize war and justify ineffective strategies, see George Lakoff, "Metaphor and War, Again," *Alternet*, March 18, 2003, https://escholarship.org/uc/item/32b962zb; George Lakoff and Mark Johnson, *Philosophy in the Flesh: The Embodied Mind and Its Challenge to Western Thought* (New York: Basic Books, 1999).
13. This project resulted in two publications: Peter T. Coleman, Antony G. Hacking, Mark A. Stover, Beth Fisher-Yoshida, and Andrzej Nowak, "Reconstructing Ripeness I: A Study of Constructive Engagement in Protracted Social Conflicts," *Conflict Resolution Quarterly* 26, no. 1 (2008): 3–42; Peter T. Coleman, Beth Fisher-Yoshida, Mark A. Stover, Antony G. Hacking, and Andrea Bartoli, "Reconstructing Ripeness II: Models and Methods for Fostering Constructive Stakeholder Engagement Across Protracted Divides," *Conflict Resolution Quarterly* 26, no. 1 (2008): 43–69.
14. For more on implicit theories, see Carol S. Dweck, *Mindset: The New Psychology of Success* (New York: Ballantine, 2008); Peter T. Coleman, "Implicit Theories of Organizational Power and Priming Effects on Managerial Power Sharing Decisions: An Experimental

Study," *Journal of Applied Social Psychology* 34, no. 2 (2004): 297–321; Peter T. Coleman, "A Tale of Two Theories: Implicit Theories of Power and Power-Sharing in Organizations," in *Power and Interdependence in Organizations*, ed. Dean Tjosvold and BarbaraWiesse (Cambridge: Cambridge University Press, 2009).

15. For more on the way our implicit theories or beliefs about intelligence affect life outcomes, specifically, whether we believe that it is "fixed" or something that can be developed through effort, see Dweck, *Mindset.*
16. To read more about the wide range of implicit theories we hold about what makes a leader, see Lynn R. Offerman, John K. Kennedy Jr., and Philip W. Wirtz, "Implicit Leadership Theories: Content, Structure, and Generalizability," *Leadership Quarterly* 5, no. l (1994): 43–58.
17. For a fascinating study on the way beliefs about relationships—whether relationships are "meant to be" or the product of growth and development over time—influence our interactions, how we react to challenges, and relationship length, see C. Raymond Knee, "Implicit Theories of Relationships: Assessment and Prediction of Romantic Relationship Initiation, Coping, and Longevity," *Journal of Personality and Social Psychology* 74, no. 2 (1998): 360–70.
18. For more on implicit theories and conflict resolution, see Carol S. Dweck and Joyce Ehrlinger, "Implicit Theories and Conflict Resolution," in *The Handbook of Conflict Resolution: Theory and Practice*, 2nd ed., ed. Morton Deutsch, Peter T. Coleman, and Eric C. Marcus (Hoboken, NJ: Wiley, 2006), 317–30.
19. For more on the way our implicit theories of our own emotions—specifically, whether we see our emotions as fixed or malleable—affect our sense of well-being and emotional experience over time, see Maya Tamir, Oliver John Sanjay Srivastava, and James J. Gross, "Implicit Theories of Emotion: Affective and Social Outcomes Across a Major Life Transition," *Journal of Personality and Social Psychology* 92, no. 4 (2007): 731–44.
20. Dexter Dunphy, "Organizational Change in Corporate Settings," *Human Relations* 49, no. 5 (1996): 541–52; Peter T. Coleman, "Paradigmatic Framing of Protracted, Intractable Conflict: Towards the Development of a Meta-Framework-II," *Peace and Conflict: Journal of Peace Psychology* 10, no. 3 (2004): 197–235.
21. See Roger Fisher, William Ury, and Bruce Patton, *Getting to Yes: Negotiating Agreement Without Giving In* (1981; updated and repr. New York: Penguin Books, 2011).
22. Peter T. Coleman, *The Five Percent: Finding Solutions to (Seemingly) Impossible Conflicts* (New York: Perseus Books, 2011).
23. See the brilliant treatise by Paul Diesing, "Economic Rationality," in *Reason in Society: Five Types of Decisions and Their Social Conditions* (Urbana: University of Illinois Press, 1962), 14–64.
24. Peter T. Coleman, Jennifer Goldman, and Katharina Kugler, "Emotional Intractability: Gender, Anger, Aggression, and Rumination in Conflict," *International Journal of Conflict Management* 20 (2009): 113–31.
25. Peter T. Coleman and J. Krister Lowe, "Conflict, Identity, and Resilience: Negotiating Collective Identities Within the Palestinian and Israeli Diasporas," *Conflict Resolution Quarterly* 24, no. 4 (2007): 377–412.

26. Peter T. Coleman, "Fostering Ripeness in Seemingly Intractable Conflict: An Experimental Study," *International Journal of Conflict Management* 11, no. 4 (2000): 300–317.
27. Coleman, *The 5 percent*; Robin R. Vallacher, Peter T. Coleman, Andrzej Nowak, and Lan Bui-Wroszinka, "Rethinking Intractable Conflict: The Perspective of Dynamical Systems," *American Psychologist* 65, no. 4 (2010): 262–78; Robin R. Vallacher, Peter T. Coleman, Andrzej Nowak, Lan Bui-Wrzosinska, Larry Liebovitch, Katharina Kugler, and Andrea Bartoli, *Attracted to Conflict: Dynamic Foundations of Destructive Social Relations* (New York: Springer, 2013).
28. Katharina Kugler and Peter T. Coleman, "Get Complicated: The Effects of Complexity on Conversations over Potentially Intractable Moral Conflicts," *Negotiation and Conflict Management Research* 13, no. 3 (August 2020): 211–230; Levent Kurt, Katharina Kugler, Peter T. Coleman, and Larry S. Liebovitch, "Behavioral and Emotional Dynamics of Two People Struggling to Reach a Consensus on a Topic on Which They Disagree," *PLOS ONE* 9, no. 1 (2014).
29. Dr. Martin Luther King Jr., "Beyond Vietnam" (speech), April 4, 1967, a year to the day before he was assassinated in Memphis. You can access the audio and text of the speech through Stanford University's Martin Luther King Jr. Research and Education Institute website at https://kinginstitute.stanford.edu/king-papers/documents/beyond-vietnam.
30. George Mead, *Mind, Self, and Society* (Chicago: University of Chicago Press, 1934); Peter T. Coleman, "Conflict Intelligence and Systemic Wisdom: Meta-Competencies for Engaging Conflict in a Complex, Dynamic World," *Negotiation Journal* 34, no. 1 (2018): 7–35.
31. Kaiping Peng and Richard E. Nisbett, "Culture, Dialectics, and Reasoning About Contradiction," *American Psychologist* 54, no. 9 (1999): 741–54; François Jullien, *A Treatise on Efficacy: Between Western and Chinese Thinking*, trans. J. Lloyd (Honolulu: University of Hawai'i Press, 2004), x–202; Orit Gal, "About Social Acupuncture," Social Acupuncture, 2017, http://www.socialacupuncture.co.uk/about/.
32. Florence R. Kluckhohn and Fred L. Strodtbeck, *Variations in Value Orientations* (Evanston, IL: Row, Peterson, 1961).
33. Brandt C. Gardner, Brandon K. Burr, and Sara E. Wiedower, "Reconceptualizing Strategic Family Therapy: Insights from a Dynamic Systems Perspective," *Contemporary Family Therapy* 28, no. 3 (2006): 339–52.
34. Daniel J. Svyantek and Linda L. Brown, "A Complex-Systems Approach to Organizations," *Current Directions in Psychological Science* 9, no. 2 (2000): 69–74.
35. Cedric H. De Coning, "Complexity Thinking and Adaptive Peacebuilding," *Accord: An International Review of Peace Initiatives* 28 (2019): 36–39; Ben Ramalingam, *Aid on the Edge of Chaos: Rethinking International Cooperation in a Complex World* (Oxford: Oxford University Press, 2013).
36. Peter T. Coleman, Nicholas Redding, and Joshua Fisher, "Understanding Intractable Conflict," in *Negotiators Desk Reference*, ed. Andrea Schneider and Chris Honeyman (Chicago: American Bar Association Books, 2017), 489-508; Peter T. Coleman, Nicholas Redding, and Joshua Fisher, "Influencing Intractable Conflict," in *Negotiators Desk Reference*, ed. Andrea Schneider and Chris Honeyman (Chicago: American Bar Association Books, 2017), 509–28.

37. Yuval Noah Harari, *Sapiens: A Brief History of Humankind* (New York: Harper, 2018).
38. In fact, some scholars refer to these types of problems as *infinite games* because they do not have consistent rules or a beginning and an end where someone "wins." Rather, they are ongoing, evolving games with mutating rules that require different types of play. See James P. Carse, *Finite and Infinite Games: A Vision of Life and Play and Possibility* (New York: Free Press, 1986).

5. RESET—CAPTURE THE POWER OF NEW BEGINNINGS

1. In addition, the regime worked to establish woman's suffrage, strengthen the electoral tribunal, identify and address institutionalized racism, and nationalize the banking system. Gary S. Elbow, "Costa Rica," *Encyclopædia Britannica*, March 17, 2020, https://www.britannica.com/place/Costa-Rica/Transition-to-democracy.
2. Peter T. Coleman and Jaclyn Donahue, "Costa Rica: Choosing a Path to Build and Sustain Peace," *International Peace Institute's Global Observatory*, September 7, 2018, https://theglobalobservatory.org/2018/09/costa-rica-choosing-path-to-build-sustain-peace/.
3. A number of interesting resources describe the power of destabilizing shocks for transforming long-term patterns of conflict. Paul F. Diehl and Gary Goertz, *War and Peace in International Rivalry* (Ann Arbor: University of Michigan Press, 2001); Connie J. G. Gersick, "Revolutionary Change Theories: A Multilevel Exploration of the Punctuated Equilibrium Paradigm," *Academy of Management Review* 16, no. 1 (1991): 10–36; James P. Klein, Gary Goertz, and Paul F. Diehl, "The New Rivalry Dataset: Procedures and Patterns," *Journal of Peace Research* 43, no. 3 (2006): 331–48.
4. Kurt Lewin, "Frontiers in Group Dynamics: Concept, Method and Reality in Social Science; Equilibrium and Social Change," *Human Relations* 1, no. 1 (1947): 5–41.
5. Gersick, "Revolutionary Change Theories."
6. Diehl and Goertz, *War and Peace in International Rivalry*.
7. Nolan McCarty, Keith T. Poole, and Howard Rosenthal, *Polarized America: The Dance of Ideology and Unequal Riches* (Cambridge, MA: MIT Press, 2006).
8. Stephen Jay Gould, *Under the Panda's Thumb: More Reflections in Natural History* (New York: Norton, 1980).
9. Among the many examples of this phenomenon in writings about human and organizational development, I recommend Daniel J. Levinson, "A Conception of Adult Development," *American Psychologist* 41, no. 1 (1986): 3. See also Connie J. G. Gersick, "Time and Transition in Work Teams: Toward a New Model of Group Development," *Academy of Management Journal* 31, no. 1 (1988): 9–41; Michael L. Tushman and Elaine Romanelli, "Organizational Evolution: A Metamorphosis Model of Convergence and Reorientation," *Research in Organizational Behavior* 7 (1985): 171–222.
10. For more reading on the role of destabilizing forces in driving forward scientific advancements, I recommend Thomas S. Kuhn, *The Structure of Scientific Revolution*, 2nd ed. (Chicago: University of Chicago Press, 1970); Ilya Prigogine and Isabelle Stengers, *Order Out of Chaos: Man's New Dialogue with Nature* (New York: Bantam Books, 1984).
11. Gould, *Under the Panda's Thumb*.

12. Visit scholar.google.com and search for "punctuated equilibrium research" to get a flavor of the studies to date and a sense of the vast cross-disciplinary range of research that has been done.
13. Elaine Romanelli and Michael L. Tushman, "Organizational Transformation as Punctuated Equilibrium: An Empirical Test," *Academy of Management Journal* 37, no. 5 (1994): 1141–66.
14. Jack Mezirow and Victoria Marsick, *Education for Perspective Transformation: Women's Reentry Programs in Community Colleges* (New York: Center for Adult Education, Teachers College, Columbia University, 1978); Jack Mezirow, *Transformative Dimensions of Adult Learning* (San Francisco: Jossey-Bass, 1991).
15. Diehl and Goertz, *War and Peace in International Rivalry*.
16. See Connie Gersick, "Reflections on Revolutionary Change," *Journal of Change Management* 20, no. 1 (2020): 7–23.
17. Gersick, "Revolutionary Change Theories," 12.
18. Gersick went on to elaborate: "Deep structures are highly stable for two general reasons. First, like a decision tree, the trail of choices made by a system rules many options out, at the same time as it rules mutually contingent options in. This characterization accords with organizational research on the tenacity of initial choices, and the fact that early steps in decision trees are most fateful." Gersick, "Revolutionary Change Theories," 14–16. See also Kathleen M. Eisenhardt and Claudia Bird Schoonhoven, "Organizational Growth: Linking Founding Team, Strategy, Environment, and Growth Among U.S. Semiconductor Ventures, 1978–1988," *Administrative Science Quarterly* 35, no. 3 (1990): 504–29; Robert C. Ginnett, "First Encounters of the Close Kind: The Formation Process of Airline Flight Crews" (PhD diss., Yale University, 1987); Arthur L. Stinchcombe, "Social Structure and Organizations," in *Handbook of Organizations*, ed. J. P. March (Chicago: Rand McNally, 1965), 142–93.

    In addition, researchers find that the activity patterns of a system's deep structure reinforce the system as a whole through mutual feedback loops. David B. Wake, Gerhard Roth, and Marvalee H. Wake, "On the Problem of Stasis in Organismal Evolution," *Journal of Theoretical Biology* 101, no. 2 (1983): 211–24; Gersick, "Reflections on Revolutionary Change."
19. Gersick, "Revolutionary Change Theories," 23.
20. This is a reference to the American Western film classic *Shane*, set in the post–Civil War era and featuring a mysterious lone gunslinger who rides into a town in the Wyoming Territory. If the reference was lost on you but you have a soft spot for nostalgia films, I recommend watching it.
21. Thomas S. Kuhn, *The Structure of Scientific Revolutions* (Chicago: University of Chicago Press, 1996).
22. Romanelli and Tushman, "Organizational Transformation as Punctuated Equilibrium."
23. For more information about the work of the nonprofit Hope in the Cities, visit their website at https://us.iofc.org/hope-in-the-cities.
24. For a list compiled by our team of organizations working to transform polarization and division, visit https://icccr.tc.columbia.edu/resources/organizations-bridging-divides/.

25. The Harlem Children's Zone's goal is for every child to graduate from college. To see their outcomes to date, visit the website at https://hcz.org/results/.
26. Michael G. Wessells, "Bottom-Up Approaches to Strengthening Child Protection Systems: Placing Children, Families, and Communities at the Center," *Child Abuse and Neglect* 43 (2015): 8–21.
27. Gersick, "Reflections on Revolutionary Change."
28. Ryszard Praszkier, Andrzej Nowak, and Peter T. Coleman, "Social Entrepreneurs and Constructive Change: The Wisdom of Circumventing Conflict," *Peace and Conflict: Journal of Peace Psychology* 16, no. 2 (2010): 153–74.
29. Read more about Tim Shriver's initiative, The Call to Unite, at https://unite.us/.
30. This phenomenon also accounts for what economists refer to as *path dependence*, such as when suboptimal products and designs (like VHS videotapes and the QWERTY layout in computer keyboards) capture the market over clearly superior products (such as Betamax tapes and the Dvorak keyboard) because of the conditions of their early entry into a market. See W. Brian Arthur, "Complexity and the Economy," *Science*, 284, no. 5411 (1999): 107–9.
31. John M. Gottman, Catherine Swanson, and Kristin R. Swanson, "A General Systems Theory of Marriage: Nonlinear Difference Equation Modeling of Marital Interaction," *Personality and Social Psychology Review* 6, no. 4 (2002): 326–40.
32. Barbara L. Fredrickson and Thomas Joiner, "Positive Emotions Trigger Upward Spirals Toward Emotional Well-Being," *Psychological Science* 13, no. 2 (2002): 172–75.
33. To read more about the positivity effect, see Fredrickson and Joiner, "Positive Emotions Trigger Upward Spirals"; Barbara L. Fredrickson, Stephanie L. Brown, Michael A. Cohn, Anne M. Conway, and Joseph A. Mikels, "Happiness Unpacked: Positive Emotions Increase Life Satisfaction by Building Resilience," *Emotion* 9, no. 3 (2009): 361–68.

    Research also shows that initial positive attitudes (e.g., interest and curiosity about a topic) tend to produce more accurate subsequent knowledge about the topic than do initial negative attitudes (e.g., boredom and cynicism). By prompting more exploration of issues, positive attitudes create learning opportunities that can confirm or correct initial expectations. Because negative attitudes tend to promote avoidance of a topic, opportunities to correct false impressions and learn are often missed. Russell H. Fazio, J. Richard Eiser, and Natalie J. Shook, "Attitude Formation Through Exploration: Valence Asymmetries," *Journal of Personality and Social Psychology* 87, no. 3 (2004): 293–311.
34. Peter T. Coleman, Antony G. Hacking, Mark A. Stover, Beth Fisher-Yoshida, and Andrzej Nowak, "Reconstructing Ripeness I: A Study of Constructive Engagement in Protracted Social Conflicts," *Conflict Resolution Quarterly*, 26, no. 1 (2008): 3–42.
35. Larry S. Liebovitch, Vincent Naudot, Robin Vallacher, Andrzej Nowak, Lan Bui-Wrzosinska, and Peter T. Coleman, "Dynamics of Two-Actor Cooperation-Competition Conflict Models," *Physica A: Statistical Mechanics and Its Applications* 387, no. 25 (2008): 6360–78.
36. For background on this, I recommend Yuval Noah Harari, *Sapiens: A Brief History of Humankind* (New York: Harper, 2018).

37. This brings to mind the example of Derek Black—the former heir apparent to the white nationalist movement, the godson of David Duke—whose views fundamentally changed after being invited, over the course of a couple of years, to Shabbat dinners by an Orthodox Jewish classmate, Matthew Stevenson. When Stevenson was asked why he was compelled to invite Black to Shabbat dinners, he shared a bit about his implicit theory of change:

    I think that, for me, from a very early age, my mom was very involved in AA, Alcoholics Anonymous. And it's one thing to say that people could change, but it's another to see somebody who had been engaged in enormously destructive behaviors not only cease doing those behaviors but do a complete about-face and to actively help other people in the same situation that they had been; actively try to make the world a better place. And I think that Derek's example, and those, convince me beyond a shadow of a doubt that no matter how deeply involved somebody is in a negative pattern of behavior or a negative ideology, they're never in too deep. There is always a chance for redemption.

    To listen to or read the full interview, see Derek Black and Matthew Stevenson, "Befriending Radical Disagreement" (podcast), hosted by Krista Tippett, https://onbeing.org/programs/derek-black-and-matthew-stevenson-befriending-radical-disagreement/.

38. Implicit beliefs we hold about how human beings work have a profound impact on how we navigate the world ourselves. To learn more about

    a. how beliefs about intelligence being "fixed" versus something that can be grown and develop impact responses to setbacks, see Carol S. Dweck, "Implicit Theories as Organizers of Goals and Behavior," in *The Psychology of Action: Linking Cognition and Motivation to Behavior*, ed. Peter M. Gollwitzer and John A. Bargh (New York: Guilford Press, 1996), 69–90; Daniel C. Molden and Carol S. Dweck, "Finding 'Meaning' in Psychology: A Lay Theories Approach to Self-Regulation, Social Perception, and Social Development," *American Psychologist* 61, no. 3 (2003): 192.
    b. how fixed or malleable facets of personality are, see E. Lowell Kelly, "Consistency of the Adult Personality," *American Psychologist* 10, no. 11 (1955): 659–81.
    c. how we often explain our own motivations differently than we perceive and explain the motivations for other people's behaviors, called the fundamental attribution error, see Fritz Heider, *The Psychology of Interpersonal Relations* (New York: Wiley, 1958).

39. Lara K. Kammrath and Carol Dweck, "Voicing Conflict: Preferred Conflict Strategies Among Incremental and Entity Theorists," *Personality and Social Psychology Bulletin* 32, no. 11 (2006): 1497–1508; Laura J. Kray and Michael P. Haselhuhn, "Implicit Negotiation Beliefs and Performance: Experimental and Longitudinal Evidence," *Journal of Personality and Social Psychology* 93, no. 1 (2007): 49–64.
40. Mary Parker Follett, known as the Mother of Modern Management, wrote extensively about how more fixed, competitive, zero-sum views of authority relations in organizations

could be replaced by more dynamic, cooperative, win-win views—to the benefit of all. Mary Parker Follett, *Creative Experience* (New York: Longmans Green, 1924). Mary Parker Follett, "Power," in *Dynamic Administration: The Collected Papers of Mary Parker Follett*, ed. Elliot M. Fox and L. Urwick (London: Pitman, 1973): 66–84. Pauline Graham, ed., *Mary Parker Follett: Prophet of Management* (Boston, MA: Harvard Business School Press, 1995).

41. To learn more about how interventions to encourage disputants to make "cognitive reappraisals" of the Israeli-Palestinian conflict led to more endorsement of conciliatory policies and less endorsement of aggressive policies, see Eran Halperin, Roni Porat, Maya Tamir, and James J. Gross, "Can Emotion Regulation Change Political Attitudes in Intractable Conflicts? From the Laboratory to the Field," *Psychological Science* 24, no. 1 (2012): 106–11.
42. To learn more about interventions that encourage adolescents to believe in the potential for personal change and the impact on behavioral issues and coping skills, see David Scott Yeager, Kali H. Trzesniewski, and Carol S. Dweck, "An Implicit Theories of Personality Intervention Reduces Adolescent Aggression in Response to Victimization and Exclusion," *Child Development* 84, no. 3 (2013): 970–88.
43. Roy F. Baumeister, Ellen Bratslavsky, Mark Muraven, and Dianne M. Tice, "Ego Depletion: Is the Active Self a Limited Resource?," *Journal of Personality and Social Psychology* 74, no. 5 (1998): 1252–65.
44. Daniel Kahneman, *Thinking Fast and Slow* (New York: Farrar, Straus and Giroux, 2011).
45. Paschal Sheeran and Thomas L. Webb, "The Intention-Behavior Gap," *Social and Personality Psychology Compass* 10, no. 9 (2016): 503–18.
46. The Way Out website, https://www.thewayoutofpolarization.com/, lists a few questions to ask yourself in the warm-up to the encounter.
47. Jennifer S. Lerner, Ye Li, Piercarlo Valdesolo, and Karim S. Kassam, "Emotion and Decision Making," *Annual Review of Psychology* 66 (January 2015): 799–823.
48. Barbara L. Fredrickson and Marcial F. Losada, "Positive Affect and the Complex Dynamics of Human Flourishing," *America Psychologist* 60, no. 7 (2005): 678–86.
49. It is important to cultivate positive emotions, but you can also de-escalate and temper the destructive potential of negative emotions just by becoming aware of them. To get through negative emotions, you need to "name it to tame it" and acknowledge the useful information negative emotional responses tell us about our concerns, without feeling compelled to act out of anger, frustration, or sadness. Schwartz suggests that "we can't change what we don't notice. Denying or avoiding feelings doesn't make them go away, nor does it lessen their impact on us, even if it's unconscious. Noticing and naming emotions gives us the chance to take a step back and make choices about what to do with them." See Tony Schwartz, "The Importance of Naming Your Emotions," *New York Times*, April 3, 2015, https://www.nytimes.com/2015/04/04/business/dealbook/the-importance-of-naming-your-emotions.html. Furthermore, there is research on how "accepting" our emotions leads to more emotional well-being: "acceptance helps keep individuals from reacting to—and thus exacerbating—their negative mental experiences." See Brett Q. Ford, Phoebe Lam, Oliver P. John, and Iris B. Mauss, "The Psychological Health Benefits of Accepting Negative Emotions and Thoughts: Laboratory, Diary, and Longitudinal Evidence," *Journal of Personality and Social Psychology* 115, no. 6 (2018): 1075–92.

50. Brad J. Bushman, "Does Venting Anger Feed or Extinguish the Flame? Catharsis, Rumination, Distraction, Anger, and Aggressive Responding," *Personality and Social Psychology Bulletin* 28, no. 6 (2002): 724–31.
51. Peter T. Coleman, Anthea Chan, and Rebecca Bass, "Development of the Conflict Anxiety Response Scale" (working paper). The Morton Deutsch International Center for Cooperation and Conflict Resolution, Teachers College, Columbia University, http://conflictintelligence.org/CARS.html.
52. John M. Gottman and Nan Silver, *The Seven Principles for Making Marriage Work* (New York: Three Rivers Press, 1999).
53. For recent research on the nature of our divided political landscape, see Stephen Hawkins, Daniel Yudkin, Mirian Juan-Torres, and Tim Dixon, "Hidden Tribes: A Study of America's Polarized Landscape," *Hidden Tribes*, 2018, https://hiddentribes.us/pdf/hidden_tribes_report.pdf. After talking to those with differing views, a recent Pew Research poll (https://www.pewresearch.org/politics/2018/11/05/more-now-say-its-stressful-to-discuss-politics-with-people-they-disagree-with/) found that most red and blue Americans find they have *less* in common with the other side than they thought. Ugh.
54. Amos Tversky and Daniel Kahneman, "The Framing of Decisions and the Psychology of Choice," *Science* 211, no. 4481 (January 30, 1981): 453–458, https://science.sciencemag.org/content/211/4481/453.abstract.
55. Roi Ben-Yehuda and Tania Luna, "When Surprise Is a Good Negotiation Tactic," *Harvard Business Review*, October 3, 2019, https://hbr.org/2019/10/when-surprise-is-a-good-negotiation-tactic.

6. BOLSTER AND BREAK—LOCATE LATENT BUBBLES

1. Read a full account of this story in the autobiography of Norman Cousins, *Anatomy of an Illness as Perceived by the Patient: Reflections on Healing and Regeneration* (Boston, MA: Norton, 1979).
2. Ten years earlier, Cousins had read a classic book that provided evidence that adrenal exhaustion could be caused by extreme forms of emotional tension, frustration, or rage. This is a book that all Americans should read today. Hans Selye, *The Stress of Life* (1957; repr. New York: McGraw-Hill Education, 1979).
3. It was later discovered that high doses of aspirin were in fact harmful in the treatment of collagen illnesses, one of which Cousins was suffering.
4. Chip Heath and Dan Heath, "Switch: Don't Solve Problems—Copy Success," *Fast Company*, February 1, 2010, https://www.fastcompany.com/1514493/switch-dont-solve-problems-copy-success; Chip Heath and Dan Heath, *Switch: How to Change Things When Change Is Hard* (New York: Crown Business, 2011).
5. Richard Pascale, Jerry Sternin, and Monique Sternin, *The Power of Positive Deviance: How Unlikely Innovators Solve the World's Toughest Problems* (Cambridge, MA: Harvard Business Review Press, 2010).
6. Bibb Latané and Andrzej Nowak, "Attitudes as Catastrophes: From Dimensions to Categories with Increasing Involvement," in *Dynamical Systems in Social Psychology*, ed. Robin R. Vallacher and Andrzej Nowak (San Diego, CA: Academic Press, 1994), 219–49.

7. Horowitz claimed that his intention in placing the ads was to expose "the intolerance of political correctness" on university campuses that "suffered from a prevailing liberal orthodoxy that treated conservative views, and those who expound them, like toxic waste: fit for burying or burning but not for engaging in dialogue." See Diana Jean Schemo, "Ad Intended to Stir Up Campuses More Than Succeeds in Its Mission," *New York Times*, March 21, 2001, https://www.nytimes.com/2001/03/21/us/ad-intended-to-stir-up-campuses-more-than-succeeds-in-its-mission.html. Most campus newspapers declined the request to run the ad. Some accepted. At Brown University, the University of Wisconsin, the University of California Berkeley, Duke University, and elsewhere, the ad ran, and angry protests erupted. Thousands of copies of the papers were destroyed, apologies were demanded and received from editors, and reparations were demanded from some of the papers that ran the ad.
8. To read more about the controversy over Horowitz's list of "dangerous" professors nationwide, read Scott Jaschik, "David Horowitz Has a List," *Inside Higher Ed*, February 13, 2006, https://www.insidehighered.com/news/2006/02/13/david-horowitz-has-list.
9. For a documentary focused on the psychological dynamics of various forms of extremism, see Patricia Bush, *Facing Extremism* (video), 2013, https://www.visiontv.ca/shows/facing-extremism/. See also Arno Michaelis, *My Life After Hate* (Milwaukee, WI: Authentic Presence, 2012). This memoir is about Michaelis's own journey from skinhead to antiracist activist.
10. Witness the Price sisters' journey into paramilitary service for the Irish Republican Army in Patrick Radden Keefe, *Say Nothing: A True Story of Murder and Memory in Northern Ireland* (New York: Doubleday, 2019).
11. See the captivating TED talk of Megan Phelps-Roper, a former member of the infamous Westboro Baptist Church and a writer and educator on issues such as extremism, bullying, and empathy. Megan Phelps-Roper, "I Grew Up in the Westboro Baptist Church. Here's Why I Left," *TED*, February 2017, https://www.ted.com/talks/megan_phelps_roper_i_grew_up_in_the_westboro_baptist_church_here_s_why_i_left.
12. Andrzej Nowak and Robin R. Vallacher, "Nonlinear Societal Change: The Perspective of Dynamical Systems," *British Journal of Social Psychology* 58, no. 1 (2019): 105–28; Andrzej Nowak, Jacek Szamrej, and Bibb Latané, "From Private Attitude to Public Opinion: A Dynamic Theory of Social Impact," *Psychological Review* 97, no. 3 (1990): 362–76.
13. These results were maintained after accounting for age; demographic factors such as educational attainment, chronic diseases, and depression; and health behaviors such as alcohol use, exercise, diet, and primary care visits. Lewina O. Lee, Peter James, Emily S. Zevon, Eric S. Kim, Claudia Trudel-Fitzgerald, Avron Spiro III, Francine Grodstein, and Laura D. Kubzansky, "Optimism Is Associated with Exceptional Longevity in 2 Epidemiologic Cohorts of Men and Women," *Proceedings of the National Academy of Sciences of the United States of America* 116, no. 37 (2019): 18357–62.
14. John Gottman, Julie S. Gottman, Andy Greendorfer, and Mirabai Wahbe, "An Empirically Based Approach to Couples' Conflict," in *The Handbook of Conflict Resolution: Theory and Practice*, 3rd ed., eds. Peter T. Coleman, Morton Deutsch, and Eric C. Marcus (San Francisco: Jossey-Bass, 2014), 898–920.
15. Gottman et al., "An Empirically Based Approach to Couples' Conflict," 907.

16. Gabriella Blum, *Islands of Agreement: Managing Enduring Armed Rivalries* (Cambridge, MA: Harvard University Press, 2007).
17. Michael G. Wessells, "Bottom-Up Approaches to Strengthening Child Protection Systems: Placing Children, Families, and Communities at the Center," *Child Abuse & Neglect* 43 (2015): 8–21; David Marsh, Dirk G. Schroeder, Kirk A. Dearden, Jerry Sternin, and Monique Sternin, "The Power of Positive Deviance," *BMJ* 329, no. 7475 (2004): 1177–79.
18. E. Tory Higgins, "Making a Good Decision: Value from Fit," *American Psychologist* 55, no. 11 (2000): 1217–30.
19. Ezra Klein, *Why We're Polarized* (London: Profile Books, 2020).
20. Peter T. Coleman, "Half the Peace: The Fear Challenge and the Case for Promoting Peace," *International Peace Institute's Global Observatory*, March 19, 2018, https://theglobal-observatory.org/2018/03/half-the-peace-fear-challenge-promoting-peace/.
21. For an informative and practical guide to building a healthy marriage, see John Gottman and Nan Silver, *The Seven Principles for Making Marriage Work* (New York: Harmony Books, 2000). This book summarizes decades of Gottman's research at his "Love Lab."
22. Gary Goertz, Paul F. Diehl, and Alexandru Balas, *The Puzzle of Peace: The Evolution of Peace in the International System* (New York: Oxford University Press, 2016).
23. Signithia Fordham and John U. Ogbu, "Black Students' School Success: Coping with the 'Burden' of 'Acting White'," *Urban Review* 18, no. 3 (1986): 176–206.
24. Ben Sasse, *Them: Why We Hate Each Other—And How to Heal* (New York: Macmillan, 2018).
25. See David Dorsey's thoughtful profile of Jerry Sternin, a former country director at Save the Children, and current director of the Positive Deviance Initiative. David Dorsey, "Positive Deviant," *Fast Company*, November 30, 2000, https://www.fastcompany.com/42075/positive-deviant.
26. For a more in-depth interview, see Jerry Sternin, *The Positive Deviance Initiative Story* (interview), Carnegie Council for Ethics in International Affairs, January 5, 2007, https://www.carnegiecouncil.org/publications/archive/policy_innovations/innovations/PositiveDeviance.
27. Ashutosh Varshney, *Ethnic Conflict and Civic Life: Hindus and Muslims in India* (New Haven, CT: Yale University Press, 2002).
28. Leslie Riopel, "The Research on Appreciative Inquiry and Its Fields of Application," *PositivePsychology.com*, October 28, 2019, https://positivepsychology.com/appreciative-inquiry-research/.
29. To read more about the work of Ashoka around the world, visit ashoka.org.
30. Ryszard Praszkier, Andrzej Nowak, and Peter T. Coleman, "Social Entrepreneurs and Constructive Change: The Wisdom of Circumventing Conflict," *Peace and Conflict: Journal of Peace Psychology* 16, no. 2 (2010): 153–74.
31. Praszkier, Nowak, and Coleman, "Social Entrepreneurs and Constructive Change," 153.
32. Sternin, *The Positive Deviance Initiative Story*.
33. Marsh, Schroeder, Dearden, Sternin, and Sternin, "The Power of Positive Deviance," 1177–1179.
34. For the full report about our work in Colombia, see Josh Fisher, Kyong Mazzaro, Nick Redding, and Christine Straw, *The Contribution of Reconciliation and Victim Memory to*

Sustainable Peace in Colombia, Advanced Consortium on Cooperation, Conflict, and Complexity, Earth Institute, Columbia University, July 2015, https://ac4.earth.columbia.edu/sites/default/files/content/2015%20Fisher%2C%20Mazarro%2C%20Redding%2C%20and%20Straw%20WORLD%20BANK%20COLOMBIA.pdf.

35. For more on the concept of resonance and its relevance for the field of peace and conflict resolution, see Kyong Mazzaro, Nicholas Redding, Ben Yahuda, Danny Burns, and Jay Rothman, "Resonance, Conflict and Systems Change," *DTS Innovation Lab*, November 6, 2015, https://conflictinnovationlab.wordpress.com/2015/11/06/test-digest1/.
36. Danny Burns, *Systemic Action Research: A Strategy for Whole System Change* (Bristol, UK: Policy Press, 2007); Danny Burns, "Facilitating Systemic Conflict Transformation Through Systemic Action Research," in *The Non-linearity of Peace Processes—Theory and Practice of Systemic Conflict Transformation*, ed. Daniela Korppen, Norbert Ropers, and Hans J. Giessmann (Farmington Hills, MI: Verlag Barbara Budrich, 2011), 97–109.
37. Amra Lee, "Crisis-Mapping and New Technologies: Harnessing the Potential and Mitigating Unintended Consequences," *Humanitarian Practice Network*, July 12, 2013, https://odihpn.org/blog/crisis-mapping-and-new-technologies-%C2%96-harnessing-the-potential-and-mitigating-unintended-consequences/.
38. David Newman, "How Israel's Peace Movement Fell Apart," *New York Times*, August 30, 2002, https://www.nytimes.com/2002/08/30/opinion/how-israel-s-peace-movement-fell-apart.html.
39. Elaine Romanelli and Michael L. Tushman, "Organizational Transformation as Punctuated Equilibrium: An Empirical Test," *Academy of Management Journal* 37, no. 5 (1994): 1141–66.
40. Andrew Mercer, Claudia Deane, and Kyley McGeeney, "Why 2016 Election Polls Missed Their Mark," *Pew Research Center*, November 9, 2016, https://www.pewresearch.org/fact-tank/2016/11/09/why-2016-election-polls-missed-their-mark/.
41. Jay D. Hmielowski, Myiah J. Hutchens, and Michael A. Beam, "Asymmetry of Partisan Media Effects?: Examining the Reinforcing Process of Conservative and Liberal Media with Political Beliefs," *Political Communication*, May 23, 2020, https://doi.org/10.1080/10584609.2020.1763525.
42. The Flip Side, "About Us" (webpage), accessed September 9, 2020, https://www.theflipside.io/about-us.
43. More information about:
    - Solutions Journalism's "Guide to Deeper Connection" is available at https://thewholestory.solutionsjournalism.org/a-guide-to-deeper-connections-36c9f94fb035;
    - The Aspen Institute's "Weave: The Social Fabric Project" is available at https://www.aspeninstitute.org/programs/weave-the-social-fabric-initiative/;
    - StoryCorps "Take One Small Step" initiative is available at: https://storycorps.org/discover/onesmallstep/
    - BBC News' "Crossing Divides" is available at: https://www.bbc.com/news/world-43160365
    - Unite's "Join the Movement to Unite as One" is available at: https://unite.us/

44. Kurt Lewin, *Resolving Social Conflicts: Selected Papers on Group Dynamics* (New York: Harper and Row, 1948), 47.
45. I. William Zartman and Johan Aurik, "Power Strategies in De-escalation," in *Timing the De-escalation of International Conflicts*, ed. Louis Kriesberg and Stuart J. Thorson (Syracuse, NY: Syracuse University Press, 1991), 152–81.
46. Diane L Coutu, "Edgar Schein: The Anxiety of Learning," *Harvard Business Review* 80, no. 3 (March 2002); Diane L Coutu, "Edgar Schein: The Anxiety of Learning: The Darker Side of Organizational Learning" (interview), April 15, 2002, https://hbswk.hbs.edu/archive/edgar-schein-the-anxiety-of-learning-the-darker-side-of-organizational-learning; Marc Pilisuk and Paul Skolnick, "Inducing Trust: A Test of the Osgood Proposal," *Journal of Personality and Social Psychology* 8, no. 2 (1968): 121–33.
47. The scenario was based on an actual incident in a school system but was developed as a simulation case for this study. Peter T. Coleman, "Fostering Ripeness in Seemingly Intractable Conflict: An Experimental Study," *International Journal of Conflict Management* 11, no. 4 (2000): 300–317.
48. Boaz Hameiri, Daniel Bar-Tal, and Eran Halperin, "Paradoxical Thinking Interventions: A Paradigm for Societal Change," *Social Issues and Policy Review* 13, no. 1 (2019): 36–62.
49. Douglas P. Fry, *War, Peace and Human Nature: The Convergence of Evolutionary and Cultural Views* (New York: Oxford University Press, 2015).
50. Douglas P. Fry, *Beyond War: The Human Potential for Peace* (New York: Oxford University Press, 2007).
51. Bruce Drake and Jocelyn Kiley, "Americans Say the Nation's Political Debate Has Grown More Toxic and 'Heated' Rhetoric Could Lead to Violence," *Pew Research Center, FactTank* (blog), July 18, 2019, https://www.pewresearch.org/fact-tank/2019/07/18/americans-say-the-nations-political-debate-has-grown-more-toxic-and-heated-rhetoric-could-lead-to-violence/.

7. COMPLICATE—EMBRACE CONTRADICTORY COMPLEXITY

1. Megan Phelps-Roper, "Head Full of Doubt/Road Full of Promise," *Medium* (blog), February 6, 2013, https://medium.com/@meganphelps/head-full-of-doubt-road-full-of-promise-83d2ef8ba4f5.
2. Watch Megan Phelps-Roper's captivating TED talk: Megan Phelps-Roper, "I Grew Up in the Westboro Baptist Church. Here's Why I Left," February 2017, https://www.ted.com/talks/megan_phelps_roper_i_grew_up_in_the_westboro_baptist_church_here_s_why_i_left.
3. Read Robert Kegan's *In Over Our Heads: The Mental Demands of Modern Life* (Cambridge, MA: Harvard University Press, 1998).
4. Katharina G. Kugler and Peter T. Coleman, "Get Complicated: The Effects of Complexity on Conversations over Potentially Intractable Moral Conflicts," *Negotiation and Conflict Management Research* 13, no. 1 (July 2020).
5. For more on the effects of confirmation bias, see Scott Plous, *The Psychology of Judgment and Decision Making* (New York: McGraw Hill, 1993), 233; Elizabeth Kolbert, "Why Facts Don't Change Our Minds," *New Yorker*, February 27, 2017, https://www.newyorker.com/magazine/2017/02/27/why-facts-dont-change-our-minds.

6. Lucien Gideon Conway III, Peter Suedfeld, and Philip E. Tetlock, "Integrative Complexity and Political Decisions That Lead to War or Peace," in *Peace, Conflict, and Violence: Peace Psychology for the 21st Century*, ed. Daniel J. Christie, Richard V. Wagner, and Deborah DuNann Winter (Upper Saddle River, NJ: Prentice Hall, 2001), 66–75. Philip E. Tetlock and Dan Gardner, *Superforecasting: The Art and Science of Prediction* (New York: Broadway Books, 2015).
7. Shawn W. Rosenberg, *Reason, Ideology and Politics* (Princeton, NJ: Princeton University Press, 1988); Agnieszka Golec and Christopher M. Federico, "Understanding Responses to Political Conflict: Interactive Effects of the Need for Closure and Salient Conflict Schemas," *Journal of Personality & Social Psychology* 87, no. 6 (2004): 750–62.
8. Kugler and Coleman, "Get Complicated"; John M. Gottman, James D. Murray, Catherine C. Swanson, Rebecca Tyson, and Kristin Swanson, *The Mathematics of Marriage: Dynamic Nonlinear Models* (Cambridge, MA: MIT Press, 2005); Barbara L. Fredrickson and Marcial F. Losada, " 'Positive Affect and the Complex Dynamics of Human Flourishing': Correction to Fredrickson and Losada (2005)," *American Psychologist* 68, no. 9 (2013): 822.
9. See Katherine A. Lawrence, Peter Lenk, and Robert E. Quinn, "Behavioral Complexity in Leadership: The Psychometric Properties of a New Instrument to Measure Behavioral Repertoire," *Leadership Quarterly* 20, no. 2 (2009): 87–102.
10. Kugler and Coleman, "Get Complicated."
11. Sonia Roccas and Marilynn B. Brewer, "Social Identity Complexity," *Personality and Social Psychology Review* 6, no. 2 (2002): 88–106.
12. Irving L. Janis, *Groupthink: Psychological Studies of Policy Decisions and Fiascos* (Boston, MA: Houghton Mifflin, 1982); Marlene E. Turner and Anthony R. Pratkanis, "A Social Identity Maintenance Model of Groupthink," *Organizational Behavior and Human Decision Processes* 73, no. 2–3 (1998): 210–35.
13. Sarah E. Gaither, Jessica D. Remedios, Diana T. Sanchez, and Samuel R. Sommers, "Thinking Outside the Box: Multiple Identity Mind-Sets Affect Creative Problem Solving," *Social Psychological and Personality Science* 6, no. 5 (2015): 596–603.
14. Robert D. Putnam, *Bowling Alone: The Collapse and Revival of American Community* (New York: Touchstone Books, 2000); Elif Erisen and Cengiz Erisen, "The Effect of Social Networks on the Quality of Political Thinking," *Political Psychology* 33, no. 6 (2012): 839–65, https://www.jstor.org/stable/23324195. Rochelle R. Cote and Bonnie H. Erickson, "Untangling the Roots of Tolerance: How Forms of Social Capital Shape Attitudes Toward Ethnic Minorities and Immigrants," *American Behavioral Scientist*, 52, no. 12 (2009): 1664–89; Penny S. Visser and Robert R. Mirabile, "Attitudes in the Social Context: The Impact of Social Network Composition on Individual-Level Attitude Strength," *Journal of Personality and Social Psychology* 87, no. 6 (2004): 779–95.
15. Robert A. LeVine and Donald T. Campbell, *Ethnocentrism: Theories of Conflict, Ethnic Attitudes, and Group Behavior* (New York: Wiley, 1972). Ashutosh Varshney, *Ethnic Conflict and Civic Life: Hindus and Muslims in India* (New Haven, CT: Yale University Press, 2002).
16. I call this the crude law of complexity, coherence, and conflict (C^3); namely, that humans are driven toward consistency and coherence in their perception, thinking, feeling, behavior, and social relationships, and this is natural and functional. Conflict, however,

intensifies this drive, which can become dysfunctional during prolonged conflicts. Developing more complex patterns of thinking, feeling, acting, and social organizing can mitigate this, resulting in more constructive responses to conflict. See Peter T. Coleman, *The Five Percent: Finding Solutions to (Seemingly) Impossible Conflicts* (New York: Perseus Books, 2011).

17. "Cognitive Dissonance," *Psychology Today*, July 10, 2020, https://www.psychologytoday .com/us/basics/cognitive-dissonance. See also foundational research by Leon Festinger, *A Theory of Cognitive Dissonance* (Stanford, CA: Stanford University Press, 1957).
18. This has been found to be a particularly Western value, see Kaiping Peng and Richard E. Nisbett, "Culture, Dialectics, and Reasoning About Contradiction," *American Psychologist* 54, no. 9 (1999): 741–54.
19. Dan W. Grupe and Jack B. Nitschke, "Uncertainty and Anticipation in Anxiety: An Integrated Neurobiological and Psychological Perspective," *Nature Reviews. Neuroscience* 14, no. 7 (2013): 488–501.
20. Peng and Nisbett, "Culture, Dialectics, and Reasoning About Contradiction."
21. William Blake, *The Marriage of Heaven and Hell* (London, 1790).
22. Sonia Roccas and Marilynn B. Brewer, "Social Identity Complexity," *Personality and Social Psychology Review* 6, no. 2 (2002): 88–106.
23. Natalie R. Hall and Richard J. Crisp, "Considering Multiple Criteria for Social Categorization Can Reduce Intergroup Bias," *Personality and Social Psychology Bulletin* 31, no. 10 (2005): 1435–44.
24. Megan L. Endres, Sanjib Chowdhury, and Morgan Milner, "Ambiguity Tolerance and Accurate Assessment of Self-Efficacy in a Complex Decision Task," *Journal of Management & Organization* 15, no. 1 (2009): 31–46.
25. Anne Maydan Nicotera, Michael Smilowitz, and Judy C. Pearson, "Ambiguity Tolerance, Conflict Management Style and Argumentativeness as Predictors of Innovativeness," *Communication Research Reports* 7, no. 2 (1990): 125–31.
26. Daniel J. Siegel, *Mindsight: The New Science of Personal Transformation* (New York: Random House, 2010).
27. Alan Jacobs, *How to Think: A Survival Guide for a World at Odds* (New York: Currency Press, 2017).
28. Peter Berger and Thomas Luckmann, *The Social Construction of Reality: A Treatise in the Sociology of Knowledge* (Garden City, NY: Doubleday, 1966).
29. William Hart, Dolores Albarracín, Alice H. Eagly, Inge Brechan, Matthew J. Lindberg, and Lisa Merrill, "Feeling Validated Versus Being Correct: A Meta-analysis of Selective Exposure to Information," *Psychological Bulletin* 135, no. 4 (2009): 555–88.
30. In a 2012 TEDx Talk, I made the mistake of proposing a more general, indiscriminate exercise of intentionally tuning in to the television channels representing the other sides of debate (MSNBC and FOX) in order to mitigate against this type of insular thinking. I *was wrong*. The educator Alan Jacobs got it right—seek out the *best* thought leaders on the other side, and leave the popular political puppets and hacks in the dust.
31. Tetlock and Gardner, *Superforecasting*.

32. Magoroh Maruyama, "The Second Cybernetics: Deviation-Amplifying Mutual Causal Processes," *American Scientist* 51, no. 2 (1963): 164–79, https://www.jstor.org/stable/27838689. Magoroh Maruyama, ed., *Context and Complexity: Cultivating Contextual Understanding* (New York: Springer-Verlag, 1991).
33. Philippe Vandenbroeck, Jo Goossens, and Marshall Clemens, "Tackling Obesities: Future Choices—Obesity System Atlas," *UK Government 's Foresight Programme*, October 2007, https://www.gov.uk/government/uploads/system/uploads/attachment_data/file/295153/07-1177-obesity-system-atlas.pdf.
34. Danny Burns. *Systemic Action Research: A Strategy for Whole System Change* (Bristol, UK: Policy Press, 2007).
35. Eric Berlow, "Simplifying Complexity," *TEDGlobal* (video), July 2010, https://www.ted.com/talks/eric_berlow_simplifying_complexity?language=en.
36. Alex Mintz and Carly Wayne, *The Polythink Syndrome: U.S. Foreign Policy Decisions on 9/11, Afghanistan, Iraq, Iran, Syria, and ISIS* (Stanford, CA: Stanford University Press, 2016).
37. Andrzej Nowak, "Dynamical Minimalism: Why Less Is More in Psychology," *Personality and Social Psychology Review* 8, no. 2 (2004): 183–93.
38. Emile G. Bruneau and Rebecca Saxe, "The Power of Being Heard: The Benefits of 'Perspective-Giving' in the Context of Intergroup Conflict," *Journal of Experimental Social Psychology* 48, no. 4 (2012): 855–66.
39. Susan Fiske, "Controlling Other People: The Impact of Power on Stereotyping," *American Psychologist* 48, no. 6 (1993): 621–28.
40. Amanda Ripley, "Complicating the Narratives: What If Journalists Covered Controversial Issues Differently—Based on How Humans Actually Behave When They Are Polarized and Suspicious?," *Solutions Journalism Network*, June 27, 2018, https://thewholestory.solutionsjournalism.org/complicating-the-narratives-b91ea06ddf63.
41. Hélène Biandudi Hofer, "Complicating the Narratives: How We're Moving This Work Forward," *Solutions Journalism Network*, August 23, 2019, https://thewholestory.solutions-journalism.org/narratives-in-the-media-frustrate-journalists-too-so-lets-loop-and-figure-it-out-together-7ae6978f115d.
42. Between 1949 and 1987, the U.S. Federal Communications Commission required media companies to follow the FCC Fairness Doctrine, a policy that required the holders of broadcast licenses to present controversial issues of public importance and to do so in a manner that was—in the FCC's view—honest, equitable, and balanced. The Regan administration ended this policy.
43. The Flipside (website), https://www.theflipside.io/; AllSides (website), https://www.allsides.com/.
44. Peter T. Coleman, "Lawmakers, to Repair Our Polarized Congress, Make DC Your Home," *The Hill*, May 16, 2018, http://thehill.com/opinion/campaign/388007-lawmakers-to-help-repair-our-polarized-congress-make-dc-your-home.
45. Erin Duffin, "U.S. Congress—Public Approval Rating 2019–2020," *Statista*, October 5, 2020, https://www.statista.com/statistics/207579/public-approval-rating-of-the-us-congress/.
46. LeVine and Campbell, *Ethnocentrism*; Michael Taylor and Douglas Rae, "An Analysis of Crosscutting Between Political Cleavages," *Comparative Politics* 1, no. 4 (1969):

534–47; Varshney, *Ethnic Conflict and Civic Life*; Joel Sawat Selway, "The Measurement of Cross-Cutting Cleavages and Other Multidimensional Cleavage Structures," *Political Analysis* 19, no. 1 (2011): 48–65; Thad Dunning and Lauren Harrison, "Cross-Cutting Cleavages and Ethnic Voting: An Experimental Study of Cuisinage in Mali," *American Political Science Review* 104, no. 1 (2010): 21–39.

47. Amnda Ripley, Rekha Tenjarla, and Angela Y. He, "The Geography of Partisan Prejudice: A Guide to the Most—and Least—Politically Open-Minded Counties in America," *The Atlantic*, March 4, 2019, https://www.theatlantic.com/politics/archive/2019/03/us-counties-vary-their-degree-partisan-prejudice/583072/.

8. MOVE—ACTIVATE NOVEL PATHWAYS AND RHYTHMS

1. A small Jewish community was present in the city from the time of Casimir III the Great in the fourteenth century. The king granted the Jews a writ of rights that caused the town to become a focal point for Jewish immigration.
2. This presentation eventually became a case analysis of the outbreak of peace in Mozambique. See Andrea Bartoli, Lan Bui-Wrzosinska, and Andrzej Nowak, "Peace Is in Movement: A Dynamical Systems Perspective on the Emergence of Peace in Mozambique," *Peace and Conflict: Journal of Peace Psychology* 16, no. 2 (2010): 211–30.
3. See Andrzej Nowak, Morton Deutsch, Wieslaw Bartkowski, and Sorin Solomon, "From Crude Law to Civil Relations: The Dynamics and Potential Resolution of Intractable Conflict," *Peace and Conflict: Journal of Peace Psychology* 16, no. 2 (2010): 189–209.
4. Vamik Volkan describes these as local "hot spots," areas in communities that come to symbolically represent the deepest resentments and loyalties associated with a conflict. Vamik Volkan, *Killing in the Name of Identity: A Study of Bloody Conflicts* (Durham, NC: Pitchstone, 2006).
5. This is an instance of Morton Deutsch's Crude Law of Social Relations. See Morton Deutsch, *The Resolution of Conflict: Constructive and Destructive Processes* (New Haven, CT: Yale University Press, 1973).
6. For an excellent summary, see Christine Webb, Maya Rossignac-Milon, and E. Tory Higgins, "Stepping Forward Together: Could Walking Facilitate Interpersonal Conflict Resolution?," *American Psychologist* 72, no. 4 (2017): 374–85.
7. Michelle LeBaron, "The Alchemy of Change: Cultural Fluency in Conflict Resolution," in *The Handbook of Conflict Resolution: Theory and Practice*, 3rd ed., ed. Peter T. Coleman, Morton Deutsch, and Eric Marcus (San Francisco: Jossey-Bass, 2014), 581–603.
8. LeBaron, "The Alchemy of Change," 594.
9. Norman Doidge, *The Brain That Changes Itself: Stories of Personal Triumph from the Frontiers of Brain Science* (New York: Penguin, 2007).
10. LeBaron, "The Alchemy of Change."
11. Arie W. Kruglanski, Eric P. Thompson, E. Tory Higgins, M. Nadir Atash, Antonio Pierro, James Y. Shah, and Scott Spiegel, "To 'Do the Right Thing' or to 'Just Do It': Locomotion and Assessment as Distinct Self-Regulatory Imperatives," *Journal of Personality and Social Psychology* 79, no. 5 (2000): 793–815.

12. Filippo Aureli and Frans B. M. De Waal, eds., *Natural Conflict Resolution* (Berkeley: University of California Press, 2000).
13. If you're *really* interested in field theory, read Morton Deutch, "Field Theory in Social Psychology," in *Handbook of Social Psychology*, ed. Gardner Lindzey (Cambridge, MA: Addison Wesley, 1954), 181–222. Chapter 6 can be retrieved at https://docs.google.com/viewer?a=v&pid=sites&srcid=ZGVmYXVsdGRvbWFpbnxpbnZlc3RpZ2FjaW9uZW-50ZmV8Z3g6MjI1ODdmOTVmOTRmOTFhZA.
14. The idea of attractor landscapes is to some degree an updated notion of the life space. We experience these landscapes psychologically and can move across their contours cognitively and physically. They can be transformed by us or by external actors or events.
15. Victor Daniels, "Kurt Lewin Notes," Sonoma State University, December 3, 2003, http://web.sonoma.edu/users/d/daniels/lewinnotes.html.
16. Kruglanski et al., "To 'Do the Right Thing' or to 'Just Do It'."
17. Christine E. Webb, Peter T. Coleman, Maya Rossignac-Milon, Stephen J. Tomasulo, and E. Tory Higgins, "Moving On or Digging Deeper: Regulatory Mode and Interpersonal Conflict Resolution," *Journal of Personality and Social Psychology* 112, no. 4 (2017): 621–41; Webb, Rossignac-Milon, and Higgins, "Stepping Forward Together."
18. The primate work was published separately. See Christine E. Webb, "Moving Past Conflict: How Locomotion Facilitates Reconciliation in Humans and Chimpanzees (*Pan troglodytes*)" (PhD diss., New York, Columbia University, 2015).
19. Katharina Kugler and Peter T. Coleman, "Get Complicated: The Effects of Complexity on Conversations over Potentially Intractable Moral Conflicts," *Negotiation and Conflict Management Research* 13, no. 3 (July 2020).
20. This method uses computer software to track the curser on a computer screen to assess the dynamics of changing emotions over time. See Robin R. Vallacher, Paul Van Geert, and Andrzej Nowak, "The Intrinsic Dynamics of Psychological Process," *Current Directions in Psychological Science* 24, no. 1 (2015): 58–64.
21. We refer to this as a more *optimal ratio* because both positivity and negativity are necessary for learning and growth in conflictual encounters. See John Gottman, Julie S. Gottman, Andy Greendorfer, and Mirabai Wahbe, "An Empirically Based Approach to Couples' Conflict," in *The Handbook of Conflict Resolution: Theory and Practice*, 3rd ed., ed. Peter T. Coleman, Morton Deutsch, and Eric M. Marcus (San Francisco: Jossey-Bass, 2014), 898–920.
22. See, for example, Peter T. Coleman and Robert Ferguson, *Making Conflict Work: Harnessing the Power of Disagreement* (New York: Houghton-Mifflin-Harcourt, 2014); Peter T. Coleman and Katharina G. Kugler, "Tracking Adaptivity: Introducing a Dynamic Measure of Adaptive Conflict Orientations in Organizations," *Journal of Organizational Behavior* 35, no. 7 (2014): 945–68; Peter T. Coleman, Katharina G. Kugler, and Ljubica Chatman, "Adaptive Mediation: An Evidence-Based Contingency Approach to Mediating Conflict," *International Journal of Conflict Management* 28, no. 3 (2017): 383–406.
23. Daniel Bar-Tal, Arie W. Kruglanski, and Yechiel Klar, "Conflict Termination: An Epistemological Analysis of International Cases," *Political Psychology* 10, no. 2 (1989): 233–55.
24. Marily Oppezzo and Daniel L. Schwartz, "Give Your Ideas Some Legs: The Positive Effect of Walking on Creative Thinking," *Journal of Experimental Psychology* 40, no. 4 (2014): 1142–52.

25. Stuart J. H. Biddle, Ken Fox, and Steve Boutcher, *Physical Activity and Psychological Well-Being* (London: Routledge, 2001).
26. Phillip D. Tomporowski, "Effects of Acute Bouts of Exercise on Cognition," *Acta Psychologica* 112, no. 3 (2003): 297–324.
27. Marc G. Berman, John Jonides, and Stephen Kaplan, "The Cognitive Benefits of Interacting with Nature," *Psychological Science* 19, no. 12 (2009): 1207–12.
28. See J. Russell Boulding, "The Dynamics of Imaging Futures (1978)," in *Elise Boulding: Writings on Peace Research, Peacemaking, and the Future*, ed. J. Russell Boulding (Cham, Switzerland: Springer, 2017), 159–71.
29. See Tamar Avnet and E. Tory Higgins, "Locomotion, Assessment, and Regulatory Fit: Value Transfer from 'How' to 'What'," *Journal of Experimental Social Psychology* 39, no. 5 (2003): 525–30.
30. Scientists have long struggled with this as well. The great management theorist Mary Parker Follett was among the first to point out that most scientists take a strange approach to the study of human interactions: they see them as static things. They typically investigate how particular attitudes, personality characteristics, rewards, or opportunity structures predict how people will treat each other. Although such causes may sometimes be valid, this kind of thinking neglects the one thing we know to be constant in life: *change*. As Follett said, "They are comparing fixed things to fluid things." Mary P. Follett. *Dynamic Administration: The Collected Papers of Mary Parker Follett*, ed. E. M. Fox and L. Urwick (London: Pitman Publishing, 1940).
31. see Joshua Conrad Jackson, Jonathan Jong, David Bilkey, Harvey Whitehouse, Stefanie Zollmann, Craig McNaughton, and Jamin Halberstadt, "Synchrony and Physiological Arousal Increase Cohesion and Cooperation in Large Naturalistic Groups," *Scientific Reports* 8, no. 127 (2018): 18023–24; Jean-Jacques E. Slotine and Wei Wang, "A Study of Synchronization and Group Cooperation Using Partial Contraction Theory," in *Cooperative Control*, ed. Vijay Kumar, Naomi Leonard, and A. Stephen Morse (Berlin: Springer, 2004), 207–28; Daniel M. T. Fessler and Colin Holbrook, "Marching Into Battle: Synchronized Walking Diminishes the Conceptualized Formidability of an Antagonist in Men," *Biology Letters* 10, no. 8 (August 2014).
32. For examples of complexity mapping, see Danny Burns, *Systemic Action Research: A Strategy for Whole System Change* (Bristol, UK: Policy Press, 2007); Robert Ricigliano, *Making Peace Last: A Toolbox for Sustainable Peacebuilding* (Boulder, CO: Paradigm Press, 2012); Glenda H. Eoyang and Royce J. Holladay, *Adaptive Action: Leveraging Uncertainty in Your Organization* (Stanford, CA: Stanford University Press, 2013); Peter T. Coleman, *The Five Percent: Finding Solutions to Seemingly Impossible Conflicts* (New York: Public Affairs, 2011).
33. Julia Zimmermann and Franz J. Neyer, "Do We Become a Different Person When Hitting the Road? Personality Development of Sojourners," *Journal of Personality and Social Psychology* 105, no. 3 (2013): 515–30.
34. Jiyin Cao, Adam D. Galinsky, and William W. Maddux, "Does Travel Broaden the Mind? Breadth of Foreign Experiences Increases Generalized Trust," *Social Psychological and Personality Science* 5, no. 5 (2014): 517–25.
35. Audra D. S. Burch, "A Youth Camp Where No Issue Is Off Limits," *New York Times*, August 29, 2019, https://www.nytimes.com/2019/08/29/us/summer-camp-etgar.html.

36. This account was largely informed by reporting shared by my colleague Bastian Berbner, "Beer Summit," *This American Life* (video), episode 683, September 20, 2019, https://www.thisamericanlife.org/683/beer-summit.
37. By the way, it is estimated that there are approximately fifteen thousand "tribes" in our world today.
38. See, for example, Andrzej Nowak, Robin R. Vallacher, Michal Zochowski, and Agnieszka Rychwalska, "Functional Synchronization: The Emergence of Coordinated Activity in Human Systems," *Frontiers in Psychology* 8, no. 945 (June 2017); see also Andrzej Nowak and Robin R. Vallacher, "Synchronization Dynamics in Close Relationships: Coupled Logistic Maps as a Model of Interpersonal Phenomena," in *From Quanta to Societies*, ed. Wlodzimierz Klonowski (Lengerich, Germany: Pabst Science Editors, 2003), 165–80.
39. Frank J. Bernieri and Robert Rosenthal, "Interpersonal Coordination: Behavior Matching and Interactional Synchrony," in *Fundamentals of Nonverbal Behavior*, ed. Robert S. Feldman and Bernard Rimé (Cambridge: Cambridge University Press, 1991), 401–32.
40. Webb, Rossignac-Milon, and Higgins, "Stepping Forward Together."
41. Svenja Koehne, Alexander Hatri, John T. Cacioppo, and Isabel Dziobek, "Perceived Interpersonal Synchrony Increases Empathy: Insights from Autism Spectrum Disorder," *Cognition* 146 (January 2016): 8–15.
42. Stephanie Cacioppo, Haotian Zhou, George Monteleone, Elizabeth A. Majka, Kimberly A. Quinn, Aaron B. Ball, Gregory J. Norman, Gun R. Semin, and John T. Cacioppo, "You Are In Sync with Me: Neural Correlates of Interpersonal Synchrony with a Partner," *Neuroscience* 277 (September 2014): 842–58.
43. Ryszard Praskier writes, "In the early 1990s, Italian researcher Vittorio Gallese, part of Prof. Giacomo Rizzolatti's group from the University of Parma, made a remarkable and quite unexpected discovery. One day, Gallese was working in a room with a macaque monkey with electrodes implanted in its brain. As Gallese reached for his food, he noticed neurons begin to fire in the monkey's premotor cortex—the same area that showed activity when the animal made a similar gesture (Iacoboni 2009; Society for Neuroscience 2008). How could this happen, when the monkey was sitting still and merely watching him? This opened the gateway to the discovery of mirror neurons, which revolutionized psychology, providing a unifying framework and helping explain a host of mental abilities that have, hitherto, remained mysterious (Ramachandran 2000). Some use vivid names such as 'empathy neurons' or 'Dalai Lama neurons,' to describe mirror neurons, holding that they dissolve the barrier between self and others (Ramachandran 2006)." See Ryszard Praszkier, "Empathy, Mirror Neurons and SYNC," *Mind and Society* 15 (2016): 1–25.
44. Katharina G. Kugler, Peter T. Coleman, and Anna M. Fuchs, "Moral Conflict and Complexity: The Dynamics of Constructive Versus Destructive Discussions over Polarizing Issues" (paper presented at the 24th Annual Conference of the International Association of Conflict Management, Istanbul, Turkey, 2011), https://ssrn.com/abstract=1872654.
45. John Gottman, Catherine Swanson, and James Murray, "The Mathematics of Marital Conflict: Dynamic Mathematical Nonlinear Modeling of Newlywed Marital Interaction," Journal of Family Psychology 13, no. 1 (1999): 3–19; Julian Cook, Rebecca Tyson, Jane White, Regina Rushe, John Gottman, and James Murray, "Mathematics of Marital

Conflict: Qualitative Dynamic Mathematical Modeling of Marital Interaction," *Journal of Family Psychology* 9, no. 2 (1995): 110–30; John M. Gottman, James D. Murray, Catherine C. Swanson, Rebecca Tyson, and Kristin Swanson, *The Mathematics of Marriage: Dynamic Nonlinear Models* (Cambridge, MA: MIT Press, 2002).

46. See Marcial Losada and Emily Heaphy, "The Role of Positivity and Connectivity in the Performance of Business Teams: A Nonlinear Dynamics Model," *American Behavioral Scientist* 47, no. 6 (2004): 740–65.
47. Webb, Rossignac-Milon, and Higgins, "Stepping Forward Together."
48. Scott S. Wiltermuth and Chris Heath, "Synchrony and Cooperation," *Psychological Science* 20, no. 1 (2009): 1–5.
49. Sebastian Kirschner and Michael Tomasello, "Joint Music Making Promotes Prosocial Behavior in 4-Year-Old Children," *Evolution and Human Behavior* 31, no. 5 (2010): 354–64; Laura K. Cirelli, Kathleen M. Einarson, and Laurel J. Trainor, "Interpersonal Synchrony Increases Prosocial Behavior in Infants," *Developmental Science* 17, no. 6 (2014): 1003–11.
50. Frank J. Bernieri, Janet M. Davis, Robert Rosenthal, and C. Raymond Knee, "Interactional Synchrony and Rapport: Measuring Synchrony in Displays Devoid of Sound and Facial Affect," *Personality and Social Psychology Bulletin* 20, no. 3 (1994): 303–11.
51. Peter J. Carnevale, Dean G. Pruitt, and Steven D. Seilheimer, "Looking and Competing: Accountability and Visual Access in Integrative Bargaining," *Journal of Personality and Social Psychology*, 40, no. 1 (1981): 111–20.
52. Tim Smith and John Henderson, "Attentional Synchrony in Static and Dynamic Scenes," *Journal of Vision* 8, no. 6 (2008): 773.
53. Emma E. Cohen, Robin Ejsmond-Frey, Nicola Knight, and R. I. M. Dunbar, "Rowers' High: Behavioural Synchrony Is Correlated with Elevated Pain Thresholds," *Biology Letters* 6, no. 1 (2010): 106–8.
54. Nowak, Vallacher, Zochowski, and Rychwalska, "Functional Synchronization."
55. This encounter was later made into a 1988 stage play by Lee Blessing called *A Walk in the Woods*.
56. However, it was later rejected by government officials.
57. For example, see Ali Al-Ghamby, "Walking Diplomacy," *Saudi Gazette*, May 30, 2012, https://saudigazette.com.sa/article/4643.
58. Anthony G. Delli Paoli, Alan L. Smith, and Matthew B. Pontifex, "Does Walking Mitigate Affective and Cognitive Responses to Social Exclusion?," *Journal of Sport & Exercise Psychology* 39, no. 2 (2017): 97–108.
59. Read about "Conflict Cafés"—or "pop-ups that serve peace through food"— at https://www.international-alert.org/conflict-cafe. Read about the "Conflict Kitchen," a Pittsburgh-based restaurant that "only serves food from countries with which the United States is in conflict," at https://www.conflictkitchen.org/. See Siobhan Norton, "Conflict Kitchen: How Food Can Unite Us All," *Independent*, September 22, 2014, https://www.independent.co.uk/life-style/food-and-drink/features/conflict-kitchen-how-food-can-unite-us-all-9748599.html.
60. Read about the Make America Dinner Again initiative, designed to bring people with disparate views on current political issues together over intimate home-cooked meals, at http://www.makeamericadinneragain.com/index.html.

61. To read more about the Abraham's Path initiative, visit their website at https://www.abrahampath.org/. You can also read more on William Ury's personal website at https://www.williamury.com/story/. Watch William Ury, "The Walk from No to Yes" (video), TEDxMidwest, October 2010, https://www.ted.com/talks/william_ury_the_walk_from_no_to_yes.
62. Gray Atherton, Natalie Sebanz, and Liam Cross, "Imagine All the Synchrony: The Effects of Actual and Imagined Synchronous Walking on Attitudes Towards Marginalised Groups," *PLoS ONE* 14, no. 7 (2019): e0220-64, https://doi.org/10.1371/journal.pone.0216585.

9. ADAPT—SEEK EVOLUTION FOR REVOLUTION

The chapter title is adapted from the inimitable Nicky Case and his unique and original approach to comprehending complexity and change. Read his engaging blog post /illustrated lesson on the history and internal dynamics of revolution. Nicky Case, "Evolution, Not Revolution," *Nicky Case's Blog*, August 12, 2016, https://blog.ncase.me/evolution-not-revolution/.

1. To learn more about this "micro world" game developed by Impact Games—and to play it yourself!—visit http://www.peacemakergame.com/.
2. Philip E. Tetlock, *Expert Political Judgment: How Good Is It? How Can We Know?* (Oxford: Princeton University Press, 2005).
3. As I have outlined, there is a tremendous amount of research on all the psychological and biological reasons we aren't all that good at making decisions, as well as a lot of research on the consequences of those limitations. For further reading on the studies I reference, see Jerome S. Bruner and Cecile C. Goodman, "Value and Need as Organizing Factors in Perception," *Journal of Abnormal and Social Psychology* 42, no. 1 (1947): 33–44, https://doi.org/10.1037/h0058484. Jerome S. Bruner and Leo Postman, "On the Perception of Incongruity: A Paradigm," *Journal of Personality* 18, no. 2 (1949): 206–23 https://doi.org/10.1111/j.1467-6494.1949.tb01241.x. James G. March and Herbert A. Simon, *Organizations* (New York: Wiley, 1958); Daniel Kahneman, *Thinking Fast and Slow* (New York: Farrar, Straus and Giroux, 2011); Dietrich Dörner, *The Logic of Failure: Recognizing and Avoiding Error in Complex Situations* (New York: Metropolitan Books, 1996); Tetlock, *Expert Political Judgment*; Philip E. Tetlock and Dan Gardner, *Superforecasting: The Art and Science of Prediction* (New York: Crown, 2015).
4. For a deeper look at the "existence" effect—or the idea that it can be challenging to comprehend and plan for daunting contingencies that have not yet occurred, specifically ahead of 9/11—I recommend Kurt Eichenwald, "The Deafness Before the Storm," *New York Times*, September 11, 2012, https://www.nytimes.com/2012/09/11/opinion/the-bush-white-house-was-deaf-to-9-11-warnings.html.
5. See, for example, Shelly Chaiken, Roger Giner-Sorolla, and Serena Chen, "Beyond Accuracy: Defense and Impression Motives in Heuristic and Systematic Information Processing," in *The Psychology of Action: Linking Cognition and Motivation to Behavior*, ed. Peter M. Goldwitzer and John A. Bargh (New York: Guilford Press, 1996), 553–87.
6. To read Dörner's own account of the findings in his lab, I recommend Dörner, *The Logic of Failure*.

7. For a real-world illustration of a well-intentioned "fix" that failed, see David Bamberger, "What Happens When an NGO Admits Failure" (video), *TEDxYYC*, April 2011, https://www.ted.com/talks/david_damberger_what_happens_when_an_ngo_admits_failure. Bamberger worked for Engineers Without Borders and speaks helpfully about the blind spots that undermined the organization's impact—and what they did to better adapt going forward.
8. Dietrich Dörner, *The Logic of Failure, Recognizing and Avoiding Error in Complex Situations* (New York: Metropolitan Books, 1996), 8.
9. Dörner, *Logic of Failure*, 33
10. Some scholars refer to these types of problems as *infinite games*; however, I hesitate to use the metaphor of "games" to characterize social-emotional-political relationship dynamics because games tend to be associated with more strategic, rational types of interactions. See James P. Carse, *Finite and Infinite Games: A Vision of Life and Play and Possibility* (New York: Simon and Schuster, 1986).
11. In Latin, revolution or *revolutio* means "a turnaround."
12. For more on the "negativity effect" or our tendency to focus more on the negative, and for negative events to have more power and impact than positive events, see Roy F. Baumeister, Ellen Bratslavsky, Catrin Finkenauer, and Kathleen D. Vohs, "Bad Is Stronger Than Good," *Review of General Psychology* 5, no. 4 (2001): 323–70.
13. For an overview of decades of research on the factors that contribute to stable, healthy relationships, and for an introduction to a wide range of research-backed strategies for repairing damaged relationships, I suggest John Gottman, Julie S. Gottman, Andy Greendorfer, and Mirabai Wahbe, "An Empirically Based Approach to Couples' Conflict," in *The Handbook of Conflict Resolution: Theory and Practice*, 3rd ed., ed. Peter T. Coleman, Morton Deutsch, and Eric M. Marcus (San Francisco: Jossey-Bass, 2014), 898–920.
14. Nicholas Redding and Peter T. Coleman, "Leadership Competencies for Addressing Complex, Dynamic Conflicts" (paper presented at a conference of the International Association of Conflict Management, Berlin, Germany, June 2016).
15. The website for this book, thewayoutofpolarization.com, provides a set of assessments for each of the competencies discussed here as well as a set of exercises and reflection questions for enhancing them in your life.
16. Karl Popper, "Of Clouds and Clocks," in *Objective Knowledge: An Evolutionary Approach* (Boston: Allyn and Bacon, 1972), 4.
17. Carol S. Dweck and Ellen L. Leggett, "A Social-Cognitive Approach to Motivation and Personality," *Psychological Review* 95, no 2 (1988): 256–73.
18. Carol Dweck translated her decades of research on the impact of beliefs about intelligence into a helpful and accessible book. Carol Dweck, *Mindset: The New Psychology of Success* (New York: Ballantine, 2008).
19. David B. Miele, Bridgid Finn, and Daniel C. Molden, "Does Easily Learned Mean Easily Remembered? It Depends on Your Beliefs About Intelligence," *Psychological Science* 22, no. 3 (2011): 320–24.
20. For information focused on supporting teachers' better understanding of the impact of beliefs about intelligence on student performance, see Implicit Beliefs About Intelligence

and Implications for Educators (website), https://implicitbeliefsofintelligencetu-torial.weebly.com/home.html. This online repository of explanations, case studies, and self-assessments is designed to support the development of "growth" mindsets. Mindset Works, "Decades of Scientific Research That Started a Growth Mindset Revolution" (website), https://www.mindsetworks.com/science/.

21. John Gottman, Kimberly Ryan, Catherine Swanson, and Kristin Swanson, "Proximal Change Experiments with Couples: A Methodology for Empirically Building a Science of Effective Interventions for Changing Couples' Interaction," *Journal of Family Communication* 5, no. 3 (2009): 163–90.
22. Computer scientist Herb Morreale has distilled his thoughts and ideas about how individuals can make an impact for the greater good into what he calls his "domino theory." Herb Morreale, "Domino Theory: Small Steps Can Lead to Big Results," *Psys.org* (blog), April 30, 2012, https://phys.org/news/2012-04-domino-theory-small-big-results.html.
23. See also Teresa Amabile and Steven J. Kramer, "The Power of Small Changes," *Harvard Business Review*, May 2011, https://hbr.org/2011/05/the-power-of-small-wins.
24. The Good Judgment Project is an initiative "harnessing the wisdom of the crowd to forecast world events." It was co-created by Phillip Tetlock, decision scientist Batbara Mellers, and Don Moore, in cooperation with the Intelligence Advanced Research Projects Activity (IARPA) of the U.S. government. IARPA, "The Good Judgment Project" (website), https://www.iarpa.gov/index.php/newsroom/iarpa-in-the-news/2015/439-the-good-judgment-project.

10. CONCLUSION: NEW RULES FOR *THE WAY OUT*

1. "2020 Election Report," *Jefferson County, NY*, https://co.jefferson.ny.us/media/Elections/Summary%20report.html.
2. Amanda Ripley, Rekha Tenjarla, and Angela Y. He, "The Geography of Partisan Prejudice," *The Atlantic*, March 4, 2019, https://www.theatlantic.com/politics/archive/2019/03/us-counties-vary-their-degree-partisan-prejudice/583072/.
3. Cook County, Illinois, where I was born, is highly intolerant (95th percentile), whereas New York County, where I live now, is not much better (81st percentile). Interestingly, Suffolk and Norfolk counties in Massachusetts, which include the cities of Boston and Brookline, respectively, appear to be the most *intolerant* of all—both in the 100th percentile!
4. See Ripley, Tenharla, and He, "The Geography of Partisan Prejudice"; Amanda Ripley, "The Least Politically Prejudiced Place in America," *The Atlantic*, March 4, 2019, https://www.theatlantic.com/politics/archive/2019/03/watertown-new-york-tops-scale-political-tolerance/582106/.
5. You can see a world map of peaceful societies and peace systems (clusters of societies that do not make war) at http://sustainingpeaceproject.com/.
6. In 1948, Costa Rica's president, Jose Figueres Ferrer, the former leader of an armed revolution, chose peace. Although in power for only eighteen months, he chose to grant women and Blacks the right to vote, preserved and expanded the country's social welfare system,

and completely demilitarized. See Peter T. Coleman and Jaclyn Donahue, "Costa Rica: Choosing a Path to Peace," *Stanley Center for Peace and Security Courier*, August 26, 2018.

7. The same law included a commitment to peaceful conflict resolution and endorsing mediation whenever possible, and Costa Rica has established such practices in areas of its foreign affairs.
8. Costa Rica ranks high on the Global Peace Index, very high on the Positive Peace Index, and thirteenth (of 156 nations) in the 2018 World Happiness Report. Costa Rica has been referred to as "a model in terms of the development of a culture of peace." See Benjamin A. Peters, "Costa Rica," in *The SAGE Encyclopedia of War: Social Science Perspectives*, ed. Paul Joseph (Thousand Oaks, CA: Sage, 2017), 401–2.
9. In terms of the population, 74 percent of New Zealanders identify as being of European descent, 14.9 percent as Māori, 11.8 percent as Asian, 7.4 percent as Pacific Peoples, and 1.2 percent as Middle Eastern/Latin American/African (MELA). All of these statistics are based on 2019 data from the website of Stats NZ (www.stats.govt.nz), the nation's official data agency. The country's three official languages are Māori, English, and Sign Language.
10. New Zealand was ranked "very high" on the 2018 Global Peace Index of the Institute for Economics and Peace. On the 2018 Positive Peace Index, New Zealand ranked eighth highest for Positive Peace, and second highest for equitable distribution. Transparency International's 2018 Corruption Percentage Index ranked New Zealand second highest ("very clean"), and the 2018 Happiness Index Report ranked New Zealand eighth highest. The country also scores six out of eight on the Multiculturalism Policy Index (higher than most countries—the United States scores three). According to the Government Restrictions Index (GRI), New Zealand has one of the lowest restrictions on religions in the world, as well as a "low" Religious-Related Social Hostilities Index. Finally, the 2019 Freedom House Index measuring political rights and civil liberties ranked New Zealand seventh highest.
11. Anine Hagemann and Isabel Bramsen, "New Nordic Peace: Nordic Peace and Conflict Resolution Efforts," *Nordic Council of Ministers*, 2019, https://norden.diva-portal.org/smash/get/diva2:1302296/FULLTEXT01.pdf.
12. Ripley, Tenjarla, and He, "The Geography of Partisan Prejudice."
13. Mina Cikara, Emile G. Bruneau, Jay Van Bavel, and Rebecca Saxe, "Their Pain Gives Us Pleasure: Understanding Empathic Failures and Counter-Empathic Responses in Intergroup Competition," *Journal of Experimental Social Psychology* 55 (November 2014): 110–25.
14. Here are a few examples of evidence of these rule overrides:

    a. Neuroscience research with brain imaging has found that exposure to simple images of members of out-groups stimulates the amygdala (the fear center in the brain) and increases out-group negativity. This is a main driver of the tendency to "move away from different others." However, this research has also found that these effects can be mitigated when the out-group member is also seen to be a member of an in-group or to share common goals with the perceiver. Emile Bruneau, "Putting Neuroscience to Work for Peace," in *Social Psychology of*

Intractable Conflicts, ed. Eran Halperin and Keren Sharvit (Switzerland: Springer International, 2015), 143–55.

b. Research from our Difficult Conversations Lab has consistently shown that conversations over polarizing moral issues are much more constructive and lead to better outcomes when information about the topic of discussion is presented as a set of complex interrelated issues than when it is presented in more simple, pro/con terms. More complex framing of the issues helps to override Rule 1: Simplify. See Katharina G. Kugler and Peter T. Coleman, "Get Complicated: The Effects of Complexity on Conversations over Potentially Intractable Moral Conflicts," *Negotiation and Conflict Management Research* 13, no. 3 (July 2020).
c. Research on self-regulation of emotions in conflict has documented how "hot" emotional arousal easily triggers reflective reactions such as aggression and flight. However, it has also shown that intentionally employing "cooling" techniques such as time-outs, reflection, constructive modeling, planning, and role playing can override these reactions and promote more effective forms of problem solving. See Evelin Linder, "Emotion and Conflict: Why It Is Important to Understand How Emotions Affect Conflict and How Conflict Affects Emotions," in *Handbook of Conflict Resolution: Theory and Practice*, 2nd ed., ed. Morton Deutsch, Peter T. Coleman, and Eric C. Marcus (Hoboken, NJ; Wiley, 2006): 268–93.
d. Experimental research on stereotyping shows that even our more automatic, implicit forms of prejudice can be controlled and overridden by gaining an awareness of the bias and choosing intentionally not to act on it. Margo J. Monteith and Aimee Y. Mark, "Changing One's Prejudiced Ways: Awareness, Affect, and Self-Regulation," *European Review of Social Psychology* 16, no. 1 (2005): 113–54.
e. Experimental research on the effects of mortality salience (heightened awareness of one's own inevitable death) on increasing out-group bias and discrimination has found that the effect disappears when the subject becomes consciously aware of the experimental manipulation. Tom Pyszczynski, Jeff Greenberg, and Sheldon Solomon, "A Dual-Process Model of Defense Against Conscious and Unconscious Death-Related Thoughts: An Extension of Terror Management Theory," *Psychological Review* 106, no. 4 (1999): 835–45.
f. Ethnographic research on violent societies has shown that the chances of escalating intergroup hostilities and violence can be markedly reduced when members of communities develop cross-cutting ties or meaningful relationships across the groups. This is greatly enhanced by building cross-cutting structures (multiethnic work teams, sport teams, labor unions, social groups, etc.) for connecting members of different ethnic groups. John F. Dovidi, Samuel L. Gaertner, Melissa-Sue John, Samer Halabi, Tamar Saguy, Adam R. Pearson, and Blake M. Riek, "Majority and Minority Perspectives in Intergroup Relations: The Role of Contact, Group Representation, Threat, and Trust in Intergroup Conflict and Reconciliation," in *Social Psychology of Intergroup Reconciliation*, ed. Arie Nadler, Thomas Malloy, and Jeffrey D. Fisher (New York: Oxford University Press, 2008), 227–53.

AFTERWORD

1. Nelson Mandela, *Long Walk to Freedom: The Autobiography of Nelson Mandela* (New York: Little Brown, 1994), 544.
2. John Lewis, "Together, You Can Redeem the Soul of Our Nation," *New York Times*, July 30, 2020, https://www.nytimes.com/2020/07/30/opinion/john-lewis-civil-rights-america.html.

INDEX

Page numbers in *italics* indicate figures or tables

AA. *See* Alcoholics Anonymous
abortion, 9–12, 19, 235n36; bombshell effect and, 85; resistance reduction and, 131; worldviews and, 140, 142
Abraham's Path, 180–81
Adams, Jane, 181
adapting, 77, 184, 210, 223, 226; with distant vision, 200–203; to failure, 79
adaptive decision making, 200, *200*
adaptivity: complex, 192, *193–94*; conflict, 169; conflict response, 239n35; in failure response, 184
addiction, 83
adrenal exhaustion, 252n2
advocating, 146
affective polarization, 21, 23, 205, 222
affiliative interactions, 168
agreeableness, 173
Alcoholics Anonymous (AA), 83, 250n37
alienation, 120
Allport, Gordon, 66
AllSides, 158
America in One Room, 65, 243n4
American Federation of Musicians, 153
American National Election Studies (ANES), 22, 23
American Psychiatric Association, 6
AmeriCorps, 175
amygdala, 149, 213, 268n14
analytic framework, 69
ANES. *See* American National Election Studies
antagonistic interactions, 168
anxiety, 6, 104, 139; adaptive and maladaptive responses to, 239n35; attractors and, 46; uncertainty and, 149
appreciative inquiry, 122
artificial intelligence, 37
Ashoka, 123
Asimov, Isaac, 37, 211
Aspen Institute, 130
aspirin, 252n3
assessment, 167
assumptions, 108
Atlantic, The (magazine), 18, 205; Geography of Partisan Prejudice, 159
attitudes: divergence in, 21; learning and, 249n33; toward mainstream media, 115; negative, 249n33; polarization and, 115; polarization and out-group, 115; positive, 249n33; reversals in, 114; self-defining, 113, 114
attractor-induced conflicts, 67
attractor landscapes: changes in, 61; conflict development and, 51–58; polarization and, 51; simplification of, 51–52, 55–56

attractors, 15, 18, 240n4; anxiety and, 46; cloud problems becoming, 40, 222; complex processes and, 45; conflict, 43, 47–51, 54; current, 50; defining, 44–45; depth of, 48; developing alternative, 112; emergence of concept, 44; energy and, 46, 222; initial conditions and, 58–59; landscapes and, 47, *47*, 222, 261n14; latent, 50; manifest, 61; occurrences of, 45; outside influence resistance, 59–60; shocks to, 60; understanding conflict with, 46; width of, 47–48
Augustine (Saint), 149
authoritarianism, 28
authority, 25; zero-sum views of, 250n40
automatic writing, 69

Babcock, Julia, 199
ballistic behavior, 187–90
Bartoli, Andrea, 99, 161
BBC. *See* British Broadcasting Corporation
behavioral complexity, 146, *193–94*, 195
being heard, 156
Belfast, Northern Ireland, 165–66
Belichick, Bill, 1
belief: in change, 98; clusters of, 115; conflict-supporting, 131; implicit, 250n38; self-defining, 113, 114
belonging, 24
Benghazi, ix
Berlow, Eric, 154
Bertrand Russell Peace Foundation, 114
best practices, 124
Better Angels, 65, 217, 243n5
bias: cognitive processing and, 101–2; confirmation, 30, 144, 157
big collapse, 38–39, 138, 162, 204, 225
big data, 37
"Big Five" personality traits, 173
Bin-Laden, Osama, 99
bipartisanship, 22
birtherism, ix
Black, Derek, 250n37
Black History Month, 114
Black Lives Matter, 3, 64, 93
Blake, William, 149
bolstering, 77, 77–78, 111–13, 117–19, 210, 223, 224
bombshell effect, 77, 84, 85–89, 95, 128, 223
Boston, Massachusetts, 1–3, 9, 13–14, 84, 85, 97, 140, 221, 235n36; resistance reduction and, 131
Boston Globe (newspaper), 10, 13
Boston Red Sox, 2, 3, 7
Boston Tea Party, 1
Botswana, 174–75
bottom-up insider catalysts, 92–94
Boulding, Elise, 171
breaking down, 77, 78, 111, 113, 128, 210, 223, 224
Brexit, ix
bridge-building media initiatives, 129–30
bright spots, 77, 112, 224
British Broadcasting Corporation (BBC), 130, 158
Brookline, Massachusetts, 9–10, 84, 118
Brooks, David, 157
Bruneau, Emile, 156
Bruner, Jerome S., 185
bubble theory, 115, 116, 127–28
Buckley, Steve, 2
Bui-Wrzosinska, Lan, 71
Burns, Danny, 126
butterfly effect, 84, 95–98, 224

C3. *See* complexity, coherence, and conflict
Camp David, 108
Canada, Geoffrey, 197–98
catalysts: bottom-up insider, 92–94; middle-out joint, 94–95; top-down outsider, 91–92
categorical complexity, 150
Catholic Church, 10, 84, 142
CBOs. *See* community-based organizations
cellular automata, 162
Central Intelligence Agency, 201
change: belief in, 98; human interaction study and, 262n30; implicit assumptions about, 100; nonlinear, 80, 223; revolutionary, 90–92
changeable mindsets, 100
change agents: community-centered, 126; role of, 69
changing course, 215, *216*
Chasin, Laura, 10–11, 97, 106, 118, 131
choosing time and place, 107–8
civic culture, 206
civil rights movement, 3
civil unrest, ix
Civil War, U.S., 3, 22
clarity of meaning and purpose, 46
Clinton, Hillary, 29, 129
clock problems, 34–38, *35*; conflict as, 70–71
cloudlike thinking, 74–75
cloud problems, 34–38, *35*, 58; becoming attractors, 40, 222; conflict as, 71–72;

decision-making errors in, 187; as infinite problems, 190
clusters of beliefs, 115
cognition, 28; bias and, 101–2; System 1 and System 2 processes in, 101–2
cognitive complexity, 38, *193*, 194–95
cognitive dissonance, 149
cognitive reappraisals, 251n41
cognitive rigidity, 38
cognitive shortcuts, 28
coherence: C3, 257n16; tendency towards, 59
Colbert, Stephen, 5
collapse of complexity, 39
collective action, 73
Colombia: complexity mapping in, 125; resistance to change in, 94
community: complicating, 158–60; social network complexity and, 146–47; structural complexity and, 147
community-based organizations (CBOs), 125
community-centered change makers, 126
community leaders, dialogue among, 13
Community of Sant'Egidio, 99, 100, 217
compassion, 73
complex adaptive competencies, 192, *193–94*
complexity, 137; behavioral, 146, *193–94*, 195; categorical, 150; cognitive, 38, *193*, 194–95; collapse of, 39; consistent, 138, 140, 224–25; contradictory, 78, 138–43, 160, 224–25; emotional, 39, 145–46, *193*, 195; group, 146; initial conditions and, 77; integrative, 145, 154, *193*; political, 145; social identity, 146, 150; of social networks, 146–47, 152; structural, 147
complexity, coherence, and conflict (C3), 257n16
complexity mapping, 125, 153–54; flow and, 172; physical aspects of, 172–73
complexity science, 44, 71, 79
complex problems, 36, 222
complex processes, attractors and, 45
complex systems: changes in, 61; coherence and integration tendencies and, 59; initial conditions and, 77; interaction rules in, 60–61; small difference sensitivity of, 95; unintended consequences of changes in, 61–62
complicating, 77, 78, 210, 217, 224–25
"Complicating the Narrative" (Ripley), 157
Complicating the Narrative project, 130
Confessions (Augustine), 149
confirmation bias, 30, 144, 157
conflict: adaptive and maladaptive responses, 239n35; attractor-induced, 67; attractors and understanding, 46; C3 and, 257n16; circumventing, 123; constructive, 225; context and, 66; R2 and, 73; simulating societal, 162–64, *163*; theories of change about, 67, *72*; tribalism and, 148
"Conflict, The" (video campaign), 131–32
conflict adaptivity, 169
Conflict Anxiety Response Scale, 239n35
conflict attractors, 43, 47–51, 54; fractal dynamics in, 56
Conflict Café, 180
conflict clock theory, 70–71
Conflict Kitchen, 180
conflict landscape, 49, 51; contradictory complexity and reconfiguring, 138–47; development of, 51–58
conflict-supporting beliefs, 131
conformity: groupthink and, 146; in-groups and, 28, 60
congenial information, 151
Congress, U.S.: crosscutting ties and, 158–59; voting patterns in, 22, *22*, 45, 86, *86*
connecting, 210
consideration of future consequences, 39, *194*, 195
consistency principle, 19, 59
consistent complexity, 138, 140, 224–25
constructive conflict, 225
constructive containers, 80
context: conflict and, 66; engaging with, 112; flow of forces within, 73; mapping, 153–54; R2 and, 73
contradiction: acknowledging personal, 149–51; group complexity and, 146
contradictory complexity, 78, 160, 224–25; DCL evidence, 143–45; embracing, 138–43; evidence across levels, 145–47; practices for, 148–60
conversations: complicating, 155–56; framing difficult, 143. *See also* Difficult Conversation Lab; Public Conversations Project
cooking, 179–80
cooling techniques, 269n14
Coons, Chris, 175
cooperative contact, 147
Cora, Alex, 2
core dynamics, 154
CORPS Act, 175
corrective feedback, 201

Corruption Percentage Index, 268n10
Costa Rica, 208, 267n6, 268nn7–8; civil war in, 84
Cousins, Norman, 109–11, 117, 252n3
COVID-19, ix, 180, 189, 219
crisis mapping, 127
critical evaluators, 146
crosscutting ties, 158, 269n14
Crossing Divides project, 130
Crossing Party Lines, 65, 217
crude laws, 58–62, 223
cults, 59
current attractor, 50
current state: attractors and, 47; of conflict, 50; landscapes and, 61; self-organization and maintaining, 59; of systems, 47, 61
cybernetics, 153
Cyprus, 127

Darwin, Charles, 87
DCL. *See* Difficult Conversation Lab
deadlock, 4
debate: in Boston, 13; dialogue difference from, 17, 155; perceptions of political, 133; synchrony and, 178
decision making, 200, *200*, 202, 265n3; errors in, 187
decoupling of emotions, 177
deep rules, 211–14
deep structure, 85, 90, 223, 248n18
depolarization, 95, 225, 227, 235n36
depression, 6, 104
destabilizing shocks, 74, 247n3
Detroit Symphony Orchestra, 152–53
Deutsch, Morton, 163, 239n35
development aid scenario, 188
devil's advocates, 146
De Waal, Frans, 167
dialogue, 13, 155–56; defining, 16–17
Die Zeit (*The Time*) (newspaper), 63, 107, 189
Difficult Conversation Lab (DCL), 39, 64, 72, 104, 137, 168, 178; contradictory complexity evidence from, 143–45
difficult encounters, preparing for, 98–108
disease task, 106
disorienting dilemmas, 88
divorce, 120
Dixon, Tim, 7
domino theory, 267n22
Dörner, Dietrich, 185, 186–87, 189–90, 192, 200–202
driving forces, 130
DST. *See* dynamical systems theory
Dweck, Carol, 196
dynamical systems theory (DST), 71, 76, 240n4

E4vortex, 184–86, 189, 226
echo-chamber effect, 152
efficiency, 185, 226
Eldredge, Niles, 87, 92
electromagnetism, 20, 34
emergence, 61
emergency rules, 213–14
emotional complexity, 39, 145–46, *193*, 195
emotional locomotion, 168
emotional positivity, reservoirs of, 104
emotional reservoirs, 103–5, 108, 224
emotional synchronization, 177
emotional synchrony and inertia, 177
emotions: conflict clock theory and, 70; decoupling of, 177; negative, 251n49; noticing and naming, 251n49; positive, 251n49; self-regulation of, 269n14; toxic, 71, 104
employment location transfers, 174
energy: attractors and, 46, 222; flow of, 224
entertainmentization, 158
entity theorists, 196
environment, 185, 226
escalation, 225
esteem, 185, 226
Etgar 36, 65, 174
ethnic violence, 175
evolution: punctuated equilibrium and, 87; seeking, for revolution, 79, 190–92
exhausted majority, 8
existence, 185, 226, 265n4
extreme behavioral reactions, 104
extremity, in-groups and, 28

Facebook, 16, 235n2, 236n3; founding of, 17; mission, 17–18
Fafo Institute, 108
failing smart, 197
failure: adapting to, 79; adaptivity in response to, 184; planning for, 195–98
Fairness Doctrine, 259n42
family systems therapy, 74, 243n5
Faraday, Michael, 20, 34
FCC. *See* Federal Communications Commission, U.S.
fear problem, 119–20, 122, 224
Federal Communications Commission, U.S. (FCC), 259n42

feedback: corrective, 201; vicious cycles and, 30–31
Ferrer, Jose Figueres, 84, 267n6
Festinger, Leon, 236n7
field theory, 167
Fisher, Josh, 76
fit problem, 119, 224
fixed mindsets, 100, 196
fixer problem, 120–21, 123, 224
flexibility, 225
Flip Side, The, 129, 158
flow: of energy, 224; of forces, 73, 224; mapping and, 172–73
focusing on problems, 122
focus of interest, 153
Follett, Mary Parker, xi, 250n40, 262n30
foreign travel, 173–74
forward framing, 170–72
fossil records, 87
FOX News, 5, 48, 129
fractal dynamics, 56, 223
fractionalization, 39
Fragility, Conflict and Violence unit, 125
framing, 108, 269n14; of difficult conversations, 143; forward, 170–72; semantic, 106; unfamiliar, 105–7
France, World War II and, 18–19
Fredrickson, Barbara, 96, 145
Freedom House Index, 268n10
friend problem, 120, 224
Funt, Alan, 110
future imaging, 171

Gallese, Vittorio, 263n43
gamers approach, 79
Gandhi, Mahatma, 92
Garry, Fred, 206
gender discrimination, 82, 102
generalized trust, 173
genetic engineering, 37
Gentzkow, Matthew, 24
Geography of Partisan Prejudice, 159
Gersick, Connie, 90, 91, 248n18
Gestalt psychology, 44, 167, 236n7
getting ready, 215, *216*
getting small, 198–99
Getting to Yes (Ury), 180
Gingrich, Newt, 158
Global Peace Index, 268n8, 268n10
Good Friday Peace Agreement, 68, 165
Good Judgment Project, 201, 267n24
Gottman, John, 96, 105, 117, 145, 198–99
Gould, Stephen Jay, 87, 92
Government Restrictions Index (GRI), 268n10
Great Attractor, 45
Great Depression, 219
GRI. *See* Government Restrictions Index
group affiliations, 146
group complexity and contradiction, 146
group identities, 148
group polarization, 237n10
group preferences, 28
groups: hierarchical structure tendencies, 29; intergroup contact theory, 65–66; intergroup enmity, 34; polarization factors, 28; self-help, 83. *See also* in-groups; out-groups
groupthink, 146, 154
growth mindsets, 196
guiding star, 201

Hadjipavlou, Maria, 127
hanging out, 151
Hannity, Sean, 5
Happiness Index Report, 268n10
Harlem Children's Zone (HCZ), 198
harmony orientation, 73–74
hate speech, 16
Havel, Vaclav, 155
Hawking, Stephen, 37
HCZ. *See* Harlem Children's Zone
hearing others, 156
Heaven's Gate, 59
Heider, Fritz, 236n7
"Hidden Tribes" study, 105
hierarchical group structures, tendency toward, 29
Higgins, Tory, 167
Hindu-Muslim communal violence, 121–22
Hitzig, William, 109–10
homophily, 29
Hope in the Cities, 93
Horowitz, David, 114, 116, 253n7
humanitarian development simulations, 188
Hunter, Torii, 3

identity issues, 43
ideological consistency, 238n24; attractors and, 44; scale for, 24; trends toward, 233n12
ideological polarization, 21, 222, 232n8
imaginative exploration, 171
implicit beliefs, 250n38
implicit theories, 68–69, 250n37

incremental theorists, 196
India, 209; Hindu-Muslim communal violence in, 121–22
infinite games, 247n38, 266n10
infinite problems, 190
in-groups, 28, 120; group polarization and, 237n10; socialization, 31
initial assumptions, 98–101
initial conditions, 98; attractor sensitivity to, 58–59; complex systems and, 77; R2 and, 74
initiating crisis, 93
Innocents Abroad (Twain), 173
inquiring, 146
inside-out partnerships, 94
insider catalysts, 92–94
instability, 7
Instability4, 8
integrating moving together, 226
integration, tendency towards, 59
integrative complexity, 145, 154, *193*
intentions, 101–3, 108
interactional synchrony, 176–77
interactive activities, 225
intergroup contact theory, 65–66
intergroup enmity, 34
internal contradictions, 150
international conflicts: political shocks and ending, 60, 89; reaching out and, 99
International Justice System, 76
internet, 37
internet sorting algorithms, 151
interventions, 69
intimate partner violence (IPV), 199
intractable polarization, 65, 85
IPV. *See* intimate partner violence
I Robot stories (Asimov), 211
islands of agreement, 118
Israeli-Palestinian conflict, 43, 99, 131–32, 164–66, 251n41; resistance to change in, 94; simulating, 183

Janjaweed, 99, 100
Jefferson County, New York, 205
joint catalysts, 94–95
joint movement, 225
joint synchrony, 175
journalism, 157

Kaepernick, Colin, 2, 64–65
Kahneman, Daniel, 101, 106, 185
King, Martin Luther, Jr., 73, 92, 181
King Philip's War (First Indian War), 1
kneeling protests, 64
Know Nothing movement, 1
Kristoff, Nicholas, 157
Kugler, Katharina, 143
Kuhn, Thomas, 92
Kvitsinsky, Yuli A., 179

labor-management conflicts, 152–53
landscapes: attractors and, 47, *47*, 222, 261n14; conflict, 49, 51–58. *See also* attractor landscapes; radical relandscaping
latent attractors, 50, 61
latent bubbles, 78; locating, 113–17
Law, Bernard (Cardinal), 10
laws of nature, 36
League of American Orchestras, 152
learnable competencies, 226
learning: attitudes and, 249n33; failure and, 195–98
learning orientation, 196
LeBaron, Michelle, 164–66
left-versus-right tribalism, 7
legislative voting, 4
Lewin, Kurt, 44, 85, 130, 167, 168, 176, 236n7
Lewis, John, 220
Liebovitch, Larry, 71, 97
life space, 167
Limbaugh, Rush, 5, 129
Lincoln, Abraham, 92, 181
locomotion, 164, 167; emotional, 168; forward framing and, 170–72; mandating, 174–75; mapping and, 172–73; in nature, 179; practices for, 179–81; strategic, 169; travel, 173–74
long game, R2 and, 74, 79
loosely coupled systems, 40
Lorenz, Edward, 95
Los Angeles Dodgers, 2
Love Lab, 96, 145, 198–99
lower-energy states, 46, 222
Lowney, Shannon, 10

Maddow, Rachel, 5
magnetic polarization, 20, *20*
mainstream media: attitudes toward, 115; hyperpoliticization of, 129; vilification of, 34
major depression, 6
Make America Dinner Again, 65, 180
malnutrition, 124
Mandela, Nelson, 92, 101, 220

manifest attractor, 61
mapping, 225; complexity, 125, 153–54, 172–73; crisis, 127; physical aspects of, 172–73; problem-context, 153–54
March, James G., 185
marital conflict, 145
Maruyama, Magoroh, 153
mass national psychosis, 5–6, 15
mastery orientation, 70, 73, 196
McChrystal, Stanley, 239n33
Mead, George Herbert, 73
meaning: clarity of, 46; social construction of, 151
mechanical clock theory, 223
mediation, 268n7
MENA. *See* Middle East and North Africa
mercy, 136
metaphor, 69
micro-cultures, 80
Middle East and North Africa (MENA), 41–43, 164; locomotion and, 180; reaching out in, 99–100; United States military incursions in, 89
middle-out joint catalysts, 94–95
mindsets: fixed, 100, 196; growth, 196; shifting, 100; tribal, 44
mirror neurons, 177, 263n43
miserable middle majority, 8–9
Mitchell, George J., 68
modes of practice, 76–79, 77
moral disputes, polarizing, 96
moral scope, 39
moral values, 239n28
More in Common, 7, 232n11
mortality salience, 269n14
motivational orientations, 119
motivational threshold, 209
moving, 77, 78–79, 161–62, 210, 223, 226
MSNBC, 5, 48
Mueller inquiry, ix
Multiculturalism Policy Index, 268n10
multistability, 49
Musk, Elon, 37
mutually enticing opportunity, 8, 9
mutually hurting stalemate, 8
Myanmar, 236n3

narratives: complicating, 156–58, 217; science and, 37
national exit polls, 232n8
National Institute of Health, psychosis definition by, 5–6
National Public Radio (NPR), 157, 158
National Unity March for America, 181
nativism, 1
nature: laws of, 36; locomotion in, 179
need for closure, 38
negative attitudes, 249n33
negative emotions, 251n49
negative frame condition, 106
negative partisanship, 23
negativity effect, 191, 266n12
networks of effective action, 118
neuroplasticity, 166, 225
neuroticism, 173
New Left, 114
new species story, 92–94, 112
Newtonian Revolution, 35, 36
New York Times (newspaper), 19
New York Yankees, 2
New Zealand, 208–9, 268n10
Nichols, Leanne, 10
Nitze, Paul H., 179
nonlinear change, 80, 223
nonlinear systems, 61–62
normative patterns, 7
Northern Ireland, 68
North Star, 69, 201, 205–7, 227
noticing and naming emotions, 251n49
novel pathways and rhythms, 79
Nowak, Andrzej, 71, 123, 162, 176
NPR. *See* National Public Radio
nudge tactics, 172

Occupy movement, 93
Oersted, Hans Christian, 20, 34
One Small Step, 130
openness to experience, 173
optimism, 117
organizational development, 74; strengths-based approaches, 122
organizational transformation, 87
out-groups, 120, 268n14; cooperative contact with, 147; future imaging and, 171; mobilizing power of threats of, 58
outsider catalysts, 91–92
oversimplification, 39, 139, 222
Oxford Group, 93

pain management, 110
pandemics, 88
paradoxical thinking interventions, 131
partisan violence, opinions on, 6

path dependence, 249n30
PBS. *See* Public Broadcasting Service
PCP. *See* Public Conversations Project
peacebuilding, 118
"Peace Is in the Movement" (Bartoli), 161
PeaceMaker, 183–84, 192, 194, 201
pecking order dynamics, 44
Perception Gap, 232n11
perceptions: of political divide, 4; selective, 144
perceptual polarization, 21, 222
performance orientation, 196
personal change, 251n42
personality factors, 28
perspective, 156
Pew Research Center, 23, 66, 232n9; ideological consistency scale, 24, 238n24; polarization research, 238n20
phase transition, 115
Phelps Fred, 135
Phelps-Roper, Megan, 135-37, 139, 150
physical activity: benefits of, 169, 170; in mapping exercises, 172–73; moving in sync, 177–78
physical determinism, 36
physical indeterminism, 36, 37
place: choosing, 107–8; resets and, 83
Planned Parenthood, 10
Podziba, Susan, 10–12, 97, 131
polarization, ix, 3, 8, 11, 13–16, 221; affective, 205; attraction of, 18–20; attractor landscapes and, 51; attractors and, 15; defining, 20–21; group, 237n10; ideological, 232n8; intractable, *65*, 85; out-group attitudes and, 115; patterns of, 25–29; shocks and, 85; superstorms of, 31, *33*, 138, 204; theories of, 25, 27; toxic, 222, 223; trends in America in, 21–25, 222; types of, 20–21, 222
polarizing moral disputes, 96
political assassinations, 89
political complexity, 145
political divides, 232n9
political intolerance, 3
political perceptions, 4
political polarization, 21, 222; drivers of, 25, *26*; historical trends and, 86, 88–89
political tolerance, 207–9
polythink, 154
Popper, Karl, 34–36, 70, 75, 195
positive attitudes, 249n33
positive deviance, 77, 112, 121, *121*, 124, 126, 224
positive emotions: benefits of, 104; cultivating, 251n49
Positive Emotions and Psychophysiology Lab, 96, 145
positive frame condition, 106
Positive Peace Index, 268n8, 268n10
positivity, 96, 117, 224, 225
positivity effect, 249n33
potentials, 50
power of negativity, 57
power of situations, 73
PowerPoint, 239n33
Praszkier, Ryszard, 123
PredictWise, 205
premotor cortex, 263n43
Preterm Health Services, 10
Price, David, 2
problem-context mapping, 153–54
problems: clock, 34–38, *35*; cloud, 34–38, *35*, 40, 58, 71–72, 187, 190, 222; complex, 36, 222; complicating, 152–55; fear, 119–20, 122, 224; fit, 119, 224; fixer, 120–21, 123, 224; focusing on, 122; friend, 120, 224; infinite, 190
pro-choice community, 9, 10, 97, 141, 142
progressivism, 114
pro-life community, 9, 10, 97, 141, 142
proximal change experiments, 198–99, 202
psychosis, defining, 5–6
Public Broadcasting Service (PBS), 158
Public Conversations Project (PCP), 10, 106–7, 118, 131, 235n36
public forums, 11–12
public scandals, 87
punctuated equilibrium, 60, 87, 90

Al-Qaeda, 99, 100
quantum theory, *35*

R2. *See* radical relandscaping
racial discrimination, 82, 102
racial injustice, 3
racial segregation, 44
radical relandscaping (R2), 73–74, 223; long game and, 74; modes of practice for, 76–79, *77*
Ramparts Magazine, 114
rationality, 195
Reagan, Ronald, 89
Redding, Nick, 76
reinforcing cycles, *30*
reinforcing feedback: complex systems and, 59; initial condition impact on attractors and, 59; loops of, 30
reinforcing repellers, 132–34
relational repair, 191

relevance gap, 41
Religious-Related Social Hostilities Index, 268n10
reparations, 114
repellers, 51, 224; reinforcing, 132–34
resets, 76–77, 77, 83–85, 210, 223
resistance, 224; of attractors, to outside influence, 59–60; reducing, 130–32
resonance, 126
reversals, 114
revolution: conservative, 89; in MENA countries, 89; Newtonian, 35, 36; scientific, 92, 98; seeking evolution for, 79, 190–92
revolutionary change, 90–92
Revolutionary War (U.S.), 1
Ripley, Amanda, 156–58, 205
riptides, 112
risky shift effects, 237n10
Rizzolatti, Giacomo, 263n43
Roe v. Wade, 9, 142
Rohingya, 236n3
role of change agents, 69
Roosevelt, Eleanor, 92
rules, 211–14
rules-based cultures, 211
Runaround (Asimov), 211
ruptures, 128–30, 224

Salvi, John C., III, 9–10
Sandberg, Sheryl, 16
Sanders, Bernie, 92
Sartre, Jean-Paul, 18–19, 25, 138
savior complex, 120
Schwartz, Morrie, 80, 251n49
scientific revolution, 98
Scientology, 59
selective perception, 144
self-defining beliefs and attitudes, 113, 114
self-help groups, 83
self-organization, 59
self-other information processing, 177
self-regulation, 269n14
self-reported well-being, 239n35
semantic framing, 106
Senate, U.S., 48–49
sensitivity to small differences, 95
settings, choosing, 107–8
sexual orientation, 233n22
shocks: attractor destabilization by, 60; destabilizing, 74, 247n3; international conflict and, 60, 89; interstate conflicts and, 86; intractable polarization and, 85; Trump as, 88
shock waves, 128–30
Shriver, Tim, 95, 130
Siege of Boston, 1
Simon, Herbert A., 185
simulated communities, 186
single sovereign theory fallacy, 27
sketching, 172
smartphones, 37
social construction of meaning, 151
social dominance orientation, 28
"Social Entrepreneurs and Constructive Change" (Praszkier, Nowak, and Coleman), 123
social identity complexity, 146, 150
social isolation, 120
social justice, 82
social media, 16, 17; vicious cycles and, 31
social networks: complexity of, 146–47, 152; homogenous, 31
social relations: altering patterns in, 111; attractors and, 45; promoting constructive, 145
social rules, 212
societal conflicts, simulating, 162–64, *163*
society: long-term trends in, 4; polarization factors, 29; virtual, 16–17
Solution Journalism, 130
sorting algorithms, 151
sound relationship house theory, 117
South Sudan, 94
Spanish flu of 1918, 86
Special Olympics, 95
speciation, 87, 92
split ticket voting, 238n18
starting small, 79
State of the Unions speech of 2019, 4
stereotyping, 269n14
Sternin, Jerry, 121, 124
Stevenson, Matthew, 250n37
Storycorps, 130
stranger story, 91–92
strategic inside-out partnerships, 94
strategic locomotion, 169
strengths-based approaches, 122
structural complexity, 147
substance abuse, 83
suicide rates, 6
superforecasters, 152, 201
superstorms of polarization, 31, 33, 138, 204, 222
sustainable political tolerance, 207–9

symbolic interactionism, 151
synchronization story, 94–95, 164, 176–78
Syria, 94
System 1 and 2 processing, 101–2
systemic wisdom, 73

taboos, 132–34, 224
"Talking with the Enemy" article, 10, 13
Tanaland, 186–88, 190
Task Force on Community and Diversity, 217
Tea Party, 64, 93
"Ten Reasons Why Reparations for Slavery Is a Bad Idea—and Racist Too." (Horowitz), 114
Tetlock, Philip, 152, 184, 185, 192, 200, 201
theory of change: changing, 74–75; defining, 67; fixing conflict clocks, 70–71; implicit, 68–69, 250n37
Theory X management, xi
Thinking Fast and Slow (Kahneman), 101
threat sensitivity, 28
threshold-effect changes, 114
tightly coupled complex systems, unintended consequences of changes in, 61–62
time, 190; building positivity and, 191; choosing, 107–8
Tippett, Krisata, 157
tolerance, 267n3; for ambiguity, 150, *193*, 194; political, 207–9
top-down outsider catalysts, 91–92
topological psychology, 44
toxic emotions, 71, 104
toxic polarization, 222, 223
transfer policies, 174–75
travel, 173–74, 225, 243n3
Treaty of Waitangi, 208
tribal conflicts, 120
tribalism: conflict and, 148; left-versus-right, 7
Trump, Donald, x, 2, 3, 29, 39, 64, 205; "American Carnage" philosophy, 30; COVID-19 response, 189; impeachment of, ix; as shock, 88; shock wave from election of, 129; stranger story and, 92; as symptom, 4
Tudy-Jackson, Janice, 179
Tversky, Amos, 106, 185
Twain, Mark, 173
twenty-four-hour news cycle, 30
Twitter, 30

UN. *See* United Nations
uncertainty: fear and, 149; tolerance for, 150
uncertainty principle, 37
uncongenial information, 151
unfamiliar framing, 105–7
unfreezing, 85, 131
unintended consequences, 61–62, 79, 187
Unite, 95, 130
United Nations (UN), 107
United States: MENA military incursions by, 89; polarization trends in, 21–25; presidential election of 2016, 16, 232n9; Senate, 48–49. *See also* Congress, U.S.
Ury, William, 180
Ushahidi, 127
us-versus-them patterns, 56–57, 225

Vallacher, Robin, 71, 176
value-behavior inconsistencies, 150
Varshney, Ashutosh, 121–22
verbal intelligence, 201
vicious cycles, 29–34, *31*, *32*, 138, 160, 222, 225
vicious cyclones, 31, 138, 222
Vietnam War, 3
views of authority, 250n40
virtual society, 16–17
virtuous cycles, 160, 199, 208

Wahed, Annafi, 129
Watergate, 3
Watertown, New York, 205–7
Weave Social Fabric Project, 130
Webb, Christine, 167, 168
Weld, William F., 10
well-being, self-reported, 239n35
Westboro Baptist Church, 135–37
Wheeler, John Archibald, 37, 195
Wicker, Roger, 175
worker-management enmity, xi
World Bank, 181; Fragility, Conflict and Violence unit, 125; International Justice System of, 76
World Economic Forum, 7
World Happiness Report, 268n8
World War I, 86
World War II, 18–19

YouTube, 131

Zoom, 17
Zuckerberg, Mark, 16, 17